All the programs from Complete Turbo Pascal, 2/e are also available on diskette for the IBM PC. This diskette has been given to many major national IBM PC user groups and to TUG, the Turbo Users Group. These groups will provide this diskette as part of their own ongoing software library programs. Contact your local user group or TUG for current prices and ordering information.

Or, you can order this diskette directly from the author for $10.00, using the order form below.

D1605128

Order Form

Shipping information—please print

Name _____

Street _____

City _____ State _____ Zip _____

Date _____

Please send me

_____ diskettes to accompany **Complete Turbo Pascal, 2/e,** at $10.00 each; $15.00 each outside U.S. and Canada.

Check method of payment:

☐ check   ☐ money order   ☐ cash

(Credit cards and C.O.D. payments are not accepted.)

Amount enclosed $ _____

Mail to: Jeff Duntemann
            805 Seaword Road
            Towson, MD 21204

Price includes postage and handling and applicable sales tax. Price and availability subject to change without notice.

COMPLETE TURBO PASCAL

SECOND EDITION, REVISED AND ENLARGED

COMPLETE TURBO PASCAL

SECOND EDITION, REVISED AND ENLARGED

JEFF DUNTEMANN

Scott, Foresman and Company
Glenview, Illinois   London

ISBN 0-673-18600-8

Copyright © 1987, 1986 Scott, Foresman and Company.
All Rights Reserved.
Printed in the United States of America.

Library of Congress Cataloging-in-Publication Data

Duntemann, Jeff.
  Complete Turbo Pascal.

  Includes index.
  1. PASCAL (Computer program language) 2. Turbo
Pascal (Computer program) I. Title.
QA76.73.P2D86 1986b   005.36′9   86-17801
ISBN 0-673-18600-8

        3   4   5   6   KPF   91   90   89   87

Scott, Foresman Professional Publishing Group books are available for bulk sales at quantity
discounts. For information, please contact Marketing Manager, Professional Books,
Professional Publishing Group, Scott, Foresman and Company, 1900 East Lake Avenue,
Glenview, IL 60025.

Turbo Pascal is a trademark of Borland International, Inc. CP/M and CP/M-86 are
trademarks of Digital Research, Inc. Xerox and Xerox 820-II are trademarks of Xerox
Corporation. IBM and IBM PC are trademarks of IBM Corporation.

Notice of Liability

Introduction

This is a book about Pascal, and about a Pascal compiler.

The Pascal language definition was released by Niklaus Wirth early in 1971. Borland International's Turbo Pascal compiler was released on November 15, 1983. The first draft of this book was completed almost precisely one year later, and to date—March 1986—Borland has sold more than 400,000 copies of Turbo Pascal, probably more copies than all other Pascal compilers put together. There simply is no other mass market Pascal compiler for CP/M-80 and the IBM PC/MS DOS computer family, nor is there ever likely to be. The price/performance ratio of Turbo Pascal would be supremely difficult to duplicate. I think that in the long run virtually everyone who learns Pascal will learn using Turbo Pascal. There are larger and more powerful Pascal compilers for doing the more difficult work of the world. But back at square one, where the beginner begins to write his BEGINs, there will be Turbo and precious little else.

When the first edition of this book appeared, it was a clean break with Pascal texts in the past, which took care to place distance between themselves and any particular machine, or even any particular Pascal compiler. Today, few if any books on any popular language attempt to remain "generic." The audience demands more than theory at the highest level of abstraction. A book, to be considered useful, must treat both the high-level abstractions of the

Pascal language, and the gritty, low-level details of dealing with specific computers and operating systems. Computers were built to be *used*. My mission is to tell you how to use your computer. With any luck, you will learn Pascal in the process.

By the luck of the draw, I turned my first manuscript in two weeks before the announcement of Turbo Pascal V3.0. The book had been delayed once already—I had written it originally about Pascal/MT+, which had the bad manners to sink out of sight even as I wrote—and I did not want to delay it further for yet another rewrite. This second edition came about primarily to address V3.0's additional features, and to bring my code capitalization in line with the emerging Turbo Pascal standard. It is now indeed *complete* Turbo Pascal, with the sole exception of Turtle Graphics. My apologies, but Turtle Graphics is a very, *very* bad idea, and I do not want to encourage its use. Graphics in general is too large a subject to cover along with all of Turbo Pascal. It is not enough to speak only of graphics primitives—how they go together is far more important. I have only touched on it here, but I will give it its due in *Turbo Pascal Solutions: Graphics*, which should appear sometime in 1987.

The blizzard of letters I received on the first edition was gratifying. I can't promise to answer all of them, but I keep every one and enjoy them.

This is square one

You have it in your head to learn Pascal. To that end, you have this book in your hand. In front of you is your personal computer. It can be most any personal computer running any of the CP/M and PC/MS DOS families of operating systems. For real-life examples we'll be speaking of the Xerox 820 using CP/M-80 and the IBM Personal Computer using PC DOS.

I'll have to assume that you have learned the basics of operating your computer. This includes how to boot up the system, how to format diskettes, how to interpret a directory listing, how to copy files from one diskette to another, and so on. I'll assume you understand the importance of making backup copies of anything which has any value to you. *Anything which you don't back up you will eventually lose.*

As I mentioned earlier, this book is about a specific Pascal compiler: Turbo Pascal from Borland International. So finally, I will assume that you own Turbo Pascal for your computer.

Given those few assumptions, this book and your own common sense can teach you how to program in Pascal.

—Jeff Duntemann
Towson, Maryland

Acknowledgements

Many thanks to Larry Stone for his (brilliant) assembly-language assistance; to Dave Smereski of Xerox Corporation for help with interrupt theory and real numbers; to Mike Bentley and John Hall for needed advice; to Jim Dunn for media conversion; and to Nancy Kress for frequent booster shots of sanity.

For Carol,
who builds structures of love

Contents

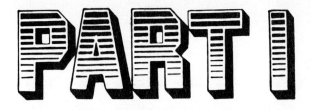

PART I

THE IDEA OF PASCAL

The Pascal process

1.1   Programs are blueprints for action

That eccentric wizard Ted Nelson, author of *Computer Lib* and guru of the amazing Xanadu Hypertext system, defines a computer simply as "a box that follows a plan." And way down deep, that's all it is: The computer is a box that represents numbers, letters, and words as electronic symbols and understands a limited repertoire of instructions for manipulating those symbols. The plan is a sequence of those instructions, arranged so that the computer, in following the sequence of instructions, will get something done.

The instructions themselves are almost ridiculously minute. Translated out of their jargon, computer instructions sound something like this:

> Put the number 6 into Box A.
> Put the number stored at memory location X into Box B.
> Add Box A to Box B. Put the result into Box B.
> Store the contents of Box B at Memory Location Y.
> If the contents of Box B is 0, perform Instruction #Z instead of the next instruction.

As you might imagine, it takes thousands of these little instructions to do anything useful. Because computers are so fast, they can, in fact, do thousands of these instructions in a second and make it look as though they are executing a small number of large steps, when really they are executing an enormous number of *very* small steps. This sequence of steps, so carefully arranged and followed, is a computer program. It is the computer's action plan. You write it. The computer follows it.

HIGH-LEVEL COMPUTER LANGUAGES

Writing programs using the minuscule instructions paraphrased above is called "assembly language programming." It is done when necessary, for various reasons. It should not be done unless it *must* be done. There are infinitely easier ways to tell computers what to do.

The most important is the use of "high-level" computer languages, like Pascal, BASIC, FORTRAN, COBOL, and such. In a nutshell, such languages cobble together big program steps out of many little program steps and then allow you to write programs by arranging the big program steps and not worrying about writing hordes of tiny program steps. For example, the simple action

```
Beep
```

toots a tone on your computer's speaker. The actual sequence of instructions for making this tone might be dozens of tiny instructions long. But you don't care about that; if you can write the word **Beep** and let someone else worry about setting up those dozens of tiny instructions, so much the better.

That "someone else" is a high-level computer language. Pascal is such a language. Pascal allows you to write a series of large instructions like this

```
Remainder := Remainder - 1;
IF Remainder = 0 THEN
BEGIN
  Beep;
  Write('Warning!  Your time has run out!');
END;
```

in perhaps fifteen seconds. The sequence of actual "machine" instructions to do these things may be 100 instructions long. No problem. Pascal does the converting. It arranges the machine instructions automatically while you run out to the kitchen for another bagel and prune juice.

Converting a series of large, English-language steps into a series of tiny (usually incomprehensible) machine instructions is what Pascal does. So do BASIC and COBOL, as well as all the others. The idea is the same, no matter how it happens to be expressed.

1.2   Programs that make other programs

What we call Pascal is actually itself a computer program. Like all other entities that are run or manipulated on a computer, it is stored on a floppy disk. You run it as you would run any other computer program.

When you program in Pascal, what you actually do is edit a text file (a file of human-readable words) and store it on a floppy disk. The computer itself can do nothing with this text file; to the computer it is just a jumble of letters, numbers, and punctuation marks:

```
PROGRAM Genesis;

BEGIN
  Writeln('In the beginning God created Adam.');
  Writeln('--or was it Coleco?')
END.
```

The Pascal compiler program, however, understands this (rather absurd) little program very well. The compiler program reads the text file from disk and looks at every word and symbol. Based on which words they are and what order they are in, it builds a stream of those minute machine instructions and stores the stream as a file on floppy disk. This file becomes a real computer program, which

can be loaded into your computer and run. When run, it will print
these words on your CRT screen:

```
In the beginning God created Adam.
--or was it Coleco?
```

and quit.

So, in fact, the Pascal compiler is a computer program that
creates other computer programs. The words *you* write (your
"program") are actually instructions to the Pascal compiler and *not*
to the computer itself.

1.3 Setting up work disks

Most of what you've read so far applies to any Pascal compiler. The
focus of this book is on a specific compiler, Turbo Pascal from
Borland International. From now on, assume that what is said
applies to Turbo Pascal, although the broader concepts of Pascal go
beyond any individual implementation of the language.

I recommend that you prepare two work disks for learning and
using Turbo Pascal. One disk (which I will refer to as your
compiler disk) should contain the compiler and a few other files
that the compiler needs to operate. You should also put on this disk
any utility programs that you use frequently, such as a disk formatting program, PIP and STAT (for CP/M-80) and a debugger (DDT
for CP/M-80 or DEBUG for PC/MS DOS.) This disk will reside in
disk drive A:.

The other disk (which I will call your program disk) will reside
in drive B:, and will contain your program source files, "include"
files (we'll explain them in a while), and compiled runnable object
files. You will, in time, have a number of program disks for drive
B:. It makes a good deal of sense to confine each major programming project to its own disk. With diskettes now available for as
little as fifty cents each in quantity (get together with your friends

and buy them by the hundred!) the cost of one disk per project is small compared with the confusion you will avoid.

You've heard this before, I'm sure, but it is important: The distribution disks that come from Borland International should be considered *read-only*. Under *no* circumstances should you try to write to a distribution master disk, and you should read from it as infrequently as possible. Once you've made your compiler working disk, put the master in a plastic diskette case at the bottom of the bureau drawer that contains your stamp collection and last year's Sears catalogs.

Not all of the files on the distribution disks are necessary for you to work with Turbo Pascal. In addition to the compiler itself, there are several example programs written in Turbo Pascal and a READ.ME file that contains latebreaking notes on your release of the compiler.

At *minimum* you must copy the following files from the distribution master to your compiler work disk:

TURBO.COM   The compiler program itself
TURBO.MSG   The English-language error messages

If your version of Turbo Pascal is for CP/M-80, there will be a third file called TURBO.OVR. This file allows you to "jump out" of the Turbo environment to execute another CP/M-80 program and then jump back in again. Unless you need that ability, you may omit TURBO.OVR from your compiler disk.

1.4 Turbo Pascal as a programming environment

The "Turbo environment" is a phrase I will be using frequently to describe the Turbo Pascal system. I call it an "environment" because it is more than just a Pascal compiler. It is a place to get your work done.

Traditionally, a Pascal compiler is a separate program in itself. To develop programs in Pascal you must load and run a text editor to edit your text. Then you must exit the text editor and load and run the Pascal compiler to compile the program text you have just edited. After that (in most cases) you must load and run a linker program that prepares the compiled object code for running. Then and only then, once you exit the linker program, can you load and run your compiled program to see if it works correctly.

This is a lot of loading and jumping into and out of programs. It takes a fair amount of time to move all of that information to and from a floppy disk. The Turbo Pascal environment, by contrast, is *one* program that loads once from disk and lets you do *everything* from inside it. What we call Turbo Pascal includes an editor, a Pascal compiler, a means of running compiled programs, and some simple debugging utilities, all in one program.

You run Turbo Pascal by typing its name:

```
A>TURBO
```

Turbo will ask you if you wish to load error messages; until you are an expert or desperately need the extra memory (especially on an 8-bit computer like the Xerox 820) *always* answer *Yes*.

The screen will clear and the Turbo Menu will appear. For MS DOS machines (including the IBM PC) it looks like this:

```
Logged drive: A
Active directory: \

Work file:
Main file:

Edit    Compile  Run   Save

Dir     Quit  compiler Options

Text:    0 bytes
Free: 62635 bytes

>
```

The Turbo Menu looks a little different for 8-bit CP/M-80 machines like the Xerox 820:

```
Logged drive: A

Work file:
Main file:

Edit      Compile   Run    Save

eXecute   Dir       Quit   compiler Options

Text:      0 bytes (802A-802A)
Free: 22491 bytes (802B-D806)

    >
```

In the list of commands, the capital letter in each command is the only letter you need press to begin that particular command. For example, to compile a program, press C. The execute command is spelled "eXecute" to show you that you must type "X" to invoke it.

The greater than symbol, >, indicates that Turbo Pascal is waiting for a command.

THE WORK FILE

In the Turbo environment, you work on one program at a time. The name of this program is displayed on the Turbo menu after "Work file:" When you Edit, Compile, or Run from the Turbo menu, the work file names the program that will be edited, compiled, or run.

When you first run Turbo, no work file is displayed. You must enter a work file name before you try to edit or compile anything. Entering a work file is done by pressing W and typing a name in response to the prompt:

```
Work file name: GENESIS.PAS
```

As soon as you enter the file name, Turbo will try to load the text file into memory for you to work with it.

```
Loading A:GENESIS.PAS
```

If it cannot find the file on disk, it will create an empty text file with that name, and display the message:

```
New file
```

The work file remains in memory until you load a new work file over it or until you leave the Turbo Pascal environment.

1.5   Editing, compiling, and running a simple program

The best way to learn anything is by doing it, and you can get some Turbo Pascal practice by typing in some of the small programs from this book and then compiling and running them.

Part III of *Complete Turbo Pascal* is a complete reference to installing, modifying, and using Turbo Pascal. It contains everything you will need to know to run the compiler and editor, from elementary practice programs up to large, complicated programs with multiple overlays. Since a beginner could easily drown in Part III's ocean of technical details, this short section will describe the fundamentals of editing, compiling, and running small simple programs such as the examples given in this book.

As you gain expertise in Pascal, you might spend some time reading through Part III. It's not the sort of thing you'd want to curl up with on a rainy night, but when you must reference some minuscule arcane detail, it will help to have reviewed Part III in advance.

EDITING

To edit your work file, simply press E. Turbo Pascal will clear the screen and display the file. (A new file, of course, will be empty and the screen will show nothing.) Your cursor will be resting at the top of the screen, ready for you to enter new text or change text that already exists.

Type the lines of the GENESIS program, pressing RETURN after each line:

```
PROGRAM Genesis;

BEGIN
  Writeln('In the beginning God created Adam.')
  Writeln('--or was it Coleco?')
END.
```

(Yes, there is a bug in the preceding program. Be a sport and type it in verbatim, just to see what happens . . .)

If you make a mistake in typing, you can use the arrow keys to move the cursor back to your misplaced characters and delete them or add what's missing. (It is possible that your arrow keys will not work correctly as they do on the IBM PC. The Xerox 820, for example, will not move the cursor correctly if you use the arrow keys. You may be able to change key assignments to correct this by using Turbo's TINST utility—see the *Turbo Pascal Reference Manual*, Appendix L.)

There are quite a number of commands that you can use to build your program file with the Turbo Pascal editor. These will be explained in detail in Chapter 22.

Finally, you will decide that your program is finished and ready to be compiled. To exit the editor, hold down the CTRL key, then (while holding it) press (one at a time) K and D. The Turbo Pascal prompt, >, will reappear.

Your source program is still in memory. If you turned off the computer right now, you would lose it for good, since you have not yet saved it out to disk. For safety's sake, press S. Your program source file will be saved to disk. It is a good idea to press S every time you exit the editor.

COMPILING

Your program is ready to compile. Press C. Turbo Pascal will print a running display of the line numbers it is compiling. Programs shorter than 50 lines will compile almost too quickly to follow.

When the compilation is complete, the Turbo Pascal prompt, >, will appear again.

Now, if during the compilation Turbo Pascal detects an error in your program, it will display the error and its error number on the screen:

```
Error 1: ';' expected. Press <ESC>:
```

If you typed in program **Genesis** exactly as it was given above, you will see the preceding message when you try to compile it. A semicolon should have been placed after the first **Writeln** statement. Press the ESC key.

The editor screen will reappear, displaying your file. The cursor will be flashing under the W in the second **Writeln.** This isn't exactly where the semicolon should go; it is where Turbo became quite certain that a semicolon was missing. Semicolons serve to separate statements (see Section 13.8) and there is nothing to separate the two **Writeln** statements. Once Turbo ran into the second **Writeln** statement, it realized no semicolon was going to be encountered and it started to get confused, hence the error.

To correct the error you should move the cursor to the immediate right of the first **Writeln** statement and type a semicolon. Then exit the editor (hint: CTRL-K/D), save your corrected program file back out to disk (the S command), and compile it once again.

RUNNING   Once a program compiles correctly it may be run. This is as easy as pressing R. Some early versions of Turbo Pascal for the IBM PC will clear the screen before running any program. Others will simply print the word "Running . . ." and begin executing your program. Program **Genesis** doesn't do much; it only displays these two lines:

```
In the beginning God created Adam.
--Or was it Coleco?
```

When the program is finished running, you will see the Turbo menu prompt, >, appear again.

A FORK IN THE ROAD

With that quick overview you should be able to type in any of the short example programs found in this book, compile them, and run them.

Where to now?

That depends on your frame of mind. The rest of Part I deals with the *idea* of Pascal. There is a philosophy behind the language that goes well beyond the simple stringing of program statements together. If you are a patient, methodical person, and most especially if you want to write large, easily-readable programs, I strongly suggest reading the rest of Part I before doing anything else.

If you are fundamentally a practical person and want to learn more about how the system runs, read Part III now. Part III is a detailed reference manual for the Turbo Pascal environment. Much of it is dry reading, but you will have to learn all its material thoroughly to get the most out of Turbo Pascal. *Then,* do come back and finish Part I.

Finally, if you are impatient to get down and hack Pascal and are willing to make lots of mistakes in the process, go directly to Part II and have at it. Part II is the description of the language itself, feature by feature. Digest that, and the How of Pascal will be in your pocket.

I trust you will then return to Part I and find out the Why. By doing so, you will save yourself enormous amounts of time, CRT phosphor, and torn hair. You will also write better programs.

The choice is yours.

The secret is structure

Pascal, by design, is a structured language.

Unlike BASIC and FORTRAN, it imposes a structure on its programs. Pascal will not let you string statements together haphazardly, even if every one, taken alone, is syntactically correct. There is a detailed master plan that every Pascal program must follow and the compiler is pretty stiff about enforcing the rules. A program must be coded in certain parts. Some parts must go *here,* and others must go *there*. Everything must be in a certain order. Some things cannot work together. Other things *must* work together.

Aside from some concessions to compiler designers (Pascal makes their task easier in some respects), Pascal's structure exists solely to reinforce a certain way of thinking about programming. This way of thinking represents Niklaus Wirth's emphasis on creating programs that are understandable without scores of pages of flowcharts and thousands of lines of explication. This way of thinking championed by Wirth and others is frequently called "structured programming." Although structured programming can be accomplished in any computer language (even BASIC!) Pascal is one of only a few computer languages that *require* it.

2.1   Basic elements of a Pascal program

A structure must be made of something. A crystal is a structure of atoms in a particular orderly arrangement. A Pascal program is made of "atoms" that are simply English words formed from the

Reserved words in Turbo Pascal				
ABSOLUTE	END	LABEL	REPEAT	WHILE
AND	EXTERNAL	MOD	SET	WITH
ARRAY	FILE	NIL	SHL	XOR
BEGIN	FOR	NOT	SHR	
CASE	FORWARD	OF	STRING	
CONST	FUNCTION	OR	THEN	
DIV	GOTO	PACKED	TO	
DO	IF	PROCEDURE	TYPE	
DOWNTO	IN	PROGRAM	UNTIL	
ELSE	INLINE	RECORD	VAR	

ASCII character set. These program atoms fall into three categories. There is a very small number of words (only 43 in Turbo Pascal) called "reserved words," a larger number of words called "standard identifiers," and then the unlimited multitude of ordinary identifiers created by you, the programmer. Reserved words are words that have special meanings within Pascal. They cannot be used by the programmer except to stand for those particular meanings. The compiler will immediately error-flag any use of a reserved word that is not rigidly in line with that word's meaning. Examples would include **BEGIN**, **END**, **PROCEDURE**, **ARRAY**, and that old devil **GOTO**.

Everything that is not a reserved word is an "identifier." Some identifiers have predefined meanings to the compiler. These "standard identifiers," like reserved words, have a particular meaning to the compiler. However, under certain circumstances you can redefine their meanings for your own purposes. I shouldn't have to say that redefining a standard identifier is not something you should attempt until you know the Pascal language and your compiler inside and out.

Any name you apply to an entity in a program is an ordinary identifier. The names of variables, of procedures and functions, and of the program itself are identifiers. An identifier you create can mean what you want it to mean (within Pascal's own rules and limits) as long as it is unique. That is, if you have a variable named **Counter**, you cannot have a procedure named **Counter**. Nor can you have another variable named **Counter**. You can give a particular identifier to only *one* entity of your program. The compiler will flag an error as soon as it spots the second usage.

Standard identifiers in Turbo Pascal

Addr	Delete	Length	Readln
Append	Dispose	LN	Real
ArcTan	EOF	Lo	Release
Assign	EOLN	LowVideo	Rename
Aux	Erase	Lst	Reset
AuxInPtr	Execute	LstOutPtr	Rewrite
AuxOutPtr	Exit	Mark	Round
BlockRead	Exp	MaxAvail	Seek
BlockWrite	External	MaxInt	SeekEOF
Boolean	False	Mem	SeekEOLN
BufLen	FilePos	MemAvail	Sin
Byte	FileSize	Move	SizeOf
Chain	FillChar	New	Sqr
Char	Flush	NormVideo	Sqrt
Chr	Frac	Odd	Str
Close	FreeMem	Ord	Succ
ClrEOL	GetMem	Output	Swap
ClrScr	GotoXY	OvrDrive	Text
Con	Halt	OvrPath	Trm
ConInPtr	HeapPtr	ParamCount	True
ConOutPtr	Hi	ParamStr	Trunc
Concat	IOResult	Pi	Truncate
ConstPtr	Input	Port	UpCase
Copy	InsLine	Pos	Usr
Cos	Insert	Pred	UsrInPtr
CrtExit	Int	Ptr	UsrOutPtr
CrtInit	Integer	Random	Val
DelLine	Kbd	Randomize	Write
Delay	Keypressed	Read	Writeln

Identifiers specific to CP/M-80 Turbo Pascal

BDOS	BIOS	RecurPtr	
BDOSHL	BIOSH	StackPtr	

Identifiers specific to MS-DOS & CP/M-86 Turbo Pascal

CSeg	Intr	Ofs	Seg
DSeg	MeMW	PortW	SSeg

Identifiers specific to MS-DOS Turbo Pascal

ChDir	LongFilePos	LongSeek	MSDOS
GetDir	LongFileSize	MkDir	RmDir

Identifiers specific to CP/M-86 Turbo Pascal

BDOS

Identifiers specific to IBM PC Turbo Pascal

Black	Brown	Cyan	DarkGray
Blink	BW40	CW40	Draw
Blue	BW80	CW80	GraphBackground

Standard identifiers in Turbo Pascal (*continued*)			
Identifiers specific to IBM PC Turbo Pascal			
GraphColorMode	LightCyan	Plot	WhereY
GraphMode	LightGray	Red	White
GraphWindow	LightGreen	Sound	Window
Green	LightMagenta	TextBackground	Yellow
HiRes	LightRed	TextColor	
HiResColor	Magenta	TextMode	
LightBlue	NoSound	WhereX	

Combining reserved words and identifiers gives you statements. **IF**, **THEN**, =, and **GOTO** are reserved words. (The equal sign, =, is called an "operator," which is a special kind of reserved word.) **Chain** is a standard identifier. **Counter**, **Limit**, and **NextProg** are programmer-defined (that is, by you) identifiers.

```
IF Counter = Limit THEN Chain(NextProg);
```

is a statement.

Combining statements in a fashion that respects Pascal's structure gives you a program.

2.2 Data and structures made of data

There are other programming languages that enforce a program structure, such as Algol and PL/1. Pascal goes beyond both, in that it allows a programmer to build structures of data as well as structures of program statements. Understanding this will require a look at the Pascal concept of "data."

Data are chunks of information that your program manipulates. There are different "types" of data, depending on what the data is intended to represent. How your program handles your variables depends completely on what type you decide they are. Every variable used in a Pascal program must be declared to be of some type, with a notation like this:

```
CreditHours : Integer;
```

This will allow you to manipulate integer values in a variable called **CreditHours**, subject to PASCAL's explicit limitations on what can be done with integers.

At the lowest level, all data in a Pascal program (or any program, really) are stored as binary numbers somewhere in your computer's RAM space. The data type to some extent dictates the way those binary numbers are arranged in RAM, and to a greater extent dictates how you, as a human being, will use that data. The concept of data type is much more important in Pascal than it is in BASIC. Numbers and strings are the only common data types used in BASIC. Pascal goes much further in the different types of data it recognizes. It defines certain fundamental types of data:

Integers are numbers (including negative numbers) that cannot have decimal points, like 1, –17, and 4529.

Characters (indicated by predefined identifier **Char**) consist of the ASCII character codes from 0 to 127. These include all the common letters, numbers, and symbols used by all modern computers. Turbo Pascal extends that to include those 128 ASCII characters plus an additional 128 characters that your computer may or may not use.

Boolean type variables have only two possible values, **True** and **False**. They are sometimes called "flags." Pascal uses them in conditional statements like **IF/THEN/ELSE** and **REPEAT/UNTIL** to determine whether to take some action or not.

Real type variables are used to express "real numbers," numbers that may include a decimal part. Numbers such as 1.16, –3240.0, 6.338, and –74.0457 are all real numbers.

In addition to these elementary data types understood by all Pascals, Turbo Pascal adds two of its own: **Byte** and **String**. A detailed discussion of all basic data types appears in Part II.

Virtually any task can be accomplished using these fundamental data types alone. However, creating structures of data by using these fundamental data types as building blocks can help you to develop a program design and to code the program once the design is complete. Using the basic data types, Pascal allows a programmer to build special-purpose types that are valid only within the program in which they are defined.

One way to build new special-purpose data types is by defining "subranges." A subrange is a type that may have as its values only certain values from the range of the fundamental data type. For example, academic grades are usually expressed as letters. Not all letters are grades, however. You might define a subrange of the basic type **Char** that can have as values only the letters from A through F. Such a type would be defined this way:

```
Grade = 'A'..'F';
```

Now, to create a variable to hold grades, you would declare a variable this way:

```
History : Grade;
```

Subranges provide a modicum of protection against certain coding mistakes. For example, if you tried to assign a grade of W to the variable **History**, the compiler would tell you during compilation that W is not a legal value of the subrange **Grade**.

Another powerful tool for building types is called a "record." A record is a grouping of fundamental types into a larger structure that is given a name as a new type. Variables can be declared to be of this type. Those variables can be assigned, compared, and written to files just as integers or characters can.

For example, if you are writing a program that keeps track of student grades and test results, you might group together basic data types in this arrangement:

```
TYPE
    SemesterGrades = RECORD
                    StudentID   : String[9];
                    SemesterID  : String[6];
```

(continues)

```
    Math        : Grade;
    English     : Grade;
    Drafting    : Grade;
    History     : Grade;
    Spanish     : Grade;
    Gym         : Grade;
    SemesterGPA : Real
END;
```

(concluded)

Now you can define a variable as having the type **SemesterGrades**. By a single variable name you now can control nine separate data chunks that you would otherwise have had to deal with separately. This can make certain programming tasks a *great* deal simpler. Even more important, however, it allows you to treat logically-connected data as a single unit to clarify your program's design and foster clear thinking about its function. For example, when you need to write the semester's grades out to a disk file, you needn't fuss with individual subjects separately. The whole record goes out to disk at once, as though it were a single variable, without any reference to the individual variables from which the record is built. The alternative is a series of statements that write the student ID to disk, followed by the semester ID, followed by the math grade, followed by the English grade, and so on.

When you need to think of all of a student's grades taken together, you can think of them as a unit. When you need to deal with them separately, Pascal has a simple way of picking out any individual variable within the record. (We'll be treating all these subjects in detail in Part II.) How you think of the data now depends on how you *need* to think of the data. Pascal encourages you to structure your data in ways like this, which encourage clear thinking about your problem at a high level (all grades taken together) or at a low level (each grade a separate data item).

Much of the skill of programming in Pascal is learning how to structure your data so that details are hidden by the structure until they are needed. It is much like being able to step back and see your data as a forest without being distracted by the individual trees.

Like most tools, the structuring of data is an edge that cuts two ways. It is all too easy to create data structures of Byzantine complexity that add nothing to a program's usefulness while obscuring its ultimate purpose. If the data structure you create for your program makes the program *harder* to understand from "three steps back," you've either done it the wrong way, or done it too much.

The rule of thumb I use is this: *Don't create data structures for data structure's sake.* Unless there's a reason for it, resist. Simplicity, when scrutinized, is not a simple thing.

2.3   The "master plan" of a Pascal program

The preceding overview has described the elements of a Pascal program. The program itself must be constructed from these elements in a very particular way. To some extent, this is done to make life easier for the compiler program. However, the bottom-line reason for the plan of a Pascal program is to make it easy to think of the program's task in a clear, structured way.

From the top:

THE PROGRAM STATEMENT

The *program statement* gives your program a name and tells the compiler that the work begins *here*. This name need not be the same name as your source file, nor the same name as the machine code file the compiler produces as an end product. This is a program statement:

```
PROGRAM Logbook;
```

THE LABEL DECLARATION PART

The *label declaration part* of the program comes next. It consists of the reserved word **LABEL** followed by your labels. Labels are markers in your program to which a **GOTO** statement may go. They are whole, non-negative numbers. They need not be in any particular order nor in any particular range. Each one must be unique, however. This is a sample label declaration (the program it came from probably uses too many **GOTO**'s!):

```
LABEL
    50,100,150,200,250;
```

If you have no **GOTO**'s in your program (and that is generally a very good idea) you won't need labels. Not having labels means the label declaration part of your program is unnecessary. But if you have one, it must be the first non-comment following the program statement.

THE CONSTANT DECLARATION PART

If you intend to use any constants in your program, the compiler expects them to follow the label declaration part. Constants are values that are defined at compile time and never changed while the program is running. The *constant declaration part* consists of the reserved word **CONST** followed by your constant declarations. Declaring a constant consists of the constant's identifier and its value, separated by an = symbol.

```
CONST
    LIMIT      = 255;
    GName      = '3-D Bar Graph';
    UsePlotter = True;
```

In the above example, **Limit** is an integer constant, **GName** is a string constant, and **UsePlotter** is a boolean constant. Standard Pascal and Turbo Pascal differ significantly in what may be a constant and what may not. We will be speaking of constants in detail in Part II.

THE TYPE DECLARATION PART

Following the constant declaration part of your program comes *type declaration*. The type declaration part consists of the reserved word **TYPE** followed by your type declarations. A type declaration is the type identifier and its declaration, separated by an = symbol. Pascal predeclares fundamental types like **Integer**, **Boolean**, **Char**, **Byte**, and **Real**. You don't have to declare these. You need only declare types that you build from other types or subranges of other types.

You can build types out of other types that you have already defined. However, you can't use a type as an ingredient in a new type unless the compiler already "knows" what that type is. The compiler knows a type either because that type is predeclared

(**Integer**, **Byte**, etc.) or because it has already compiled a statement defining that type in terms of other previously known types.

```
TYPE
   TeamTag  = 'A'..'G';              { Subrange }

   Callsign = String[8];

   USHam    = RECORD
                 OpCall    : Callsign;
                 LicClass  : Char
              END;

   Contact  = RECORD
                 HisCall   : Callsign;
                 RST       : Integer;
                 Band      : Integer;
                 Frequency : Real;
                 Emission  : String[2];
                 Date      : Integer;
                 ZuluTime  : Integer
              END;

   LogEntry = RECORD
                 OurOp     : USHam;
                 Team      : TeamTag;
                 QSO       : Contact
              END;
```

Above are a series of type declarations as they might appear in a ham radio logging program. If the details of notation are still strange to you, don't worry. We'll be covering all of this material in detail in Part II. The important thing to notice is that all types are defined in terms of fundamental types or subranges (through a statement containing a = symbol) before they are used.

For example, all of the types that make up **LogEntry** are programmer-defined types. Each must have been defined prior to the definition of **LogEntry**, and each was. If **TeamTag** had been defined *after* **LogEntry**, the compiler would have flagged it as an error during compilation of the program. It would not have known what the identifier **TeamTag** stood for. **TeamTag** is actually a subrange of type **Char** (it includes the characters from A to G), and once defined in those terms the compiler is perfectly comfortable dealing with it.

As with label declarations, the type declaration part is optional. If you have defined no types yourself, you don't need to include any type declarations.

Ordinarily, the constant declaration part of your program comes before the type declaration part. Turbo Pascal allows you to declare constants *after* types. This is done in connection with array constants and record constants. See Section 9.6.

THE VARIABLE DECLARATION PART

Following your type declarations must be your *variable declarations*. Strictly speaking, a program does not need a variable declaration part to compile or run. However, although you might be able to get away without having any label declarations or type declarations, it would not be much of a program without some variables to work with!

The variable declaration part consists of the reserved word **VAR** followed by your variable declarations. Every variable you use must have a valid type, either a predefined type (**Integer, Char, Boolean,** etc.) or a type you define yourself in the type declaration part of the program. Unlike type declarations, variable declarations use a colon symbol : to separate the variable name from its type:

```
VAR
  Counter : Integer;
  Tag     : Char;
  Grid    : XY Pair;
```

If several variables have the same type, you can group them on one line, separating them by commas like this:

```
VAR
  I,J,K : Integer;
```

I should point out that the reserved word **VAR** should appear only once, *not* on every line that declares a variable.

PROCEDURE AND FUNCTION DEFINITIONS

After all your variables have been declared, you must define any procedures and functions your program is to include. Procedures and functions are Pascal's subroutines. In form they are miniature programs, identical in structure to the program itself except that procedures and functions begin with **PROCEDURE** or **FUNCTION** rather than **PROGRAM** and do not end with a period but with a semicolon. Functions, additionally, return a value.

The rest of the structure remains the same. Procedures and functions may have their own "private" label declarations, constants, programmer-defined types, variables, and even their own procedures and functions. This nesting of structures can theoretically go on forever, but there are always "implementation restrictions," which mean (ultimately) that the machine eventually runs out of RAM to work with. There are practical hardware-dictated limits to any compiler feature. Be aware of them as you work out solutions to your programming problems.

The Pascal compiler enforces a calling hierarchy among procedures and functions. A procedure or function may call any procedure or function *above* itself in the source file. No procedure or function may call any procedure or function *below* itself without special authorization. (We'll treat that later on.) The reason is similar to the reason you must define a type before you use it: The compiler is travelling down the source file, building a list of identifiers it encounters as it goes. It will not allow a procedure to call another procedure unless the name of the called procedure is already on that list. This can only happen if the called procedure was encountered earlier by the compiler—meaning it exists *above* the calling procedure in the source file.

By this hierarchy, the first procedure the compiler encounters can't call anything—and the last procedure can call any procedure or function in the program. That's easy to understand why: they are all above the last procedure, and the compiler already has all the other procedures on its list by the time it gets down to that last procedure.

Think of it as a hostess travelling down a line of guests, taking names. By the time she meets the last man in line, she already knows the names of all the others and can introduce the last man to anyone else he wishes to meet; but if the first poor chap wishes to know who else is in line, the hostess can only shrug her shoulders. She simply doesn't know yet.

THE MAIN PROGRAM

And of course, the main program, being at the very bottom of the source file, is Boss—it calls anybody it wants. As we said above, the main body of your program is treated very much like the body of a procedure or function by the compiler, save that it must always come last—and it must end with a period ".".

When the computer begins executing your compiled program, it "enters" the program, not at the top of the source file but at the **BEGIN** that begins the main program. When it encounters the **END** at the end of the main program, it leaves the program and returns control to your operating system. In between, it does all the work the program must do, by calling functions and procedures and following the program's flow of control.

```
PROGRAM Tiny;               PROCEDURE Tiny;

CONST                       CONST
  TEN = 10;                   Ten = 10;

VAR                         VAR
  I   : Integer;              I   : Integer;

BEGIN                       BEGIN
  I:=Ten;                     I:=Ten;
  Writeln('>>I am now ',I)    Writeln('>>I am now',I)
END.                        END;
```

There's not much difference between **PROGRAM Tiny** and **PROCEDURE Tiny**, is there? Aside from the reserved words **PROGRAM** and **PROCEDURE** and the period or semicolon at the end, there is none. The two useless little things have the same structure and do the same work. The *really* big difference between them is that only **PROGRAM Tiny** can stand on its own. **PROCEDURE Tiny** *must* exist within some other program, or the compiler will kick it out as an error.

So the structure of a procedure or function is actually the structure of a program in miniature. A Pascal program is much like a collection of nested Chinese boxes, one (or more) inside another, all cubical and made of the same material. But only one box is big enough to contain the others, and that box is always on the outside. You can only "get at" the inside boxes by picking up the largest box and opening it.

The following program is a real, functioning program. It performs a nonsense function on a text file, producing a "foo factor" for any given text file. It's not intended to be useful, nor is the programming method ideal. (No program this small should have **LABEL**s or **GOTO**s. I put them in to show you how such creatures fit into program structure.) Ignore what it does for now and simply look at how the different parts are put together.

Look first at the main program. It's short—only a few statements long. And the statements are relatively general ones, mostly function and procedure calls. Reading down the main program, you can quickly understand what the program has to do: Open a file, calculate a foo factor for that file, display the foo factor, and close the file. Notice that the details for opening the file or calculating the foo factor are not given in the main program. They don't have to be there. In fact, if they were there it would be harder to understand what the program does.

To find those details you have to go up into the list of procedures and functions. Function **CrunchFile** calculates the foo factor for the entire file. It does this by reading lines from the file and calculating a foo factor for each line. But calculating a foo factor for a line is a relatively involved process in itself, so those details are extracted and put into yet another function called **CrunchLine**. By putting the details for crunching a line into a separate procedure, we make the process for crunching the whole file easier to understand.

CrunchFile can call **CrunchLine**, and does. But **CrunchLine** cannot call **CrunchFile**. **CrunchLine** lies above **CrunchFile** in the source file and in the hierarchy. **CrunchLine** could call **OpenAFile** if it needed to, but it does not.

```
1          PROGRAM Generic;
2
3
4          LABEL
```

(continues)

```
5              100;
6
7          CONST
8            Iterations = 25;
9
10         TYPE
11           InputFile  = TEXT;
12           String80   = String[80];
13
14         VAR
15           Counter    : Integer;
16           OK         : Boolean;
17           LIMIT      : Integer;
18           FooFactor  : Integer;
19           Buffer     : String80;
20           DoFile     : InputFile;
21
22
23         PROCEDURE OpenAFile(VAR OK : Boolean);
24
25         VAR
26           I : Integer;
27
28         BEGIN
29           Assign(DoFile,'MYTEXT.TXT');
30           {$I-} Reset(DoFile); {$I+}
31           I := IOResult;
32           IF I = 0 THEN OK := True ELSE OK := False;
33         END;
34
35
36         FUNCTION CrunchLine(Buffer : String80) : Integer;
37
38         VAR
39           I      : Integer;
40           Bucket : Integer;
41
42         BEGIN
43           CrunchLine := 0;
```

(continues)

```
44              IF Length(Buffer) > 0 THEN
45                BEGIN
46                  Bucket := 0;
47                  FOR I := 1 TO Length(Buffer) DO Bucket := Bucket +
48                    Ord(Buffer[I]);
49                  Bucket := Bucket DIV LENGTH(Buffer);
50                  CrunchLine := Bucket
51                END
52           END;
53
54
55        FUNCTION CrunchFile(VAR DoFile : InputFile) : Integer;
56
57        VAR
58           Passes : Integer;
59           Temp   : Integer;
60
61        BEGIN
62           Temp := 0;
63           FOR Passes := 1 TO Iterations DO
64             BEGIN
65               Reset(DoFile);
66               WHILE NOT EOF(DoFile) DO
67                 BEGIN
68                   Readln(DoFile,Buffer);
69                   Temp := Temp+CrunchLine(Buffer);
70                 END
71             END;
72           CrunchFile := Temp DIV Iterations
73        END;
74
75
76
77        BEGIN     { Main Program }
78           OpenAFile(OK);
79           IF NOT OK THEN
80             BEGIN
81               Writeln('>>The file cannot be opened.');
82               GOTO 100
```

(continues)

```
83              END;
84           FooFactor := CrunchFile(DoFile);
85           Writeln('>>Foo Factor for Input File is ',FooFactor);
86           Close(DoFile);
87           Writeln('>>Processing completed.');
88              100:
89         END.
```

(concluded)

The calling hierarchy forces the details of the structure to the top and the "broad strokes" of the program structure to the bottom. As you move upward from the main program, the level of detail increases. This gives you a clear method to begin understanding a Pascal program: Read and understand the main program first, which gives you the broadest picture of the program with the fewest details to distract you. From there move upward to the major procedures and functions, and still further upward, until by the time you understand the topmost procedures and functions on the source file, you have it all, and you learned it in the right order: the order most conducive to clear thought about the program and what it does.

This sort of approach to designing and understanding programs—large structure first, details last—has often been called "top-down programming." Pascal, to a large extent, enforces a top-down method on its users. I object to the term "top-down programming" because when working with a Pascal source file, it is really "bottom-up programming." Your design and understanding really work from the bottom of the source file upward.

I prefer to think of a Pascal program as a pyramid. You must climb it (and *build* it!) from the base upward. If you attempt to build the details at the top without a well-designed base on which to rest them, the whole thing will collapse all over you.

This, in brief, is the master plan of a Pascal program. Some programmers object to the admittedly rigid nature of this plan. I'll be the first to admit that it makes "clever hacks" difficult to achieve. On the other hand, if you feel (as I do) that it is important to produce code that is as easy to understand (and fix!) next year as it is today, you'll design your programs along the Pascal plan even without a whip-wielding compiler to enforce it.

Remember: The pyramids are not an especially clever hack. But they've been around a *long* time.

Nesting and scope

The notion of "scope" in a Pascal program is often a peculiar and slippery one to beginning programmers, and it's worth a little space all by itself.

Scope is an attribute of an identifier, be it variable, constant, data type, procedure, or function. The scope of an identifier is the region of a program that "knows" that identifier and can gain access to it. It has to do with levels of "nesting."

As we mentioned in the previous section, a program can be thought of as a Chinese box containing smaller programs built to the same general Pascal structure. These smaller programs are the procedures and functions of the main program. They are "nested" within the main program.

What we didn't emphasize (for clarity's sake) was that any procedure or function can have other procedures and functions nested within it. Like the Chinese boxes, this nesting of procedures and functions can continue until your computer system runs out of memory to contain it all.

The constants, variables, procedures, functions, or other identifiers that are declared within a procedure or function are said to be "local" to that procedure or function.

```
PROGRAM Hollow;

VAR
  Z    : Integer;
  Ch, Q : Char;
  Gonk  : String[80];

PROCEDURE LITTLE1;

VAR
  Z : Integer;

BEGIN
END;

PROCEDURE LITTLE2;

VAR
  Z : Integer;
  Q : Char;

BEGIN
END;

BEGIN     { Main for Hollow }
  Little1;
  Writeln('>>We are the hollow programs,');
  Little2;
  Writeln('>>We are the stuffed programs.')
END.
```

The program **Hollow** is nothing more than the merest skeleton of a program, constructed to illustrate the concept of scope and nesting. If you're sharp and have looked closely at **Hollow**, you may be objecting to the fact that there are three instances of a variable named **Z**—and I already told you that Pascal does not tolerate duplicate identifiers. Well, due to Pascal's notion of scope, the three **Z**'s are not duplicates at all.

Up near the top of the source file, in **Hollow**'s own variable list, is a variable named **Z**. In **Little1** is a variable named **Z**, but *this* **Z** is local to **Little1**. **Little2** also has a **Z** that is local to **Little2**. Each **Z** is "known" only in its own neighborhood, and the extent of that neighborhood is its scope. The scope of **Little1**'s Z is *only* within **Little1**. Likewise, **Little2**'s **Z** is known only within **Little2**. You *cannot* access the value of **Little2**'s **Z** (or, for that matter, *any* variable declared within **Little2**) from within **Little1**. Furthermore, while you are in the main program, you cannot access either of the two **Z**'s that are local to **Little1** and **Little2**. They might as well not exist until you enter one of the two procedures in which those local **Z**'s are declared.

This gets a little more slippery when you consider the **Z** belonging to program **Hollow** itself. That **Z**'s neighborhood encompasses the entire program, which includes both **Little1** and **Little2**. So while we're within **Little1** or **Little2**, which **Z** is the real **Z**? Plainly, we need a rule here, and the rule is call "precedence." *When the scopes of two identical identifiers overlap, the most local identifier takes precedence.* In other words, while you're within **Little1**, **Little1**'s own local **Z** is the only **Z** you can "see." The **Z** belonging to **Hollow** is hidden from you while you're within the scope of a more local **Z**. **Hollow**'s **Z** doesn't go away and doesn't change; you simply can't look at it or change it while **Little1**'s **Z** takes precedence.

Try this metaphor: There are too many Mike Smiths in the world. A national liquor company based in New York City has a vice president named Mike Smith. The company also has two regional salesmen named Mike Smith, one in Chicago and one in Geneseo, New York. When you are at corporate headquarters in New York and mention Mike Smith, everyone assumes you mean the Vice President of Whiskey Keg Procurement. However, if you're in Chicago and mention Mike Smith to a liquor store owner, he thinks you mean the skinny chap who sells him Rasputin Vodka. He's never heard of the VP or the salesman in Geneseo. Furthermore, if you're in Geneseo and mention Mike Smith, the restaurant owners think of the fellow with the red beard who distributes Old Tank Car wines. They don't know (and could care less about) the VP or the vodka salesman in Chicago.

Look back at **Hollow** for a moment and consider the variable **Q**. **Hollow** has a **Q**. **Little2** also has one. **Little1** does not. Within **Little2**, **Little2**'s **Q** is king, and **Hollow**'s **Q** is hidden away. However, **Little1** can read and change **Hollow**'s **Q**. There is no precedence conflict here because there is no **Q** in **Little1**. Since the scope of **Hollow**'s **Q** is the entire program, any function or procedure within **Hollow** can access **Hollow**'s **Q** as long as there is no conflict of precedence. We say that **Hollow**'s **Q** is "global" to the entire program. In the absence of precedence conflicts, **Hollow**'s **Q** is "known" throughout **Hollow**.

Hollow has a variable named **Gonk** that can be accessed from either **Little1** or **Little2** because it is the only **Gonk** anywhere within **Hollow**. With **Gonk**, the question of precedence does not arise at all.

Unless you can't possibly avoid it, don't make your procedures and functions read or change global variables (like **Ch** or **Gonk**) *unless* those variables are passed to the procedure or function through the parameter line. This prevents data "sneak paths" among your main program and procedures and functions. Such sneak paths are easy to forget when you modify a program, and may bollix up legitimate changes to the program in (apparently) inexplicable ways.

To sum up: An identifier is local to the block (procedure, function, module, or program) in which it is defined. This block is the *scope* of that identifier.

You cannot access a local identifier unless you are *within* that block or are *contained by* that block.

Where a duplicate identifier conflict of scope exists, the *more local* of *the two* is the identifier that you can access.

Programming by understanding the problem first

4.1 The problem of impatience

The number one killer of computer programs is impatience. The number one waster of data processing dollars is impatience. The number one mass-producer of program bugs is impatience. If you can conquer impatience, you have computer programming, in Pascal or any other language, right in your hip pocket.

The problem is simple enough: Planning is dull and difficult. Coding is fun. Following a natural enough human tendency, planning often gets short shrift during a programming project. Programmers dive into coding long before they have a really clear notion of what the project entails. The project definition (or "requirements") may not even be finished before the coding begins.

The hazards of working this way should be obvious, but a real-world (and true!) example should make it abundantly clear.

A school district sets out to create a student database. The programmers, going on a handwritten data structure sketched out in half an hour by the project manager, begin work on the excuse that keying in the data will take weeks, and having a "little module" to accept data will allow the keypunchers to get going. The little module is done in a week, and the keypunchers start punching. Days and thousands of student entries later, the project manager realizes that he will need several new fields on each student to comply with federal aid regulations. The incomplete data structure is now enshrined in 2000 lines of code and 4000 records of data. Adding in the support for the additional data fields is done hastily, and a second "little module" is created to accept the keypunchers' input for the missing fields. The patches to the code prove bug-ridden, and matching the additional data to the student records is faulty. Bottom line (when all the tangles are untangled): three months of additional (unnecessary) effort to get the system running. Bugs are still haunting the users three years after implementation.

Knowledgeable people in the software engineering field claim that there is a certain irreducible amount of effort required to design and implement a computer system. If that effort is not expended in planning, it will be expended two or many times over in scrapping and rewriting program modules and patching what the writers do not have the intestinal fortitude to scrap and rewrite.

Sadly, many textbooks on programming start new programmers off on the wrong foot, by showing them this single line program on page 2:

```
10 PRINT "HI! I'M A BASIC PROGRAM!"
```

On page 3 they add another line of text output. On page 4 they add some sort of numerical calculation. On page 5 they add a branch of some sort, and so it goes through all the features of BASIC, tacking line after line onto the poor program. The purpose is to reinforce the tutorial on BASIC by showing the programmer how the statements work. The lesson that isn't supposed to come across but does is that it's perfectly all right to design and write a program by sticking little pieces together without any planning beforehand. Not one word (or maybe a paragraph or two on page 279) is given to the process of planning out a program before the coding begins. Thus, it doesn't surprise me that impatience ruins so many programming efforts. Impatience is built right into the way we teach programmers their craft.

There is a method of programming championed by Niklaus Wirth that works extremely well on small to medium sized programming projects. It's called "programming by successive refinement." The gist of the method is this: Begin with a single clear statement of the purpose of the program you want to write, and then gradually refine that statement (breaking it down into subsidiary statements) until the last statement is compilable code in your language of choice. The first several iterations can (and should) be written without assuming you know what language the program will eventually be written in.

Because this method begins with a single broad statement and adds detail to the statement in a structured, orderly fashion, it fits in particularly well with the Pascal language.

I have found that the method breaks down when the system is so large as to encompass several very large programs, many necessary manual operations, and concurrent processes. If you find yourself faced with creating such a system, you are much better off following the method of structured analysis and design as outlined by Yourdon and Constantine.[1] This is *especially* true if your system is to be written and implemented by a team of programmers in addition to yourself.

For working on your own in developing reasonably straightforward programs, however, successive refinement will do nicely. The example I'm about to show you is a real, useable program written in Turbo Pascal. If you're reading this book in a strictly serial fashion without any previous knowledge of Pascal, you may not fully understand all of the code used. Don't worry about it right now. Look past the actual code and pay closer attention to the *method* involved in developing the code. Then come back after you've read Part II, which explains the Pascal language in detail, and read this short section again.

4.2 An example of successive refinement

Even the longest programming project begins with a single step. It's a big one and an important one: *Formulate a one-sentence statement of what the program must do.*

[1]Edward Yourdon and Larry L. Constantine, *Structured Design* (Englewood Cliffs, NJ: Prentice-Hall, Inc., 1979)

Make it *one* sentence. Why? It will help you decide what belongs in the program and what does not. In the early, muddled stages of formulation, it is often unclear just what a program has to do. Should all the work you desire be done by a single program? Do the various tasks belong together?

If you cannot describe the program in the broadest terms with fewer than two sentences, see if the tasks represented by the two sentences have anything in common. If not, you're better off splitting your single proposed program into two. Or, check to see if you're beginning to describe how the process is to be done, rather than stating what the process *is*. In that case, you have not used the broadest terms to describe your program. Look to your sentences and work backwards from their *how* to the *what*.

Now, back to our example. To keep the example program down to manageable size, its task must be relatively simple: *To chart the frequency of different word lengths appearing in a text file.*

```
PROGRAM STATEMENT ITERATION #1:

Collect and display the relative frequency of
different word lengths appearing in a text file.
```

This is the first iteration of your program statement, the single-sentence statement emphasized above. Very simply, you want to see which lengths of words appear most frequently in various textfiles you happen to have.

This will involve reading the text file, tallying the instances of each word length, and finally displaying the tallies in a meaningful way. In fact, the previous sentence lies at the heart of iteration #2. You might have been tempted to use this sentence as your single-sentence program statement, but you should not: Yes, it's a single sentence, but it tells *how* to do something, not simply what needs to be done. Rule of thumb: Once you begin talking *how* instead of *what,* you're already beyond the first iteration.

```
        PROGRAM STATEMENT ITERATION #2:

1. Select a text file and open it.

2. Set up a counter for each reasonable word length.

3. Scan the text file line by line, incrementing the
   appropriate counter for the length of each word
   read from the file.

4. Display histograms for each word length,
   reflecting the relative frequency of word lengths
   in the file.
```

At each stage in the process, look hard at each step in your current iteration and ask yourself: Do I really know what each statement means? If you don't understand the broad sense of each of your steps, you can hardly be expected to break each step down into the more detailed descriptions that your next iteration will demand.

At about iteration #3 (perhaps a little later if the problem is large and complex), your program statement will begin to take on some of the characteristics of your chosen language. Look for likely statements that can become procedures and functions. Begin to express the problem's need for data as real data items, even if they are not completely, rigorously defined in their first appearance. Indicate loops with indentation.

Avoid the temptation to write code at this point. You're not quite ready yet.

```
        PROGRAM STATEMENT ITERATION #3:

Opener(FileName, ErrorFlag)
  Open the file.
  If an error occurs, return an error flag.

Grapher (Counters)
  For each word length:
    Display the length as a number.
    Display a line of *'s proportional to counter.
```

```
MAIN PROGRAM
  Get a filename from somewhere.
  Opener(FileName, ErrorFlag)
  If ErrorFlag, print error message and exit.
  Set up an array of 40 integers.
  Until you hit EOF on the file:
    Read a line.
      Until the line is empty:
        Identify the first word in the line.
        Determine the length of the word.
        Increment that length's counter in array.
        Delete the word from the line.
  Close the file.
  Grapher(Counters)
  Display a message indicating process is complete.
```

Iteration #3 is still not anything like code, though it's plain that we're heading in the direction of Pascal. Keep refining the statement, watching for hidden "gotchas" that indicate some incomplete area of your understanding of the problem.

For example, there's a "gotcha" in iteration #3 that you'll find when you begin to refine the statement for the **Grapher** procedure. **Grapher** must display a line of asterisks proportional to the value in each of your counters. If you scan a large file, you may find the counter for four-letter words (the polite kind, of course) has a value of several hundred. Your printer prints only 80 columns. You have to *scale* the counters such that the line of asterisks for the largest counter will still fit across your printer's page.

You must decide how this scaling function is going to be done and where it must fit into the program. You may find in working out the details that you have defined a few more program steps and a few more data items. Add these to your next iteration. For example, a file and its name are two separate data items, yet iteration #3 treats them as though they were one. In your next iteration you must deal with both the "logical" (Pascal) and physical (disk resident) file.

In the process you'll discover that here and there things have begun to "fall into" real Pascal code. One of the first places this will happen is with loops. Once you understand how a loop is to be tested and terminated, it's natural to write that loop's statement as though it were Pascal code. Again, unless you are truly comfortable committing a statement to real code, it may mean you are unsure of what that statement means and how it works.

```
            PROGRAM STATEMENT ITERATION #4:

Variables
  I,J         : general purpose integers
  Counters    : array of 40 integers
  FileName    : a string
  TestFile    : a text file
  Line        : a string
  AWord       : a string
  WordLength  : an integer
  Scale       : a real number

KillJunk(AWord)
  BEGIN
    Take off bad characters in front of the word.
    Take off bad characters at the end of the word.
  END

Opener(FileName, ErrorFlag)
  BEGIN
    Associate TestFile with FileName
    Open TestFile for read.
    If an error occurs, return an error flag.
  END

Grapher(Counters, Scale)
  BEGIN
    FOR I = 1 TO 40 DO
      BEGIN
        Display word length I
        Display counter / Scale asterisks
      END
  END

FUNCTION Scaler(Counter) returns real
  BEGIN
    Scan CounterS for largest counter.
```

```
            IF largest count < printer width THEN exit
               ELSE Scaler := largest count / printer width
         END
BEGIN MAIN PROGRAM
   Extract FileName from the DOS command tail.
   Opener(FileName, TestFile, ErrorFlag)
   IF ErrorFlag is true, THEN
      BEGIN
         print error message
         exit
      END

   Set up an array of 40 integers.
   WHILE NOT EOF on TestFile
      BEGIN
         Read Line
         Increment LineCount
            WHILE there's still words in Line DO
               BEGIN
                  Extract AWord from Line
                  KillJunk(AWord)
                  Increment the total word counter
                  Limit length of humungous words to 40
                  Increment counter for AWord's length
                  Delete AWord from Line
               END

      END
   Close TestFile
   Scale := Scaler(Counters)
   Grapher(Counters, Scale)
   Display a message indicating process is complete.
END
```

Iteration #4 is starting to look something like a structured program. The first edition of this book, and a great many Pascal programs you'll find in books and on user group disks, show identifiers as well as reserved words in upper case. There is nothing sacred about upper or lower case in Pascal; the compiler forces all program text into upper case before it attempts to compile it. You

may write a program wholly in upper case, lower case, or mixed case as you like. The programs in this book reflect the mixed-case conventions that prevail in Turbo Pascal circles: Reserved words remain in upper case and all identifiers (including predefined identifiers) are in mixed case. Many people "spread out" their identifiers by interspersing underscores within the identifiers:

```
ERROR_FLAG
RETURN_TO_DOS
```

This is legal, but I do not do it because I also program in Modula 2, which does not allow underscores in identifiers.

The scaling problem was dealt with by adding a function named **Scaler** that returns a scale factor in the variable named **Scale**. Iteration #4 of **Scaler** has a logic bug (not a code bug; this isn't code yet) in it. Can you find it? If you can't, compare that expression of **Scaler** with the final Pascal code below.

An additional procedure has been added to take care of removing punctuation, tab characters, and other "junk" from the file, where "junk" is defined as anything that is not a countable letter or number in a word. The exclamation point after "Goodness!" should not be counted as part of the word, for example, nor quotes around the word "protection" in "copy 'protection.'"

Deciding when an iteration may take the final leap into code depends heavily on how fully you understand how every part of the program must work, and how comfortable you are with Pascal itself. Above all else, avoid this trap: You are still a touch fuzzy on how some detail in the program is supposed to work, so you make a fuzzy guess as to how it should be coded, making a mental note that "this probably won't work, but I'll pound it into shape once the rest of it works." *That's impatience talking!* A fuzzily-understood part of your program will invariably propagate its fuzziness to other parts of the program that depend upon it. Bugs that are the consequence of fuzzy design are the hardest to find and the most work to remove.

The more confident you are in your knowledge of Pascal, the larger the jump may be from your last iteration to actual code. If you are unsure about Pascal, it is best to take smaller jumps. Don't let impatience masquerade as false confidence.

When you decide you are ready, pull out your Pascal reference and copy your penultimate iteration to the final iteration (either on paper or on disk), making sure all statements have been converted to compilable Pascal code. Print a hardcopy of the program, and finally, turn the compiler loose on it.

The final program in Pascal is shown below. I have only printed five iterations for brevity's sake and because it took me five iterations to produce the program. A beginner might go a little slower and do the job in seven or eight iterations. Certainly, one additional iteration beyond 4 would be a good idea if you are unsure of Pascal's syntax.

Again, if you don't fully understand all the details of the code in the final program, don't worry about it just yet. All actual code details will be covered in Part II.

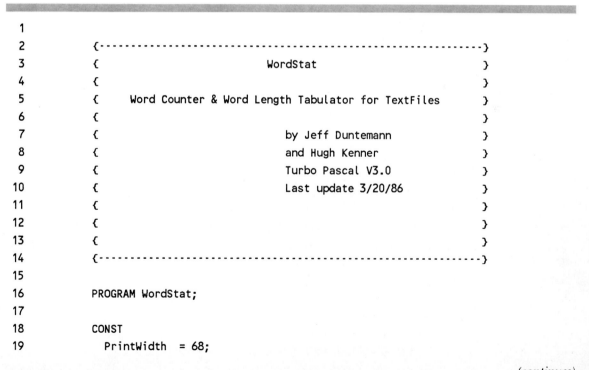

```
 1
 2          {----------------------------------------------------------}
 3          {                        WordStat                          }
 4          {                                                          }
 5          {    Word Counter & Word Length Tabulator for TextFiles     }
 6          {                                                          }
 7          {                          by Jeff Duntemann              }
 8          {                          and Hugh Kenner                }
 9          {                          Turbo Pascal V3.0              }
10          {                          Last update 3/20/86            }
11          {                                                          }
12          {                                                          }
13          {                                                          }
14          {----------------------------------------------------------}
15
16          PROGRAM WordStat;
17
18          CONST
19            PrintWidth  = 68;
```

(continues)

```
20              Tab         = #9;
21
22
23         TYPE
24             Array40     = ARRAY[0..40] OF Integer;
25             String80    = String[80];
26
27         VAR
28             I,J         : Integer;
29             Scale       : Real;
30             Ch          : Char;
31             Opened      : Boolean;
32             TestFile    : Text;
33             FName       : String80;
34             Counters    : Array40;
35             Line        : String80;
36             AWord       : String80;
37             WordLength  : Integer;
38             LineCount   : Integer;
39             WhiteSpace  : SET OF Char;
40             GoodChars   : SET OF Char;
41
42
43         PROCEDURE KillJunk(VAR AString : String80);
44
45         BEGIN
46           WhiteSpace := [#8,#9,#10,#12,#13,#32];
47           GoodChars  := ['A'..'Z','a'..'z','0'..'9'];
48           REPEAT       { Clean up leading end of word }
49             IF Length(AString) > 0 THEN
50               IF (AString[1] IN WhiteSpace) OR (NOT(AString[1] IN GoodChars))
51                 THEN Delete(AString,1,1)
52           UNTIL ((NOT (AString[1] IN WhiteSpace)) AND (AString[1] IN GoodChars))
53             OR (Length(AString) <= 0);
54           REPEAT       { Clean up trailing end of word }
55             IF Length(AString) > 0 THEN
56               IF (AString[Length(AString)] IN WhiteSpace)
57                 OR (NOT(AString[Length(AString)] IN GoodChars))
```

(continues)

```
58               THEN Delete(AString,Length(AString),1)
59         UNTIL ((NOT(AString[Length(AString)] IN WhiteSpace)
60           AND (AString[Length(AString)] IN GoodChars))
61           OR  (Length(AString) <= 0))
62     END;  { KillJunk }
63
64
65
66     PROCEDURE Opener(    FileName : String80;
67                      VAR TFile    : Text;
68                      VAR OpenFlag : Boolean);
69
70     VAR
71       I : Integer;
72
73     BEGIN
74       Assign(TFile,FileName);        { Associate logical to physical }
75       {$I-} Reset(TFile); {$I+}      { Open file for read     }
76       I := IOResult;                 { I <> 0 = File Not Found }
77       IF I = 0 THEN OpenFlag := True ELSE OpenFlag := False;
78     END;  { Opener }
79
80
81
82     FUNCTION Scaler(Counters : Array40) : Real;
83
84     VAR
85       I,MaxCount : Integer;
86
87     BEGIN
88       MaxCount := 0;           { Set initial count to 0 }
89       FOR I := 1 TO 40 DO
90         IF Counters[I] > MaxCount THEN MaxCount := Counters[I];
91       IF MaxCount > PrintWidth THEN Scaler := PrintWidth / MaxCount
92         ELSE Scaler := 1.0;    { Scale=1 if max < printer width}
93     END;  { Scaler }
94
95
```

(continues)

```
96
97          PROCEDURE Grapher(Counters : Array40; Scale : Real);
98
99      VAR
100       I,J : Integer;
101
102     BEGIN
103       FOR I := 1 TO 40 DO
104         BEGIN
105           Write(Lst,'[',I:3,']: ');        { Show count }
106           FOR J:=1 TO Round(Counters[I] * Scale) DO Write(Lst,'*');
107           Writeln(Lst,'')                  { Add (CR) at end of *'s}
108         END
109     END;
110
111
112     BEGIN   { WordStat Main }
113
114       FName := ParamStr(1);            { We must pick up command tail first, }
115       KillJunk(FName);                 {    before opening any files! }
116       FOR I:=0 TO 40 DO Counters[I]:=0;        { Init Counters }
117       LineCount := 0;
118
119       Opener(FName,TestFile,Opened);   { Attempt to open input file }
120       IF NOT Opened THEN               { If we can't open it...      }
121         BEGIN
122           Writeln('>>>Input file ',FName,' is missing or damaged.');
123           Writeln('   Please Check this file''s status and try again.');
124         END
125       ELSE                             { If you've got a file, run with it! }
126         BEGIN
127           WHILE NOT EOF(TestFile) DO   { While there's stuff in the file }
128             BEGIN
129               Readln(TestFile,Line);         { Read a Line }
130               LineCount := LineCount + 1;   { Count the Line }
131               Write('.');                    { Display a progress indicator }
132               FOR I := 1 TO Length(Line) DO
133                 IF Line[I] = Tab THEN Line[I] := ' ';
```

(continues)

```
134                    WHILE Length(Line) > 0 DO      { While there are words in the Line }
135                      BEGIN
136                        KillJunk(Line);              { Remove any non-text characters }
137                        IF POS(' ',Line) > 0 THEN
138                          AWord := Copy(Line,1,POS(' ',Line)) ELSE AWord := Line;
139                        KillJunk(AWord);             { Clean up the individual word }
140                        Counters[0] := Succ(Counters[0]);    { Count the word }
141                        WordLength := Length(AWord);
142                        IF WordLength > 40 THEN WordLength := 40;
143                        J := Counters[WordLength]; { Get counter for that Length }
144                        J := Succ(J);                { Increment it...        }
145                        Counters[WordLength] := J; { ...and put it back. }
146                        Delete(Line,1,Length(AWord));  { Remove the word from the Line }
147                      END
148                  END;
149                Writeln;
150                Close(TestFile);                 { Close the input file }
151                { The count itself is done.  Now to display it: }
152                Scale := Scaler(Counters);       { Scale the Counters }
153                Writeln(Lst,
154                '>>Text file ',FName,
155                ' has ',Counters[0],
156                ' words in ',LineCount,' Lines.');
157                Writeln(Lst,
158                '  Word size histogram follows:');
159                Grapher(Counters,Scale);         { Display Scaled histograms  }
160                Writeln(Lst,Chr(12));            { Send a formfeed to printer }
161              END
162         END.
```

(concluded)

PART II

LEARNING THE LANGUAGE

Introduction

In Part I of this book, we took a roller coaster ride through the idea of Pascal, in the hope of getting a bird's eye view of the large issues of the language, without stopping too long for individual details.

Now it's time for the details.

At this point I want to emphasize the difference between a language *definition* and a language *implementation*. In 1971, Niklaus Wirth wrote the language definition of Pascal, in a well-known (and impossible to read) book entitled *Pascal: User Manual and Report*. The book contained a meticulously detailed description of what the language should do. However, at that time there was no actual compiler program in existence that would actually take a Pascal source file and produce a runnable code file from it. Someone (many someones, actually) had to take Wirth's book and write a compiler program that obeyed the language definition as Wirth set it out. Such programs first appeared for large mainframe computers like the CDC6600, and have appeared for microcomputers only in the last few years.

Those compiler programs that functionally embody the Pascal language definition are called implementations of the Pascal language.

The formal definition of the Pascal language as Wirth defined it has a lot of holes and weak spots, rendering it of only limited use. Wirth's definition does not address string handling, random files, operating system calls, and many other things. People who actually implement the language on a particular computer usually expand beyond the language definition to make the compiler program capable of compiling more useful programs.

Furthermore, some implementations are forced to impose some limits on the programmer that Wirth's definition does not. To make use of small memory systems, real-world limits must be placed on identifier size, procedure and function size, maximum legal values for integers and real numbers, maximum member counts for sets, and so on. None of these things is present in the definition of the language, but all are critical to their particular implementation.

While Part I dealt mostly with the language's definition, Part II describes a particular implementation: Turbo Pascal. To allow you to do useful programming with this implementation of Pascal, we have to deal with implementation details, such as data range limitations, language extensions, and many other things.

It's important to remember, especially if you find yourself using other compilers on other computers, that Pascal as implemented in Turbo Pascal is only broadly the same as Pascal as implemented in the UCSD P-System, or MS Pascal, or Pascal/MT+. The details are likely to be different.

And details, in computer science, are everything.

Identifiers and the naming of names

God created the animals and Adam gave them names.

The animals were, after all, for Adam's use, and he had to have some way of keeping them all straight. God doesn't have problems like that.

Your computer creates programs for your use. Programs are collections of things (data) and steps to be taken in storing, changing, and displaying those things (statements). The computer knows such things by their addresses in memory. The readable, English-language names of data, of programs, and of functions and procedures are for your benefit. We call such names, taken as a group, *identifiers*. They exist in the source code only. *Identifiers do not exist in the final code file.*

Identifiers are sequences of characters of any length up to 127 characters that obey these few rules.

1. Legal characters include letters, digits, and underscores. Spaces and symbols like &,!,*, or % (or any symbol not a letter or digit) are not allowed.
2. Symbols or digits (0 to 9) may *not* be used as the first character in an identifier. All identifiers must begin with a letter from A to Z (or lower-case a to z) or an underscore.
3. Identifiers may not be identical to any reserved word.
4. Case differences are ignored. "A" is the same as "a" to the compiler.

5. Underscores are legal and significant. Note that this differs from most other Pascal compilers, in which underscores are legal but ignored. You may use underscores to "spread out" a long identifier and make it more readable; for example, SORT_ON_ZIP_CODE rather than SORTONZIPCODE. (A better method is to use mixed case to accomplish the same thing: SortOnZIPCode.)

6. *All* characters are significant, no matter how long the identifier is, up to 127 characters. Many other Pascals ignore all characters after the eighth character in an identifier.

These are all invalid identifiers that will generate errors:

Fox&Hound	Contains an invalid character
FOO BAR	Contains a space
7Eleven	Begins with a number
RECORD	"RECORD" is a reserved word

Simple constants

Constants are data values that are "baked into" your source code and do not change during the execution of a program. There are two kinds of constants in Standard Pascal: literal and named. Turbo Pascal provides a third kind of constant that is not really a constant: structured constants, which are constants that are data structures like arrays and records. We will discuss structured constants in Section 9.6.

A literal constant is a value of some sort that is stated as a value where it is used in your code. For example:

```
SphereVolume := (4/3)*PI*(Radius*Radius*Radius);
```

In this line of code, "4" and "3" are literal constants, representing the values of 4 and 3.

There is another constant in that statement: The identifier **PI** was previously declared a constant in the constant declaration part of the program:

```
CONST
  PI = 3.14159;
```

We could as well have used the literal constant 3.14159 in the statement, but "**PI**" is shorter and makes the expression less cluttered and more readable. Especially where numbers are concerned, named constants almost always make a program more readable.

Another use for constants is in the setting of program parameters that need changing only very rarely. They still *might* be changed someday, and if you use a named constant, changing the constant *anywhere in the program* is only a matter of changing the constant's declaration *once* in the declaration part of the program and then recompiling.

The alternative is to hunt through hundreds or thousands of lines of source code to find every instance of a literal constant to change it. You will almost certainly miss at least one, and the resultant bug farm may cost you dearly.

In short, don't use literal constants anywhere you will *ever* anticipate needing changes. In mathematical formulae, literal constants are usually all right; the value of PI hasn't changed recently.

TYPES OF CONSTANTS

In Standard Pascal, constants may be simple types and sets only. That includes real numbers, integers, bytes, characters, strings, sets, and Booleans. Individual enumerated types may also be considered constants, although they are not declared the same way as other constants. (We'll speak more fully of enumerated types in Section 8.2.) Structured types such as records, pointers, and arrays may *not* be constants in Standard Pascal. Turbo Pascal supports structured constants, but we must cover data structures first before we can speak of them.

Here are some sample named constants of various types:

```
CONST
    PI           = 3.14159;      { Floating point real }
    Threshold    = -71.47;       { Negative FP real     }
    PenIOAddress = $06;          { Hexadecimal value    }
    Using8087    = True;         { Boolean              }
    DriveUnit    = 'A';          { Character            }
    Revision     = 'V2.61B';     { String               }
    Answer       = 42;           { Integer              }
    NotAnswer    = -42;          { Negative integer     }
    YesSet       = ['Y','y'];    { Set                  }
    NullString   = '';           { Null (empty) string  }
```

**CONSTANTS
VS. DATA**

How is a constant different from a variable? The obvious difference is that the value of a constant is set at compile time. You cannot assign a value to a constant. Given the list of constants above, you could not legally code:

```
Answer := 47;
```

because **Answer** is a constant with a value of 42.

In Turbo Pascal, constants are written into the code by the compiler as immediate data. Variables are kept separate from the code portion of a program. Constants, therefore, do not take up room in your data segment (8086) or data area (Z80).

The type of a constant depends, to some extent, on its context. Consider:

```
VAR
    Tiny   : BYTE;       { One byte                  }
    Little : INTEGER;    { An integer (2 bytes)      }
    Bit    : REAL;       { A real number (6 bytes)   }

    Tiny   := ANSWER;
    Little := ANSWER;
    Big    := ANSWER;
```

From the constants above, **Answer**'s value is 42. But it is perfectly legal to assign the value of **Answer** to type **Byte**, type **Integer**, or type **Real**. The code the compiler generates to do the assignment in each case is a little different. But the end result is that all three variables of three different types will each express a value of 42 in its own fashion.

Except under very special (and peculiar) circumstances, the type of a variable is fixed and unambiguous.

**NOTES ON
LITERAL
CONSTANTS**

A dollar sign ($) in front of a numeric literal means that the compiler will interpret the literal as a hexadecimal number. The numeric literal may *not* have a decimal point if it is to be considered hexadecimal.

Inside string literals, lower case and upper case characters are distinct. If you wish to include a single quote mark inside a string literal, you must use two single quotes together:

```
Writeln('>>You haven''t gotten it right yet...');
```

This line of code will display the following line on your CRT:

```
>>You haven't gotten it right yet...
```

Simple data types

Data is the information that your program manipulates. Data can be numbers, characters, character strings, and other easy-to-visualize symbols, or it can be highly abstract, like conditions of Boolean truth or falsehood, sets of concepts like days of the week, or elaborate structures built out of simpler items.

The richness of expression with which Pascal can treat data places it far apart from earlier languages such as BASIC and FORTRAN. Modern versions of BASIC may have strings and different types of numerics, but no BASIC allows you to build complex data structures from simple data types.

The "type" of a data item is actually a set of rules governing the storage and use of that data item. Data takes up space in RAM memory. The type of a data item dictates how much space is needed and how the data is represented in that space. An integer, for example, always occupies two bytes of memory. The more significant bit of an integer carries the sign of the number the integer represents.

Type also governs how a data item may be used. Type **Char** and type **Byte** are both single bytes in RAM, but you can add or multiply two variables of type **Byte**. Attempting to use variables of type **Char** in an arithmetic expression will generate an error.

The Pascal language uses "strong typing," which means that there are strict limitations on how individual types may be used, and especially on how variables of one type may be assigned to variables of another type. In most cases, a variable of one type may not be assigned to a variable of a different type. Transferring information between variables across type boundaries is usually done with "transfer functions" that depend upon well-defined relationships between types. Transfer functions are described in Chapter 16.

Simple types, which we will describe in this section, are "unstructured"; that is, they are data "atoms" that cannot be broken down into simpler data types.

7.1 Characters

Type **Char** (character) is an ISO Standard Pascal type, present in all implementations of Pascal.

Type **Char** includes the familiar ASCII character set: letters, numbers, common symbols, and the "unprintable" control characters like carriage return, backspace, tab, and so on. There are 128 characters in the ASCII character set. But type **Char** actually includes 256 different values, since a character is expressed as an eight-bit byte. (Eight bits may encode 256 different values.) The "other" 128 characters have no names or meanings as standard as the ASCII character set. When printed to the CRT of the IBM PC, the "high" 128 characters display as foreign language characters, segments of boxes, or mathematical symbols. On other computers, however, the high 128 characters may display as flashing or underlined variants of the normal ASCII character set, or they may be the ASCII character set expressed in reverse video. How the high 128 characters are displayed is completely dependent on your own computer hardware. In fact, there are occasional differences in representing the supposedly "standard" ASCII character set.

How, then, to represent characters in your program? The key lies in the concept of *ordinality*. There are 256 different characters included in type **Char**. These characters exist in a specific ordered sequence numbered 0,1,2,3 and onward up to 255. The 65th character (counting from 0, remember) is always capital A. The 32nd character is always a space, and so on.

An ordinal number is a number indicating a position in an ordered series. A character's position in the sequence of type **Char** is its ordinality. The ordinality of capital A is 65. The ordinality of capital B is 66, and so on. Any character in type **Char** can be unambiguously expressed by its ordinality, using the "transfer function" **Chr**.

A capital A may be expressed as the character literal 'A.' It may also be expressed as **Chr(65)**. The expression **Chr(65)** may be used anywhere you would use the character literal 'A.'

Beyond the limits of the ASCII character set, the **Chr** function is the only reasonable way to express a character. The character expressed as **Chr(234)** will display on the IBM PC screen as the Greek capital letter omega (Ω), but it will probably be displayed as something else on another computer. It is best to express such characters using the function **Chr**.

Characters are stored in memory as single bytes, expressed as binary numbers from 0 to 255.

What will Pascal allow you to do with variables of type **Char**?

1. You can write them to the screen or printer using **Write** and **Writeln**:

```
Writeln('A');
Write(Chr(234));
Write(UnitChar);   { UnitChar is type Char }
```

2. You can concatenate them with string variables using the string concatenation operator (+) or the **Concat** built-in function (see Section 15.1):

```
ErrorString := Concat('Disk error on drive ',UnitChar);
DriveSpec   := UnitChar + ':' + FileName;
```

3. You can derive the ordinality of characters with the **Ord** transfer function:

```
BounceValue := 31+Ord(UnitChar);
```

Ord returns a numeric value giving the ordinality of the character parameter. **Ord** allows you to perform arithmetic operations on the ordinality of a character.

4.   You can compare characters with one another using relational operators such as =, >, <, >=, <=, and <>. This is due to the way characters are ordered in a series. What you are actually comparing is the ordinality of the two characters in their series when you use relational operators. For example, when you see:

```
'a' > 'A'
```

(which evaluates to a Boolean value of **True**) the computer is actually performing a comparison of the ordinalities of 'a' and 'A':

```
97 > 65
```

Since 'a' is positioned *after* 'A' in the series of characters, its ordinality is larger, and therefore 'a' is in fact "greater than" 'A.'

7.2 Bytes

Type **Byte** is *not* present in ISO Standard Pascal, although most microcomputer implementations of Pascal include it. Like **Char**, **Byte** is stored in memory as an eight-bit byte. On the lowest machine level, therefore, **Byte** and **Char** are exactly the same. They only differ in what the compiler will allow you to do with them.

Type **Byte** may be thought of as an unsigned "half-precision" integer. **Byte** variables may not share an assignment statement with any type other than **Integer**. Mixing type **Byte** with **Boolean, Char,** or any other type will cause error 44, Type Mismatch.

7.3 Integers

Type **Integer** is a part of ISO Standard Pascal. It is the most efficient way to handle relatively small numbers. Integers range from −32768 to 32767. Integers are always whole numbers. They cannot have decimal parts. In Pascal, only real number types can have decimal parts.

Integers are stored in memory as two bytes. The highest order bit of the two bytes is the sign bit, which indicates whether the value expressed by the integer is positive or negative. If this high bit is a binary 1, then the integer has a negative sign. If the high bit is a binary 0, the integer is positive.

MAXINT

The predefined identifier **MaxInt** is a constant containing the maximum value an integer may express: 32767. **MaxInt**, which is a feature of ISO Standard Pascal, exists to help make programs more nearly portable. Turbo Pascal uses a two-byte integer with a **MaxInt** value of 32767. Other computers, particularly computers with larger word sizes, may be able to express a much larger value in an integer variable. (Computers with 32 bit words define **MaxInt** as 2,147,483,647.) For any Pascal compiler, **MaxInt** contains the largest value legally assignable to an integer. By testing **MaxInt**, your program can determine how large a value may be stored in an integer, and alter its workings to allow use of all values up to **MaxInt**, whatever **MaxInt** may happen to be for that compiler.

The **MaxInt** limitation for integers is due to their having to exist in a fixed amount of memory; in our case, only two bytes.

7.4 Booleans

Type Boolean is part of ISO Standard Pascal. A Boolean variable has only two possible values, **True** and **False**. Like type **Char**, type **Boolean** is an ordinal type, which means it has a fixed number of possible values that exist in a definite order. In this order, **False** comes before **True**. By using the transfer function **Ord** you would find that:

Ord(False) returns the value 0.
Ord(True) returns the value 1.

The words **True** and **False** are predefined identifiers in Pascal. The compiler predefines them as constants of type **Boolean**. As with any predefined identifier, the compiler will allow you to define them as something other than Boolean constants, but that is a thoroughly bad idea.

A Boolean variable occupies only a single byte in memory. The actual words **True** and **False** are not physically present in a Boolean variable. When a Boolean variable contains the value **True**, it actually contains the binary number 01. When a Boolean variable contains the value **False**, it actually contains the binary number 00. If you write a Boolean variable to a disk file, the binary values 00 or 01 will be physically written to the disk. However, when you print or display a Boolean variable using **Write** or **Writeln**, the binary values are recognized by program code and the words "**TRUE**" or "**FALSE**" (in upper case ASCII characters) will be substituted for the binary 00 and 01.

Boolean variables are used to store the results of expressions using the relational operators =, >, <, <>, >=, and <=, and the set operators +, *, -. (Operators and expressions will be discussed more fully in Chapter 11.) An expression such as "**2 < 3**" is easy enough to evaluate; logically you would say that the statement "two is less than three" is "true." If this were put as an expression in Pascal, the expression would return a Boolean value of **True**, which could be assigned to a Boolean variable and saved for later processing:

```
OK := 2 < 3;
```

This assignment statement stores a Boolean value of **True** into the Boolean variable **OK**. The value of **OK** can later be tested with an **IF..THEN..ELSE** statement, with different actions taken by the code depending on the value assigned to **OK**:

```
OK := 2 < 3;
IF OK THEN
   Writeln('>>Two comes before three, not after!')
ELSE
   Writeln('>>We are all in very serious trouble...');
```

Boolean variables are also used to alter the flow of program control in the **WHILE..DO** statement and the **REPEAT..UNTIL** statement (see Sections 13.5 and 13.6).

7.5 Floating point real numbers

All the data types described up to this point have been ordinal types. Ordinal types are types with a limited number of possible values, existing in a definite order. Integers are an ordinal type, since there are exactly 65,535 of them. They are ordered and sharply defined: After 6 comes 7, after 7 comes 8, and so on, with no possible values in between. Integers have absolute precision; that is, the value of the integer 6 is exactly six.

The real world demands a way to deal with fractions. So ISO Standard Pascal supports type **Real**, which can express numbers with fractions and exponents. Real numbers, especially very large ones or very small ones, do not have absolute precision. For example, **1.6125E10** is a real number having an exponent. You might expand the exponent and write it as 16,125,000,000. This notation implies that we know the value precisely—yet we do not. A real number offers a fixed number of "significant figures" and an exponent giving us an order of magnitude, but there is a certain amount of "fuzz" in the value. The digits after the 5 in 16,125,000,000 are zeroes because we do not know what they really are. The measurements that produced the number were not precise enough to pin down the last six digits—so they are left as zeroes to express the order of magnitude that the exponent expressed in the exponential form **1.6125E10**.

Real numbers are "real" in that they are most often used in the scientific and engineering community to represent measurements made of things in the real world. Integers, by contrast, are largely mathematical in nature, and express abstract values usually generated by logic and not by physical measurement.

Real numbers may be expressed two ways in Turbo Pascal. One way, as we have seen, is with a mantissa (1.6125) giving the significant figures, and an exponent (E10) giving the order of magnitude. This form is used for very large and very small numbers. For very small numbers, the exponent would be negative:

1.6125E-10. You would read this number as "One point six one two five times ten to the negative tenth."

The second way to express a real number is with a decimal point: **121.402**, **3.14159**, **0.0056**, **–16.6**, and so on.

INTERNAL REPRESENTATION OF REAL NUMBERS

Floating point real numbers are represented as six bytes in Turbo Pascal, giving real numbers a range of 10^{-38} to 10^{38}. From low memory to high: The exponent is stored in the first byte, followed by the least significant byte of the mantissa, the next most significant byte, and so on for five bytes of mantissa. Forty bits worth of mantissa will give you 11 significant figures. Beyond that point, additional precision will be lost, although the exponent will always give you the correct order of magnitude to the limits of the range of a Turbo Pascal real.

A real number actually has two signs. The most significant bit of the mantissa (bit seven of the most significant byte of the real number) is the traditional sign bit, which indicates to which side of zero the number lies. A one bit indicates that the number is negative.

The other sign is the sign of the exponent, which indicates to which direction the decimal point moves when converting from scientific notation to decimal notation. The value of the exponent is offset by $80. Exponents greater than $80 indicate that the decimal point must move rightward. Exponents less than $80 indicate that the decimal point must move leftward. $80 must be subtracted from the exponent byte before the exponent can be evaluated.

Real numbers in Turbo Pascal are represented internally as base two logarithms. In other words, to represent the number 4,673.450, Turbo Pascal stores the exponent to which the number two must be raised to yield 4,673.450. This makes multiplying and dividing real numbers much easier on the compiler, since numbers may be multiplied by adding their logarithms, and they may be divided by subtracting their logarithms.

The representation of Turbo Pascal's real numbers in memory is shown in Figure 7.1.

MANIPULATING REAL NUMBERS

Turbo Pascal includes a number of built-in mathematical and trigonometric functions that return real number values. These are discussed at length in Chapter 16.

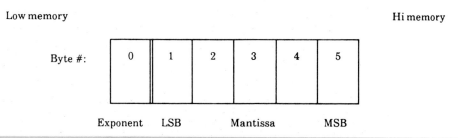

FIGURE 7.1 Floating point real representation

The arithmetic operators +, -, *, and / may all be used with type **Real**. The integer division operators **DIV** and **MOD** may *not* be used with real numbers. (See Section 11.2 for a complete discussion of arithmetic operators.) Integers and real numbers may be mixed within expressions; however, the result of an expression containing a real number is always of type **Real** and must be assigned to a variable of type **Real**:

```
VAR
   Radius    : Integer;
   Area,PI   : Real;

PI := 3.14159;
Area := PI * Radius * Radius;
```

Here, **PI** (real) and **Radius** (integer) exist peaceably in the same expression, as long as the result of the expression is assigned to **Area**, a real number.

The inherent "fuzziness" of real numbers presents a few problems with using reals. One caution is that computed reals should *not* be compared for equality. For example, 1/3 times 3 equals 1, right? Well . . . no:

```
VAR
  Q,R,S : REAL;

R := 1.0;
S := R / 3;
Q := S * 3;
IF R = Q THEN Write('3 x 1/3 equals 1!') ELSE
  Write('Something funny is going on here...');
```

Common sense would tell you that 3 × 1/3 is indeed 1, but Turbo Pascal will tell you (as you would see if you were to execute this code fragment) that something funny is going on: R <> Q.

The fraction 1/3 is an infinitely repeating fraction. It cannot be expressed exactly without an infinitely long series of threes following the decimal point: 0.33333333333 *ad infinitum*. Your computer truncates the decimal fraction to some reasonable number of threes and that's all it keeps. It expresses the fraction 1/3 not as 1/3 but as a number slightly less than 1/3. So multiplying the computer's *expression* of 1/3 by 3 will *not* produce a result of 1 but of some number slightly less than 1. The problem should be obvious by now, as should the reason why Turbo evaluates R as not equal to Q. But there's more . . .

If you were to display all 11 significant figures of the value of Q in the example above, you would see:

```
1.0000000000
```

Strange indeed! 1.0 <> 1.000000000? Turbo Pascal (rather sadly, I think) rounds up to 1 for display purposes even when the number it is displaying is not truly equal to 1.

Keep the problems of rounding and precision in mind as you program with real numbers. Expecting too much precision from real numbers (or even believing too uncritically in what you see on the screen) will cost you a great deal of headscratching time.

Subranges and enumerated types

All the types we have discussed to this point have been simple types, predefined by Turbo Pascal and ready to use. Much of the power of Pascal lies in its ability to create structures of data out of these simple types. Data structures can make your programs both easier to write and, later on, easier to read as well.

Defining your own custom data types is easy to do. The reserved word **TYPE** begins the type definition part of your program, and that's where you lay out the plan of your data structures:

```
TYPE
    YourType = ItsDefinition;
```

From now on, the types we're going to discuss must all be declared and defined in the type definition part of your program.

A type definition does not, by itself, occupy space in your program's data area. A type definition provides instructions to the compiler, telling it how to deal with variables of type **YourType** when it encounters them further down in your program source file.

With some exceptions (strings and subranges, for example), you cannot write structured types to your screen or printer with **Write** or

Writeln. If you want to display structured types somehow, you must write procedures specifically to display some representation of the type on your CRT or printer.

8.1 Subranges

The simplest data structure you can define is a subset of an ordinal type called a "subrange." If you choose any two legal values in an ordinal type, these two values plus all values that lie between them define a subrange of that ordinal type. For example, these are subranges of type **Char**:

```
TYPE
    Uppercase = 'A'..'Z';
    Lowercase = 'a'..'z';
    Digits    = '0'..'9';
```

Uppercase is the range of characters A,B,C,D,E,F and so on to Z. **Digits** includes the numeral characters 0,1,2,3, and 4, on up to 9. The quotes are important. They tell the compiler that the values in the subrange are of type **Char**. If you left out the quote marks from the type definition for type **Digits**:

```
Digits = 0..9;
```

you would have, instead, a subrange of type **Integer**, because '7' is not the same as 7.

An expression in the form **'A'..'Z'** or **3..6** is called a "closed interval." A closed interval is a range of ordinal values including the two stated boundary values and all values falling between them. We will return to closed intervals later on while discussing sets in Chapter 9.

8.2 Enumerated types

Newcomers to Pascal frequently find the notion of enumerated types hard to grasp. The Turbo Pascal Reference Manual calls enumerated types "user-defined scalar types." Most Pascal texts refer to them as enumerated types. An enumerated type is an ordinal type that you define. It consists of an ordered list of values with unique names. One of the best ways to approach enumerated types is through comparison with type **Boolean**.

Type **Boolean** is, in fact, an enumerated type that is predefined by the compiler and used in special ways. Type **Boolean** is an ordered list of two values with unique names: **False**, or **True**. It is *not* a pair of ASCII strings containing the English words "False" and "True." As we mentioned earlier, a Boolean value is actually a binary number with a value of either 00 or 01. We "name" the binary code 00 within type **Boolean** as **False** and the binary code 01 within type **Boolean** as **True**.

Consider another list of values with unique names: the colors of the spectrum. (Remember that colorful chap Roy G. Biv?) Let's create an enumerated type in which the list of values includes the colors of the spectrum, in order:

```
TYPE
    Spectrum = (Red, Orange, Yellow, Green, Blue,
                Indigo, Violet);
```

The list of an enumerated type is always given within parentheses. The order you place the values within the parentheses defines their ordinal value, which you can test using the **Ord(X)** function. For example, **Ord(Yellow)** would return a value of 2. **Ord(Red)** would return a value of 0.

You can compare values of an enumerated type with other values of that same type. It may be helpful to substitute the ordinal value of enumerated constants for the words that name them when evaluating such comparisons. The statement **Yellow > Red** (think: 2 > 0) would return a Boolean value of **True**. **Green > Violet** or **Blue < Orange** would both return Boolean values of **False**.

The values of type **Spectrum** are all constants. They may be assigned to variables of type **Spectrum**. For example:

```
VAR
   Color1, Color2 : Spectrum;

Color1 := Yellow;
Color2 := Indigo;
```

You cannot, however, assign anything to one of the values of type **Spectrum**. **Red := 2** or **Red := Yellow** make no sense.

Enumerated types may index arrays. For example, each color of the rainbow has a frequency (of that color of light) associated with it. These frequencies could be stored in an array, indexed by the enumerated type **Spectrum**:

```
Wavelength : ARRAY[Red..Violet] OF Real;
Frequency  : ARRAY[Red..Violet] OF Real;
Color      : Spectrum;
Lightspeed : Real;

Wavelength[Red]    := 6.2E-7;     { All in meters }
Wavelength[Orange] := 5.9E-7;
Wavelength[Yellow] := 5.6E-7;
Wavelength[Green]  := 5.4E-7;
Wavelength[Blue]   := 5.15E-7;
Wavelength[Indigo] := 4.8E-7;
Wavelength[Violet] := 4.5E-7;
```

The functions **Ord** and **Odd** work with enumerated types, as do the **Succ** and **Pred** functions. This is so because an enumerated type has a fixed number of elements in a definite order that does not change. **Succ(Green)** will return the value **Blue**. **Pred(Yellow)** returns the value **Orange**. Be aware that **Pred(Red)** and **Succ(Violet)** are undefined. You should test for the two ends of the **Spectrum** type

CHAPTER 8 SUBRANGES AND ENUMERATED TYPES   71

while using **Succ** and **Pred** to avoid assigning an undefined value to a variable.

Enumerated types may also be control variables in **FOR/NEXT** loops. In continuing with the example begun above, we might calculate the frequencies of light for each of the colors of type **Spectrum** this way:

```
Lightspeed := 3.0E08              { Meters/second }
FOR Color := Red TO Violet DO
Frequency[Color] := Lightspeed / Wavelength[Color];
```

One great disadvantage to enumerated types is that they cannot be printed to the console or printer. You cannot, for example, code up

```
Writeln(Orange);
```

and expect to see the ASCII word "Orange" appear on the screen. Turbo Pascal will flag this as Error 66: I/O are not allowed. In cases where you must print an enumerated type to the screen or printer, set up an array of strings that is indexed by the enumerated type:

```
Names : ARRAY[Red..Violet] OF String80;

Names[Red] := 'Red';
Writeln(Names[Red]);
```

The **Writeln** statement above will print the string "Red" to the screen. You might also set up an array constant containing the names of the items in an enumerated type. This feature is unique to Turbo Pascal and will make your programs thoroughly non-portable, so caution is advised. Array constants are covered in Section 9.6.

Data structures

Allowing you, the programmer, to build structures of data out of simple data types was perhaps the greatest advance made by Pascal over earlier computer languages like FORTRAN and Algol.

We've covered simple data types like **Integer** and **Boolean**, and user-defined subranges and enumerated types. Subranges involve "building down" from a simple type. Now let's take a look at "building up" larger structures from the same simple types.

9.1 Sets

Sets are collections of elements picked from simple types. An element is either in a set, or it is not in the set. The letters "A," "Q," "W," and "Z" may be taken together as a set of characters. "Q" is in the set, and "L" is not.

Expressed in Pascal's notation:

```
VAR
   CharSet : SET OF Char;

CharSet := ['A','Q','W','Z'];
```

A pair of square brackets, when used to define a set, is called a "set constructor."

Is this useful? Very. For example, sets in Pascal provide an easy way to sift valid user responses from invalid ones. In answering even a simple yes/no question, a user may, in fact, type two equally valid characters for yes and two for no: Y/y and N/n. Ordinarily, you would have to test for each one individually:

```
IF (Ch='Y') OR (Ch='y') THEN DoSomething;
```

With sets, you could replace this notation with:

```
IF Ch IN ['Y','y'] THEN DoSomething;
```

The operator **IN** checks only if **Ch** is present in the set. This method is not only shorter and more readable than using ordinary equality tests; it actually takes less machine time to execute.

In Turbo Pascal, a set type may be defined for any simple type having 256 or fewer individual values. Type **Char** qualifies, as does **Byte**. The enumerated type **Spectrum** we created in the last section also qualifies, since it has only seven separate values:

```
VAR
   LowColors : SET OF Spectrum;

LowColors := [Red,Orange,Yellow];
```

Type **Integer**, however, does not qualify as a set. There are 65,535 different values available in type **Integer**, and a set may only be defined for "base types" having 256 or fewer individual values. If you define an integer subrange spanning 256 or fewer values, you may define a set within that subrange type as the set's base type:

```
TYPE
   ShoeSizes    = 5..17;

VAR
   SizesInStock : SET OF ShoeSizes;
```

You may also assign a range of elements to a set, assuming the elements are of an acceptable base type:

```
VAR
  Uppercase, Lowercase,
  Whitespace, Controls : SET OF Char;

Uppercase  := ['A'..'Z'];
Lowercase  := ['a'..'z'];
Controls   := [Chr(1)..Chr(31)];
Whitespace := [Chr(9),Chr(10),Chr(12),Chr(13),Chr(32)];
```

This is certainly easier than explicitly naming all the characters from A to Z to assign them to a set. A range of elements containing no gaps (like 'A'..'Z') is called a "closed interval." The list of members within the set constructor can include single elements, closed intervals, and expressions that yield an element of the base type of the set. These must all be separated by commas, but they do not have to be in any sort of order:

```
GradeSet := ['A'..'F','a'..'f'];
BadChars := [Chr(1)..Chr(8),Chr(11),Chr(X+4),'Q','x'..'z'];
NullSet  := [];
```

You should take care that expressions do not yield a value that is outside the range of the set's base type. If X in **BadChars** grows to 252 or higher, the result of the expression **Chr(X+4)** will no longer be a legal character. The results of such an expression will be unpredictable, other than to say they won't do you very much good.

Sets like **Uppercase**, **Lowercase**, and **Whitespace** defined above can be very useful when manipulating characters coming in from the keyboard or other unpredictable source:

```
FUNCTION CapsLock(Ch : Char) : Char;

BEGIN
  IF Ch IN Lowercase THEN CapsLock := Chr(Ord(Ch)-32)
    ELSE CapsLock := Ch
END;

FUNCTION DownCase(Ch : Char) : Char;

BEGIN
  IF Ch IN Uppercase THEN Capslock := Chr(Ord(Ch)+32)
    ELSE DownCase := Ch
END;

FUNCTION IsWhite(Ch : Char) : Boolean;

BEGIN
  IsWhite := Ch IN WhiteSpace
END;
```

All three of these routines assume that **Uppercase**, **Lowercase**, and **Whitespace** have already been declared and filled with the proper values. Actually, the way to ensure that this is done is to do it *inside* each routine by the use of set constants, as we will do in Section 9.6. **CapsLock** returns all characters passed to it in uppercase. **DownCase** returns all characters passed to it as lowercase. **IsWhite** returns a **True** value if the character passed to it is "whitespace," that is, a tab, carriage return, linefeed, or space character.

The **IN** operator we used above is not the only operator you can use with sets. There are two classes of set operators: Operators that build sets from other sets, and operators that test relationships between sets and yield a boolean result.

The set builder operators are:

+ Union of two sets; all elements in both sets.
* Intersection of two sets; all elements that are present in both sets.
- Exclusion ("set difference" in the Turbo Pascal Reference Manual), which yields a set of the elements in the set on the right, once all the elements in the set on the left have been removed from it.

The set relational operators are:

IN **True** if the given element is present in the set.
= **True** if both sets contain *exactly* the same elements.
<> **True** if the two given sets do not contain exactly the same elements.
<= **True** if all the elements in the set on the left are present in the set on the right.
>= **True** if all the elements in the set on the right are present in the set on the left.

More details on these set operators, including examples, will be given in Section 11.3, Set Operators.

INTERNAL REPRESENTA-TION OF SETS

Turbo Pascal implements set types as bitmaps. The memory required by any given set type depends on the number of elements in that set's base type. Since no set may have more than 256 elements, the largest legal set type will be 32 bytes in size (32 bytes × 8 bits = 256 possible set elements.) Unlike most Pascals, sets whose base types have fewer elements will be smaller.

I must emphasize here that all sets of a given set type will *always* be the same size in memory. This figure is set at compile-time and does not change as elements are included in or excluded from a set.

The size in memory of a given set type will be:

```
(Max DIV 8) - (Min DIV 8) + 1
```

where **Max** and **Min** are the ordinal values of the largest and smallest items in the set. A set of **Char**, for example, runs from character 0 to character 255:

```
(255 DIV 8) - (0 DIV 8) + 1

31 - 0 + 1

32 bytes occupied by a set of Char
```

Now, consider a set with a smaller base type:

```
TYPE
   Printables = ' '..'^';
   SymbolSet = SET OF Printables;
```

Here, **Min** will be 32 (**Ord(' ')**) and **Max** will be 126 (**Ord('^')**):

```
(126 DIV 8) - (32 DIV 8) + 1

15 - 4 + 1

12 bytes occupied by set type SymbolSet;
```

Each possible set element has a bit in the bitmap. If a particular element is present in the set, its bit is set to binary 1; otherwise its bit remains binary 0.

The set **Uppercase** defined above is a set of **Char**. Its base type (**Char**) has 256 different elements. The set must then be represented in memory as the following sequence of 32 hex bytes:

```
00 00 00 00 00 00 00 00 FE FF FF 07 00 00 00 00
00 00 00 00 00 00 00 00 00 00 00 00 00 00 00 00

    Low memory      -->      High memory
```

This is a bitmap of the 256 possible elements in a set of **Char**. The bit that represents 'A' is bit 1 of byte 8. The bit representing 'Z' is bit 2 of byte 11. (Both bits and bytes are numbered from zero.) This might seem confusing at first, since the byte order is numbered from left to right while the order of the bits within each byte is numbered from right to left. If it still seems strange, write out the sequence of bytes from 8 to 11 as binary patterns, but with the bits reading from left to right instead of right to left:

```
            Byte #8 of set Uppercase

Hex FE:    11111110            01111111
            ^       ^           ^       ^
Bits:       7       0           0       7

Read:   Right-to-left      Left-to-right
```

If all the bytes in the set were expressed as binary patterns reading from left to right, the set could be written as a true bitmap.

This information on the internal representation of sets will not be especially useful to you until you need to pass a set variable to a machine language subroutine. Then you will need to know exactly which binary bit corresponds to which element in the set, so that your machine language routine will be manipulating the correct elements of the set it receives from your Pascal program.

9.2 Arrays

An array is a data structure consisting of a fixed number of identical elements, with the whole collection given a single identifier as its name. The program keeps track of them by number. Sometimes you name the entire array to work with it. Most of the time you identify

one of the individual elements, by number, and work with that
element alone. This number identifying an array element is called
an "index." In Pascal, an index need not be a traditional number.
Enumerated types, characters, and subranges may also act as array
indices, allowing a tremendous richness of expression not matched
by any other computer language.

It may be helpful to think of an array as a row of identical empty
boxes in memory, side by side. The program allocates the boxes, but
it is your job as programmer to fill them and manipulate their
contents. The elements in an array are, in fact, set side by side in
order in memory.

An array element may be of any data type except a file. Arrays
may consist of data structures; you may have arrays of records and
arrays of arrays. An array index must be a member or a subrange of
an ordinal type, or a programmer-defined enumerated type. Real
numbers may *not* act as array indices. Type **Integer**, **Byte**, **Char**, and
Boolean may all index arrays.

Here are some valid array declarations, just to give you a flavor of
what is possible (if you don't understand for now what a "record"
is, bear with us for the time being, or look ahead to Section 9.3):

```
CONST
   Districts  = 14;

TYPE
   String80   = String[80];
   Grades     = 'A'..'F';                         { Subrange   }
   Percentile = 1..99;                            { Ditto      }
                                                  { Enum. type }
   Levels     = (K,G1,G2,G3,G4,G5,G6,G7,G8,G9,G10,G11,G12);
                                                  { Ditto      }
   Subjects   = (English,Math,Spelling,Reading,Art,Gym);

   Profile    = RECORD
                   Name     : String80;
                   SSID     : String80;
                   IQ       : Integer;
                   Standing : Percentile;
                   Finals   : ARRAY[Subjects] OF Grades
                End;
```

(continues)

```
GradeDef  = ARRAY[Grades] OF String80;
VAR
  K12Profile : ARRAY[Levels] OF Profile;
  Passed     : ARRAY[Levels] OF Boolean;
  Subtotals  : ARRAY[1..24] OF Integer;
  AreaPerc   : ARRAY[1..Districts] OF Percentile;
  AreaLevels : ARRAY[1..Districts] OF ARRAY[Levels] OF
                  Percentile;
  RoomGrid   : ARRAY[1..3,Levels] OF Integer;
```

(concluded)

The declarations shown above are part of an imaginary school district records manager program written in Pascal. Note that **Passed** is an array whose index is an enumerated type. **Passed[G5]** would contain a Boolean value (**True** or **False**), indicating whether a student had passed or failed the fifth grade. Remember, "**G5**" is *not* a variable; it is a constant value, one value of an enumerated type.

The low limit and high limit of an array's index are called its "bounds." *The bounds of an ordinary array in Pascal must be fixed at compile time.* The Pascal compiler must know when it compiles the program exactly how large all data items are going to be. You cannot **REDIM** an ordinary array as you might in BASIC, nor change its shape as you might in APL.

With this in mind, the variable **AreaPerc** deserves a closer look. At first glance, you might think it has a variable for a high bound, but actually, **Districts** is a constant with a value of 14. Writing [1..**Districts**] is no different from writing [1..14], but within the context of the program it assists your understanding of what the array actually represents.

Most of the arrays shown in the above example are one-dimensional. A one-dimensional array has only one index. A two-dimensional array (like **RoomGrid**, above) has two indices. An array may have any number of dimensions, but it edges toward bad practice to define an array with more than two or three. (See Figure 9.1.) Also, the more dimensions an array has, the larger it tends to be—and the more likely that parts of it are empty or full of duplicate or rarely-accessed information that does nothing for you but waste memory. There are better, less memory-wasteful ways to handle large, complicated data structures, like pointers.

When Turbo Pascal allocates an array in memory, it does not zero the elements of the array, as BASIC would. In general, *Pascal does not initialize data items for you.* If there was garbage in RAM where the compiler went out to set up an array, the array elements will contain the garbage when the array is allocated. If you wish to zero out or otherwise initialize the elements of an array, you must do it

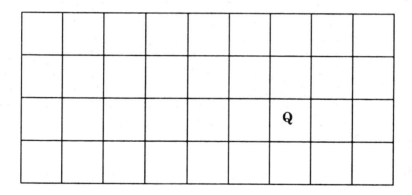

D1 : ARRAY[0..8] OF CHAR;
D1[6] contains the "Q"

D2 : ARRAY[0..8,1..4] OF CHAR;
D2[6,3] contains the "Q"

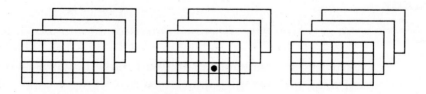

D4 : ARRAY[0..7,1..4,0..3,0..2] OF CHAR;
D4[5,3,0,1] contains the "Q"

FIGURE 9.1 Multi-dimensional arrays

yourself in your program, before you use the array. This is not difficult, using a **FOR** loop (see Section 13.4 for more on **FOR** loops):

```
FOR I := 1 TO 24 DO Subtotals[I] := 0;
```

If portability is not a consideration, arrays (especially *large* arrays) may be initialized even more quickly with Turbo Pascal's **FillChar** statement:

```
FillChar(Subtotals,SizeOf(Subtotals),Chr(0));
```

Details on using **FillChar** will be found in Section 20.3.

INTERNAL REPRESENTA-TION OF ARRAYS

Arrays are sequences of the same data type. Turbo Pascal allocates array elements from low memory to high. In other words, the first byte in the first element of an array has the lowest address of any byte in the array.

For multidimensional arrays, the elements are stored with the rightmost dimension increasing first. This is best shown as a diagram. (see Figure 9.2, page 83.)

9.3 Records

An array is a data structure composed of a number of identical data items all in a row and referenced by number. This sort of data structure is handy for dealing with large numbers of the same type of data, for example, values returned from an experiment of some sort. You might have a collection of 500 temperature readings and need to average them and perform analysis of variance on them. The easiest way to do that is to load them into an array and work with the temperature readings as elements of the array.

A data structure composed of data items that are *not* of the same type is called a record, which gets its name from its origins as one line of data in a data file.

A *record* is a structure composed of several data items of different types grouped together. These data items are called the "fields" of the record. An auto-repair shop might keep a file on its spare parts inventory. For each part they keep in stock, they need to record its part number, its description, its wholesale cost, retail price, customary stock level and current stock level. All these items are intimately linked to a single physical gadget (a car part), so to

ARRAY[0..8] OF CHAR

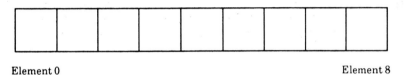

Element 0   Element 8

Low memory   High memory

ARRAY[0..2,0..7] OF CHAR

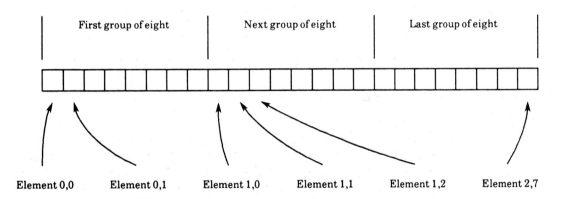

Multidimensional arrays are stored in memory with the rightmost dimensions increasing first.

FIGURE 9.2 Arrays in memory

simplify their programming the shop puts the fields together to form a record:

```
TYPE
  PartRec  =   RECORD
                  PartNum, Class   : Integer;
                  PartDescription  : String 80;
                  OurCost          : Real;    { Best done using }
                  ListPrice        : Real;    { Turbo-BCD! }
                  StockLevel       : Integer;
                  OnHand           : Integer
               END
VAR
  CurrentPart,  NextPart   : PartRec;
  PartFile      : FILE OF  PartRec;
  CurrentStock  : Integer;
  MustOrder     : Boolean;
```

The entire structure becomes a new type with its own name. Data items of the record type can then be assigned, written to files, and otherwise worked with as a single entity without having to mention explicitly all the various fields within the record.

```
CurrentPart := NextPart; { Assign part record to another }
Read(PartFile,NextPart); { Read next record from file     }
```

When you need to work with the individual fields within a record, the notation consists of the record identifier followed by a period (".") followed by the field identifier:

```
CurrentStock := CurrentPart.OnHand;
IF CurrentStock < CurrentPart.StockLevel
  THEN MustOrder := True;
```

Relational operators may *not* be used on records. To say that one record is "greater than" or "less than" another cannot be defined, since there are an infinite number of possible record structures with no well-defined and unambiguous order for them to follow. In the example above we are comparing the *fields* of two records, not the records themselves. The fields are both integers and can therefore be compared by the "<" operator.

**THE WITH
STATEMENT**

Fields within a record are accessed this way:

```
CurrentPart.OurCost := 10.75;
CurrentPart.ListPrice := 41.85;
CurrentPart.OnHand := 4;
```

There's some unnecessary repetition here. If you have to go down a list of fields within the same record and work with each field, you can avoid specifying the identifier of the record each and every time by using a special statement called the **WITH** statement.

We could simplify assigning values to several fields of the same record by writing the above snippet of code this way:

```
WITH CurrentPart DO
  BEGIN
    OurCost := 10.75;
    ListPrice := 41.85;
    OnHand := 4
  END;
```

The space between the **BEGIN** and **END** is the "scope" of the **WITH** statement. Within that scope, the record identifier need not be given to work with the fields of the record named in the **WITH** statement. (If you are very new to Pascal, you might return to this section after reading the general discussion on statements in Chapter 12. **WITH** statements are subject to the same rules that all types of Pascal statements obey.)

WITH statements need not have a **BEGIN/END**. A single statement is sufficient:

```
WITH CurrentPart DO VerifyCost(OurCost,ListPrice,Check);
```

In this example, **VerifyCost** is a procedure that takes as input two price figures and returns a value in **Check**. (Procedures are covered fully in Chapter 14.) Without the **WITH** statement, calling **VerifyCost** would have to be done this way:

```
VerifyCost(CurrentPart.OurCost,
          CurrentPart.ListPrice,Check);
```

The **WITH** statement makes the statement crisper and easier to understand.

NESTED RECORDS

A record is a group of data items taken together as a named data structure. A record is itself a data item, and so records may themselves be fields of larger records. Suppose the repair shop we've been speaking of expands its parts inventory so much that finding a part bin by memory gets to be difficult. There are ten aisles with letters from A through J, with the bins in each aisle numbered from 1 up. To specify a location for a part requires an aisle character and a bin number. The best way to do it is by defining a new record type:

```
TYPE
  PartLocation = RECORD
                   Aisle : 'A'..'J';
                   Bin   : Integer
                 END;
```

Since each part has a location, **PartRec** needs a new field:

```
TYPE
  PartRec = RECORD
              PartNum, Class  : Integer;
              PartDescription : String80;
              OurCost         : Real;
              ListPrice       : Real;
              StockLevel      : Integer;
              OnHand          : Integer;
              Location        : PartLocation { A record! }
            END;
```

Location is "nested" within the larger record. To access the fields of **Location** you need *two* periods:

```
LookAisle := CurrentPart.Location.Aisle
```

If the outermost record is specified by a **WITH** statement, you might have an equivalent statement like this:

```
WITH CurrentPart DO LookAisle := Location.Aisle;
```

WITH statements are fully capable of handling many levels of record nesting. You may, first of all, nest **WITH** statements one within another. The following compound statement is equivalent to the previous statement:

```
WITH CurrentPart DO
  WITH Location DO LookAisle := Aisle;
```

The **WITH** statement also allows a slightly terser form to express the same thing:

```
WITH CurrentPart, Location DO LookAisle := Aisle;
```

For this syntax you must place the record identifiers after the **WITH** reserved word, separated by commas, *in nesting order*. That is, the name of the outermost record is on the left, and the names of records nested within it are placed to its right, with the "innermost" nested record placed last.

Records are often used as "slices" of a disk file. We will explore this use of records much more fully in the general discussion of binary file I/O in Section 18.9.

9.4 Variant records

In the previous section we looked at Pascal's way of grouping several different data types together and calling them a record. In a "fixed" record type (which we have been discussing) the fields which make up a record are always the same data items in the same order and never change.

In a program doing real work in the real world, a record usually represents some real entity—and the real world is a varied and messy place. Pascal makes a major concession to the messiness of the real world by allowing "variant records," the fields of which may be different data types depending on the contents of the other fields.

The notion of variant records is a subtle one. You might wish to come back to this section after reading the rest of Part II, having paid particular attention to the discussion of **CASE OF** statements in Section 13.3. The definition of every variant record contains a **CASE OF** construct, and without a reasonable understanding of **CASE OF** you will not understand how variant records work.

Let's continue with the example of the auto repair shop's parts inventory system. In their system, each part kept in stock has a record in a file containing price information, stocks levels, and a location in their storage room. However, in some cars there are parts that break so rarely that they are practically never needed, so it would be financially foolish to keep such parts in stock.

Still, if one breaks, the shop must have some means of ordering the part quickly. It is necessary to store (for those parts only) a vendor name and phone number for emergency ordering, and a suspected lead time on the order based on previous discussions with the vendor. If the part has to come all the way from Japan, better the customer know about it up front rather than have him haunt the repair shop for weeks while the part is in shipment.

We can see that there are two types of parts: Those kept in stock and those obtainable via emergency order only. Both types have a part number, class, description, and cost values. But there the similarity ends. We might have two separate record definitions, one for each type of part:

```
TYPE
  STPartRec = RECORD
                PartNum, Class  : Integer;
                PartDescription : String;
                OurCost         : Real;
                ListPrice       : Real;
                StockLevel      : Integer;
                OnHand          : Integer;
                Location        : PartLocation
              END;

  EOPartRec  = RECORD
                PartNum, Class  : Integer;
                PartDescription : String:
                OurCost         : Real;
                ListPrice       : Real;
                Vendor          : String[50];
                OrderPhone      : String[20];
                OrderLead       : Integer
              END;
```

The new part record type handles all information for emergency-order parts quite nicely. *But* (as we will see in Section 18.9) a binary file may store only one record type, not two. Need we now keep two separate parts files, one for stocked parts and one for emergency-order only parts?

No. The two fixed record types may be combined into a single variant record type. The new record looks like this:

```
PartRec  = RECORD
              PartNum, Class  : Integer;
              PartDescription : String80;
              OurCost         : Real;
              ListPrice       : Real;
              CASE Stocked : Boolean OF
                True :
                  (StockLevel  : Integer;
                   OnHand      : Integer;
                   Location    : PartLocation);
                False :
                  (Vendor      : String50;
                   OrderPhone  : String20;
                   OrderLead   : Integer)
          END;
```

The new record type has two distinct parts. The first part, including the fields from **PartNum** to **ListPrice**, is called the "fixed part" of the record type. The rest of the record, from the reserved word **CASE** to the end, is the "variant part" of the record type. The variant part of a variant record must always be the last part of the record. You cannot have more fixed part fields after the variant part.

The difference turns around the **CASE** construct. The **CASE** construct provides two or more alternative field definitions based on the value of what is called the "tag field." The tag field of **PartRec** is the Boolean variable **Stocked**.

Stocked, being a Boolean variable, has only two possible values, **True** and **False**. In those **CASE**s where **Stocked** is **True** (if the record refers to a part kept in stock) the record contains the fields **Stock-Level**, **OnHand**, and **Location**. In those **CASE**s where **Stocked** is **False** (for emergency-order parts), the record instead contains the fields **Vendor**, **OrderPhone**, and **OrderLead**.

Note the use of parentheses to set off the separate variant parts of a variant record. Parentheses *must* surround the field definitions of each variant part. Do not include the tag field value constants (**True** and **False** in our example) within the parentheses.

It is not just a matter of the record actually containing both variant parts and "hiding" the one that is not currently selected by **Stocked**. *Variant parts of a variant record that are not selected by the tag field are inaccessible and their values undefined.* Such fields are literally "not there," and data that was previously contained in those fields vanishes when the tag field changes.

You must keep this in mind to stay out of certain kinds of trouble. For example, if **Stocked** = **True** and you perform this assignment:

```
CurrentPart.OnHand := 6;
```

and then later in the program perform this assignment on that same record:

```
CurrentPart.Stocked := False;
```

CurrentPart.OnHand is now inaccessible. If you try to read the field **OnHand** the code may present you with garbage. Furthermore, if you then assign

```
CurrentPart.Stocked := True;
```

although the field **OnHand** is now accessible, it does not retain its old value. It is undefined until you assign a new value to it. Turbo Pascal will *not* give you run-time errors for attempting to access fields in unselected variant parts of a variant record. It will place either garbage data or parts of other unrelated fields in the fields you access.

Although for simplicity our example record type has only two variants (because the tag field is Boolean and has only two possible values), a variant record may have up to 256 different variants, and any ordinal type may act as a tag field. This allows the (hazardous) possibility of a tag field assuming a value for which there is no defined variant. For example, if your tag field is of type **Char** and you define variants only for cases in which the tag field contains 'A', 'B', or 'C', what happens if the tag field is assigned a value of 'Z'? The variant part of the record becomes undefined, and attempts to access a field in a variant part may return garbage. *Avoid this possibility at all costs.* The best way is to make sure that *all* possible values of a tag field have a defined variant. Instead of making a tag field of type **Char**, define a subrange type

```
TYPE
  TagChar = 'A'..'C';
```

and make the tag field type **TagChar** instead. Enumerated types (see Section 8.2) are also extremely useful in creating data structures incorporating variant records.

It is perfectly legal for the variant parts of a variant record to be of different sizes. So how does the compiler allocate space for a variant record in memory? Every instance of a variant record type is allocated as much memory as required by the largest variant. (See Figure 9.3.) If data storage space is short, you might check to see whether you are wasting space by defining an enormous variant of a record and then rarely (or never) using it. Every time you define a record of that type, the record will use all the space needed by that enormous variant even if that variant is never selected by the tag field. Rearranging your data structure to break out that enormous variant as a separate type could save you a lot of memory and disk space!

FREE UNION VARIANT RECORDS

There are actually two types of variant records defined by the Pascal language, and both of them are implemented in Turbo Pascal. The variant record we have just described is called a "discriminated union." Discriminated union variant records always have a tag field. It is possible to define a variant record *without* a tag field. Such a data structure is called a "free union" variant record.

At first glance, a variant record without a tag field would appear to be a call to chaos. (Some experts do consider it exactly that.)

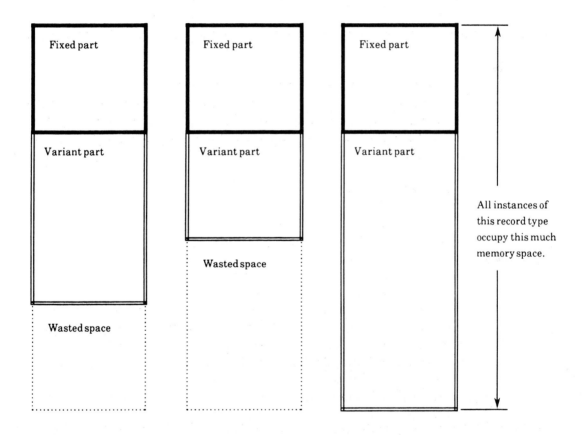

Three instances of the same variant record type, each with a different variant in force

FIGURE 9.3 Variant records

Without a tag field to select one variant part from the many, how can the compiler know which variant part is currently in force?

The answer is easy: They are *all* in force, all at once.

It is a peculiar concept, and one which should not be used without complete understanding of its implications. An example will help:

```
TYPE
   Halfer = RECORD
                CASE Boolean OF
                   True  : (I : Integer);
                   False : (HiByte : Byte;
                             LoByte : Byte);
                END;

VAR
   Porter : Halfer;
```

As you can see, there is no tag field present. There is, however (and this is the most peculiar thing about a free union) a tag field *type,* which in this case is **Boolean**. The tag field type must be present, and it must be an ordinal type with 256 or fewer values.

The tag field type is given only to specify the number of possible variant parts of the record, and the values by which the variants are selected.

You'll remember that any time the tag field changes in an ordinary discriminated union variant record, the values of the fields in the previously selected variant part go away, and the values of the fields in the newly selected variant part are undefined until some new values are assigned to those fields. (To add to the confusion, Turbo Pascal does not enforce this. There *might* be some carryover in the values as variants are selected and deselected, but there might not. The compiler makes no promises.)

Here the tag field cannot change because it does not exist. Any value assigned to any field of any variant part of a free union remains, and that value will be interpreted by all the other variant parts that share that same region of memory.

To understand that, you must break a prime taboo in ISO Standard Pascal and look at the actual memory locations underlying a program's data area. All variant parts of a free union are mapped onto the same region of memory. Our free union type **Halfer** has two variant parts: One has a single **Integer** field, and the other has two **Byte** fields. We know that an integer is stored as two bytes in memory. Values assigned to **Porter.HiByte** occupy the same physical byte of memory where the high-order byte of **Porter.I** exists. Values assigned to **Porter.LoByte** occupy the same physical byte of memory where the low-order byte of **Porter.I** exists.

When we assign a value to **Porter.I** (the details of port I/O are covered in Section 20.5):

```
Porter.I := 21217;
```

and then examine the value of **Porter.HiByte**, we will find that **Porter.HiByte** contains the high-order byte of **Porter.I**, in this case, 82. In similar fashion, we can change the high-order byte of **Porter.I** without disturbing the value of the low-order byte, and vice versa.

What good is all this? Free unions can get you out of some tight spots. For example, some CPUs can only move one 8-bit byte at a time to an I/O port. (The Z80 has this limitation.) To send a 16-bit quantity to an I/O port, you must break it down into two bytes. There are mathematical ways of deriving the values of the individual high- and low-order bytes of an integer, but they involve arithmetic, which takes time. A faster way is simply assigning your integer to a data type that can *simultaneously* be treated as both a single integer and as two 8-bit bytes. To send an integer to an 8080 I/O port using the **Halfer** free union variant record, you would do this:

```
J := 21217;
Porter.I := J;              { Porter is type Halfer }
OUT[$A0] := Porter.HIByte;  { Out to I/O port $A0    }
OUT[$A0] := Porter.LOByte;  { one byte at a time... }
```

The free union variant record is actually a trick to circumvent the strong typing restrictions Pascal places upon you. It is a way of mapping one type upon another so that any type can be converted to any other type *if you know what you are doing*. Free unions are actually a concession to the vagaries of the standard-less hardware world and should only be used to defeat problems imposed by the hardware itself.

There are terser and less "magical" ways of doing this sort of thing, mainly with absolute variables. (See Section 20.1.) Free unions are your best choice when portability is a consideration, however. They are often not portable in their effects but are probably more portable than absolute variables.

9.5   Strings

Manipulating words and lines of text is a fundamental function of a computer program. At minimum, a program must display messages like "Press RETURN to continue:" and "Processing completed." In Pascal, as in most computer languages, a line of characters to be taken together as a single entity is called a "string."

STANDARD PASCAL STRINGS (FIXED LENGTH)

ISO Standard Pascal has very little power to manipulate strings. In Standard Pascal, there is nothing formally referred to as type **String**. To hold text strings, Standard Pascal uses a packed array of characters, sometimes abbreviated as **PAOC**:

```
TYPE
    PAOC25 = PACKED ARRAY[1..25] OF Char;
```

This is a typical definition of a **PAOC** type. Of course, it doesn't have to be 25 characters in size; it can be as large as you like. The word **PACKED** is a holdover from large mainframe computers; on 8- and 16-bit computers it serves no purpose. In mainframe computers with 32- and 64-bit words, the word **PACKED** instructs the compiler to store as many characters as will fit in one machine word, rather than using one machine word per character. Using

PACKED on a mainframe could reduce the size of a string by a factor of four to eight times. Turbo Pascal always stores a **Char** value in one byte no matter what the word size of the computer it runs on. The word **PACKED** is still necessary, however, to define a Standard Pascal string.

What can be done with a **PAOC**-type string? Not much. A string constant can be assigned to it, if the string constant is *exactly* the same size as the definition of the **PAOC**:

```
VAR
  ErrorMsg : PAOC25;

ErrorMsg := 'Warning! Bracket missing!';   { This is OK }
ErrorMsg := 'Warning! Comma missing!';     { Illegal!   }
```

The second string constant is two characters short of 25 long, so the compiler will flag error #44: Type mismatch. The second string constant could not be considered a **PAOC25** because it is only 23 characters long; hence, the type mismatch error. Of course, you could have padded out the second constant with spaces, and the padded constant would have been acceptable.

You can compare two **PAOC**-type strings with the relational operators, read and write them from files, and print them to the screen. And that's where it ends. All other manipulations have to be done on a character-by-character basis, as though the string were just another array of any simple type.

The only reason to use **PAOC**-type strings is in situations where you are writing code for a Pascal compiler that does not understand variable-length (sometimes called "dynamic") strings. Such compilers are rare and getting rarer. As you might expect, they seem to be found mainly on enormous mainframe computers.

TURBO PASCAL VARIABLE-LENGTH STRINGS

Most modern Pascal implementors, including those who wrote Turbo Pascal, have filled this hole in the language definition by providing what are called "variable-length" strings. Like **PAOC**-type strings, variable-length strings are arrays of characters, but they are treated by the compiler in a special way. Variable-length strings have a "logical length" that varies, depending on what you put into the string. Strings of different logical lengths may be assigned to one another as long as the real physical lengths of the strings are not exceeded. The method of implementing variable-length strings in Turbo Pascal is identical to their implementation in Pascal/MT+ and UCSD Pascal.

A string type in Turbo Pascal has two lengths: A physical length and a logical length. The physical length is the amount of memory the string actually takes up. This length is set at compile time and never changes. The logical length is the number of characters currently stored in the string. This can change as you work with the string. The logical length (which from now on we will simply call the length) is stored as part of the string itself and can be read in several ways.

A string variable is defined using the reserved word **String**. A physical size must be specified in brackets after the word **String**. The legal range of physical lengths is 1 to 255 characters. Unlike Pascal/MT+, there is no default physical size for strings. You *must* specify a physical size or Turbo Pascal will flag error #8: '[' expected.

```
VAR
  Message : String[80];  { Physical size = 80 }
  Name    : String[30];  { Physical size = 30 }
  Address : String[30];  { Physical size = 30 }
  State   : String[2];   { Physical size = 2  }
```

You may also define string types as strings of different physical lengths. This is a much better way to deal with strings having a physical length longer or shorter than 80 characters:

```
TYPE
  String80 = String[80];
  String30 = String[30];
  Buffer   = String[255];
```

Once you have defined these types, declare all string variables that are to have a physical length of 30 characters as type **String30**. This way, all such strings will have identical types and not simply compatible types. This becomes critical when you have to pass string variables as reference parameters. (See Section 12.2 for a discussion of compatible and identical types, and Section 14.2 for a discussion of reference parameters.)

What is a string, physically? A string is an array of characters indexed from 0 to the physical length. Character 0 is special, however; it is the "length byte" and it holds the logical length of the string at any given time. The length byte is set by the runtime code when you perform an operation on a string that changes its logical length:

```
MyString := '';                        { MyString[0] = 0  }
MyString := 'Frodo';                   { MyString[0] = 5  }
MyString := 'Alfred E. ' + 'Neuman';   { MyString[0] = 17 }
```

The actual text contained in the string begins at **MyString[1]**. See Figure 9.4.

Strings may be accessed as though they were, in fact, arrays of characters. You can reference any character in the string, including the length byte, with a normal array reference:

```
VAR
   MyString  : String[15];
   CharS     : Integer;
   OUTChar   : Char;

MyString  := 'Galadriel';
Chars     := ORD(MyString[0]);  { Chars now equals 9     }
OUTChar   := MyString[6];       { OUTChar now holds 'r' }
```

Even though the Turbo Pascal runtime code treats the length byte as a number, it is still an element in an array of **Char** and thus cannot be assigned directly to type **Byte** or **Integer**. To assign the length byte to a numeric variable, you must use the **Ord** transfer function, which is Pascal's orderly way of transferring a character value to a numeric value. (See Section 16.5.)

This, however, is doing it the hard way. Many predefined string-handling functions and procedures are built into Turbo Pascal. The **Length** function is a good example. It returns the current logical length of a string variable:

```
Chars := Length(MyString);     { Chars now equals 9   }
```

We will discuss **Length** and all the other built-in string-handling functions and procedures in Chapter 15.

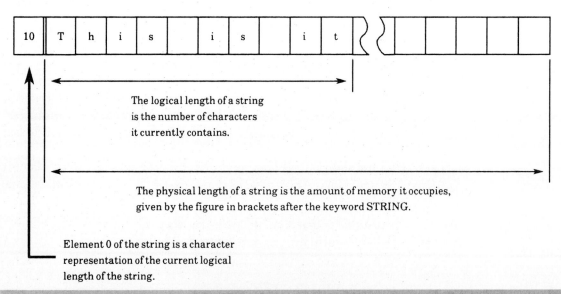

VAR MYSTRING : STRING[80];
MYSTRING := 'This is it';

The logical length of a string
is the number of characters
it currently contains.

The physical length of a string is the amount of memory it occupies,
given by the figure in brackets after the keyword STRING.

Element 0 of the string is a character
representation of the current logical
length of the string.

FIGURE 9.4 String representation

Characters and strings are compatible in some limited ways. You can assign a character value to a string variable. The string variable then has a logical length of 1:

```
MyString := 'A'          { Logical length = 1 }
MyString := OUTChar;     { Ditto }
```

A string (even one having a length of 0 or 1) cannot be assigned to a character variable. You can compare a string variable to a character literal:

```
IF MyString = 'A' THEN StartProcess;
```

It is possible to assign a string to another string with a shorter physical length. This will cause neither a compile time nor a runtime error. What it *will* do is truncate the data from the larger string to the maximum physical length of the smaller string.

9.6   Structured constants

Standard Pascal only allows simple constants: Integers, characters, reals, Booleans, and strings. Turbo Pascal provides "structured" constants, meaning constants in the form of arrays, records, and sets.

Calling Turbo Pascal's structured constants "constants" is not entirely fair. Real constants are hardcoded into the machine code produced by the compiler and exist at no single address. Turbo Pascal's structured constants are actually static variables that are initialized at runtime to values taken from the source code. They exist at one single address, which is referenced anytime the structured constant is used.

Structured constants also violate the most fundamental proscription of constants in all languages: They may be changed during the course of a program run. Of course, you are not obligated to alter structured constants at runtime, but the compiler will not stop you if you try. In this, Turbo Pascal provides less protection than in the area of simple constants. If you attempt to write to a simple constant, Turbo Pascal will flag Error #41: Unknown identifier or syntax error.

With that in mind, it might be better to think of structured constants as a means of forcing the compiler to initialize complicated data structures. Standard Pascal has *no* means of initializing variables automatically. If values are to be placed into variables, *you* must place them there somehow, either from assignment statements or by reading values in from a file. For example, you could initialize an array of 15 integers this way:

```
VAR
   Weights : ARRAY[1..15] OF Integer;

Weights[1]  := 17;
Weights[2]  := 5;
Weights[3]  := 91;
Weights[4]  := 111;
Weights[5]  := 0;
Weights[6]  := 44;
Weights[7]  := 16;
Weights[8]  := 3;
Weights[9]  := 472;
Weights[10] := 66;
Weights[11] := 14;
Weights[12] := 38;
Weights[13] := 57;
Weights[14] := 8;
Weights[15] := 10;
```

For 15 values this may seem manageable, but suppose you had 50 values or 100? At that point Turbo's structured constants become *very* attractive. This same array could be initialized as a structured constant:

```
CONST
  Weights : ARRAY[1..15] OF Integer =
    (17,5,91,111,0,44,16,3,472,66,14,38,57,8,10);
```

The form of a structured constant definition is:

```
<identifier> : <type> = <values>
```

Because Turbo Pascal allows multiple **CONST** keywords within a single program, you may have a separate **CONST** declaration section for structured constants *after* the type declaration section. This allows you to declare your own custom type definitions and then create constants of your custom types.

ARRAY CONSTANTS

The example above is a simple, one-dimensional array constant. Its values are placed, in order, between parentheses, with commas separating the values. *You must give one value for each element of the array constant.* Turbo Pascal will not allow you to initialize some values of an array and leave the rest "blank." You must do all of them or none. If the number of values you give does not match the number of elements in the array, Turbo Pascal will respond with Error #3 : ',' expected. It is literally looking for another comma and more values in the list.

If you only need to initialize a few values of a large array, it might be more effective to go back to individual assignment statements.

You may also define multi-dimensional array constants. The trick here is to enclose each dimension in parentheses, with commas separating both the dimensions and the items. A single pair of parentheses must enclose the entire constant. The innermost nesting level represents the rightmost dimension from the array declaration. An example will help:

```
CONST
    Grid : Array[0..4,0..3] OF Boolean =
                ((4,6,2,1),
                 (3,9,8,3),
                 (1,7,7,5),
                 (4,1,7,7),
                 (3,1,3,1));
```

This is a two-dimensional array of integer constants, arranged as five rows of four columns. It might represent game pieces on a grid. Adding a third dimension to the game (and the grid) would be done this way:

```
CONST
    Space : Array[0..7,0..4,0..3] OF Integer =

(((4,6,2,1),(3,9,6,1),(1,7,7,5),(4,1,7,7),(3,1,3,1)),
 ((1,1,1,1),(1,1,1,1),(1,1,1,1),(1,1,1,1),(1,1,1,1)),
 ((2,2,2,2),(2,2,2,2),(2,2,2,2),(2,2,2,2),(2,2,2,2)),
 ((3,3,3,3),(3,3,3,3),(3,3,3,3),(3,3,3,3),(3,3,3,3)),
 ((4,4,4,4),(4,4,4,4),(4,4,4,4),(4,4,4,4),(4,4,4,4)),
 ((5,5,5,5),(5,5,5,5),(5,5,5,5),(5,5,5,5),(5,5,5,5)),
 ((6,6,6,6),(6,6,6,6),(6,6,6,6),(6,6,6,6),(6,6,6,6)),
 ((7,7,7,7),(7,7,7,7),(7,7,7,7),(7,7,7,7),(7,7,7,7)));
```

The values given for the two-dimensional array have been retained here to see how the array has been extended by one dimension. Note that the list of values in an array constant must begin with the same number of left parentheses as the array has dimensions. Remember, also, that *every* element in the array must have a value in the array constant declaration.

Notice that this feature of Turbo Pascal allows you to initialize 160 different integer values in a relatively small space. Imagine what it would have taken to initialize this array with assignment statements!

RECORD CONSTANTS

Record constants are handled a little bit differently. You must first declare a record type and then a constant containing values for each field in the record. The list of values must include the name of each field followed by a colon and then the value for that field. Items in the list are separated by semicolons. As an example, consider a record containing configuration values for a terminal program:

```
TYPE
  BPS        = (B110,B300,B1200,B2400,B4800,B9600);
  ParityType = (EvenParity,OddParity,NoParity);
  TermCFG    = RECORD
                 LocalAreaCode : String[3];
                 UseTouchtones : Boolean;
                 DialOneFirst  : Boolean;
                 BaudRate      : BPS;
                 BitsPerChar   : Integer;
                 Parity        : ParityType
               END;

CONST
  Config : TermCFG =
               (LocalAreaCode : '716';
                UseTouchtones : True;
                DialOneFirst  : True;
                BaudRate      : B1200;
                BitsPerChar   : 7;
                Parity        : Even Parity);
```

The structured constant declaration for **Config** must come after the type definition for **TermCFG**, otherwise the compiler would not know what a **TermCFG** was. Note that there is no **BEGIN/END** bracketing in the declaration of **Config**. The parentheses serve to set off the list of field values from the rest of your source code.

SET CONSTANTS

Declaring a set constant is not very different from assigning a set value to a set variable:

```
CONST
     Uppercase : SET OF Char = ['A'..'Z'];
```

The major difference is the notation used to represent non-printable characters in a set of **Char**. Characters that do not have a printable symbol associated with them may ordinarily be represented in a set builder by the **Chr** transfer function:

```
MySet := [Chr(7),Chr(10),Chr(13)];
```

The **Chr** notation above is invalid when declaring set constants. You have two alternatives:

1. Express the character as a control character by placing a caret symbol (^) in front of the appropriate character. The bell character, **Chr(7)**, would be expressed as **^G**.
2. Express the character as its ordinal value preceded by a pound sign (#). The bell character would be expressed as **#7**. This notation is more useful for expressing characters falling in the "high" 128 bytes of type **Char**, corresponding to the line drawing and foreign language characters on the IBM PC and many compatibles.
   For example, the set of whitespace characters is a useful set constant:

```
CONST
  Whitespace : SET OF Char = [#8,#10,#12,#13,' '];
```

or, alternatively:

```
CONST
  Whitespace : SET OF Char = [^H,^J,^L,^M,' '];
```

The following three routines show you how to use set constants in simple character-manipulation tools. If you do a *lot* of character manipulation and find a great deal of use for these three set constants, you might also declare them at the global program level so that any part of the program can use them. Remember that, declared as they are here locally to their individual functions, they *cannot* be accessed from outside the function!

```
FUNCTION CapsLock(Ch : Char) : Char;

CONST
  Lowercase : SET OF Char = ['a'..'z'];

BEGIN
  IF Ch IN Lowercase THEN CapsLock := Chr(Ord(Ch)-32)
    ELSE CapsLock := Ch
END;

FUNCTION DownCase(Ch : Char) : Char;

CONST
  Uppercase : SET OF Char = ['A'..'Z'];

BEGIN
  IF Ch IN Uppercase THEN DownCase := Chr(Ord(Ch)+32)
    ELSE DownCase := Ch
End;

FUNCTION IsWhite(Ch : Char) : Boolean;

CONST
  Whitespace : SET OF Char = [#8,#10,#12,#13,' '];

BEGIN
  IsWhite := Ch IN WhiteSpace
END;
```

Pointers

10.1 Static and dynamic variables

Up to this point, we've made the assumption that all data items used in a Pascal program are known to the compiler when it compiles the program. That is, in order to use three integer variables I, J, and K, those three variables must be declared in the program source code:

```
VAR
    I,J,K : Integer;
```

The compiler uses this line to create three integer variables, which remain available as long as the program is running. The three variables are each given their proper place in the program's data area and there they remain. The program (assuming it has only these three variables) cannot decide on the basis of its work that it needs another variable and so create it. What it gets at compile time is what it has, period.

Variables of this sort are called "static variables." Pascal allows another kind of variable that the program can, in fact, create as needed. These variables are called "dynamic variables."

Dynamic variables are identical in form to static variables. What is different about them is how they are created and how they are accessed. To understand that we must understand a new kind of data item: the pointer.

Almost by definition, the static data area of a program is set at compile time and can never change while the program is running. Dynamic variables, if they can be created and destroyed during a program's run, must exist somewhere else.

This "somewhere else" is a region of computer memory set aside by the compiler specifically to hold dynamic variables. It is called "heapspace" or "the heap." The word "heap" was coined in contrast to the word "stack," which is a memory-management method in which items are stored in strict order and must be stored and retrieved in that order, like plates placed in a stack: The top one must come off first, then the next-to-top, and so on. In a heap of plates, the plates are in no special order. If you want a plate, you can reach in and take any of them you like in any order.

So it is with dynamic variables placed in heapspace. They are in no order and can be created and fetched at random.

10.2 Defining pointer types

The major purpose of pointer variables is to act as the bridge between the static data area and the heap. You must keep one thing in mind: *Dynamic variables have no names!* A pointer variable is in one sense a way of naming a dynamic variable; the only way, in fact, of "getting at" a dynamic variable. Pointer types are defined by the programmer just as enumerated types and structured types are:

```
TYPE
  AType = String[20];

  APtr  = ^AType;
```

A pointer type is *always* defined as a pointer to some other type The notation ^**AType** is read, "pointer to **ATYPE**." Pointers may point to any type except a file type.

One peculiarity of defining pointer types is that a pointer may be defined as pointing to a type that has itself not been defined yet. Consider the problem of defining a pointer variable that points to a record type containing (as a field) a pointer like itself, which points to a record of that type:

```
TYPE
   RecPtr  = ^DynaRec;
   DynaRec = RECORD
                Datapart : String;
                Next     : RecPtr
             END;
```

Ordinarily, you cannot use an identifier until the compiler already knows what it is. But there is a "chicken and egg" conflict here: If we define **RecPtr** first, the compiler doesn't know what **DynaRec** means. If we define **DynaRec** first, the compiler doesn't know what **RecPtr** means. By convention, therefore, Pascal allows us to define a pointer to a type that will later be defined. (Of course, if you never get around to defining that type, an error will be generated and the compilation will fail.)

Records like **DynaRec** are central to the notion of "linked lists," which we will return to in Section 19.2.

10.3 Creating dynamic variables

When a pointer variable is allocated by the compiler, its value is undefined, as with any static variable. It is even incorrect to say that it points to nothing; there is a way to explicitly force a pointer to point to nothing. An undefined pointer is simply undefined and should not be used until it has been given something (or nothing—see below) to point to.

Dynamic variables are created by a predefined Pascal procedure called **NEW**:

```
VAR
   APtr : RecPtr;

NEW(APtr);
```

The type **RecPtr** (as we saw above) was previously defined as a pointer to type **DynaRec**. Because **APtr** is of type **RecPtr**, the program (*not* the compiler; this is done at runtime) knows to create a variable of type **DynaRec** in heapspace. It then sets up **APtr** to point to the new dynamic variable of type **DynaRec**. **APtr**, which was previously undefined, now indeed points to something: to a brand new **DynaRec**.

Figure 10.1 shows a generalized diagram of this way of using **NEW**. Note in the diagram that **DynaRec** is not the *name* of the new dynamic variable, but its *type*.

Accessing a dynamic variable is done through its pointer. Going back to the text example, if we wish to assign some value to the **DataPart** field of the new **DynaRec**, we must use this notation:

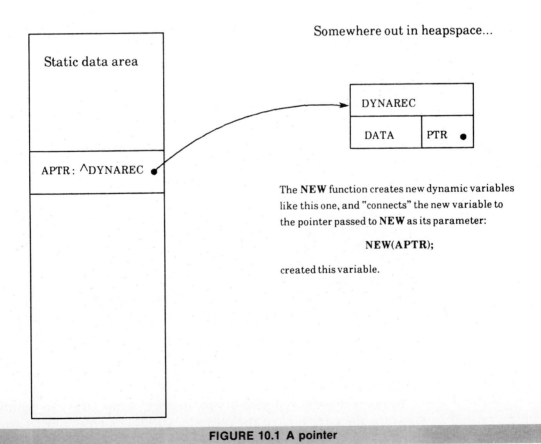

Somewhere out in heapspace...

Static data area

DYNAREC

DATA   PTR

APTR: ^DYNAREC

The **NEW** function creates new dynamic variables like this one, and "connects" the new variable to the pointer passed to **NEW** as its parameter:

NEW(APTR);

created this variable.

FIGURE 10.1 A pointer

```
APtr^.DataPart := 'Be dynamic!';
```

Assigning a dynamic variable (or a field of a dynamic record) to a static variable is done just as easily:

```
AString := APtr^.DataPart;
```

There is no "clean" way to pronounce **APtr^** other than "that which pointer **APtr** points to." **APtr^** is the closest the new dynamic variable will ever come to having a name.

10.4   Operations on pointers

A pointer is either undefined or it points to a dynamic variable or it points to nothing. Making a pointer point to nothing involves assigning it a special predefined value called **NIL**:

```
APtr := NIL;
```

It can now be said that **APtr** points to nothing. It is a good idea to assign **NIL** to all pointers soon after a program begins running. Using a pointer with a value of **NIL** is safer than using a pointer that is undefined.

Pointers may be compared for equality. When two pointers are said to be equal, it means that they both point to the identical dynamic variable or that they both have a value of **NIL**. Both pointers must be of the same type to be compared.

Comparing two undefined pointers will return an undefined value. *Don't do it.*

Pointers may be assigned to one another. Again, the two pointers must be the same type or the compiler will flag a type conflict error.

The logic with pointer assignment is that when you assign one pointer to a second pointer, the second pointer now points to the identical dynamic variable to which the first pointer was pointing:

```
VAR
  APtr,BPtr := RecPtr;

NEW(APtr);          { APtr^ is a dynamic record       }
NEW(BPtr);          { BPtr^ is another dynamic record }
BPtr := APtr;       { What used to be BPtr^ is lost!  }
```

In this example, two pointers are each set to point to a new dynamic variable. You must keep in mind that each call to **NEW** produces a separate and distinct dynamic variable in heapspace. Then, however, in the assignment statement **BPtr** is assigned the value of **APtr**. Both pointers now point to the same dynamic record, which is the record **APtr** pointed to originally. **APtr^** and **BPtr^** are now the identical record. Furthermore, the record created by the call **NEW(BPtr)** is now lost forever. *Once you "break" a pointer away from its dynamic variable, that variable is utterly inaccessible.*

This situation is even worse, in fact, than it sounds. Even though the original **BPtr^** is inaccessible, *it still exists,* and occupies memory, which now cannot be used for anything else. Do *not* just cut a dynamic variable loose—unlike a kite or balloon, which will fly away and cease being a problem, a "lost" dynamic variable will remain as long as the program that created it continues running. If you cut loose too many dynamic variables you could conceivably run out of heapspace and cause a "stack collision."

In the way Turbo Pascal allocates memory, the stack grows downward from high memory, while the heap grows upward from low memory. If the two collide, your system will crash hard.

10.5   Disposing of dynamic variables

The way out is to clean house correctly when dynamic variables are no longer needed. Turbo Pascal contains a predefined procedure called **Dispose**, which is much the opposite of **NEW**:

```
Dispose(APtr);
```

The **Dispose** procedure takes a pointer as its parameter. **Dispose** releases the memory occupied by **APtr^** (the dynamic variable pointed to by **APtr**) and causes the value of **APtr** to become undefined. Don't make the mistake of thinking that **Dispose** forces the value of its pointer parameter to **NIL**. The value becomes undefined, just as it was before you assigned a value to the pointer when the program began running.

The memory once occupied by **APtr^** now becomes available for **NEW** to allocate to other dynamic variables.

There's not a whole lot more to pointer variables themselves. Pointers are actually the glue that can hold together elaborate data structures formed from dynamic variables. There's a fair amount of Pascal to be learned before you should take on dynamic data structures such as linked lists. Later on, in Section 19.2, we'll look at them in greater detail.

Physically, a pointer is a machine address of some location in memory; specifically, of the first byte of the dynamic variable the pointer points to. You must keep in mind that pointers are implemented in different ways in different machine environments. Turbo Pascal pointers are 16-bit absolute addresses in 8080/Z80 environments, and 32-bit segment/offset addresses in 8086 environments. In both environments a **NIL** pointer has all bits set to binary zero.

You should avoid tinkering with pointers beneath the level of the language itself. If you do, you lose any protection against stray memory references that Turbo Pascal's runtime library provides. A pointer is, after all, just a memory reference. If you accidentally create a pointer that points somewhere in the middle of your operating system and then store a dynamic variable at that location, you will crash resoundingly.

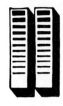

Operators and expressions

So far we have covered, in depth, the various data types that Pascal offers you. Data are representations of concepts that we want a program to manipulate. From this point on, we will be speaking largely of how the Pascal language manipulates its data.

As we explained previously, a variable is a container in memory laid out by the compiler. It has a particular size and shape defined by its type. Into a variable you load an item of data that conforms to the size and shape of the variable. This data is called a "value."

You are probably familiar with this symbol, perhaps the most fundamental operator in Pascal: " := " It is the assignment operator. The assignment operator is (usually) how values are placed into variables. We've been using it informally all along and will discuss it in some detail in Section 12.1. In case you aren't sure by now how it works, consider this simple assignment statement:

```
I := 17;
```

A value on the right side of the assignment operator is assigned to the variable on the left side of the assignment operator. In an assignment statement, there is always a variable on the left side of the assignment operator. On the right side may be a constant, a variable, or an expression.

An expression in Pascal is a combination of data items and operators that eventually "cooks down" to a single value. Data items are constants and variables. Operators are special symbols that perform some action involving the value or values given to it. These values are called an operator's "operands."

The simplest and most familiar examples of expressions come to us from arithmetic. This is an expression:

   17 + 3

The addition operator performs an add operation on its two operands, 17 and 3. The value of the expression is 20.

An expression like "17 + 3," while valid, would not be used in a real program, where the value "20" would suffice. Considerably more useful are expressions that involve variables. For example:

   3.14159 * Radius * Radius

This expression's value is recognizable as the area of the circle defined by whatever value is contained in **Radius**.

ISO Standard Pascal includes a good many different operators for building expressions, and Turbo Pascal enhances ISO Pascal with a few additional operators. They fall into a number of related groups, depending on what sort of result they return: Relational, arithmetic, set, and logical (also called "bitwise") operators.

11.1   Relational operators

Relational operators are used to build Boolean expressions, that is, expressions that evaluate down to a Boolean value of **True** or **False**. Boolean expressions are the most widely used of all expressions in Pascal. All of the looping and branching statements in Pascal depend on Boolean expressions.

A relational operator causes the compiler to compare its two operands for some sort of relationship. The resulting Boolean value is calculated according to a set of well-defined rules concerning how data items of various sorts relate to one another.

The following table summarizes the relational operators implemented in Turbo Pascal. All return Boolean results:

Relational operations in Turbo Pascal			
Operator	Symbol	Operand type	Precedence
Equality	=	scalar, set, string, pointer, record	5
Inequality	<>	scalar, set, string, pointer, record	5
Less than	<	scalar, string	5
Greater than	>	scalar, string	5
Less than or equal	<=	scalar, string	5
Greater than or equal	>=	scalar, string	5
Set membership	IN	set, set members	5
Set inclusion, left in right	<=	set	5
Set inclusion, right in left	>=	set	5
Negation	NOT	Boolean	2
Conjunction	AND	Boolean	3
Disjunction	OR	Boolean	4
Exclusive OR	XOR	Boolean	4

Scalar types, if you recall, are types with a limited number of ordered values. **Char**, **Boolean**, **Integer**, **Byte**, and enumerated types are all scalars. Real numbers, strings, structured types (records and arrays), and sets are *not* scalars.

The three relational operators that involve sets, set membership and the two set inclusion operators, will be discussed along with the operators that return set values in Section 11.3. Note that the set inclusion operators share symbols with the greater than or equal to/less than or equal to operators, but the sense of these two types of operations is radically different.

EQUALITY

If two values compared for equality are the same, the expression will evaluate as **True**. In general, for two values to be considered equal by Turbo Pascal's runtime code, they must be identical on a bit-by-bit basis. This is true for comparisons between like types. Most comparisons must be done between values of the same type.

The exceptions are comparisons done between numeric values expressed as different types. Turbo Pascal allows comparisons rather freely among types **Integer**, **Byte**, and **Real**, but this sort of type-crossing must be done with great care. In particular, do not compare calculated reals (real number results of a real number arithmetic operation) for equality, either to other reals or to numeric values of other types. Rounding effects may cause real numbers to appear unequal to compiled code, even though the mathematical sense of the calculation would seem to make them equal. (For an example of this problem, see Section 7.5.)

Type **Byte** may be compared with integers.

Two sets are considered equal if they both contain exactly the same members. Two pointers are considered equal if they both point to the same dynamic variable. Two pointers are also considered equal if they both point to **NIL**.

Two records are considered equal if they are of the same type (you cannot compare records of different types) and each field in one record is bit-by-bit identical to its corresponding field in the other record.

Two strings are considered equal if they both have the same logical length (see Section 9.5) and contain the same characters. This makes them bit-by-bit identical as far out as the logical length, which is the touchstone for all like-type equality comparisons under Turbo Pascal. Remember that this makes leading and trailing blanks significant:

```
'   Eriador' <> 'Eriador'    { True! }
'Eriador   ' <> 'Eriador'    { True! }
```

INEQUALITY

The rules for testing for inequality are exactly the same as the rules for equality. The only difference is that the Boolean state of the result is reversed:

```
17 = 17         { True  }
17 <> 17        { False }
42 = 17         { False }
42 <> 16        { True  }
```

In general, you can use the inequality operator anywhere you can use the equality operator.

Pointers are considered unequal when they point to different dynamic variables, or when one points to **NIL** and the other does not. The bit-by-bit rule is again applied: Even one bit's difference found during a like-type comparison means the two compared operands are unequal. The warning applied to rounding errors produced in calculated reals applies to inequality comparisons as well.

GREATER THAN/LESS THAN

The four operators greater than, less than, greater than or equal to, and less than or equal to add a new dimension to the notion of comparison. They assume that their operands always exist in some well-defined order by which the comparison can be made.

This immediately disqualifies pointers, sets, and records. Saying one pointer is greater than another simply makes no sense, given the definition of pointers. You could argue that since pointers are physical addresses, one pointer will always be greater or less than another non-equal pointer. This may be true, but in the spirit of the Pascal language, details about how pointers are implemented are hidden from the programmer at the level of Pascal.

The same applies to sets and records. Ordering them makes no logical sense, so operators involving an implied order cannot be used with them.

With scalar types, a definite order is part of the type definition. For integers, the order is obvious from our experience with arithmetic; integers model negative and positive whole numbers between specific bounds.

The **Char** and **Byte** types are both limited to 256 possible values, and both have an order implied by the sequence of binary numbers from 0 to 255. The **Char** type is ordered (at least for the lower 128 values) by the ASCII character set, which makes the following expressions evaluate to **True**:

```
'A' < 'B'
'a' > 'A'
'@' < '['
```

The higher 128 values assignable to **Char** variables have no standard characters, but they still exist in fixed order and are numbered from 128 to 255.

Enumerated types are limited to no more than 255 different values, and usually have fewer than 10 or 12. Their fixed order is the order the values were given in the definition of the enumerated type:

```
TYPE
  Spectrum = (Red,Orange,Yellow,Green,Blue,Indigo,Violet);
```

This order makes the following expressions evaluate to **True**:

```
Red < Green
Blue > Yellow
Indigo < Violet
```

The ordering of string values involves two components: The length of the string and the ASCII values of the characters present in the string. Essentially, Turbo Pascal begins by comparing the first characters in the two strings being compared. If those two characters are different, the test stops there, and the ordering of the two strings is based upon the relation of those two first characters. If the two characters are the same, the second characters in each string are compared. If they turn out to be the same, then the third characters in both strings are compared.

This process continues until the code finds two characters that differ, or until one string runs out of characters. In that case, the longer of the two is considered to be greater than the shorter. All of the following expressions evaluate to **True**:

```
'AAAAA' > 'AAA'
'B' > 'AAAAAAAAAAAA'
'AAAAB' > 'AAAAAAAAAA'
```

NOT, AND,
OR, AND XOR

Four operators work only on Boolean operands: **NOT**, **AND**, **OR**, and **XOR**. These four operators are sometimes set apart as a separate group called Boolean operators. In some ways, they have more in common with the arithmetic operators than with the relational operators. They do not test a relationship that already exists between two operands. Rather, they combine their operands according to the rules of Boolean algebra to produce a new value that becomes the value of the expression.

The simplest of the four is **NOT**, which takes only one Boolean operand. The operand must be placed after the **NOT** reserved word. **NOT** negates the Boolean value of its operand:

```
NOT False    { Expression is True    }
NOT True     { Expression is False   }
```

Some slightly less simplistic examples:

```
NOT (6 > I)   { True for I < 6   }
NOT (J = K)   { True for J <> K  }
```

The parentheses indicate that the expression within the parentheses is evaluated first, and only then is the resultant value acted upon by **NOT**. This expression is an instance where "order of evaluation" becomes important. We will discuss this in detail in Section 11.5.

AND (also known as "conjunction") requires two operands, and follows this rule: *If both operands are **True**, the expression returns **True**; else the expression returns **False**.* If either operand or both operands have the value **False**, the value of the expression as a whole will be **False**.

Some examples:

```
True AND True            { Expression is True  }
True AND False           { Expression is False }
False AND True           { Expression is False }
False AND False          { Expression is False }

(7 > 4) AND (5 <> 3)     { Expression is True  }
(16 = (4 * 4)) AND (2 <> 2)  { Expression is False }
```

All of these sample expressions use constants, and thus are not realistic uses of **AND** within a program. We present them this way so the logic of the statement is obvious without having to remember what value is currently in a variable present in an expression. We'll be presenting some real-life coding examples of the use of **NOT**, **AND**, and **OR** in connection with the discussion of order of evaluation in Section 11.5.

OR (also known as "disjunction") also requires two operands, and follows this rule: *If either (or both) operands is **True**, the expression returns **True**; only if both operands are **False** will the expression return **False**.*

Some examples, again using constants:

```
True OR True             { Expression is True  }
True OR False            { Expression is True  }
False OR True            { Expression is True  }
False OR False           { Expression is False }

(7 > 4) OR (5 = 3)       { Expression is True  }
(2 < 1) OR (6 <> 6)      { Expression is False }
```

Finally, **XOR**, which also requires two operands, follows this rule: *If both operands are the same Boolean value, **XOR** returns **False**; only if the operands have unlike Boolean values will **XOR** return **True**.*

Some examples:

```
True XOR True        { Expression is False }
True XOR False       { Expression is True  }
False XOR True       { Expression is True  }
False XOR False      { Expression is False }
```

GREATER THAN OR EQUAL TO/ LESS THAN OR EQUAL TO

These two operators are each combinations of two operators. These combinations are so convenient and so frequently used that they were welded together to form two single operators with unique symbols: >= (read, "greater than or equal to") and <= (read, "less than or equal to").

When you wish to say:

```
X >= Y
```

you are in fact saying

```
(X > Y) OR (X = Y)
```

and when you wish to say

```
X <= Y
```

you are in fact saying

```
(X < Y) OR (X = Y)
```

The rules for applying **>=** and **<=** are exactly the same as those for **<** and **>**. They may take only scalars or strings as operands.

11.2   Arithmetic operators

Manipulating numbers is done with arithmetic operators, which, along with numeric variables, form arithmetic expressions. About the only common arithmetic operator not found in Pascal is the exponentiation operator, that is, the raising of one number to a given power. (We will, however, build a function that raises one number to the power of another in Section 18.4.) The following table summarizes the arithmetic operators implemented in Turbo Pascal:

Arithmetic operations in Turbo Pascal				
Operator	Symbol	Operand types	Result type	Precedence
Addition	+	Integer, real, byte	same	4
Sign inversion	−	Integer, real	same	1
Subtraction	−	Integer, real, byte	same	4
Multiplication	*	Integer, real, byte	same	3
Integer division	DIV	Integer, byte	same	3
Real division	/	Integer, real, byte	real	3
Modulus	MOD	Integer, byte	same	3

The "operands" column lists those data types that a given operator may take as operands. The compiler is fairly free about allowing you to mix types of numeric variables within an expression. In other words, you may multiply bytes by integers, add reals to bytes, multiply integers by bytes, and so on. For example, these are all legal expressions in Turbo Pascal:

```
VAR
   I,J,K  : Integer;
   R,S,T  : Real;
   A,B,C  : Byte;
```

(continues)

```
I * B          { Integer multiplied by byte }
R + J          { Integer added to real      }
C + (R * I)    { Etc. }
J * (A / S)
```

(concluded)

The "result type" column in the table indicates the data type that the value of an expression incorporating that operator may take on. Pascal is ordinarily very picky about the assignment of different types to one another in assignment statements. This "strict type checking" is relaxed to some extent in simple arithmetic expressions. Numeric types may, in fact, be mixed fairly freely within expressions as long as a few rules are obeyed:

1. Any expression including a real value may only be assigned to a real number variable.
2. Expressions containing real division (/) may only be assigned to a real number variable.

Failure to follow these rules will generate error #44: Type mismatch. Outside of the two mentioned restrictions, however, a numeric expression may be assigned to any numeric variable, assuming the variable has sufficient range to contain the value of the expression. For example, if an expression evaluates to 14,000, you should not assign the expression to a variable of type **Byte**, which can only contain values from 0 to 255. Program behavior in such a case is unpredictable.

Addition, subtraction, and multiplication are handled in the same way as ordinary arithmetic with pencil or calculator, and we won't need to describe them here.

SIGN INVERSION

Sign inversion is a "unary" operator; that is, it takes only a single operand. It reverses the sign of its operand, making a positive quantity negative, or a negative quantity positive. It does not affect the absolute value (distance from zero) of the operand.

Note that sign inversion cannot be used with bytes. Turbo Pascal's type **Byte** is "unsigned"; that is, it is never considered negative.

DIVISION

There are three division operators in Pascal. One supports real number division, and the other two support division for integers and bytes. Real number division (/) may take operands of any numeric type, but it always produces a real number value, complete with decimal part. Attempting to assign a real number division expression to a non-real type will generate error #44, *even if all numeric variables involved are integers:*

```
VAR
   I,J,K : Integer;

I := J / K;            { Won't compile!!! }
```

Division for numbers that cannot hold decimal parts is handled in much the same way as division is first taught to grade schoolers: When one number is divided by another, two numbers result. One is a whole number quotient; the other a whole number remainder.

In Pascal, integer division is actually two separate operations that do not depend upon one another. One operator, **DIV**, produces the quotient of its operands:

```
J := 17;
K := 3;
I := J DIV K;      { I is assigned the value 5  }
```

No remainder is generated at all by **DIV**, and the operation should not be considered incomplete. If you wish to compute the remainder, the modulus operator (**MOD**) is used:

```
I := J MOD K;    { I is assigned the value 2  }
```

Assuming the same values given above for **J** and **K**, the remainder of dividing **J** by **K** is computed as 2. The quotient is not calculated at all (or calculated internally and thrown away); only the remainder is returned.

11.3   Set operators

Set operators are used to manipulate values of type **SET**. To a great extent they follow the rules of set arithmetic you may have learned in grade school. The table on page 128 summarizes the set operators implemented in Turbo Pascal. All of them take set operands and return set values.

SET UNION

The union of two sets is the set that contains as members all members contained in both of the two sets. The symbol for the set union operator is the plus sign (+), as in arithmetic addition. An example:

```
VAR
   SetX, SetY, SetZ : SET OF Char;

SetX := ['Y','y','M','m'];
SetY := ['N','n','M','m'];
SetZ := SetX + SetY;
```

SetZ now contains '**Y**', '**y**', '**N**', '**n**', '**M**', and '**m**'. Note that although '**M**' and '**m**' exist in both sets, each appears but once in the union of the two sets. A set merely says whether or not a member is present in the set; it is meaningless to speak of how many times a member is present. By definition, each member is present only once or not present at all.

SET DIFFERENCE

The difference of two sets is the set that contains as members only those members that the two sets do *not* have in common. It is the opposite of set intersection, which we will come to shortly. The symbol for set difference is the dash (-) the same as in arithmetic subtraction.

Set operations in Turbo Pascal		
Operator	Symbol	Precedence
Set union	+	4
Set difference	-	4
Set intersection	*	4

```
SetX := ['Y','y','M','m'];
SetY := ['N','n','M','m'];
SetZ := SetX - SetY;
```

SetZ now contains 'Y', 'y', 'N', and 'n'. Those are the elements that **SetX** and **SetY** do not have in common.

SET INTERSECTION   The intersection of two sets is the set that contains as members only those members contained in *both* sets. It is the opposite of set difference. The symbol for set intersection is the asterisk (*), just as in arithmetic multiplication. For example:

```
SetX := ['Y','y','M','m'];
SetY := ['N','n','M','m'];
SetZ := SetX * SetY;
```

SetZ now contains 'M' and 'm,' which are the only two members contained in both sets.

THE SET RELATIONAL OPERATORS   The set operators just described work with set operands to produce new set values. We have briefly mentioned the relational operators that test relationships between sets and return Boolean values depending on those relationships.

Sets, for example, can be equal to one another, if they both have the same base type and both contain the same elements. Two sets that are not of the same base type will generate a type mismatch error at compile time if you try to compare them:

```
VAR
  SetX : SET OF Char;
  SetQ : SET OF Color;
  OK   : Boolean;

OK := SetX = SetQ;        { Will trigger error #44! }
```

This holds true for *all* set relational operators, not just equality.

The most important set relational operator is the inclusion operator **IN**. **IN** tests whether a value of a set's base type is a member of that set.

```
VAR
  Ch : Char;

Read(Ch);                 { From the keyboard }
IF Ch IN ['Y','y'] THEN
  Write('Yes indeed!');
```

This example shows a clean and easy way to tell whether a user has typed the letter Y in response to a prompt. The **IN** operator tests whether the typed-in character is a member of the set constant ['Y','y']. (**IN** works just as well with set variables.) The alternative would be to use a more complicated Boolean expression:

```
IF (Ch = 'Y') OR (Ch = 'y') THEN
  Write('Yes indeed!');
```

The **IN** operator is also faster than using a series (especially a long series) of relational expressions linked with the **OR** operator.

The greater than (>) and less than (<) operators make no sense when applied to sets, because sets have no implied order to their values. However, there are two additional set relational operators that make use of the same symbols as used by the greater than or equal to (>=) and less than or equal to (<=) operators. These are the set inclusion operators.

Inclusion of left in right (<=) tests whether all members of the set on the left are included in the set on the right. Inclusion of right in left (>=) tests whether all members of the set on the right are included in the set on the left. The action taken by these two operators is identical except for the orientation of the two operands with respect to the operator symbol. Given two sets, **Set1** and **Set2**, the expression

```
(Set1 <= Set2) = (Set2 >= Set1)
```

will always evaluate to **True**. These operators are very handy for testing and manipulating characters in a text stream. For example:

```
VAR
   Vowels,Alphabet,Samples : SET OF Char;

Vowels:=['A','E','I','O','U'];
Alphabet:=['A'..'Z'];          { Set of all UC letters }
Samples:=['A','D','I','Q','Z'];

IF Samples <= Vowels THEN Write('All samples are vowels.');
IF NOT(Samples <= Vowels) AND (Samples <= Alphabet) THEN
   Write('Some or all samples are uppercase letters.');
IF NOT(Alphabet >= Samples) THEN
   Write('Some samples are not uppercase letters.');
```

In addition to demonstrating the set inclusion operators, these examples also show some uses of the **AND** and **NOT** operators. Given the members assigned to **Samples** here, this output will be displayed:

```
Some or all samples are uppercase letters.
```

Before going on, jot down two sets of characters that would trigger the other two messages in the above example.

11.4   Bitwise operators

Turbo Pascal allows you to read and write I/O ports and other low-level data, much of which is "bit-mapped"; that is, certain bits have certain meanings apart from all other bits and must be examined, set, and interpreted individually. The way to do this is through the "bitwise" logical operators. Associated with the bitwise logical operators are the shift operators, **SHL** and **SHR**. We will speak of these shortly.

We have previously spoken of the **AND**, **OR**, and **NOT** operators, which work on Boolean operands and return Boolean values. The bitwise logical operators are another flavor of **NOT**, **AND**, **OR**, and **XOR**. They work with operands of type **Integer** and **Byte**, and they apply a logical operation (**AND**, **OR**, and **NOT**) upon their operands, done one bit at a time.

The following table summarizes the bitwise logical operators and the shift operators:

Bitwise operations in Turbo Pascal				
Operator	Symbol	Operand types	Result type	Precedence
Bitwise NOT	NOT	Integer, byte	same	2
Bitwise AND	AND	Integer, byte	same	3
Bitwise OR	OR	Integer, byte	same	4
Bitwise XOR	XOR	Integer, byte	same	4
Shift Right	SHR	Integer, byte	same	3
Shift Left	SHL	Integer, byte	same	3

The best way to approach all bitwise operators is to work in true binary notation, where all numbers are expressed in base two, and the only digits are 1 and 0. The bitwise operators work on one binary digit at a time. The result of the various operations on 0 and 1 values is best summarized by four "truth tables":

```
      NOT              AND              OR               XOR

   NOT 1 = 0      0 AND 0 = 0      0 OR 0 = 0       0 XOR 0 = 0
   NOT 0 = 1      0 AND 1 = 0      0 OR 1 = 1       0 XOR 1 = 1
                  1 AND 0 = 0      1 OR 0 = 1       1 XOR 0 = 1
                  1 AND 1 = 1      1 OR 1 = 1       1 XOR 1 = 0
```

When you apply bitwise operators to two 8-bit or two 16-bit data items, it is the same as applying the operator between each corresponding bit of the two items. For example, the following expression evaluates to **True**:

```
$80 = ($83 AND $90)     { All in hexadecimal  }
```

Why? Think of the operation $83 AND $90 this way:

```
      HEX          Binary

      $83 =   1 0 0 0 0 0 1 1
                     AND
      $90 =   1 0 0 1 0 0 0 0
                      =
      $80 =   1 0 0 0 0 0 0 0
```

Read *down* from the top of each column in the binary number, and compare the little equation to the truth table for bitwise **AND**. If you apply bitwise **AND** to each column, you will find the bit pattern for the number $80 to be the total result.

Now, what good is this? Suppose you only wanted to examine four of the eight bits in a variable of type **Byte**. The bits are numbered 0 to 7 from the right. The bits you need are bits 2 through 5. The way to do it is to use bitwise **AND** and what we call a "mask":

```
VAR
   GoodBits, AllBits : Byte;

GoodBits := AllBits AND $3E;
```

To see how this works, let's again "spread it out" into a set of binary numbers:

```
AllBits     = X X X X X X X X
                    AND
$3E (mask) = 0 0 1 1 1 1 0 0
                     =
GoodBits    = 0 0 X X X X 0 0
```

Here, "X" means *"either 1 or 0."* Again, follow the eight little operations down from the top of each column to the bottom. The zero bits present in four of the eight columns of the mask, $3E, force those columns to evaluate to zero in **GoodBits**, regardless of the state of the corresponding bits in **AllBits**. Go back to the truth table if this is not clear: *If either of the two bits in a bitwise **AND** expression is zero, the result will be zero.*

This way, we can assume that bits 0,1,7, and 8 in **GoodBits** will always be zero and we can ignore them while we test the others.

We will see more examples of the use of the bitwise logical operators in Section 20.4.

SHIFT OPERATORS

We've looked at bit patterns as stored in integers and bytes, and how we can alter those patterns by logically combining bit patterns with bitmasks. Another way to alter bit patterns in a byte or integer is with the shift operators, **SHR** and **SHL**. **SHR** stands for SHift Right; **SHL** for SHift Left.

Both operators are best understood by looking at a bit pattern before and after the operator acts upon it. Start with the value $CB (203 decimal) and shift it two bits to the right as the **SHR** operator would do:

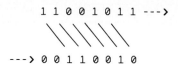

The result byte is $32 (50 decimal). The two 1-bits on the right end of the original $CB value are shifted off the end of the byte (into the "bit bucket," some say) and are lost. To take their place, two 0-bits are fed into the byte on the left end.

SHL works identically, but in the other direction. Let's shift $CB to the left with **SHL** and see what we get:

Again, we lose two bits off the end of the original value, but this time they drop off the left end, and two 0-bits are added in on the right end. What was $CB is now $2C (44 decimal.)

Syntactically, **SHL** and **SHR** are like the arithmetic operators. They act with the number of bits to be shifted to form an expression, the resulting value of which you assign to another variable:

```
Result := Operand <SHL/SHR> <number of bits to shift>;
```

Some examples:

```
VAR
  B,C : Byte;
  I,J : Integer;
I := 17;
J := I SHL 3;     { J now contains 136 }
B := $FF;
C := B SHR 4;     { C now contains $0F }
```

It would be a good exercise to work out the shifts of these two examples on paper, expressing each value as a binary pattern of bits and then shifting them.

An interesting note on the shift operators is that they are extremely fast ways to multiply and divide a number by a power of two. Shifting a number one bit to the left multiplies it by two. Shifting it two bits to the left multiplies it by four, and so on. In the example above, we shifted 17 by three bits, which multiplies it by 8. Sure enough, 17 × 8 = 136.

It works the other way, as well. Shifting a number one bit to the right divides it by two; shifting two bits to the right divides by four, and so on. The only thing to watch is that there is no remainder on divide and nothing to notify you if you overflow on a multiply. It is a somewhat limited form of arithmetic, but in time-critical applications you'll find it is *much* faster than the more generalized multiply and divide operators.

Examples of **SHL** and **SHR** in use will be found in Section 20.4.

11.5   Order of evaluation

Mixing several operators within a single expression can lead to problems for the compiler. Eventually the expression must be evaluated down to a single value, but in what order are the various operators to be applied? Consider the ambiguity in this expression:

```
7 + 6 * 9
```

How will the compiler interpret this? Which operator is applied first? As you might expect, the authors of Turbo Pascal set down rules that dictate how expressions containing more than one operator are to be evaluated. These rules define "order of evaluation."

To determine the order of evaluation of an expression, the compiler must consider three factors: Precedence of operators, left to right evaluation, and parentheses.

PRECEDENCE

All operators in Turbo Pascal have a property called "precedence." Precedence is a sort of priority evaluation system. If two operators have different precedences, the one with higher precedence is evaluated first. There are five degrees of precedence: 1 is the highest and 5 the lowest.

When we summarized the various operators in tables, the right-hand column contained each operator's precedence. The sign inversion operator has a precedence of one. No other operator has a precedence of 1. Sign inversion operations are always performed before any other operations, assuming parentheses are not present. (We'll get to that shortly.) Logical and bitwise **NOT** operators have a precedence of 2. For example:

```
VAR
  OK,FileOpen : Boolean;

IF NOT OK AND FileOpen THEN CallOperator;
```

How is the expression **"NOT OK AND FileOpen"** evaluated? **NOT OK** is evaluated first. The Boolean result is then **AND**ed with the Boolean value in **FileOpen**, to yield the final Boolean result for the expression. If that value is **True**, the procedure **CallOperator** is executed.

LEFT TO RIGHT EVALUATION

The previous example was clear-cut, since **NOT** has a higher precedence than **AND**. As you can see from the tables, however, many operators have the same precedence value; addition, subtraction, and set intersection are only a few of the operators with a precedence of 4, and *all* relational operators have a precedence of 5.

When the compiler is evaluating an expression and it confronts a choice between two operators of equal precedence, it evaluates them in order from left to right. For example:

```
VAR
   I,J,K : Integer;

J := I * 17 DIV K;
```

The * and **DIV** operators both have a precedence of 3. To evaluate the expression **I * 17 DIV K**, the compiler must first evaluate **I * 17** to an integer value, and then integer divide that value by **K**. * is to the left of **DIV**, and so it is evaluated before **DIV**.

Note that left to right evaluation happens *only* when it is not clear from precedence (or parentheses, see below) which of two operators must be evaluated first.

SETTING ORDER OF EVALUATION WITH PARENTHESES

There are situations in which the previous two rules break down. How would the compiler establish order of evaluation for this expression:

```
I > J AND K <= L
```

The idea here is to test the Boolean values of two relational expressions. The precedence of **AND** is greater than the precedence of any relational operator like > and <=. So the compiler would attempt to evaluate the subexpression **J** and **K** first.

Actually, this particular expression does not even compile; Turbo Pascal will flag error #1 as soon as it finishes compiling **J AND K** and sees another operator coming.

The only way out of this is to use parentheses. Just as in the rules of algebra, in the rules of Pascal parentheses override *all* other order of evaluation rules. To make the offending expression pass muster, you must rework it this way:

```
(I > J) AND (K <= L)
```

Now the compiler first evaluates **(I > J)** to a Boolean value, then **(K <= L)** to another Boolean value, then submits those two Boolean values as operands to **AND**. **AND** happily generates a final Boolean value for the entire expression.

This is one case (and a fairly common one) in which parentheses are required to compile the expression without errors. However, there are many occasions when parentheses will make an expression more readable, even though, strictly speaking, the parentheses are not required:

```
(PI * Radius) + 7
```

Here, not only does * have a higher precedence than +, but * is to the left of + as well. So in any case, the compiler would evaluate **PI * Radius** before adding 7 to the result. The parentheses make it immediately obvious what operation is to be done first, without having to think back to precedence tables and consider left to right evaluation.

I am something of a fanatic about program readability. Which of these (identical) expressions is easier to dope out:

```
R + 2 * PI - 6
(R + (2 * PI)) - 6
```

You have to think a little about the first. You don't have to think about the second at all. I highly recommend using parentheses in all but the most completely simpleminded expressions to indicate to all persons (including those not especially familiar with Pascal) the order of evaluation of the operations making up the expression. Parentheses cost you *nothing* in code size or code speed. Nothing at all.

To add to your program readability, that's dirt cheap.

Statements

Put as simply as possible, a Pascal program is a series of statements. Each statement is an instruction to do something: To define data, to alter data, to execute a function or procedure, to change the direction of the program's flow of control.

There are many different kinds of statements in Pascal. We'll be looking at them all in detail in this section and the next section.

Perhaps the simplest of all statements is an invocation of a procedure or function. Turbo Pascal includes several screen-control procedures for moving the cursor around, clearing the screen, and so on. Such procedures are used by naming them, and naming one constitutes a statement:

```
ClrScr;
```

The statement tells the computer to do something; in this case, to clear the screen. The computer executes the statement; the screen is cleared, and control passes to the next statement, whatever that may be.

12.1 Assignment and definition statements

We have been using assignment statements, type definition statements, and variable declaration statements all along. By now you should understand them thoroughly. Type definition statements must exist in the type definition part of a program, procedure, or function. They associate a type name with a description of a programmer-defined type. Enumerated types (see Section 8.2) are an excellent example:

```
TYPE
    Spectrum   = (Red,Orange,Yellow,Green,Blue,Indigo,Violet);
    LongColors = Red..Yellow;
    ColorSet   = SET OF Spectrum;
```

Each of these three definitions is a statement. The semicolons *separate* the statements rather than terminate them. This is a critical distinction that frequently escapes beginning Pascal programmers. We will take the matter of semicolons up again in Section 13.8.

Variable declaration statements are found only in the variable declaration part of a program, function, or procedure. They associate a variable name with the data type the variable is to have. The colon symbol (:) is used rather than the equal sign:

```
VAR
    I,J,K : Integer;
    Ch    : Char;
    R     : Real;
```

Assignment statements are used in the body of the program, function, or procedure. They copy data from the identifier on the right side of the assignment operator to the variable on the left. Only a *variable* can be to the left of the assignment operator.

Constants and literals must be on the right side. Other variables, of course, can also be to the right of the assignment operator:

```
I := 17;    { '17' is a numeric Literal           }
R := PI;    { PI was defined earlier as a constant }
K := J;     { The value of one variable assigned   }
            { to another      }
```

12.2   Type conflicts

Pascal is a strongly typed language. This means that there are rather strict limitations on how data can be moved from a variable of one data type to a variable of a different data type. Strong typing is one way Pascal helps keep nonsense out of your programs.

In Pascal, data items are not merely binary patterns in memory. The type of a data item carries a certain sense as to how that data item should be used. A Boolean variable is more than just a single byte in RAM containing a binary 1 or a binary 0. It carries a value of **True** or **False**, which has a logical rather than an arithmetic sense. To attempt to assign an integer to a Boolean variable simply makes no sense:

```
I := 42;     { Good sense... }
I := True;   { Nonsense!     }
```

To attempt this kind of assignment statement will trigger Pascal's error #44: Type mismatch. Other languages (C, notably) will allow this sort of thing. The code will take whatever binary pattern it finds in one variable and drop it into another variable, whether or not the transfer makes any kind of sense in the context of the program. Keeping "sense" in a C program is very much the responsibility of the programmer.

It is easy enough to see why Pascal would try to prevent gross errors in sense like assigning a Boolean value to an integer, and vice versa. Bugs in perfectly sensible programs will prove exasperating enough to locate; trying to debug a program that permits nonsense constructions is an order of magnitude harder.

COMPATIBLE AND IDENTICAL TYPES

In general, values assigned to a data item must be values with the same data type as the data item. A number of exceptions exist, to cover those situations where assigning one type to another *does* make sense. In such cases, the two types that may be assigned to one another are called "compatible types." For example, types **Integer** and **Byte** are compatible as long as the data they contain fall within the legal range for **Byte:** 0..255.

Types are considered identical if they resolve to the same type definition statement. For example, these two variables are *not* type-identical:

```
VAR
    GradeArray : ARRAY[1..6] OF Char;
    LevelArray : ARRAY[1..6] OF Char;
```

Even though they are defined in exactly the same way, their types are assigned in two different statements, and therefore they are considered by the compiler to be two different types. However, if you were to write:

```
VAR
  GradeArray, LevelArray : ARRAY[1..6] OF Char;
```

then the types of **GradeArray** and **LevelArray** are identical, because they both resolve to the same type definition statement. A still better way to handle the situation is this:

```
TYPE
   GradeStep = ARRAY[1..6] OF Char;

VAR
   Grades : GradeStep;
   Levels : GradeStep;
```

Now, any time you need another variable with an identical type to **Grades** and **Levels**, you can define it using the type **GradeStep**. Since all variables of type **GradeStep** refer back to a single type definition statement, the types are considered identical.

Turbo Pascal's type checking is quite strict. Unlike some other Pascals such as Pascal/MT+, Turbo's strict type checking cannot be relaxed. Strict type checking requires the use of identical types in assignment statements and in substituting variables into procedure/function parameters (see Section 14.2).

The rules for using compatible types to cross type boundaries are these:

1. Integers may be assigned to reals. There is no problem with this since any integer may be expressed as a real number. The integer 17 becomes the real number 17.0. The opposite is not true, however: Real numbers may *not* be assigned to integers.
2. Type **Byte** is assignment compatible with type **Integer**. **Byte** is most useful for low-level systems programming. For example, to output an integer to an 8-bit I/O port, you could assign the integer to a byte and then output the byte to the port. This will work only if you are sure that the value in the integer will always fall in the range 0 to 255. Assigning an integer larger than 255 to type **Byte** will *not* cause a runtime error, but the results are not reliable. The only result may be that the oversized integer is truncated to whatever happens to be in its low-order byte, but *Turbo Pascal does not guarantee it.*
3. Subranges of the same base type are compatible. This, for example, is a legal situation:

```
VAR
   Sub1 : 1..10;
   Sub2 : 0..9;

Sub1 := Sub2;
```

This assignment will not trigger a type mismatch error. However, if the value of **Sub2** is 0 when you assign **Sub2** to **Sub1**, a *range* error may be triggered at runtime. It is up to you to make sure that subrange values are range-compatible when assigning two compatible (but not identical) subrange types to one another.

TYPE CONVERSION WITH TRANSFER FUNCTIONS

To convert data cleanly between types when the conversion makes sense, use the transfer functions **Ord**, **Chr**, and **Odd**. **Ord** changes character data to integer; **Chr** changes integer data to character; and **Odd** changes integer data to Boolean.

The use of transfer functions is explained in Chapter 16.

Controlling program flow

Controlling the flow of program logic is one of the most important facets of any programming language. Conditional statements that change the direction of the flow of control, looping statements that repeat some action a number of times, and switch statements that pick one course out of many based on a controlling value, all make useful programs possible.

Pascal, furthermore, would like you the programmer to direct the flow of control in a structured, rational manner so the programs you write are easy to read and easy to change when they need changing. For this reason, wild-eyed zipping around inside a program is difficult in Pascal.

The language syntax itself suggests with some force that programs begin at the top of the page and progress generally downward, exiting at the bottom when the work is done. Multiple entry and exit points and unconditional branching via GOTO are almost literally more trouble than they are worth.

This section examines those statements that channel the flow of program logic: **IF/THEN/ELSE**, **FOR/DO**, **WHILE/DO**, **REPEAT/UNTIL**, **CASE/OF**, and that rascal **GOTO**.

13.1 BEGIN and END

We have already looked at several simple types of statements like assignment statements and data definition statements. In Pascal you frequently need to group a number of statements together and treat them as though they were a single statement. The means to do this is the pair of reserved words **BEGIN** and **END**. A group of statements between a **BEGIN** and **END** pair becomes a compound statement. The bodies of procedures and functions, and of programs themselves, are compound statements:

```
PROGRAM Rooter;

VAR
  R,S : Real;

BEGIN
  Writeln('>>Square root calculator<<');
  Writeln;
  Write('>>Enter the number: ');
  Readln(R);
  S := Sqrt (R);
  Writeln('   The square root of ',R:7:7,' is ',S:7:7,'.')
END.
```

The statements bracketed by **BEGIN** and **END** in the above example are all simple statements, but that need not be the case. Compound statements may also be parts of larger compound statements:

```
PROGRAM BetterRooter;

VAR
  R,S : Real;

BEGIN
  Writeln('>>Better square root calculator<<');
  Writeln;
  R:=1;
  WHILE R<>0 DO
    BEGIN
      Writeln('>>Enter the number (0 to exit): ');
```

(continues)

```
      Readln(R);
      IF R<>0 THEN
      BEGIN
        S := Sqrt(R);
        Writeln('  The square root of ',R:7:7,' is ',S:7:7,'.');
        Writeln
      END
    END;
  Writeln('>>Square root calculator signing off...')
END.
```

(concluded)

This program contains two compound statements, one nested inside the other, and both nested within the compound statement that is the body of the program itself.

This is a good place to point out the "prettyprinting" convention that is virtually always used when writing Pascal code. The rule on prettyprinting turns on compound statements: *Each compound statement is indented two spaces to the right of the rest of the statement in which it is nested.*

It's also crucial to remember that *prettyprinting is ignored by the compiler.* It is strictly a typographical convention to help you sort out nested compound statements by "eyeballing" rather than counting **BEGIN**s and **END**s. You could as well (as some do) indent by three or more spaces instead of two. You could also (as some do) not indent at all. The compiler doesn't care. But the readability of your program will suffer if you don't use prettyprinting.

There is one other thing about compound statements that might seem obvious to some but very unobvious to others: *Compound statements can be used anywhere a simple statement can.* Anything between a **BEGIN/END** pair is treated syntactically by the compiler just as it would a single simple statement.

13.2 IF/THEN/ELSE

A conditional statement is one that directs program flow in one of two directions based on a Boolean value. In Pascal the conditional statement is the **IF/THEN/ELSE** statement. The **ELSE** clause is optional, but every **IF** reserved word *must* have a **THEN** associated with it. In its simplest form, such a statement is constructed this way:

```
IF <Boolean expression> THEN <statement>
```

The way this statement works is almost self-explanatory from the logic of the English language: If the Boolean expression evaluates to **True**, then <statement> is executed. If the Boolean expression evaluates to **FALSE**, control "falls through" to the next statement in the program.

Adding an **ELSE** clause makes the statement look like this:

```
IF <Boolean expression> THEN <statement1>
   ELSE <statement 2>
```

Here, if the expression evaluates to **True** then <statement 1> is executed. if the expression evaluates to **False**, then <statement2> is executed. If an **ELSE** clause exists, you can be sure that one or the other of the two statements will be executed.

Either or both of the statements associated with **IF/THEN/ELSE** may be compound statements. Remember that a compound statement may be used anywhere a simple statement may. For example:

```
IF I < 0 THEN
   BEGIN
      Negative := True;      { Set negative flag     }
      I := Abs(I)            { Take abs. value of I  }
   END                       { Never semicolon here! }
ELSE Negative := False;      { Clear negative flag   }
```

An important point to remember: There is *no* semicolon after the **BEGIN/END** compound statement. The entire code fragment above is considered a single IF statement. A crucial corollary: There is *never* a semicolon immediately before an **ELSE** reserved word. Adding one will give you a "freestanding **ELSE**," which is meaningless in Pascal and will trigger a syntax error.

NESTED IF STATEMENTS

Since an IF statement is itself a perfectly valid statement, it may be one or both of the statements contained in an **IF/THEN/ELSE** statement. **IF**s may be nested as deeply as you like—but remember, that if someone reading your code must dive too deeply after the bottom-most **IF**, he may lose track of things and drown before coming up again. If the sole purpose of multiply-nested **IF**s is to choose one alternative of many, it is far better to use the **CASE OF** statement, which is covered in Section 13.3. Structurally, such a construction looks like this:

```
IF <Boolean expression1> THEN
  IF <Boolean expression2> THEN
    IF <Boolean expression3> THEN
      IF <Boolean expression4> THEN
        IF <Boolean expression5> THEN
          <statement>;
```

The bottom line here is that all Boolean expressions must evaluate to **True** before <statement> is executed.

Such a downward escalator of **IF**s is often hard to follow. Sharp readers may already be objecting that this same result could be done with **AND** operators:

```
IF <Boolean1> AND <Boolean2> AND <Boolean3>
  AND <Boolean4> AND <Boolean5> THEN
  <statement>;
```

This is entirely equivalent to the earlier nested **IF** with one sneaky catch: Here, *all* the Boolean expressions are evaluated before a decision is reached on whether or not to execute ‹statement›. (Actually, this is compiler-dependent or even code-dependent, but you can never be sure how many tests will be done, since the compiler is within its rights to try them all.) With the nested **IF**, the compiler will stop testing as soon as it encounters a Boolean expression that turns up **False**. In other words, in a nested **IF**, if ‹Boolean3› is found to be **False**, the compiler never even evaluates ‹Boolean4› or ‹Boolean5›.

Nitpicking? No! There are times when, in fact, the reason for ‹Boolean3› might be to make sure ‹Boolean4› is not tested in certain cases. Divide by zero is one of those cases. Consider this:

```
IF AllOK THEN
   IF R > PI THEN
     IF S > 1 THEN
        IF (R / ((S*S)-1) < PI) THEN
           CalculateRightAscension;
```

Here, a value of **S** = 1 will cause a divide-by-zero error if the code attempts to evaluate the next expression. So the code *must* stop testing if **S > 1** turns up **False** or risk crashing the program with a runtime divide-by-zero error.

With nested **IF**s you can determine the sequential order in which a series of tests is done. A string of **AND** operators between Boolean expressions may evaluate those expressions in any order dictated by the code generator or the optimization pass. If one of your tests carries the hazard of a runtime error, use nested **IF**s.

NESTED ELSE/IFS

The previous discussion of nested **IF**s did not include any **ELSE** clauses. Nesting **IF**s does not preclude **ELSE**s, though the use and meaning of the statement changes radically. Our previous example executed a series of tests to determine whether or not a single statement was to be executed. By using nested **ELSE/IF**s you can determine which of many statements is to be executed:

```
IF <Boolean1> THEN <statement1>
   ELSE
     IF <Boolean2> THEN <statement2>
        ELSE
          IF <Boolean3> THEN <statement3>
             ELSE
               IF <Boolean4> then <statement4>
                  ELSE <statement5>;
```

The code will descend the escalator, and as soon as it finds a Boolean with a value of **True**, it will execute the statement associated with that Boolean. The tests are performed in order, and even if <Boolean4> is **True**, it will not be executed (or <Boolean4> even evaluated) if <Boolean2> is found to be **True** first.

The final **ELSE** clause is not necessary; it provides a "none of the above" choice, in case none of the preceding Boolean expressions turned out to be true. You could simply omit it, and control would fall through to the next statement without executing any of the statements contained in the larger IF statement.

As with nested **IF**s described above, nested **ELSE/IF**s allow you to set the order of the tests performed, so that if one of them carries the danger of a runtime error, you can defuse the danger with an earlier test for the dangerous values.

The **CASE OF** statement is a shorthand form of nested **ELSE/IF**s in which all of the Boolean expressions are of this form: <value> = <value> and the type of all <value>s is identical. We'll look at **CASE OF** in the next section.

13.3 CASE/OF

Choosing between one of several alternative control paths is critical to computer programming. We've seen how **IF/THEN/ELSE** in its simplest form can choose between two alternatives based on the value of a Boolean expression. By nesting **IF/THEN/ELSE** statements one within another, we can choose among many different control paths, as we saw in the previous section.

The problem of readability appears when we nest IF statements more than two or three deep. Nested **IF/THEN/ELSE** get awkward and non-intuitive in a great hurry when more than three levels exist. Consider the problem of flashing a message on a CRT screen based on some input code number. A problem reporting system on a CRT-equipped computerized car might include a statement sequence like this:

```
Beep;
Writeln('*****WARNING*****');
IF ProblemCode = 1 THEN
  Writeln('[001] Fuel supply has fallen below 10%')
ELSE IF ProblemCode = 2 THEN
  Writeln('[002] Oil pressure has fallen below min spec')
ELSE IF ProblemCode = 3 THEN
  Writeln('[003] Engine temperature is too high')
ELSE IF ProblemCode = 4 THEN
  Writeln('[004] Battery voltage has fallen below min spec')
ELSE IF ProblemCode = 5 THEN
  Writeln('[005] Brake fluid level has fallen below min spec')
ELSE IF ProblemCode = 6 THEN
  Writeln('[006] Transmission fluid level has fallen below min spec')
ELSE IF ProblemCode = 7 THEN
  Writeln('[007] Radiator water level has fallen below min spec')
ELSE
  Writeln('[***] Logic failure in problem reporting system')
```

This will work well enough, but it takes some picking through to follow it clear to the bottom. This sort of selection of one statement from many based on a single selection value is what the **CASE/OF** statement was created for. Rewriting the above statement with **CASE/OF** gives us this:

```
Beep;
Writeln('*****WARNING*****');
CASE ProblemCode OF
  1 : Writeln('[001] Fuel supply has fallen below 10%');
  2 : Writeln('[002] Oil pressure has fallen below min spec');
```

(continues)

```
    3 : Writeln('[003] Engine temperature is too high');
    4 : Writeln('[004] Battery voltage has fallen below min spec');
    5 : Writeln('[005] Brake fluid level has fallen below min spec');
    6 : Writeln('[006] Transmission fluid level is below min spec');
    7 : Writeln('[007] Radiator water level has fallen below min spec')
ELSE
  Writeln('[***] Logic failure in problem reporting system')
END; { CASE }
```

(concluded)

Here, **ProblemCode** is called the "case selector." The case selector may be an expression or simply a variable. It holds the value upon which the choice among statements will be made. The numbers in a line beneath the word **CASE** are called "case labels." Each case label is followed by a colon : and then a statement. The statement may be simple (as in the example) or compound.

When the **CASE** statement is executed, the case selector is evaluated and its value is compared, one by one, against each of the case labels. If a case label is found that is equal to the value of the case selector, the statement associated with that case label is executed. Once the statement chosen for execution has completed executing, the work of the **CASE/OF** statement is done and control passes on to the rest of the program. Only one (or none, see below) of the several statements is executed for each pass through the **CASE/OF** statement.

If no case label matches the value of the case selector, the statement following the **ELSE** keyword is executed. **ELSE** is optional, by the way; if no **ELSE** keyword is found, control falls through to the next statement in the program.

The general form of a **CASE/OF** statement is this:

```
CASE <case selector> OF
   <constant list 1> : <statement 1>;
   <constant list 2> : <statement 2>;
   <constant list 3> : <statement 3>;
                 ....
   <constant list n> : <statement n>
   ELSE <statement>
END;
```

There may be as many case labels as you like, up to 256. You may be puzzling over the fact that what we pointed out as case labels are called "constant lists" in the general form. In our first example, each case label was only a single numeric constant. A case label may also be a list of constants separated by commas. Remember that the case label is the *list* of constants associated with a statement; each statement can only have *one* case label. And do not forget that a case label may *never* be a variable!

For another example, let's look into part of the code for a mail-in questionnaire analysis system. The responses are to be grouped together by geographical regions of the country. **State** is an enumerated type including all the two letter state name abbreviations, in alphabetical order. This particular code fragment tallies the number of responses from each geographical region:

```
TYPE
   State = (AK,AL,AR,AZ,CA,CO,CT,DE,DC,FL,GA,HI,ID,IL,IN,
           IA,KS,KY,LA,MA,MD,ME,MI,MN,MO,MS,MT,NE,NV,NH,
           NJ,NM,NY,NC,ND,OH,OK,OR,PA,RI,SC,SD,TN,TX,UT,
           VA,VT,WA,WI,WV,WY)

VAR
   FromState : State;

CASE FromState OF
CT,MA,ME,NH,
RI,VT               : CountNewEngland := CountNewEngland + 1;
DC,DE,MD,NJ,
NY,PA               : CountMidAtlantic := CountMidAtlantic + 1;
FL,GA,NC,SC         : CountSoutheast := CountSoutheast + 1;
IA,IL,IN,MI,
MN,OH,WI,WV         : CountMidwest := CountMidwest + 1;
AL,AR,KY,LA,
MO,MS,TN,VA         : CountSouth := CountSouth + 1;
KS,ND,NE,SD,
WY                  : CountPlains := CountPlains + 1;
AK,CA,CO,HI,
ID,MT,OR,UT,
WA,                 : CountWest := CountWest + 1;
AZ,NM,NV,OK,
TX                  : CountSouthwest := CountSouthwest + 1;
END; { CASE }
```

Here you can see that a case label can indeed be a list of constants. Also note that there is no **ELSE** clause here because every one of the possible values of type **State** is present in one of the case labels.

CASE/OF CAUTIONS

The most important thing to remember about case labels is that they must be constants or lists of constants. A particular value may appear only once in a **CASE/OF** statement. In other words, the value **IL** (from the last example) could not appear in both the **CountMidwest** and the **CountSouth** case labels. The reason for this should be obvious; if a value is associated with more than one statement, the **CASE/OF** logic will not know which statement to execute for that case label value.

You should be careful when using a case selector of type **Integer**. Case selectors may only have an ordinality between 0 and 255. An integer case selector may have a value much larger than 255, and when it does, the results of executing the **CASE OF** statement are undefined. If you work much with numeric codes (and intend to use **CASE/OF** structures to interpret those codes) it is a *very* good idea to define those codes as subranges of **Integer**:

```
TYPE
   Keypress = 0..255;
   Problem  = 0..32;
   Priority = 0..7;
```

Any of these named subrange types may act as case selectors.

ISO STANDARD PASCAL LACKS ELSE IN CASE/OF

I should point out an important variance between Turbo Pascal and ISO Standard Pascal here:

One of the puzzling lapses of logic in ISO Standard Pascal is the lack of an **ELSE** clause in its definition of **CASE/OF**. In Standard Pascal, a case selector value for which no case label exists is supposed to cause a runtime error. The programmer is supposed to ensure, with range testing, that each value submitted to a **CASE/OF** statement is, in fact, legal for that **CASE/OF** statement. No good explanation for why this should be necessary has ever crossed my desk.

It is not surprising, therefore, that every single commercial implementation of Pascal that I have tested includes an **ELSE** clause in its definition, to cover that "none of the above" possibility. A number of Pascal compilers (such as UCSD Pascal) use the keyword **OTHERWISE** instead of **ELSE**, but the meaning and function are exactly the same. Turbo Pascal and Pascal/MT+ both use the **ELSE** keyword.

13.4 FOR Loops

There are many occasions when you must perform the same operation or operations on a whole range of values. The most used example would be the generation of a square roots table for all the numbers from 1 to 100. Pascal provides a tidy way to loop through the same code for each value, and for dropping through to the next statement in the program when all the loops have been performed. It's called the **FOR** statement, and it is one of three ways to perform program "loops" in Pascal.

Printing the table of square roots becomes easy:

```
FOR I := 1 TO 100 DO
   BEGIN
     J := Sqrt(*I);
     Writeln('The square root of ',I,' is ',J)
   END;
```

There are better ways to lay out a square roots table, but this gets the feeling of a **FOR** loop across very well. **I** and **J** are integers. The compound statement between the **BEGIN/END** pair is executed 100 times. The first time through, **I** has the value 1. Each time the compound statement is executed, the value of **I** is increased by 1. Finally, after the compound statement has been executed with the value of **I** as 100, the **FOR** statement has done its job, and control passes on to the next statement in the program.

The preceding example is only a particular case of a **FOR** statement. The general form of a **FOR** statement is this:

```
FOR <control variable> :=
    <start value> TO <end value> DO <statement>
```

<start value> and <end value> may be expressions. <control variable> is any ordinal type, including enumerated types. When a **FOR** statement is executed, the following things happen: If <start value> and <end value> are expressions, they are evaluated and tucked away for reference. Then the control variable is assigned <start value>. Next, <statement> is executed. After <statement> is executed, the *successor value* to the value already in the control variable is placed in the control variable. The control variable is now tested. If it exceeds <end value>, execution of the **FOR** statement ceases. Otherwise <statement> is executed.

The loop repeats until the control variable is incremented past <end value.>

Note that the general definition of a **FOR** statement does not speak of "adding one to" the control variable. The control variable is incremented by assigning the successor value of the current value to the control variable. "Adding" is not really done at all, not even with integers. To obtain the successor value, the statement evaluates the expression

```
Succ(<control variable>)
```

The function **Succ** is discussed in Section 16.6. If you recall our enumerated type **Spectrum**:

```
TYPE
   Spectrum = (Red, Orange, Yellow, Green, Blue,
               Indigo, Violet);
```

the successor value to **Orange** is **Yellow**. The successor value to **Green** is **Blue**, and so on.

A variable of type **Spectrum** makes a perfectly good control variable in a **FOR** loop:

```
LightSpeed := 3.0E08;
FOR Color := Red TO Violet DO
  Frequency[Color] := LightSpeed / Wavelength[Color] ;
```

So do characters:

```
FOR Ch := 'a' to 'z' DO
  IF Ch IN CharSet DO Writeln('CharSet contains ',Ch);
```

If <start value> and <end value> are the same, the loop is executed once. If <start value> is *higher* than <end value>, the loop is not executed at all. That is, <statement> is not executed, and control immediately falls through to the next statement in the program.

CONTROL VARIABLE CAUTIONS

A control variable must be an ordinal type or a subrange of an ordinal type. Real numbers cannot be used as control variables. There is no distinct successor value to a number like 3.141592, after all. For similar reasons you cannot use sets or structured types of any kind.

A somewhat misleading error message will appear if the control variable is a formal parameter passed by reference (see Section 14.2), that is, a **VAR** parameter in the function or procedure's parameter line. You cannot do this:

```
PROCEDURE Runnerup(Hi,Lo    : Integer;
                   VAR Limit : Integer);

VAR
  Foo : Integer;
```

(continues)

```
BEGIN
  <statements>;
  FOR Limit := Lo TO Hi DO <statement>;
  Foo:=Limit;
  <statements>
END;
```

(concluded)

Turbo Pascal will respond here with Error 30: Simple type expected, with the cursor after **Limit**. What gives?

Limit is in fact a simple type, **Integer**. The error message may be a bug in Turbo Pascal. There is an error here, but it has nothing to do with simple types. ISO Pascal (and most commercial Pascals) require that control variables be local and non-formal. Turbo Pascal allows control variables to be non-local (this is, not declared in the current block) and also allows formal parameters to be control variables as long as they are passed by value, that is, if the procedure is given its own copy of the parameter to play with.

As in many of Pascal's rules and restrictions, this one was designed to keep you out of certain kinds of trouble. Understanding what kind of trouble requires a little further poking at the notion of control variables in **FOR** loops: To make procedure **Runnerup** work, some sort of local control variable would have to be declared in the data declaration section of the procedure:

```
PROCEDURE Runnerup(Hi,Lo    : Integer;
                   VAR Limit : Integer);

VAR
  Foo,I : Integer;

BEGIN
  <statements>;
  FOR I := Lo TO Hi DO <statement>;
  Foo := I;
  <statements>
END;
```

Now the **FOR** loop will compile correctly. But there is still something wrong with this procedure. What it's trying to do is make use of the control variable immediately after the loop has executed by assigning its value to **Foo**. This is also illegal. *Immediately after a **FOR** statement, the value of the control variable becomes undefined.* This is not a problem, since the end value is accessible in **Hi**. To make use of the final value of the control variable, assign **Hi** to **Foo** instead of **I**. The end result will be the same:

```
PROCEDURE Runnerup(Hi,Lo    : Integer;
                   VAR Limit : Integer);
VAR
  Foo,I : Integer;
BEGIN
  <statements>;
  FOR I := Lo TO Hi DO <statement>;
  Foo := Hi:
  <statements>
END;
```

There is a good reason for the control variable becoming undefined after its loop has run its course. After each pass through <statement> the successor value to the current value in the control variable is computed. That successor value *may in fact become undefined.* Going back to our type **Spectrum**, what is the successor value to **Violet**? There is none; **Succ(Violet)** is undefined. Consider:

```
FOR Color := Red TO Violet DO <statement>;
```

After the loop runs through its seven iterations, **Color** would hold an undefined value. If you were allowed to "pick up" the control variable's value after the run of a **FOR** loop, you might in fact be picking up an undefined nonsense value and have no way of knowing it were so. So the Standard Pascal definition declares that control variables are *always* undefined after a **FOR** loop to remove the temptation to "save" the final value of a control variable for later use.

(In some other Pascal compilers there is a **BREAK** statement that interrupts execution of a **FOR** loop before the loop has run through all the iterations called for. In such compilers you cannot always be sure that the ‹end value› will match the control variable's value at the end of the loop. In those compilers you must use a separate variable to keep track of the value in the control variable. Since Turbo Pascal does not have a **BREAK** statement, this need not concern you.)

Within the **FOR** loop (that is, within ‹statement›) the control variable must be treated as a "read-only" value. You *cannot* change the value of the control variable within the FOR loop! The **REPEAT/UNTIL** and **DO/WHILE** statements allow this kind of "moving target" loop, which will execute as often as required to make a control variable equal to some final value. **FOR** loops execute a fixed number of times, and while executing, the value of the control variable is solely under the control of the **FOR** loop itself.

Now (finally) you may understand why Turbo forbids using **VAR** parameters as control variables. Pascal reserves the right to force a control variable into an undefined state after its loop is done. Using a **VAR** parameter as a control variable might "reach up" out of the procedure and force the VAR parameter into an undefined state. Allowing a procedure to "undefine" a parameter passed to it is asking for trouble, since it may not be obvious to the calling logic that its parameter may come back undefined.

Preserve sanity in your programs. Keep your **FOR** loop control variables local.

FOR WITH DOWNTO

The **FOR** statement as we've seen it so far always increments its control variable "upward"; that is, it uses the successor value of the control variable for the next pass through ‹statement›. It is sometimes useful to go the other way: to begin with a "high" value and count down to a lower value. In this case, the *predecessor* value of the value in the control variable becomes the new control variable value for the next pass through <statement>. This predecessor value is calculated with the predefined function **Pred**(<control variable>); see Section 16.6. Otherwise, its operation is identical to that of **FOR** with **TO**:

```
FOR I := 17 DOWNTO 7 DO <statement>;

FOR Color := Indigo DOWNTO Orange DO <statement>;

FOR Ch := 'Z' DOWNTO 'X' DO <statement>;
```

When using **DOWNTO**, keep in mind that if <start value> is *lower* than <end value>, <statement> will not be executed at all. This is the reverse of the case for **FOR/TO** loops.

13.5 WHILE/DO Loops

As we have seen, a **FOR** loop executes a specific number of times, no more, no less. The control variable cannot be altered during the loop. There are many cases in which a loop must run until some condition occurs that stops it. The control variable *must* be altered during the loop, or the loop will just run forever. Pascal offers two ways to build such loops: **WHILE/DO** and **REPEAT/UNTIL**.

The general form of a **WHILE/DO** loop is this:

```
WHILE <Boolean expression> DO <statement>.
```

The <Boolean expression> can be an expression that evaluates to a Boolean value, such as **I > 17**, or it can simply be a Boolean variable. As with **FOR** loops, <statement> can be any statement including a compound statement framed between **BEGIN** and **END**.

WHILE/DO loops work like this: The code first evaluates <Boolean expression>. If the value of the expression is **True**, then

<statement> is executed. If the value is **False**, <statement> is not executed even once, and control falls through to the next statement in the program.

Assuming <Boolean expression> came out **True** the first time, then after executing <statement> the code goes back and evaluates <Boolean expression> again. If it is still true, <statement> is executed again. If it evaluates to **False**, the **WHILE/DO** loop ends and control passes on to the next statement in the program.

In short, as long as <Boolean expression> is **True**, <statement> will be executed repeatedly. Only when the expression comes up **False** will the loop end.

For example:

```
VAR
  pH : Real;

FillTank;            { Fill tank with raw water    }
Take(pH);            { Take initial pH reading     }
WHILE pH < 7.2 DO
  BEGIN
    AddAlkali;       { Drop 1 soda pellet in tank }
    AgitateTank;     { Stir }
    Take(pH)         { Read the pH sensor          }
  END;
```

This snippet of code is a part of a control system for some sort of chemical processing apparatus. All it must do is fill a tank with water, ensuring that the pH of the water is at least 7.2. If the water from the water supply comes in as too acidic (water quality varies widely in some parts of the country) its pH must be brought up to 7.2 before the water is considered useable.

First the tank is filled. Then the initial pH reading is taken. The water may in fact be useable from the start, in which case the loop is never executed. But if the water comes up acidic, the loop is executed. A small quantity of an alkali is added, the tank is stirred for a while, and then the pH is taken again. If the pH has risen to 7.2, the loop terminates. If the pH remains too low, the loop is executed again, more alkali is added, and the pH is tested once more. This will continue until the pH test returns a value in the variable pH that is higher than 7.2.

It is crucial to note that an initial pH test was performed. If the variable **pH** were not used before, its value is undefined, and testing it for **True** or **False** will not reflect any real-world meaning. *Make sure the Boolean expression is defined before the WHILE/DO loop is executed!* Every variable in the expression must be initialized somehow before the expression can be "trusted."

The most important property of a **WHILE/DO** loop is that its Boolean expression is tested *before* ‹statement› is executed. A corollary to this is that there are cases when ‹statement› will never be executed at all. Keep this in mind while we discuss **REPEAT/UNTIL** below.

WHILE/DO loops are very commonly used while performing file I/O. For some real-world examples of **WHILE/DO** in action while reading files, see Section 18.8.

13.6 REPEAT/UNTIL Loops

REPEAT/UNTIL loops are very similar to **WHILE/DO** loops. As with **WHILE/DO**, **REPEAT/UNTIL** executes a statement until a Boolean expression becomes **True**. The general form is this:

```
REPEAT <statement> UNTIL <Boolean expression>;
```

It works this way. First, ‹statement› is executed. Then ‹Boolean expression› is evaluated. If it comes up **True**, the loop terminates, and control passes on to the next statement in the program. If ‹Boolean expression› evaluates to **False**, ‹statement› is executed again. This continues until ‹Boolean expression› becomes **True**.

The important fact to notice here is that *‹statement› is always executed at least once.* So unlike **WHILE/DO**, you needn't initialize all variables in ‹Boolean expression› before the loop begins. It's quite all right to assign all values as part of executing the loop.

For an example, let's return to the chemical process controller and consider a snippet of code to handle a simple titration. Titration means adding small, carefully measured amounts of one chemical to another while watching for some chemical reaction to go to completion. Usually, when the reaction is complete, the mixture will begin changing color, or will become electrically conductive, or give some other measurable signal.

In Pascal, it might be handled this way:

```
VAR
  Drops    : Integer;
  Complete : Boolean;

Drops := 0;
REPEAT
  AddADrop;              { Opens valve for 1 drop   }
  Drops := Drops + 1;    { Increment counter        }
  Signal(Complete)       { Read the reaction sensor }
UNTIL Complete;
```

The drops counter is initialized before the loop begins. A drop is added to the test vessel, and the drop counter is incremented by one. Then the reaction sensor is read. If it senses that the reaction has gone to completion, the Boolean variable **Complete** is set to **True**.

Since it takes it least one drop to complete the reaction, this series of events must be done at least once. If the first drop completes the reaction, the loop is performed only once. Most likely, the loop will have to execute many times before the chemical reaction completes and **Complete** becomes **True**. When this happens, **Drops** will contain the number of drops required to complete the reaction. The value of **Drops** might then be displayed on an LED readout or other output device attached to the chemical apparatus.

One interesting thing about **REPEAT/UNTIL** is that the two keywords do double duty if ‹statement› is compound. Instead of bracketing the component statements between **BEGIN** and **END**, **REPEAT** and **UNTIL** perform the bracketing function themselves.

WHILE/DO OR REPEAT/UNTIL?

These two types of loops are very similar, and it is sensible to ask why both are necessary. Actually, **WHILE/DO** can accomplish anything **REPEAT/UNTIL** can, with a little extra effort and occasional rearranging of the order of the statements contained in the loop. The titration code could be written this way:

```
Drops := 0;
Complete := False;
WHILE NOT Complete DO
  BEGIN
    AddADrop;
    Drops := Drops +1;
    Signal(Complete)
  END
```

This method requires that **Complete** be set to **False** initially to ensure that it will be defined when the loop first tests it. If **Complete** were left undefined and it happened to contain garbage data that could be interpreted as **True** (if bit 0 is high, for example), the loop might never be executed, and the code would report that the titration had been accomplished with zero drops of reagent—which is chemically impossible.

Using **REPEAT/UNTIL** would prevent that sort of error in logic. Quite simply: *Use **REPEAT/UNTIL** in those cases where the loop* must *be executed at least once*. Whenever you write code with loops, always consider what might happen if the loop were never executed at all—and if anything unsavory might come of it, make sure the loop is coded as **REPEAT/UNTIL** rather than **WHILE/DO**.

13.7 Labels and GOTO

The bane of unstructured languages like BASIC, FORTRAN, and COBOL is freeform **GOTO** branching all over the program body without any sort of plan or structure. Such programs are very nearly impossible to read. The problem with such programs, however, is not the **GOTO**s themselves but bad use of them. **GOTO**s fill a certain need in Pascal, but they have a seductive power and are eminently easy to understand:

```
GOTO 150;
```

and *wham!* you're at line 150. This straightforwardness leads inexperienced programmers (especially those first schooled in BASIC, and today, almost everybody is first schooled in BASIC) to use them to get out of any programming spot that they do not fully understand how to deal with in a structured manner.

I will not caution you, as some people do, never to use a **GOTO** no matter what. I'm about to tell you about a few situations where nothing else will do. What I *will* tell you to do is never use a **GOTO** when something else will get the job done as well or better.

GOTO LIMITATIONS IN TURBO PASCAL

Use of **GOTO**s with Turbo Pascal carries a few limitations. You may **GOTO** a label *within* the current block. This means that you may *not* **GOTO** a label inside another procedure or function, or from within a procedure or function out into the main program code.

You may not **GOTO** a label within a structured statement. In other words, given this **WHILE/DO** statement:

```
WHILE NOT Finished DO
   BEGIN
     Read(MyFile,ALine);
     IF EOF(MyFile) THEN GOTO 300;
     IF ALine = 'Do not write this...' THEN GOTO 250;
     Write(YourFile,ALine);
     LineCounter := LineCounter + 1;
     250:
   END
300: Close(MyFile);
```

you could not, from some other part of the block, **GOTO** label 250. However, assuming that this snippet of code is not part of some larger structured statement, you could, in fact, **GOTO** label 300 from some other part of the current block. Whether or not that would perform any useful function is a good question.

This example is *very* bad practice, but we include it here only to indicate that you cannot branch into the middle of a **WHILE/DO** statement from somewhere outside the statement. Label 250 is accessible only from somewhere between the **BEGIN** and **END** pair.

In general, **GOTO**s are used to get *out* of somewhere, not to get *in*. Standard Pascal and Turbo Pascal (as well as Pascal/MT+) lack two general looping functions that some other Pascal implementations do have: **BREAK** and **CYCLE**. **BREAK** leaves the middle of a loop and sends control to the first statement after the loop. **CYCLE** stops executing the loop and begins the loop at the top, with the next value of the control variable. Turbo Pascal has neither.

Without **BREAK** and **CYCLE**, **GOTO** provides the only reasonably clean way to get out from inside complicated loops in which a lot is happening and more than one condition value affects exiting from the loop. You can always get out of a loop safely by using the facilities provided by the loop (exiting at the top with **WHILE/DO** and at the bottom with **REPEAT/UNTIL**), but there are cases when to do so involves tortuous combinations of **IF/THEN/ELSE** that might in fact be harder to read than simply jumping out with **GOTO**. But for clarity's sake, always **GOTO** the statement *immediately* following the loop you're exiting. (This is what the **Break** statement does.)

If a future release of Turbo Pascal includes **BREAK**, you will no longer need to use **GOTO** to get out of loops.

The other and far less frequent use of **GOTO** is to get somewhere else *NOW*, especially when the code you need to get to is code to handle some impending failure or emergency situation that requires immediate attention to accomplish an orderly shutdown of the equipment, or something of similar seriousness. This would tend to come up in system-type software that has direct control over some rather complicated hardware. In six years of working with Pascal, I have never had to do this. I suspect that if you ever do, you will know it.

13.8 Semicolons and where they go

Nothing makes newcomers to Pascal cry out in frustration quite so consistently as the question of semicolons and where they go. There are places where semicolons *must* go, places where it seems not to matter whether they go or not, and places where they cannot go without triggering an error. Worse, it seems at first to have no sensible method to it.

Of course, like everything else in Pascal, placing semicolons *does* have a method to it. Why the confusion? Two reasons:

1. Pascal is a "freeform" language that does not take line structure of the source file into account. Unfortunately, most new Pascal programmers graduate into Pascal from BASIC, which is about as line-oriented a language as ever existed.
2. Semicolons in Pascal are statement *separators,* not statement *terminators.* The difference is crucial, and made worse by the fact that the language PL/1 uses semicolons as statement terminators.

Clarifying these two issues should make semicolon placement Pascal-style second nature.

FREEFORM VERSUS LINE STRUCTURED SOURCE CODE

Pascal source code is "freeform"; that is, the boundaries of individual lines and the positioning of keywords and variables on those lines matter not at all. The prettyprinting customary to Pascal source code baffled me in my learning days until I realized that the compiler ignored it. The compiler, in fact, sucks the program up from the disk as though through a drinking straw, in one long line. The following two program listings are utterly identical as far as Turbo Pascal is concerned:

```
PROGRAM Squares;

VAR
  I,J : Integer;

BEGIN
  Writeln('Number    Its square');
  FOR I := 1 TO 10 DO
    BEGIN
      J := I * I;
      Writeln(' ',I:2,'          ',J:3)
    END;
  Writeln;
  Writeln('Processing completed!')
END.
```

(continues)

```
PROGRAM Squares;VAR I,J : Integer;BEGIN Writeln
('Number      It''s square');FOR I:=1 TO 10 DO
BEGIN J:=I*I;Writeln('  ',I:2,'          ',J:3)
END;Writeln;Writeln('Processing completed!') END.
```

(concluded)

Although the second listing appears to exist in four lines, this is only for the convenience of the printed page; the intent was to express the program as one continuous line without any "linefeed" breaks at all.

The second listing above is the compiler's eye view of your program source code. You must remember that although you see your program listing "from a height," as it were, the compiler scans it one character at a time, beginning with the **'P'** in **'PROGRAM'** and reading through to the **"."** after **END**. All unnecessary "whitespace" characters (spaces, tabs, carriage returns, linefeeds) have been removed as the compiler would remove them. Whitespace serves only to delineate the beginnings and endings of reserved words and identifiers, and as far as the compiler is concerned, one whitespace character of any kind is as good as one of any other kind. Once the compiler "grabs" a word or identifier, literal, or operator, it tosses out any following whitespace until it finds a non-whitespace character, indicating that a program element is beginning again.

SEMICOLONS AS STATEMENT SEPARATORS

Note the compound statement executed as part of the FOR loop:

```
BEGIN J:=I*I;Writeln('  ',I:2,'          ',J:3) END
```

There are two statements here, framed between **BEGIN** and **END**. "Smart" as the compiler may seem to you, it has no way to know where statements start and end unless you tell it somehow. If the ';' between **I** and **Writeln** were not there, the compiler would not know for sure if the statement that it sees (so far) as **J:=I*I** ends there or must somehow continue on with **Writeln**.

Note that there is no semicolon after the second statement. There doesn't have to be; the compiler has scanned a **BEGIN** word and knows that an **END** should be coming up eventually. The **END** word tells the compiler unambiguously that the previous statement is over and done with. **BEGIN** *and* **END** *are not statements.* They are delimiters, and only serve to tell the compiler that the group of statements between them is a compound statement.

I find it useful to think of a long line of statements as a line of boxcars on a rail siding. Separating each car from the next is a pair of linked couplers. Anywhere two couplers connect is where (if boxcars were program statements) you would need a semicolon. You don't need one at the end of the last car because the last car doesn't need to be separated from anything; behind it is just empty air.

THE NULL STATEMENT

Why, then, is it legal to have a semicolon after the last statement in a compound statement? This is perfectly all right (and adds to the confusion):

```
BEGIN
  ClrScr;
  J := J + 5;
  IF J > 100 THEN PageEject;
  DoPage;                        { ; not needed here }
END
```

The answer, of course, is that there is a statement after **DoPage;** and that statement is the null statement. This might be clearer with the example rewritten this way:

```
BEGIN
  ClrScr;
  J := J + 5;
  IF J > 100 THEN PageEject;
  DoPage;
                  { Null statement here! }
END
```

There is a semicolon between **DoPage** and the null statement, but none between the null statement and the **END** word.

The null statement is a theoretical abstraction; it does no work and generates no code, not even a **NOP** (No-Op) instruction. (Don't try to use it to pad timing loops!) It serves very little purpose other than to make certain conditional statements a little more intuitive and readable. For example:

```
IF TapeIsMounted THEN { NULL } ELSE RequestMount;
```

I find this more readable than the alternative:

```
IF NOT TapeIsMounted THEN RequestMount;
```

but I suspect it is a matter of taste. Note the convention of inserting the comment **{ NULL }** wherever you use a null statement. It's like the bandages around the Invisible Man; they keep the guy out of trouble.

Another use of the null statement is in **CASE/OF** statements, in which nothing need be done for a selector value:

```
CASE Color OF
   Red    : { NULL };        { No filter needed }
   Orange : InsertFilter(1);  { Density 1        }
   Yellow : InsertFilter(5);  { Density 5        }
   Green  : InsertFilter(11); { Density 11       }
   ELSE InsertFilter(99)      { Opaque (99)      }
END; { CASE }
```

In some sort of optical apparatus there is a mechanism for rotating a filter in front of an optical path. The density of the filter depends on the color of light being used. No filter is needed for red; for blue, indigo, or violet the test will not function and an opaque barrier is moved into the optical path instead of a filter. A null statement is used for the **Red** case label.

SEMICOLONS WITH IF/THEN/ELSE STATEMENTS

More errors are made placing semicolons within **IF/THEN/ELSE** statements than any other kind, I suspect. This sort of thing is fairly common and oh, so easy to do when you're a beginner:

```
IF TankIsEmpty THEN FillTank(Reagent,FlowRate);
  ELSE Titrate(SensorNum,Temp,Drops);
```

The temptation to put a semicolon at the end of a line is strong. Furthermore, in most dialects of BASIC you must put a colon between an **IF** clause and its associated **ELSE** clause.

Semicolons are statement *separators,* however, and the example above is *one single statement.* There is nothing to separate. Remember this rule with regard to placing semicolons in **IF/THEN/ELSE** statements. *Never place a semicolon immediately before an* **ELSE** *word!* With that in mind you will avoid 90 per cent of all semicolon placement errors.

13.9 Halt and Exit

These two statements are *not* part of Standard Pascal, and in many respects are not good practice—like **GOTO**, they are easily abused and can make your programs difficult to read and debug. But like any good tools, they have some legitimate uses.

HALT

Turbo Pascal provides a means of stopping a program in its tracks from anywhere within the program. **Halt** will terminate any running program and throw you out into Turbo Pascal's main menu (if you are running within the Turbo Pascal Environment) or into your operating system.

Halt is a creature of limited usefulness. If you have the foresight to envision a condition in which a complicated program gets so confused that it cannot continue to function meaningfully, it may be best to call a **Halt** with an appropriate error message. One example given in the next section involves a situation in which a large application consisting of multiple chain files discovers that one or more of its chain files cannot be read or may be missing from disk. This is the sort of anomalous situation from which there is no truly graceful exit—it may be better to print an informative error message and return to the operating system.

In PC DOS or MS DOS versions of Turbo Pascal V3.0 and later, the **Halt** statement may take an optional parameter:

```
Halt(ErrorCode : Integer);
```

When **Halt** returns control to DOS, it sets DOS **ERRORLEVEL** to the numeric value in the optional **ErrorCode** parameter.

If you are not familiar with **ERRORLEVEL**, it is a pseudovariable that can be tested by the **IF** batch command in order to perform conditional processing in a DOS batch file. After a program is run from a batch file, some value is set into **ERRORLEVEL**, typically zero. A program can set **ERRORLEVEL** if it wishes, and then the batch file can "branch" at that point, depending on the value set into **ERRORLEVEL** by the program.

Aside from its name, there is nothing hard-coded into **ERROR-LEVEL** connected with DOS errors. I use **Halt** with a parameter as a means of building small utilities to extend the usefulness of DOS's batch facility, typically by writing a short program to test some machine condition for which no test exists in ordinary batch commands.

For example, the following program tests whether a monochrome or graphics display is installed in the system, using the **Monochrome** function described in Section 17.2:

```
PROGRAM IsMono;

{$I MONOTEST.SRC}   {See Section 17.2}

BEGIN
  IF Monochrome THEN Halt(5)
    ELSE Halt(0)
END.
```

If a monochrome screen is present, the program returns a code of 5 to DOS **ERRORLEVEL**; otherwise it returns a 0.

A batch file can test **ERRORLEVEL** to see which display is installed in the machine:

```
ECHO off
ISMONO
IF ERRORLEVEL 5 GOTO mono
ECHO on
REM    It is a graphics screen.
GOTO exit
:mono
ECHO on
REM    It is a monochrome screen.
ECHO on
:exit
```

Your batch file could use this information to install a different set of CRT drivers for an application program, depending on the type of display adapter installed on the machine.

If you do use **Halt** in anything but the simplest programs like the one above, *highlight its presence with glow-in-the-dark comments!* Generally, Pascal programs begin at the top and end at the bottom. Ducking out in the middle via **Halt** or **Exit** (see below) is non-standard procedure and can complicate the reading and debugging of your programs.

EXIT

Version 3.0 and later of Turbo Pascal offer the **Exit** statement. **Exit** jumps out of the current block into the next highest block. In other words, if you execute an **Exit** within a function or procedure, execution of that function or procedure will cease, and control returns to the statement immediately following the invocation of the function or procedure. If **Exit** is encountered in the main program, Turbo Pascal will end the program and return to the Turbo Pascal Environment (if you were working from within the Environment) or into DOS, if the program is a standalone .COM file.

Use **Exit** with care. One of the strengths of the Pascal structure is the assurance that a block of code begins at the top and ends at the bottom. Sprinkling a block with **Exits** makes code much harder to read and debug.

13.10   Chain and execute

There is yet one more category of statements that affects program flow and should be mentioned in this section: **Chain** and **Execute**. **Chain** and **Execute** transfer control completely out of the currently running program to another program stored as a disk file. **Chain** and **Execute** are almost identical functionally. The main difference is that **Chain** will transfer control *only* to a special program file called a "chain file," created by setting the **CHN** option in the Options menu; while **Execute** will transfer control to any stand-alone .COM file whether created by Turbo Pascal or some other programming tool.

A chain file is a Turbo Pascal code file *without* the runtime support code. Code in a chain file still requires that the runtime support code be somewhere in memory, however. Any normal .COM file produced by Turbo Pascal will bring the runtime code into memory when it loads and runs. Once it is running, it can pass control to chain files (file extension .CHN) that can then use the runtime code loaded by the original file. .CHN files, since they do not include the runtime support code, are smaller and load more quickly than ordinary .COM files.

Chain is a procedure and is predeclared this way:

```
PROCEDURE Chain(VAR Prog : FILE);
```

Prog is an untyped file; that is, a file simply declared as **FILE** and not **FILE OF <type>**. **Prog** must have been previously assigned to a physical file on disk with the **Assign** statement (see Section 18.3). It should not be an *open* file, however. Don't use **Reset** or **Rewrite** on the file before you chain. (This is in contrast to the chaining scheme in Pascal/MT+, which *does* require that the program file be opened with **Reset**. Program converters take note!)

Ordinarily, if **Chain** attempts to pass control to a .CHN file that does not exist, the program will crash with an I/O error. By setting Turbo Pascal's I/O checking to passive (with the {$I-} compiler command, see Section 23.4), control will instead pass through to the next statement. This should be an assignment from the **IOResult** function, so that appropriate action may be taken if the chain fails:

```
Assign(Prog,'PAYROLL.CHN');
{$I-} Chain(Prog); {$I+}   { I/O check is passive for Chain }
I := IOResult;
IF I <> 0 THEN             { I <> 0 means File not found }
  BEGIN
    Writeln('>>Cannot chain; exiting to DOS...');
    Halt                  { *** Program terminates HERE! ***}
  END
```

Halt is one means of coping with disastrous situations, like finding a major chunk of your multiprogram system unexpectedly missing or unreadable. In such a case, **Halt** terminates the program and exits to the disk operating system.

Like **Chain**, **Execute** is a procedure:

```
PROCEDURE Execute(VAR Prog : FILE);
```

Execute works identically to **Chain**, save that **Execute** will transfer function to any complete .COM file. The target program need not have been compiled with Turbo Pascal.

CHAIN/EXECUTE CAUTIONS FOR 8086 USERS

In the Z80 world, that is all you need to consider to use **Chain** or **Execute**. In an 8086 environment, use of **Chain** and **Execute** is complicated by the fact that passing control to another program *does not change the code, data, or stack allocations set by the first* *program to be run.* In other words, if the first program has 10K of code and it passes control to another program with 20K of code, the second program's code may well overwrite its own data, heap, or stack space. Or, if a program with 10K of data passes control to another program with 20K of data, something vital in the system may be scrambled. The program may abort to DOS, or the system may lock up.

Designing an 8086-based system that consists of many programs passing control to one another requires some planning. You must set the memory allocation for each program in the system by using the commands in the Options menu, such that no program requires more memory for code, stack, or data than you have set (see Section 23.3).

In my own experience, overlays are a better way of splitting up an oversize program that will not compile in one piece.

Note that no variables are carried over to the target program. It is exactly as though you had typed the program name from the DOS prompt. The only way to pass variables between chained programs is to define a communications area at some absolute location in memory and locate your common variables there via the **ABSOLUTE** qualifier (see Section 20.1). Turbo Pascal provides *no* assurance that absolute variables will not get "stepped on" by some other code or data. *Trying to set up "common" for a group of chained programs to share is very risky stuff.*

All in all, passing variables between chained programs is a bad idea. **Execute** is best used to automatically transfer control from a program written in Turbo Pascal to a non-Turbo program without requiring the operator to invoke it from the command line. If you need to break a large program down into smaller parts, use overlays instead. Overlays require more forethought and some knowledge of your system memory map, but the accessing of variables from different overlays is well defined and safe. Overlays are discussed in detail in Chapter 24.

13.11   Runtime error trapping

(Note: This section contains advanced material that should be skipped by persons reading this book serially. Do come back to it once you've become familiar with the notion of I/O and runtime errors.)

Turbo Pascal has built-in routines for trapping runtime and I/O errors. These routines are "awakened" when an error occurs within your program that the runtime code is not prepared to handle. Such errors fall into two categories: Runtime and I/O errors. I/O errors are errors that center on the Turbo Pascal file system. Runtime errors are other kinds of errors, including divide by zero, floating point overflow, array index out of range, and so on. A complete list of runtime and I/O error messages are given in appendices C and D.

Ordinarily, in a standalone Turbo Pascal .COM file, runtime and I/O errors print out a brief error message with a numeric error code and return to the operating system. The displays look like this:

```
Run-time error 02, PC=2EFF

Program aborted

I/O error F1, PC=315B

Program aborted
```

The "PC" stands for Program Counter, and its value is either the offset into the code segment at which the error occurred (for 8086) or the absolute address where the error occurred (for Z80.)

These brief messages tell you nothing in themselves about the type of error that stopped your program. For that, you have to look up the error in the back of the **Turbo Pascal Reference Manual.**

I/O errors may be dealt with by using the $I– compiler toggle and **IORESULT**, as described in Section 18.5. You can prevent an I/O error from crashing your program by using $I– and then testing the error code returned in **IORESULT**.

Runtime errors, on the other hand, cannot be disabled with any compiler toggle and will *always* crash your program to the operating system. Some people may wonder why the program stops short in these situations, like divide-by-zero. Well, you can assume that when the runtime code evaluates an expression as a divide-by-zero (which is mathematically meaningless) it intends to assign that value to a variable. Since the expression is, in fact, meaningless, there is nothing to put into the variable. Calculations further down the program may depend on that variable. There is literally nothing meaningful to do *but* halt the program.

On the other hand, coming to a screeching halt in the middle of the execution of a program could leave some necessary housekeeping undone. In particular, open files that have been written to but not closed may not have been completely flushed to disk. If you stop the program without closing the file, some of the information that you had written to the files could be left in RAM disk buffers and lost.

Turbo Pascal offers a way out by allowing you to write a procedure that traps I/O and runtime errors. This procedure can close your files or do any other "tidying-up" that needs to be done before the program has to die. The bad news is that the program *must* die, and return control either to the operating system or to the Turbo Pascal Environment, if you were running from within the Environment. The trapping procedure cannot somehow recover control, patch up errant variables, and allow the program to carry on, nice as that would be. Think of runtime error trapping as a last will and testament rather than some kind of cure.

It's not done in the usual Pascal fashion. What you must do is this: Write a procedure to deal with the errors. Its name is not important; you can call it whatever you like. What *is* important is that the procedure have two integer parameters passed by *value, not* by reference:

```
PROCEDURE RuntimeErrorTrap(ErrorData,ErrorAddress : Integer);
```

You could as well have called it **ErrorTrapper** or **Blooie**. Your two integer parameters can also be named whatever you like. The first one will always provide an error code to the procedure, and the second will always provide the address or offset at which the error occurred.

Your procedure is not called by name. (Which is one reason its name is not especially important.) You must give Turbo Pascal a pointer to the procedure (essentially the code address of the procedure) so that when the error occurs, control will transfer directly to the procedure. The pointer has a specific name, however:

ErrorPtr. This is a predefined identifier and you should not define any identifier with the name **ErrorPtr**. Before any possible errors can occur, assign **ErrorPtr** the address of your trapping procedure. This is done differently for 8086 and Z80 versions of Turbo Pascal:

```
ErrorPtr := Ofs(RuntimeErrorTrap);   { For 8086 Turbo }

ErrorPtr := Addr(RuntimeErrorTrap);  { For Z80 Turbo }
```

You do not need to pass a separate segment address for 8086 versions because 8086 procedures always reside in the code segment, and in Turbo Pascal programs there can only be one code segment.

When an error occurs, the Turbo Pascal runtime support code will fill the procedure's first parameter with the error code and the second parameter with the error address, corresponding to the "PC=" value that would have been displayed for an untrapped error. Then the procedure is given control.

The first parameter (which I called **ErrorData**) actually contains two separate values in the two halves of the integer value. You can access these two halves by using the built-in functions **Hi** and **Lo** (see Section 16.9). The high byte of the parameter contains the error *type*, and the low byte of the parameter contains the error *number*. The error type is one of three values: 0 = user break (CTRL-C typed by the user); 1 = I/O error; and 2 = runtime error. When the error type is 0 (CTRL-C typed by user) the error number will *always* be set to 1. In other cases the error number is the number given for I/O and runtime errors in appendices C and D.

The procedure can do whatever it must to put your program's affairs in order before exiting to the operating system or Turbo Pascal Environment with a **Halt** statement (see Section 13.9). The only thing it cannot do is return to the program itself, either by using **Exit** or by reaching the terminating **END** word in the normal fashion. If you attempt to return control to the main program, another runtime error will be triggered and the program will terminate anyway.

The following program is a simple example of a runtime error trapping routine. Its function here is only to provide a more "friendly" error message before terminating the program. It could also close files, shut down peripherals, or do whatever else needs to be done. Only a few runtime error codes are accounted for in the example. You could add the others by adding additional statements to the main **CASE** statement.

```
1        {------------------------------------------------------------------}
2        {                              Trapper                             }
3        {                                                                  }
4        {        Demonstration of Turbo Pascal runtime error trapping      }
5        {                                                                  }
6        {                                    by Jeff Duntemann             }
7        {                                    Turbo Pascal V3.0             }
8        {                                    Last update 3/4/86            }
9        {                                                                  }
10       {                                                                  }
11       {                                                                  }
12       {------------------------------------------------------------------}
13
14       PROGRAM Trapper;
15
16       VAR
17         R : Real;
18
19
20       PROCEDURE RuntimeErrorTrap(ErrorData, ErrorAddress : Integer);
21
22       VAR
23         ErrorType,ErrorNumber : Byte;
24
25       BEGIN
26         ErrorType   := Hi(ErrorData);
27         ErrorNumber := Lo(ErrorData);
28         CASE ErrorType OF
29           0 : BEGIN                      { User-issued program break }
30                 Write('You typed Control-C to interrupt--');
```

(continues)

```
31                    Writeln('returning to the operating system...');
32                    Halt(1)                            { Remove parm for Z80! }
33               END;
34
35        1 : CASE ErrorNumber OF      { I/O error }
36              4 : Writeln('Block I/O attempted on closed file!');
37                  { Add other appropriate action statements here }
38            END; { CASE }
39
40        2 : CASE ErrorNumber OF      { Runtime error }
41              1 : Writeln('Floating point overflow!');
42              2 : Writeln('Divide by zero error!');
43              3 : Writeln('Square root of negative value error!');
44              4 : Writeln('Natural log argument zero or negative!');
45              255 : Writeln('Heap/stack collision!');
46            END; { CASE }
47
48      END; { CASE }
49      Halt(ErrorNumber + (ErrorType-1)*32)    { Remove parm for Z80! }
50    END;
51
52
53    BEGIN
54      ClrScr;
55      ErrorPtr := Ofs(RuntimeErrorTrap);          { 8086 error trap set }
56      {ErrorPtr := Addr(RuntimeErrorTrap);}       { Z80 error trap set }
57      Readln;
58      R := 42.0 / 0.0;      { Try to divide by zero to awaken trap }
59    END.
```

(concluded)

Procedures and functions

Some people think looping statements like **WHILE/DO** and **REPEAT/UNTIL** (and the corresponding lack of need for **GOTO**s) are the touchstone of structured programming. Not so—at the bottom of it, *structured programming is the artful hiding of details.* The human mind's ability to grasp complexity breaks down quickly unless some structure or pattern can be found in the complexity. I recall (with some embarrassment) writing a 1300 line FORTRAN program in high school, and by the time I wrote the last of it (this being done over a six-week period) I no longer remembered how the first part worked. The entire program was a mass of unstructured, undifferentiated detail.

How does one hide details in computer programs? By identifying sequences of code that do discrete tasks, and setting each sequence off somewhere, replacing it by a single word describing (or at least hinting at) the task it does. Such code sequences are properly called "subprograms."

In Pascal, there are two types of subprograms: procedures and functions. Both are sequences of Pascal statements set off from the main body of program code. Both are invoked, and their statements executed, simply by naming them. The only difference between functions and procedures is this: The identifier naming a function has a type and takes on a value when it is executed. The name of a procedure has no type and takes on no value.

Two simple examples: The procedure **ClrScr**, when executed, clears the CRT screen:

```
ClrScr;
```

ClrScr will be discussed along with the other CRT control procedures in Section 17.1. It is a complete statement in itself. Although **ClrScr** has no parameters, a procedure may have any number of parameters if it needs them.

A function, by contrast, is *not* a complete statement. It is more like an expression that returns a value that must be used somehow:

```
VAR
    Space,Radius : Real;

Radius := 4.66;
Space := Area(Radius);
```

Note that you could *not* simply have put the invocation of **Area** on a line by itself:

```
AREA(Radius);
```

This would generate an error at compile time.

Area calculates the area for the value **Radius**, which is passed to it as a parameter. After it calculates the area for the value passed to it in **Radius**, the area value is taken on by the identifier **Area**, as though **Area** were a variable.

Functions in Turbo Pascal may return values of any ordinal type (**Integer**, **Char**, **Byte**, **Real**, **Boolean**), any enumerated type, a subrange of an ordinal or enumerated type, or any pointer type. Unlike virtually all other Pascal compilers, functions in Turbo Pascal may also return values of type **String**.

Using the **Area** function hides the details of calculating areas. There aren't many details involved in calculating areas, but for other calculations (matrix inversion comes to mind) a function can hide 30 or 40 lines of complicated code. Or more. So when you're reading the program and come to a function invocation, you can think, "Ah, here's where we invert the matrix" without being concerned about *how* the matrix is actually inverted. At that level in reading the program, the *how* is not important, so those details are best kept out of sight.

The **ClrScr** function illustrates another facet of detail-hiding. The **ClrScr** function clears the CRT screen. How this is done varies widely from computer to computer. The IBM PC requires a software interrupt to clear the screen, whereas the Victor 9000 and Xerox 820 only require that a control character be sent to the system console driver. If you're writing a program that is to run on many different computers, it is best to hide machine-specific details in functions and procedures and put those functions and procedures in a machine-specific library that can be included into your main program code for each specific machine. This way, a single source file can be compiled to run on many different computers without changes, simply by including a different machine-specific library for each different computer.

THE STRUCTURE OF FUNCTIONS AND PROCEDURES

Procedures and functions are, in effect, miniature programs. They can have label declarations, constant declarations, type declarations, variable declarations, and procedure and function declarations as well as the expected code statements. Consider these two entities:

```
PROGRAM HiThere;        PROCEDURE HiThere;

BEGIN                   BEGIN
  Writeln('Hi there!')    Writeln('Hi there!')
End.                    END;
```

The only *essential* differences between a program and a procedure are the keyword **PROGRAM** and the punctuation after the final **End**.

Functions are a little different. A function has a type and takes on a value that it returns to the program logic that invokes it:

```
FUNCTION Area(R : Real) : Real;

CONST
  PI = 3.14159;

BEGIN
  Area := PI * R * R;
END;
```

The type of function **Area** is **Real**. As you can see from the function's single line of code, an expression computing area for the given radius R is evaluated, and the value is assigned to the function's name. Aside from these two distinctions, functions are identical to procedures and are also miniature programs.

14.1 Formal and actual parameters

Passing data to procedures and functions can be done two ways: By using global variables that any procedure or function can read from or write to, and through each procedure or function's parameter list. The first is a thoroughly bad idea, to be avoided unless limitations of your hardware forbid it. It is good practice to hand a procedure everything it needs through its parameter list.

The following program contains a procedure to draw boxes on the CRT screen with characters, as opposed to true pixel graphics:

```
1     {----------------------------------------------------------}
2     {                       BoxTest                            }
3     {                                                          }
4     {            Character box draw demo program               }
5     {                                                          }
6     {                          by Jeff Duntemann               }
7     {                          Turbo Pascal V3.0               }
8     {                          Last update 2/1/86              }
9     {                                                          }
10    {                                                          }
11    {                                                          }
12    {----------------------------------------------------------}
```

(continues)

```
13
14          PROGRAM BoxTest;
15
16      TYPE
17        GrafRec = RECORD
18                       ULCorner,
19                       URCorner,
20                       LLCorner,
21                       LRCorner,
22                       HBar,
23                       VBar,
24                       LineCross,
25                       TDown,
26                       TUp,
27                       TRight,
28                       TLeft : String[4]
29                     END;
30
31          String80  = String[80];
32
33
34      VAR
35        GrafChars    : GrafRec;
36        X,Y          : Integer;
37        Width,Height : Integer;
38
39
40      PROCEDURE DefineChars(VAR GrafChars : GrafRec);
41
42      BEGIN
43        WITH GrafChars DO
44          BEGIN
45            ULCorner  := Chr(201);
46            URCorner  := Chr(187);
47            LLCorner  := Chr(200);
48            LRCorner  := Chr(188);
49            HBar      := Chr(205);
50            VBar      := Chr(186);
51            LineCross := Chr(206);
```

(continues)

```
52              TDown        := Chr(203);
53              TUp          := Chr(202);
54              TRight       := Chr(185);
55              TLeft        := Chr(204)
56          END
57      END;
58
59
60      PROCEDURE MakeBox(X,Y,Width,Height : Integer;
61                        GrafChars        : GrafRec);
62
63      VAR
64          I,J : Integer;
65
66      BEGIN
67          IF X < 0 THEN X := (80-Width) DIV 2;    { Negative X centers box }
68          WITH GrafChars DO
69            BEGIN                                 { Draw top line }
70              GotoXY(X,Y); Write(ULCorner);
71              FOR I := 3 TO Width DO Write(HBar);
72              Write(URCorner);
73                                                  { Draw bottom line }
74              GotoXY(X,(Y+Height)-1); Write(LLCorner);
75              FOR I := 3 TO Width DO Write(HBar);
76              Write(LRCorner);
77                                                  { Draw sides }
78              FOR I := 1 TO Height-2 DO
79                BEGIN
80                  GotoXY(X,Y+I); Write(VBar);
81                  GotoXY((X+Width)-1,Y+I); Write(VBar)
82                END
83            END
84      END;
85
86
87
88      BEGIN
89          Randomize;                  { Seed the pseudorandom number generator }
90          ClrScr;                     { Clear the entire screen }
```

(continues)

```
91              DefineChars(GrafChars);      { Go get box-draw characters for this machine }
92              WHILE NOT KeyPressed DO       { Draw boxes until a key is pressed }
93                BEGIN
94                  X := Random(72);          { Get a Random X/Y for UL Corner of box }
95                  Y := Random(21);
96                  REPEAT Width := Random(80-72) UNTIL Width > 1;  { Get Random Height & }
97                  REPEAT Height := Random(25-Y) UNTIL Height > 1; { Width to fit on CRT }
98                  MakeBox(X,Y,Width,Height,GrafChars);             { and draw it! }
99                END
100         END.
```

(concluded)

The **GrafRec** type exists to overcome the problem that even character graphics are done in widely different ways on different computers. The IBM PC has a whole series of graphics characters in its "high" 128 character set, but the Xerox 820 has only a few drawing characters, and they can only be drawn by preceding them with a "lead-in" character. So 820 graphics characters are not characters at all, but strings—hence the types in the record are not characters but short strings. Some computers have no graphics characters at all—in those cases, plus symbols (+) can be used for the corners, cross, and T's, and the ASCII vertical bar (|) and dash (-) for vertical and horizontal lines. The important thing is that you needn't change any code to move this procedure to different computers; you need only change the values in the **GrafChars** record passed to it.

MakeBox has a parameter list with five parameters in it. In the parameter list of the procedure's declaration they are named: **X**, **Y**, **Width**, **Height**, and **GrafChars**. Notice that the types of these parameters are given in the procedure declaration. **X**, **Y**, **Width**, and **Height** are all identical types, so they may be given as a list separated by commas. You could also have defined each of the four separately, like this:

```
PROCEDURE MakeBox(X        : Integer;
                  Y        : Integer;
                  Width    : Integer;
                  Height   : Integer;
                  GrafChars : GrafRec);
```

The parameters defined in a procedure's declaration are called "formal parameters" and must always be given a type, separated from the formal parameter by a colon.

When a procedure is invoked, values are passed to the procedure through its parameters. The parameter types are not given:

```
MakeBox(25,BoxNum+2,30,3,Chars820);
```

Furthermore, in this example, the values may be values stored in variables, or values expressed as constants or expressions. The parameters that are present in the parameter list of a particular invocation of a procedure are called "actual parameters." (All parameters passed to **MakeBox** are passed by value. If they were passed by reference, the actual parameters would have to be variables of identical type to the formal parameters. This will be fully explained in the next section.)

Identifiers used as formal parameters are local to their procedure or function. As such, their names may be identical to identifiers defined in other procedures or functions, or in the main program, without any conflict. The **X** and **Y** formal parameters in **MakeBox** have no relation at all to an **X** or **Y** identifier used elsewhere in the program. Of course, the flipside of this is also true: If you are using an **X** or **Y** variable global to the entire program they will *not* be accessible from within **MakeBox.**

Also remember that formal **VAR** parameters may not act as control variables in **FOR** loops. (You'll get an anomalous Error 30 if you try it.) Local variables (such as I in **MakeBox**) should be declared for this purpose.

In the program **BoxTest**, values are loaded into **GrafChars** with assignment statements. A wiser move would be to store the **Graf-Chars** record in a file, and read the record from the file into memory at program startup. That way, nothing specific to the IBM PC is baked into the program itself, and the same source could be compiled under any installed copy of Turbo Pascal on any computer.

14.2   Passing parameters by value or by reference

When a function or a procedure is invoked, the actual parameters are "meshed" with the formal parameters, and then the function or procedure does its work. The meshing of actual parameters with formal parameters is done two ways: by value and by reference.

**PASSING
PARAMETERS
BY VALUE**

A parameter passed by value is just that: a value is copied from the actual parameter into the formal parameter. The movement of the value to the procedure is a one-way street. Nothing can come back out again and be used by the calling program. This applies whether the actual parameter is a constant, an expression, or a variable.

There are powerful advantages to one-way data movement *into* a procedure. The procedure can fold, spindle, and mutilate the parameter any way it needs to and not fear any side effects outside of the procedure. The copy of the actual parameter it gets is a truly private copy, strictly local to the procedure itself.

If a variable is passed to a procedure by value, the type of the variable must be compatible with the type of the formal parameter.

**PASSING
PARAMETERS
BY REFERENCE**

There are many occasions when the whole point of passing a parameter to a function or procedure is to have it modified and returned for further use. To have a procedure or function modify a parameter and return it, the parameter must be passed by reference.

Unlike parameters passed by value, a parameter passed by reference (often called a **VAR** parameter) cannot be a literal, a constant, or an expression. The values of constants and literals by definition cannot be changed, and the notion of changing the value of an expression and stuffing it back into the expression makes no logical sense.

To be passed by reference, an actual parameter must be a variable of the *identical* type as the formal parameter. Compatible types will not do; the types must evaluate down to the same type definition statement, as explained in Section 12.2.

The one exception to this rule in Turbo Pascal involves string types. Strings, if you recall from Section 9.5, may be defined in any physical length from 1 to 255. Under strict type checking a **VAR** string parameter passed to a procedure must be of the identical type declared in the procedure's header:

```
VAR
   String1 : String80;
   String2 : String30;

PROCEDURE Grimble(VAR WorkString : String255);
```

In this example, strict type checking would prohibit passing either **String1** or **String2** as a parameter to procedure **Grimble**.

However, strict type checking may be relaxed with the **$V** compiler command (see Section 23.4) to allow strings of any physical length to be passed as **VAR** parameters regardless of the formal **VAR** parameter's physical length. To relax strict type checking include this command in your code:

```
{$V-}
```

Note that the default for type checking is strict, and you must explicitly use the **$V–** command to relax type checking if desired.

The draconian nature of strict type checking for **VAR** parameters makes a little more sense when you realize that the variable itself is not copied into the formal parameter (as with parameters passed by value). What is passed is actually a pointer to the variable itself. Data is not being moved from one variable to another. Data is being read from one variable and written back into the same variable. To protect other data items that may exist to either side of the variable passed by reference, the compiler insists on a *perfect* match between formal and actual parameters.

The procedure **MakeBox** had several parameters, all passed by value. For an example of a parameter passed by reference, consider the Shell sort procedure below:

```
1        {<<<< ShellSort >>>>}
2
3
```

(continues)

```
4         { Described in section 14.2 -- Last mod 2/1/86   }
5
6         PROCEDURE ShellSort(VAR SortBuf : KeyArray; Recs : Integer);
7
8         VAR
9           I,J,K,L : Integer;
10          Spread  : Integer;
11
12
13        PROCEDURE KeySwap(VAR RR,SS : KeyRec);
14
15        VAR
16          T : KeyRec;
17
18        BEGIN
19          T := RR;
20          RR := SS;
21          SS := T
22        END;
23
24
25        BEGIN
26          Spread := Recs DIV 2;        { First Spread is half record count  }
27          WHILE Spread > 0 DO          { Do until Spread goes to zero:       }
28            BEGIN
29              FOR I := Spread + 1 TO Recs DO
30                BEGIN
31                  J := I - Spread;
32                  WHILE J > 0 DO
33                    BEGIN              { Test & swap across the array }
34                      L := J + Spread;
35                      IF SortBuf[J].KeyData <= SortBuf[L].KeyData THEN J := 0 ELSE
36                        KeySwap(SortBuf[J],SortBuf[L]);
37                      J := J - Spread
38                    END
39                END;
40              Spread := Spread DIV 2   { Halve Spread for next pass }
41            END
42        END;
```

(concluded)

This procedure sorts an array of sort keys. A sort key is a record type that consists of a piece of data and a pointer to a file entry from which the data came. The fastest and safest way to sort a file is not to sort the file at all, but to build an array of sort keys from information in the file and sort the array of sort keys instead.

The array can then be written out to a file. Since the data in the array is in sorted (usually alphabetical) order, it can be searched using a fast binary search function. Once a match to a desired string is found (in the **Key** field of a **KeyRec** record), the **RecNum** field contains the physical record number of the record in the file where the rest of the information is stored.

Look at the parameter line for **ShellSort**:

```
PROCEDURE ShellSort(VAR SortBuf : KeyArray; Recs : Integer);
```

The first parameter, **SortBuf**, is passed by reference. The second parameter, **Recs**, is passed by value. The difference is that **SortBuf** is preceded by the keyword **VAR**. **VAR** indicates that the parameter following it is passed by reference.

The reason for passing **SortBuf** by reference should be obvious: We want to rearrange the sort keys in **SortBuf** and put them in a certain order. **ShellSort** does this rearranging. We will need to get **SortBuf** "back" when the rearranging is done. Had we passed **SortBuf** to **ShellSort** by value, **ShellSort** would have received its own private copy of **SortBuf**, would have sorted the copy, and then would have had no way to return the sorted copy to the rest of the program.

Recs contains a count of the number of sort keys loaded into the array **SortBuf**. While knowing the value stored in **Recs** is essential to sorting **SortBuf** correctly, it need not be changed, and thus **Recs** can be passed by value. Only the *value* of **Recs** is needed.

Summing up: An actual parameter passed by value is copied into the formal parameter. The copy is local to the procedure or function and changes made to the copy do not "leak out" into the rest of the program.

Passing a parameter to a procedure by reference actually gives the procedure a pointer to the physical variable being passed. Changes made to the parameter within the procedure are actually made to the physical variable outside the procedure.

To pass a parameter by reference, precede the parameter by the keyword **VAR**. When passed by reference, actual parameters must be variables of *identical type* to the formal parameter.

14.3 Recursion

Recursion is one of those peculiar concepts that seems to defy understanding totally and depend completely on mystery for its operation, until eventually some small spark of understanding happens, and then, *wham!* It becomes simple or even obvious. A great many people have trouble understanding recursion at first glance, so if you do too, don't think less of yourself for it. For the beginner recursion is simple. But it is *not* obvious.

Recursion is what we call it when a function or procedure invokes itself. It seems somehow inituitive to beginners that having a procedure call itself is either impossible or else an invitation to disaster. Both of these fears are unfounded, of course. Let's look at them both.

Recursion is indeed possible. In fact, having a procedure call itself is no different from a coding perspective than having a procedure call any other procedure. What happens when a procedure calls another procedure? Only this: First, the called procedure is "instantiated"; that is, its formal parameters and local variables are allocated on the system stack. Next, the return address (the location in the code from which the procedure was called and to which it must return control) is "pushed" onto the system stack. Finally, control is passed to the called procedure's code.

When the called procedure is finished executing, it retrieves the return address from the system stack and then clears its variables and formal parameters off the stack by a process we call "popping." Then it returns control to the code that called it by branching to the return address.

None of this changes when a procedure calls itself. Upon a recursive call to itself, new copies of the procedure's formal parameters and local variables are instantiated on the stack. Then control is passed to the start of the procedure again.

The problem shows up when execution reaches the point in the procedure where it calls itself. A third instance of the procedure is allocated on the stack, and the procedure begins running again. A fourth instance, and a fifth . . . and after a few hundred recursive calls the stack has grown so large that it collides with something important in memory, and the system crashes. If you had this kind of procedure, such a thing would happen very quickly:

```
PROCEDURE Fatal;

BEGIN
  Fatal
END;
```

Such a situation is an unlimited feedback loop. It is this possibility that makes newcomers feel uneasy about recursion.

Obviously, the important part of recursion is knowing when to stop.

A recursive procedure must test some condition before it calls itself, to see if it still needs to call itself to complete its work. This condition could be a comparison of a counter against a predetermined number of recursive calls, or some Boolean condition that becomes true (or false) when the time is right to stop recursing and go home.

When controlled in this way, recursion becomes a very powerful and elegant way to solve certain programming problems.

Let's go through a simpleminded example of a controlled recursive procedure. Read through this code *very* carefully:

```
PROGRAM PushPop;

CONST
  Levels = 5;

VAR
  Depth : Integer;

PROCEDURE Dive(VAR Depth : Integer);
```

(continues)

```
BEGIN
  Writeln('Push!');
  Writeln('Our depth is now: ',Depth);
  Depth := Depth +1;
  IF Depth <= Levels THEN Dive(Depth);
  Writeln('Pop!')
END;

BEGIN
  Depth := 1;
  Dive(Depth)
END.
```

(concluded)

The program itself is nothing more than setting a counter to 1 and calling the recursive procedure **Dive**. Note constant **Levels**. **Dive** prints the word "Push!" when it begins executing, and the word "Pop!" when it ceases executing. In between, it prints the value of the variable **Depth** and then increments it.

If, at this point, the value of **Depth** is less than the constant **Levels**, **Dive** calls itself. Each call to **Dive** increments **Depth** by 1, until at last **Depth** is greater than **Levels**. Then recursion stops.

Running program **PushPop** produces this output. Can you tell yourself exactly why?

```
Push!
Our depth is now 1
Push!
Our depth is now 2
Push!
Our depth is now 3
Push!
Our depth is now 4
Push!
Our depth is now 5
Pop!
Pop!
Pop!
Pop!
Pop!
```

Follow the execution of **PushPop** through, with a pencil to touch each keyword, if necessary, until the output makes sense to you.

14.4   Applications of recursion

Certain programming problems simply cry out for recursive solutions. Perhaps the simplest and best known is the matter of calculating factorials. A factorial is the product of a digit and all the digits less than it, down to 1:

```
5! = 5 * 4 * 3 * 2 * 1
```

A little scrutiny here will show that 5! is the same as 5 * 4!, and 4! is the same as 4 * 3!, and so on. In the general case, N! = N * (N–1)! Whether you see it immediately or not, we have already expressed the factorial algorithm recursively by defining it in terms of a factorial. This will become a little clearer when we express it in Pascal:

```
FUNCTION Factorial(N : Integer) : Integer;

BEGIN
  IF N > 1 THEN Factorial := N * Factorial(N-1)
    ELSE Factorial := 1
END;
```

And that is it. We express it as a conditional statement because there must always be something to tell the code when to stop recursing. Without the N > 1 test the function would merrily decrement N down past zero and recurse away until the system crashed.

The way to understand this function is to work it out for N=1, then N=2, N=3, and so on. For N=1 the N > 1 test returns **FALSE**, so **Factorial** is assigned the value 1. No recursion involved. 1! = 1. For N=2 a recursive call to **Factorial** is made: **Factorial** is assigned the

value **2 * Factorial(1)**. As we saw above, **Factorial(1) = 1**. So 2! =
2 * 1, or 2. For N=3, two recursive calls are made: **Factorial** is assigned the value **3 * Factorial(2)**. **Factorial(2)** is computed (as we just
saw) by evaluating (recursively) **2 * Factorial(1)**. And **Factorial(1)** is
simply = 1. Catching on? One interesting thing to do is add (tempo-
rarily) a **Writeln** statement to **Factorial** that displays the value of
N at the beginning of each invocation.

A sidenote on the power of factorials: Calculating anything over
7! will overflow a two-byte integer.

**A RECURSIVE
QUICKSORT
PROCEDURE**

A considerably more useful application of recursion lies in the
"quicksort" method of sorting arrays, invented by C.A.R. Hoare.
Quicksort procedures can be written in a number of different ways,
but the simplest way is by using recursion.

This will not be an easy procedure to understand if you are a
beginner. If you can't make sense of it right now, come back to it
after you have had a chance to use Pascal for awhile.

The quicksort procedure below does the same job that the
procedure **ShellSort** did in the last section. **QuickSort** is passed an
array of **KeyRec** and a count of the number of records to be sorted in
the array. It rearranges the records until they are in ascending sort
order in the array:

```
1          {<<<< QuickSort >>>>}
2
3
4          { Described in section 14.4 -- Last mod 2/1/86    }
5
6          PROCEDURE QuickSort(VAR SortBuf : KeyARRAY;
7                                   Recs    : Integer);
8
9
10         PROCEDURE KeySwap(VAR RR,SS : KeyRec);
11
12         VAR
13            T : KeyRec;
14
```

(continues)

```
15          BEGIN
16            T := RR;
17            RR := SS;
18            SS := T
19          END;
20
21
22          PROCEDURE DoSort(Low, High : Integer);
23
24          VAR
25            I,J   : Integer;
26            Pivot : KeyRec;
27
28          BEGIN
29            { Can't sort if Low is greater than or equal to High... }
30            IF Low < High THEN
31              BEGIN
32                I := Low;
33                J := High;
34                Pivot := SortBuf[J];
35                REPEAT
36                  WHILE (I < J) AND (SortBuf[I].KeyData <= Pivot.KeyData) DO I := I + 1;
37                  WHILE (J > I) AND (SortBuf[J].KeyData >= Pivot.KeyData) DO J := J - 1;
38                  IF I < J THEN KeySwap(SortBuf[I],SortBuf[J]);
39                UNTIL I >= J;
40                KeySwap(SortBuf[I],SortBuf[High]);
41                IF (I - Low < High - I) THEN
42                  BEGIN
43                    DoSort(Low,I-1);      { Recursive calls to DoSort! }
44                    DoSort(I+1,High)
45                  END
46                ELSE
47                  BEGIN
48                    DoSort(I+1,High);     { Recursive calls to DoSort! }
49                    DoSort(Low,I-1)
50                  END
51              END
52          END;
53
```

(continues)

```
54
55          BEGIN
56            DoSort(1,Recs);
57          END;  { QuickSort }
```

(concluded)

QuickSort's *modus operandi* is summarized in Figure 14.1. One of the elements is chosen arbitrarily (here it is the last element in the array) to be the "pivot value." The idea is to divide the array into two partitions such that all elements on one side of the partition are greater than the pivot value, and all elements on the other side of the partition are less than the pivot value.

This is done by scanning the array from both ends toward the middle by counters **I** and **J**. **I** scans from the low end upward; **J** from the high end downward. The **I** counter samples each element, and stops when it finds an element whose value is *higher* than the pivot value. Then the scan begins from the top end down, with the **J** counter looking for a value that is *less* than the pivot value. When

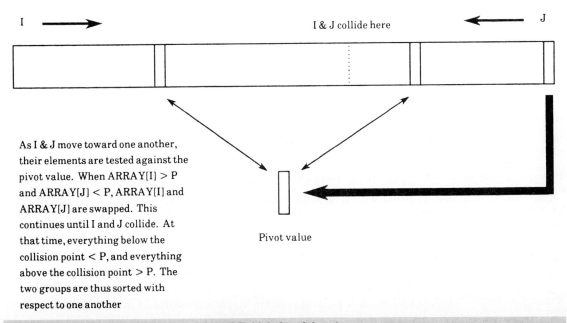

I

I & J collide here

J

As I & J move toward one another, their elements are tested against the pivot value. When ARRAY[I] > P and ARRAY[J] < P, ARRAY[I] and ARRAY[J] are swapped. This continues until I and J collide. At that time, everything below the collision point < P, and everything above the collision point > P. The two groups are thus sorted with respect to one another

Pivot value

FIGURE 14.1 A quicksort scan

it finds one, the two found elements are swapped, thus putting them on the proper side of the pivot value.

When **I** and **J** collide in the middle somewhere (*not* necessarily in the center), the array has been partitioned into two groups of elements: One that is larger than the pivot value and one that is smaller. These two groups are not necessarily equal in size. In fact, they usually will not be. The only thing that is certain is that all the elements in one group are less than the value of the pivot element, and all of the elements of the other group are greater than the pivot element. The two *groups* are sorted with respect to one another: All elements of the low group are less than all elements of the high group.

Enter recursion: This same process is now applied to each of the two groups by calling **DoSort** recursively for each group. A new pivot value is chosen for each group, and each group is partitioned around its pivot value, just as the entire array was originally. When this is done, there are four groups. A little thought will show you that low-valued elements of the array are being driven toward the low end of the array, and high-valued elements are being driven toward the high end of the array. Within each group there is no guarantee that the elements are in sorted order. What you must understand is that the *groups themselves* are in sort order. In other words, *all* the elements of one group are greater than all the elements of the group below it.

Pressing on: Each of the four groups is partitioned again by more recursive calls to **DoSort**. The groups are smaller. Each group taken as one is sorted with respect to all other groups. With each recursive call, the groups have fewer and fewer members. In time, each group will contain only one element. Since groups are always in sort order, if each group is a single element, then all elements of the array are in sorted order, and **QuickSort**'s job is finished.

How does **QuickSort** know when to stop recursing? The first conditional test in **DoSort** does it: If **Low** is greater than or equal to **High**, the sort is finished. Why? Because **Low** and **High** are the bounds of the group being partitioned. If **Low** = **High**, the group has only one member. When the groups have only one member, the array is in sort order and work is done.

If this makes your head spin, you are in good company. Follow it through a few times until it makes sense. Once you can follow **QuickSort**'s internal logic, you will have a *very* good grasp of the uses of recursion.

This particular Quicksort algorithm works best when the original order of the elements in the array is random or nearly so. It works least well when the original order is close to fully sorted. For an array of random elements, it is one of the fastest of all sorting methods. For sorting arrays that are close to being in order, the **ShellSort** procedure given earlier will be consistently faster.

The following program puts the two sort routines to the test. It generates a file of random keys, allows you to display the file (to give you an idea how random the file is), and then sorts the file by either of the two methods. Once the file is sorted, you can display the file again to satisfy yourself that the sort took place and was accurate.

```
1          {------------------------------------------------------------}
2          {                         SortTest                           }
3          {                                                            }
4          {              Data sort demonstration program               }
5          {                                                            }
6          {                              by Jeff Duntemann             }
7          {                              Turbo Pascal V3.0             }
8          {                              Last update 5/5/86            }
9          {                                                            }
10         {                                                            }
11         {                                                            }
12         {------------------------------------------------------------}
13
14         PROGRAM Sorttest;
15
16
17         CONST
18            HighLite   = True;
19            CR         = True;
20            NoHighlite = False;
21            NoCR       = False;
22            GetInteger = False;
23            Numeric    = True;
24            CapsLock   = True;
```

(continues)

```
25              Shell      = True;
26              Quick      = False;
27
28
29          TYPE
30            String255 = String[255];
31            String80  = String[80];
32            String30  = String[30];
33
34            KeyRec = RECORD
35                        Ref     : Integer;
36                        KeyData : String30
37                     END;
38
39            KeyArray = ARRAY[0..500] OF KeyRec;
40
41            KeyFile = FILE OF KeyRec;
42
43          {$I GRAFREC.DEF}    { Definition file for GrafRec record type }
44
45
46          VAR
47            I,J,Error : Integer;
48            IVAL      : Integer;
49            R         : Real;
50            Ch        : Char;
51            Response  : String80;
52            Escape    : Boolean;
53            WorkArray : KeyArray;
54            Randoms   : KeyFile;
55            GrafChars : GrafRec;
56
57
58          {$I BEEP.SRC}       { "Deedle-deedle" beeper procedure }
59          {$I UHUH.SRC}       { "Uh-uh" sound for errors }
60          {$I MONOTEST.SRC}   { Test for presence of monochrome display }
61          {$I CURSON.SRC}     { Turns IBM PC text cursor back on again }
62          {$I CURSOFF.SRC}    { Turns off IBM PC text cursor }
```

(continues)

```
63      {$I KEYSTAT.SRC}      { KEYSTAT non-echo keyboard input function }
64      {$I YES.SRC }         { YES function }
65      {$I WRITEAT.SRC}      { WRITEAT function for X/Y String display }
66
67      {$I BOXSTUFF.SRC}     { MAKEBOX procedure and associated definitions }
68      {$I GETSTRIN.SRC}     { GetString formatted String input procedure }
69      {$I SHELSORT.SRC}     { Shell sort routine }
70      {$I QUIKSORT.SRC}     { Quicksort routine }
71      {$I PULL.SRC }        { PULL random number within a given range function }
72
73
74      PROCEDURE ClearRegion(X1,Y1,X2,Y2 : Integer);
75
76      BEGIN
77        Window(X1,Y1,X2,Y2);
78        ClrScr;
79        Window(1,1,80,25)
80      END;
81
82
83      PROCEDURE GenerateRandomKeyFile(KeyQuantity : Integer);
84
85      VAR WorkKey : KeyRec;
86          I,J     : Integer;
87
88      BEGIN
89        Assign(Randoms,'RANDOMS.KEY');
90        Rewrite(Randoms);
91        FOR I := 1 TO KeyQuantity DO
92          BEGIN
93            FillChar(WorkKey,SizeOf(WorkKey),0);
94            FOR J := 1 TO SizeOf(WorkKey.KeyData)-1 DO
95              WorkKey.KeyData[J] := Chr(Pull(65,91));
96            WorkKey.KeyData[0] := Chr(30);
97            Write(Randoms,WorkKey);
98          END;
99        Close(Randoms)
100     END;
```

(continues)

```
101
102
103        PROCEDURE DisplayKeys;
104
105      VAR WorkKey : KeyRec;
106
107      BEGIN
108        Assign(Randoms,'RANDOMS.KEY');
109        Reset(Randoms);
110        Window(25,13,70,22);
111        GotoXY(1,1);
112        WHILE NOT EOF(Randoms) DO
113          BEGIN
114            Read(Randoms,WorkKey);
115            IF NOT EOF(Randoms) THEN Writeln(WorkKey.KeyData)
116          END;
117        Close(Randoms);
118        Writeln;
119        Writeln('        >>Press (CR)<<');
120        Readln;
121        ClrScr;
122        Window(1,1,80,25)
123      END;
124
125
126
127        PROCEDURE DoSort(Shell : Boolean);
128
129      VAR Counter : Integer;
130
131      BEGIN
132        Assign(Randoms,'RANDOMS.KEY');
133        Reset(Randoms);
134        Counter := 1;
135        WriteAt(20,15,NoHighlite,NoCR,'Loading...');
136        WHILE NOT EOF(Randoms) DO
137          BEGIN
138            Read(Randoms,WorkArray[Counter]);
```

(continues)

```
139              Counter := Succ(Counter)
140           END;
141        Close(Randoms);
142        Write('...sorting...');
143        IF Shell THEN ShellSort(WorkArray,Counter-1)
144           ELSE QuickSort(WorkArray,Counter-1);
145        Write('...writing...');
146        Rewrite(Randoms);
147        FOR I := 1 TO Counter-1 DO Write(Randoms,WorkArray[I]);
148        Close(Randoms);
149        Writeln('...done!');
150        WriteAt(-1,21,NoHighlite,NoCR,'>>Press (CR)<<');
151        Readln;
152        ClearRegion(2,15,77,22)
153     END;
154
155
156
157     BEGIN
158        ClrScr;
159        CursorOff;
160        DefineChars(GrafChars);
161        MakeBox(1,1,80,24,GrafChars);
162        WriteAt(24,3,HighLite,NoCR,'THE COMPLETE TURBO PASCAL SORT DEMO');
163        REPEAT
164           WriteAt(25,5,NoHighlite,NoCR,'[1] Generate file of random keys');
165           WriteAt(25,6,NoHighlite,NoCR,'[2] Display file of random keys');
166           WriteAt(25,7,NoHighlite,NoCR,'[3] Sort file via Shell sort');
167           WriteAt(25,8,NoHighlite,NoCR,'[4] Sort file via Quicksort');
168           WriteAt(30,10,NoHighlite,NoCR,'Enter 1-4: ');
169           Response := ''; IVal := 0;
170           GetString(46,10,Response,2,CapsLock,Numeric,GetInteger,
171                     R,IVal,Error,Escape);
172           CASE IVal OF
173              0 :;
174              1 : GenerateRandomKeyFile(250);
175              2 : DisplayKeys;
176              3 : DoSort(Shell);
```

(continues)

```
177              4 : DoSort(Quick);
178            ELSE
179          END; {CASE}
180        UNTIL (IVal = 0) OR Escape;
181        CursorOn
182      END.
```

(concluded)

How to use strings

ISO Standard Pascal lacks a "clean" way to deal with text. There is no **String** type in ISO Pascal; to work with strings in ISO Pascal you must confine your text to arrays of characters, keep your own logical length counters, and write all the procedures for manipulating strings yourself.

Given the pervasiveness of text in the work that computers do, it is not surprising that most implementors of Pascal have extended the language by providing a **String** data type and some built-in procedures and functions to manipulate strings.

Turbo Pascal is no exception. We looked at the **String** data type in Section 9.5. A **String** variable is actually an array of characters with a counter attached to keep tabs on how many characters have been loaded into the array. You define a string type by using the word **String** followed by the maximum physical length of the string (up to 255) in brackets. For example:

```
TYPE
    String80 = String[80];
```

The type **String80** is actually 81 physical bytes long. Byte 0 is the counter. It can hold a number from 0 to 80. Bytes 1 through 80 hold the actual text characters that make up the string.

When you assign a string literal to a string variable, the length counter is automatically updated to reflect the number of characters assigned:

```
VAR
  MyText : String80;

MyText := '';
MyText := 'Let the wookie win.';
```

Before the text assignment, **MyText** had been assigned the null string (' ') and its length counter was 0. After the assignment, the length counter was automatically updated to 19.

Turbo Pascal provides a number of powerful string procedures and functions for manipulating text stored in strings. In the next section we'll look at each in detail.

15.1   Built-in string procedures and functions

LENGTH

The length counter of a string variable is accessible two ways. One way is simply to examine element 0 of the string:

```
Count := Ord(MyText[0]);
```

This will put the length counter of string **MyText** into the integer variable **Count**. The length counter of string variables, just like the data in the string itself, is type **Char**, which needs the transfer function **Ord** to be assigned to an integer.

A somewhat better way is to use the predefined function **Length**. It is a built-in function predefined this way:

```
FUNCTION Length(Target : String) : Integer;
```

Length returns the value of the length counter byte, which indicates the logical length of string **Target**:

```
Count := Length(MyText);
```

This is functionally equivalent to accessing the length byte directly and is somewhat easier to read. **Length** is a function that returns an integer value.

The length of the null string (' ') is 0.

The following procedure **CapsLock** is a variation of a procedure originally presented in Chapter 9 in connection with sets. **CapsLock** accepts a string parameter and returns it with all lower case letters changed to their corresponding upper case letters. Note the use of the **Length** function:

```
1          {<<<< Capslock >>>>}
2
3
4
5
6          PROCEDURE Capslock(VAR MyString : String255);
7
8          VAR
9            I : Integer;
10
11         BEGIN
12           FOR I := 1 TO Length(MyString) DO
13             MyString[I] := UpCase(MyString[I]
14         END
```

This **CapsLock** makes use of a convenient Turbo Pascal built-in function, **UpCase**. **UpCase** accepts a character value as a parameter and returns the uppercase equivalent of that character, if the parameter is lowercase. If the parameter is not a lowercase character it is returned unchanged.

CONCAT

Concatenation is the process of taking two or more strings and combining them into a single string. Turbo Pascal gives you two separate ways to perform this operation.

The easiest way to concatenate two or more strings is to use Turbo Pascal's string concatenation operator (+). Many BASIC interpreters also use the plus symbol to concatenate strings. Simply place the string variables in order, separated by the string concatenation operator:

```
BigString := String1 + String2 + String3 + String4;
```

String variable **BigString** should, of course, be large enough to hold all the variables you intend to concatenate into it. If the total length of all the source strings is greater than the physical length of the destination string, all data that will not fit into the destination string is truncated and ignored. If the total length of the source strings is greater than 255, runtime error #10 occurs.

The built-in function **Concat** performs the same function as the string concatenation operator. It is included in Turbo Pascal because several older Pascal compilers (notably UCSD Pascal and Pascal/MT+) use a **Concat** function and do not have a string concatenation operator. **Concat** is a function returning a value of type **String**. It accepts any number of string variables and string literals as parameters, separated by commas.

The following example shows how both string concatenation methods work:

```
VAR
   Subject,Predicate,Sentence : String[80];

Subject := 'Kevin the hacker';
Predicate := 'crashed the system';
```

(continues)

```
Sentence  := Subject + Predicate;
Sentence :=
  Concat(Sentence,', but brought it up again.');
Writeln(Sentence);
```

(concluded)

Here, two string variables and a string literal are concatenated into a single string variable. The CRT output of the **Writeln** statement would be the concatenated string:

```
Kevin the hacker crashed the system, but brought it up again.
```

DELETE

Removing one or more characters from a string is the job done by the built-in **Delete** procedure, predefined this way:

```
PROCEDURE Delete(Target : String; Pos,Num : Integer);
```

Delete removes **Num** characters from the string **Target** beginning at character number **Pos**. The length counter of **Target** is updated to reflect the deleted characters.

```
VAR
  Magic : String;

Magic := 'Watch me make an elephant disappear...';
Delete(Magic,15,11);
Writeln(Magic);
```

Before the **Delete** operation, the string **Magic** has a length of 38 characters. When run, this example will display:

```
Watch me make disappear...
```

The new length of **Magic** is set to 27.

One use of **Delete** is to remove "leading whitespace" from a string variable. Whitespace is a set of characters that includes space, tab, carriage return, and linefeed. Whitespace is used to format text files for readability by human beings. However, when that text file is read by computer, the whitespace must be removed, as it tells the computer nothing.

The following procedure strips leading whitespace from a string variable:

```
PROCEDURE StripWhite(VAR Target : String255);

CONST
  Whitespace : SET OF Char = [#8,#10,#12,#13,' '];

BEGIN
  WHILE (Length(Target) > 0) AND (Target[1] IN Whitespace) DO
    Delete(Target,1,1)
END;
```

Whitespace is a set constant (see Section 9.6) containing the whitespace characters. Set constants are a feature unique to Turbo Pascal—keep that in mind if you intend to export your code to another Pascal compiler.

Delete(Target,1,1) deletes one character from the beginning of string **Target**. The second character is then moved up to take its place. If it, too, is a whitespace character it is also deleted, and so on until a non-whitespace character becomes the first character in **Target**, or until **Target** is emptied of characters completely.

POS

Locating a substring within a larger string is handled by the built-in function **Pos**. **Pos** is predefined this way:

```
FUNCTION
  Pos(Pattern : <string or char>; Source : String) : Integer;
```

Pos returns an integer that is the location of the first occurrence of **Pattern** in **Source**. **Pattern** may be a string variable, a **Char** variable, or a string or character literal.
For example:

```
VAR
   ChX,ChY   : Char;
   Little,Big : String;

Big := 'I am an American, Chicago-born. Chicago, that somber city.'
Little := 'Chicago';
ChX := 'g';
ChY := 'G';

Writeln('The position of ',Little,' in "Big" is ',Pos(Little,Big));
Writeln('The position of ',ChX,' in "Big" is ',Pos(ChX,Big));
Writeln('The position of ',ChY,' in "Big" is ',Pos(ChY,Big));
Writeln('The position of somber in "Big" is ',Pos('somber',Big));
Writeln('The position of r in "Big" is ',Pos('r',Big));
```

When executed, this example code will display the following:

```
The position of Chicago in "Big" is 19
The position of g in "Big" is 24
The position of G in "Big" is 0
The position of somber in "Big" is 48
The position of r in "Big" is 12
```

Pos does distinguish between upper and lower case letters. Note that if **Pos** cannot locate **Pattern** in **Source**, it returns a value of 0.

COPY

Extracting a substring from within a string is accomplished with the **Copy** built-in function. **Copy** is predefined this way:

```
FUNCTION Copy(Source : String; Pos,Num : Integer) : String;
```

Copy returns a string that contains **Size** characters from **Source**, beginning at character #**Index** within **Source**:

```
VAR
  Roland,Tower : String80;

Roland := 'Childe Roland to the Dark Tower came!';
Tower := Copy(Roland,22,10);
Writeln(Tower);
```

When run, this example will print:

```
Dark Tower
```

In this example, **Index** and **Size** are passed to **Copy** as constants. They can also be passed as integer variables or expressions. The following function accepts a string containing a file name, and returns a string value containing the file extension. (The extension is the part of a file name from the period to the end; in "TURBO.COM" the extension is ".COM").

```
1    {<<<< GetExt >>>>}
2
3
4
5
6    FUNCTION GetExt(FileName : String80) : String80;
7
8    VAR
9      DotPos : Integer;
10
```

(continues)

```
11          BEGIN
12            DotPos := Pos('.',FileName);
13            IF DotPos = 0 THEN GetExt := '' ELSE
14              GetExt := Copy(FileName,DotPos,(Length(FileName)-DotPos)+1)
15          END;
```

(concluded)

GetExt first tests to see if there is, in fact, a period in **FileName** at all. (File extensions are optional.) If there is no period, there is no extension, and **GetExt** is assigned the null string. If a period is there, **Copy** is used to assign to **GetExt** all characters from the period to the end of the string.

Since the length of a file extension may be 2, 3, or 4 characters, the expression (**Length(FileName)**-**DotPos**)+1 is needed to calculate just how long the extension is in each particular case.

Note that unlike most Pascal compilers (such as Pascal/MT+ and UCSD Pascal), Turbo Pascal allows you to write functions that return string values. Turbo Pascal is the only microcomputer Pascal compiler I know of that allows this; you should keep it in mind if portability is an important consideration to you.

If **Index** plus **Size** is greater than the logical length of **Source**, **Copy** truncates the returned string value to whatever characters lie between **Index** and the end of the string.

INSERT

A string can be added to the end of another string by using the **Concat** function. Copying a string into the middle of another string (and not simply tacking it on at the end) is done with the **Insert** procedure.

Insert is predefined this way:

```
PROCEDURE Insert(Source     : String;
                 VAR Target : String;
                 Pos        : Integer);
```

When invoked, **Insert** copies **Source** into **Target** starting at position **Pos** within **Target**. All characters in **Target** starting at position

Pos are moved forward to make room for the inserted string, and **Target**'s length counter is updated to reflect the addition of the inserted characters.

```
VAR
   Sentence,Ozzie : String [80];

Sentence := 'I am King of Kings.';
Ozzie := 'Ozymandias, ';
Insert(Ozzie,Sentence,6);
Writeln(Sentence);
```

The output from this example would be:

```
I am Ozymandias, King of Kings.
```

If inserting text into **Target** gives **Target** more characters than it can physically contain, **Target** is truncated to its maximum physical length:

```
VAR
   Fickle,GOP : String[18];

Fickle := 'I am a Democrat.';
GOP := 'Republican.';
Insert(GOP,Fickle,8);
Writeln(Fickle);
```

This prints:

```
I am a Republican.
```

Note in this example that the word "Democrat." was not overwritten; it was pushed off the end of string **Fickle** into nothingness. After the insert, **Fickle** should have contained

```
I am a Republican.Democrat.
```

however, **Fickle**, defined as **String[18]**, is only 18 physical characters long. "I am a Republican." fills it completely. "Democrat." was lost to truncation.

STR It is important to remember (and easy enough to forget) that a number and its string equivalent are *not* interchangeable. In other words, the integer 37 and its string representation, the two ASCII characters '3' and '7' look the same on your screen but are completely incompatible in all ways but that.

Unlike most other Pascals, Turbo Pascal provides a pair of procedures for translating numeric values into their string equivalents, and vice versa.

Translating a numeric value to its string equivalent is done with the procedure **Str**. **Str** is predefined this way:

```
PROCEDURE Str(<formatted numeric value>; VAR ST : String);
```

The formatted numeric value can be either an integer or a string. It is given as a "write parameter" (see Section 18.4 for a complete discussion of write parameters as they apply to all simple data types, numeric and non-numeric). Briefly, a write parameter is an expression that gives a numeric value and a format to express it in. The write parameter I:7 (assuming I was previously declared an integer) right-justifies the value of I in a field seven characters wide. R:9:3 (assuming R was declared **Real** previously) right-justifies the value of R in a field nine characters wide with three figures to the right of the decimal place.

The use of **Str** is best shown by a few examples:

```
CONST
  Bar = '|';

VAR
  R  : Real;
  I  : Integer;
  TX : String[30];

R := 45612.338;
I := 21244;

Str(I:8,TX);
Writeln(Bar,TX,Bar); { Displays:  |   21244| }

Str(I:3,TX);
Writeln(Bar,TX,Bar); { Displays:  |21244|  }

Str(R,TX);
Writeln(Bar,TX,Bar); { Displays:  |   4.5612338000E+04| }

Str(R:13:4,TX);
Writeln(Bar,TX,Bar); { Displays:  |   45612.3380| }
```

Note from the third example that if you do not specify any format for a real number, the default format will be scientific notation in a field 18 characters wide.

VAL

Going in the other direction, from string representation to numeric value, is accomplished by the **Val** procedure. **Val** is predeclared this way:

```
VAL(ST : String; VAR <numeric variable>; VAR Code : Integer);
```

Val's task is somewhat more complicated than **Str**'s. For every numeric value there is a string representation that may be constructed. The reverse is not true; there are many string constructions that cannot be evaluated as numbers. Thus, **Val** must have a means of returning an error code to signal an input string that cannot be evaluated to a number. This is the purpose of the **Code** parameter.

If the string is evaluated without any problem, **Code**'s value is 0 and the numeric equivalent of the string is returned in the numeric variable. If Turbo Pascal finds that it cannot evaluate the string to a number, **Code** returns the character position of the first character that does not jibe with Turbo Pascal's evaluation scheme. The numeric variable in that case is undefined:

```
1      {---------------------------------------------------------}
2      {                       Evaluator                          }
3      {                                                          }
4      {      String/numeric conversion demonstration program     }
5      {                                                          }
6      {                              by Jeff Duntemann            }
7      {                              Turbo Pascal V3.0            }
8      {                              Last update 1/31/86          }
9      {                                                          }
10     {                                                          }
11     {                                                          }
12     {---------------------------------------------------------}
13
14     PROGRAM Evaluator;
15
16     VAR
17       SST    : String;
18       R      : Real;
19       Result : Integer;
20
21     BEGIN
22       REPEAT
23         Write('>>Enter a number in string form: ');
24         Readln(SST);
25         IF Length(SST) > 0 THEN
26           BEGIN
27             Val(SST,R,Result);
28             IF Result <> 0 THEN
29               Writeln
```

(continues)

```
30                    ('>>Cannot evaluate that string.  Check character #',Result)
31                ELSE
32                    Writeln
33                    ('>>The numeric equivalent of that string is ',R:18:10)
34            END
35       UNTIL Length(SST) = 0
36    END.
```

(concluded)

This little program will allow you to experiment with **Val** and see what it will accept and what it will reject. One shortcoming of **Val** is that *it considers commas an error*. A string like '5,462,445.3' will generate an error on character #2.

In the next section we will be using **Val** in slightly more sophisticated surroundings to build a generalized data entry routine.

One caution on using **Str** and **Val**: If you use them in the definition of a function, that function must *never* be invoked from within a **Write** or **Writeln** statement. In order words, avoid constructs like these:

```
FUNCTION Eval(SST : String80) : Real;

BEGIN
  Val(SST,R,Result);
  IF Result <> 0 THEN Eval := R
END;

Writeln('The number is: ',Eval(SST));
```

This applies *only* to Z80 versions of Turbo Pascal. The reason for this restriction is subtle: Both **Writeln** and **Val** use the same code to handle number/string conversions, and Turbo's Z80 code is *not* re-entrant in this case. When a routine is not re-entrant, it cannot be invoked from within itself.

BUILT-IN STRING ROUTINE SUMMARY

Built-in string-handling routines
FUNCTION Concat(Source1,Source2...SourceN : String) : String
FUNCTION Copy(Source : String; Index,Size : Integer) : String
PROCEDURE Delete(Target : String; Index,Size : Integer)

PROCEDURE Insert(Source   : String;
                VAR Target : String;
                Index   : Integer)

FUNCTION Length(Source : String) : Integer
FUNCTION Pos(Pattern : String or Char;   Source : String) : Integer
PROCEDURE Str(Num : ‹write parameter›, VAR StrEquiv : String)

PROCEDURE Val(Source   : String;
             VAR NumEquiv : ‹Integer or Real›;
             VAR Code   : Integer)

15.2   A string input procedure

Pascal provides only one built-in way to enter a string from the system console. **Readln** will accept a string from the keyboard, waiting for characters to be typed until (CR) is pressed. While **Readln** is waiting for input, you can backspace over mistyped characters. This is a fairly typical example of entering a string from the console using **Readln**:

```
VAR
  Buff10 : String[10];

Write('Type up to 10 letters: ');
Readln(Buff10);
```

Here, once you've typed 10 letters, **Readln** will allow you to type as many more as you like. However, it will only return as many characters as the string has room for. If you have set up a complicated data entry form on your CRT, nothing will stop the operator from typing beyond the right boundary of any field and disrupting other fields to the right.

What you need is a slightly more disciplined string input routine. Ideally, such a routine should show you how large the string can be, accept characters up to that limit, and then ignore further characters until previous characters are deleted with backspace, or until (CR) or ESC is pressed.

The following string input routine does all this and more. First, read it over and try to understand how it works:

```
1        {<<<< GetString >>>>}
2
3
4        { Described in section 15.2 -- Last mod 2/1/86   }
5
6        PROCEDURE GetString(    X,Y      : Integer;
7                            VAR XString  : String80;
8                                MaxLen   : Integer;
9                                Capslock : Boolean;
10                               Numeric  : Boolean;
11                               GetReal  : Boolean;
12                           VAR RValue   : Real;
13                           VAR IValue   : Integer;
14                           VAR Error    : Integer;
15                           VAR Escape   : Boolean);
16
17
18       VAR I,J       : Integer;
19           Ch        : Char;
20           Cursor    : Char;
21           Dot       : Char;
22           BLength   : Byte;
```

(continues)

```
23              ClearIt    : String80;
24              Worker     : String80;
25              Printables : SET OF Char;
26              Lowercase  : SET OF Char;
27              Numerics   : SET OF Char;
28              CR         : Boolean;
29
30
31          BEGIN
32            Printables := [' '..'}'];                { Init sets }
33            Lowercase  := ['a'..'z'];
34            IF GetReal THEN Numerics := ['-','.','0'..'9','E','e']
35              ELSE Numerics := ['-','0'..'9'];
36            Cursor := '_'; Dot := '.';
37            CR := False; Escape := False;
38            FillChar(ClearIt,SizeOf(ClearIt),'.'); { Fill the clear string }
39            ClearIt[0] := Chr(MaxLen);             { Set clear string to MaxLen }
40
41                                      { Convert numbers to string if required: }
42            IF Numeric THEN           { Convert zero values to null string: }
43              IF (GetReal AND (RValue = 0.0)) OR
44                (NOT GetReal AND (IValue = 0)) THEN XString := ''
45              ELSE                    { Convert nonzero values to string equiv: }
46                IF GetReal THEN Str(RValue:MaxLen,XString)
47                  ELSE Str(IValue:MaxLen,XString);
48
49                                              { Truncate string value to MaxLen }
50            IF Length(XString) > MaxLen THEN XString[0] := Chr(MaxLen);
51            GotoXY(X,Y); Write('|',ClearIt,'|');    { Draw the field }
52            GotoXY(X+1,Y); Write(XString);
53            IF Length(XString)<MaxLen THEN
54              BEGIN
55                GotoXY(X + Length(XString) + 1,Y);
56                Write(Cursor)                       { Draw the Cursor }
57              END;
58            Worker := XString;       { Fill work string with input string     }
59
60            REPEAT                   { Until ESC or (CR) entered }
```

(continues)

```
61                                  { Wait here for keypress:   }
62              WHILE NOT KeyStat(Ch) DO BEGIN {NULL} END;
63
64              IF Ch IN Printables THEN           { If Ch is printable... }
65                IF Length(Worker) >= MaxLen THEN UhUh ELSE
66                  IF Numeric AND (NOT (Ch IN Numerics)) THEN UhUh ELSE
67                    BEGIN
68                       IF Ch IN Lowercase THEN IF Capslock THEN Ch := Chr(Ord(Ch)-32);
69                       Worker := CONCAT(Worker,Ch);
70                       GotoXY(X+1,Y); Write(Worker);
71                       IF Length(Worker) < MaxLen THEN Write(Cursor)
72                    END
73              ELSE   { If Ch is NOT printable... }
74                CASE Ord(Ch) OF
75                8,127 : IF Length(Worker) <= 0 THEN UhUH ELSE
76                        BEGIN
77                           Delete(Worker,Length(Worker),1);
78                           GotoXY(X+1,Y); Write(Worker,Cursor);
79                           IF Length(Worker) < MaxLen-1 THEN Write(Dot);
80                        END;
81
82                13 : CR := True;          { Carriage return }
83
84                24 : BEGIN               { CTRL-X : Blank the field }
85                        GotoXY(X+1,Y); Write(ClearIt);
86                        Worker := '';     { Blank out work string }
87                     END;
88
89                27 : Escape := True;      { ESC }
90                ELSE UhUh                 { CASE ELSE }
91              END; { CASE }
92
93              UNTIL CR OR Escape;         { Get keypresses until (CR) or }
94                                          { ESC pressed }
95              GotoXY(X + 1,Y); Write(ClearIt);
96              GotoXY(X + 1,Y); Write(Worker);
97              IF CR THEN                  { Don't update XString if ESC hit }
98                BEGIN
```

(continues)

```
99              XString := Worker;
100             IF Numeric THEN              { Convert string to Numeric values }
101               CASE GetReal OF
102                 True  : Val(Worker,RValue,Error);
103                 False : Val(Worker,IValue,Error)
104               END { CASE }
105             ELSE
106               BEGIN
107                 RValue := 0.0;
108                 IValue := 0
109               END
110           END
111
112       END;  { GETString }
```

(concluded)

This routine makes use of the **GotoXY** procedure to locate the cursor on your CRT screen. Turbo Pascal's CRT control procedures are described in Section 17.1.

GetString begins by drawing a field on the screen. The field consists of two vertical bar characters (ASCII character 124) with periods between them. The number of periods is the maximum length of the string you wish to enter, passed to **GetString** in **MaxLen**:

```
|.........................|
```

This example would be drawn for a **MaxLen** value of 25. The left vertical bar character is located at X,Y on the screen.

GetString can accept a string value to edit in the parameter **XString**. If **XString** has anything in it, those characters are displayed left-justified in the field:

```
|I am a man of letters....|
```

GetString then positions an underscore character for a cursor immediately after the displayed characters, or at the left margin if no characters were displayed:

```
|I am a man of letters_...|
```

At this point, **GetString** begins to accept typed characters. No **Read** or **Readln** statements are used in this procedure at all. A DOS call is performed in a tight loop to test for a keypress. If a key was pressed, the **MSDOS** or **BDOS** function (see Section 20.6) returns the character pressed; if no key was pressed, it returns character 0.

Once a keypress is accepted, **GetString** decides if it is printable or not. Control characters (ASCII 1 to 31) are never printable. If the **Numerics** parameter is **True**, only digits, decimal points, the letter 'E', and minus signs will be accepted as printable. Then, after the string has been completed by the entry of (CR), **Val** evaluates the string and places the value in **Value**.

If the **CapsLock** parameter is **True**, lowercase letters will be forced to become uppercase as they are entered.

Only a few control characters are obeyed. (CR) will end string entry and replace the previous contents of **XString** with the entered string. ESC will end string entry but leave **XString** the same as it was on entry. CTRL-X (CANcel) clears the entire string to zero length and erases it from the displayed field. BS and DEL destructively backspace over one character.

Any character that is not printable and not a recognized control character causes the **UhUh** procedure (see Section 16.11) to be invoked, signalling to the user that a keypress was ignored. Trying to backspace past the left margin of the field will trigger an error signal, as will trying to enter more characters than the field will hold.

**USING
GETSTRING
FOR SCREEN
DATA ENTRY**

GetString is the most complex piece of Pascal code we've examined so far. If you intend to write a lot of programs that interact extensively with the user, you might also find it one of the most useful tools in your software toolbox. It makes the programming of interactive data-entry screens neat and easy.

For many years all computer interaction was done on the "glass teletype" model: Computer and user took turns typing their halves of a dialog on the bottom line of a terminal, with the screen scrolling up one line after each took his turn.

Much tidier is the notion of a data entry screen. The computer "paints" one or more fields on a cleared screen, and then the user fills in the fields in some well-defined order. The computer uses some reserved portion of the screen (usually the top or bottom lines) to send messages to the user.

The following program is a simple example of a data entry screen, using the **GetString** procedure to provide several fields for the user to fill in. Nothing is done with the information after it is accepted, but in a functional program of this type the data is typically stored in a file.

GetString is another good example of hiding detail in a Pascal program. If you're programming a data entry screen, what's important is what data fields are being entered and what is done with them afterward. The excruciating details of accepting a string character-by-character and converting it (if necessary) into a numeric value are not necessary to understanding the logic of the data entry screen. The details are shoved off into a black box named **GetString**, where they will not interfere with the clarity of the code that handles the data itself.

```
 1        {--------------------------------------------------------}
 2        {                         Screen                         }
 3        {                                                        }
 4        {              Full-screen input demo program            }
 5        {                                                        }
 6        {                         by Jeff Duntemann             }
 7        {                         Turbo Pascal V3.0              }
 8        {                         Last update 2/1/86             }
 9        {                                                        }
10        {                                                        }
11        {                                                        }
12        {--------------------------------------------------------}
13
```

(continues)

```
14
15        PROGRAM Screen;
16
17        {$V-}  { Allow length mismatch for string VAR parameters.  See 23.4 }
18
19        CONST
20          Capslock     = True;
21          NoCapslock   = False;
22          Numeric      = True;
23          NonNumeric   = False;
24
25        TYPE
26          String80 = String[80];
27          String30 = String[30];
28          String6  = String[6];
29          String4  = String[4];
30          String3  = String[3];
31
32          NAPRec   = RECORD
33                        Name    : String30;
34                        Address : String30;
35                        City    : String30;
36                        State   : String3;
37                        Zip     : String6
38                     END;
39
40        TYPE
41          GrafRec = RECORD
42                        ULCorner,
43                        URCorner,
44                        LLCorner,
45                        LRCorner,
46                        HBar,
47                        VBar,
48                        LineCross,
49                        TDown,
50                        TUp,
51                        TRight,
```

(continues)

```
52                        TLeft : String[4]
53                 END;
54
55
56        VAR
57           CH             : Char;
58           CurrentRecord : NAPRec;
59           GrafChars     : GRAFREC;
60           Edit          : Boolean;
61           Quit          : Boolean;
62           Escape        : Boolean;
63           WIDTH,HEIGHT  : Integer;
64           I,J           : Integer;
65           R             : Real;
66
67
68        {$I UHUH.SRC }       { Described in Section 16.11 }
69        {$I MAKEBOX.SRC}     { Described in Section 14.1 }
70        {$I CURSOFF.SRC }    { Described in Section 17.2 }
71        {$I MONOTEST.SRC }   { Described in Section 17.2 }
72        {$I CURSON.SRC }     { Described in Section 17.2 }
73        {$I YES.SRC }        { Described in Section 17.2 }
74        {$I KEYSTAT.SRC }    { Described in Section 20.6 }
75        {$I GETSTRIN.SRC }   { Described in Section 15.2 }
76
77
78        PROCEDURE GetScreen(VAR ScreenData : NAPRec;
79                                 Edit       : Boolean;
80                            VAR Escape     : Boolean);
81
82        BEGIN
83          MakeBox(1,1,79,20,GrafChars);          { Draw the screen box }
84          IF NOT Edit THEN WITH ScreenData DO  { If not editing, clear record }
85            BEGIN
86              Name := ''; Address := ''; City := ''; State := ''; Zip := ''
87            END;
88          GotoXY(23,2);
89          Writeln('<< Name / Address Entry Screen >>');
```

(continues)

```
90          WITH ScreenData DO
91            BEGIN                        { First draw field frames: }
92              GotoXY(5,7);
93              Write('>>Customer Name:     |.............................|');
94              GotoXY(5,9);
95              Write('>>Customer Address: |.............................|');
96              GotoXY(5,11);
97              Write('>>Customer City:     |.............................|');
98              GotoXY(5,13);
99              Write('>>Customer State:    |...|');
100             GotoXY(5,15);
101             Write('>>Customer Zip:      |......| ');
102             IF Edit THEN WITH ScreenData DO  { If editing, show current values }
103               BEGIN
104                 GotoXY(26,7);  Write(Name);
105                 GotoXY(26,9);  Write(Address);
106                 GotoXY(26,11); Write(City);
107                 GotoXY(26,13); Write(State);
108                 GotoXY(26,15); Write(Zip)
109               END;                        { Now input/Edit field data: }
110             GetString(25,7,Name,30,NoCapslock,NonNumeric,False,R,I,J,Escape);
111             IF NOT Escape THEN
112               GetString(25,9,Address,30,NoCapslock,NonNumeric,False,R,I,J,Escape);
113             IF NOT Escape THEN
114               GetString(25,11,City,30,NoCapslock,NonNumeric,False,R,I,J,Escape);
115             IF NOT Escape THEN
116               GetString(25,13,State,3,Capslock,NonNumeric,False,R,I,J,Escape);
117             IF NOT Escape THEN
118               GetString(25,15,Zip,6,Capslock,NonNumeric,False,R,I,J,Escape);
119           END
120       END;
121
122
123       BEGIN        { SCREEN MAIN }
124         DefineChars(GrafChars);        { Load box drawing characters }
125         Edit := False;
126         CursorOff;
127         REPEAT
```

(continues)

```
128              ClrScr;
129              GetScreen(CurrentRecord,Edit,Escape);   { Input/Edit a data screen }
130              IF Escape THEN Quit := True ELSE        { Quit if ESC pressed }
131                BEGIN                                 { Otherwise summarize data }
132                  Quit := False;                      { and ask for approval }
133                  GotoXY(1,22);
134                  Write('>>Summary: ');
135                  WITH CurrentRecord DO
136                    BEGIN
137                      Write(Name,'/',Address,'/',Zip);
138                      GotoXY(1,23); Write('>>OK? (Y/N): ');
139                      IF YES THEN Edit := False ELSE Edit := True
140                    END
141                END
142            UNTIL Quit;
143            ClrScr;
144            CursorOn
145          END.
146
```

(concluded)

15.3 More examples of string manipulation

Perhaps the first ambitious program most beginning programmers attempt is a name/address/phone number manager. Sooner or later, in designing such a program, the problem comes up: How to sort the list on the name field, when names are stored first name first and sorted last name first?

Storing the first name in a separate field is no answer—suppose you want to store The First National Bank of East Rochester? What is its first name?

The best solution I have found is to store the name last name first, when an asterisk (*) separating the last and first names. For example, Jeff Duntemann would be stored as Duntemann*Jeff. Clive Staples Lewis would be stored as Lewis*Clive Staples. Names maintained in this order are easily sorted by last name. All we need is a routine to turn the inside-out name rightside-in again.

The following routine does just that—and uses **Pos**, **Copy**, **Delete**, and **Concat**, all in four lines!

```
1     {<<<< RvrsName >>>>}
2     { From: COMPLETE TURBO PASCAL by Jeff Duntemann  }
3
4
5
6     PROCEDURE RvrsName(VAR Name : String);
7
8     VAR
9       TName : String;
10
11    BEGIN
12      IF Pos('*',Name) <> 0 THEN
13        BEGIN
14          TName := Copy(Name,1,(Pos('*',Name)-1));
15          Delete(Name,1,Pos('*',Name));
16          Name := Concat(Name,' ',TName)
17        END
18    END;
```

The theory is simple: If there is no asterisk in the name, it's something like "Granny Maria's Pizza Palace" and needs no reversal. Hence the first test. If an asterisk is found, the last name up to (but not including) the asterisk is copied from **Name** into **TName**, a temporary string. Then the last name is deleted from **Name**, up to *and* including the asterisk. What remains in **Name** is thus the first name. Finally, concatenate **TName** (containing the last name) to **Name** with a space to separate them. The name is now in its proper first-name-first form.

A CASE ADJUSTER FUNCTION FOR STRINGS

Turbo Pascal provides a built-in character function called **UpCase**, predeclared this way:

```
FUNCTION UpCase(Ch : Char) : Char;
```

UpCase accepts a character **Ch** and returns its uppercase equivalent as the function return value. If **Ch** is already uppercase, or a character with no uppercase equivalent (numerals, symbols, and so on), the character is returned unchanged.

UpCase is a character function, but it suggests that a string function could be built that accepts an arbitrary string value and returns that value converted to uppercase. And although no "downcase" function exists in Turbo Pascal, an equivalent is not hard to put together. A two-way case adjuster function looks like this:

```
1    {<<<< ForceCase >>>>}
2
3
4    { Described in section 15.3 -- Last mod 2/1/86   }
5
6    FUNCTION ForceCase(Up : BOOLEAN; Target : String255) : String255;
7
8    CONST
9      Uppercase : SET OF Char = ['A'..'Z'];
10     Lowercase : SET OF Char = ['a'..'z'];
11
12   VAR
13     I : INTEGER;
14
15   BEGIN
16     IF Up THEN FOR I := 1 TO Length(Target) DO
17       IF Target[I] IN Lowercase THEN
18         Target[I] := UpCase(Target[I])
19       ELSE { NULL }
20     ELSE FOR I := 1 TO Length(Target) DO
21       IF Target[I] IN Uppercase THEN
22         Target[I] := Chr(Ord(Target[I])+32);
23     ForceCase := Target
24   END;
```

If you're new to Pascal in general, you may not notice anything strange about this function, but Pascal old-timers will notice that Turbo Pascal is one of the few (if not the only) Pascal implementation that allows user-defined functions to return string values.

In Turbo Pascal, functions may return string values the same as any other values. However, the string type must have been declared before the declaration of your string function. In other words, if you wish your function to return a string with a physical length of 255 (always a good idea) you must have declared a string type with that physical length:

```
TYPE
    String255 = String[255];
```

You *cannot* use the bracketed string-length notation on a string function return value. That is, you could not have declared **ForceCase** this way:

```
FUNCTION ForceCase(Up : Boolean; Target : String255) :
        String[255];          { Invalid! }
```

ForceCase will convert all uppercase characters in a string to lowercase, or all lowercase characters in a string to uppercase, depending on the Boolean value of parameter **Up**. If **Up** is true, lower case is forced to uppercase. Otherwise, uppercase is forced to lowercase. The string **Target** is scanned from character 1 to its last character, and any necessary conversion of character case is done character-by-character. The "downcase" function is done by taking advantage of the ordering of the ASCII character set, in that lower-case characters have an ASCII value 32 higher than their uppercase counterparts. Add 32 to the ordinal value of an uppercase character, and you have the ordinal value of its lowercase equivalent.

Also note that although the parameter string **Target** is modified during the scan, the modifications are not made to the actual parameter itself, since **Target** was passed by value, not by reference. **ForceCase** received its own private copy of **Target**, which it could safely change without altering the "real" **Target**. (See Section 14.2 for more on the passing of parameters by value or by reference.)

ACCESSING COMMAND-LINE STRINGS

Most operating systems allow some sort of program access to the command line tail; that is, the optional text that may be typed after the program name when invoking a program from the operating system command prompt:

```
A>CASE DOWN B:FOOFILE.TXT
```

In this example, the characters typed after the program name "CASE" constitute the command line tail:

```
DOWN B:FOOFILE.TXT
```

Turbo Pascal provides a very convenient (and operating system independent) method of getting access to the command tail. Two predefined functions are connected with the command line tail: **ParamCount** and **ParamStr**. They are predeclared this way:

```
FUNCTION ParamCount : Integer;
FUNCTION ParamStr(ParameterNumber : Integer) : String;
```

The function **ParamCount** returns the number of parameters typed after the command on the operating system command line. Parameters must have been separated by spaces or tab characters to be considered separate parameters. Commas, slashes, and other symbols will *not* delimit separate parameters!

ParamStr returns a string value that is one of the parameters. The number of the parameter is specified by **ParameterNumber**, starting from 1. If you typed several parameters on the command line, for example,

```
ParamStr(2)
```

will return the second parameter.

In CP/M, CP/M-86, and PC/MS DOS, you *must* read the command line tail before opening your first disk file! The same area used to store the tail is also used in buffer disk accesses in some cases. The best way to do this is to keep an array of strings large enough to hold the maximum number of parameters your program needs, and read the parameters into the array as soon as your program begins running. This is easy enough to do:

```
VAR
  I : Integer;
  ParmArray : ARRAY[1..8] OF String[80];

FOR I := 1 TO ParamCount DO
  ParmArray[I] := ParamStr(I);
```

Now you have the parameters safely in **ParmArray** and can examine and use them at your leisure.

For examples of **ParamCount** and **ParamStr** in use, see the **HexDump** program in Section 18.11 and the **Caser** program in Section 18.8.

Standard functions

The ISO Standard Pascal definition includes a number of "standard functions" that are built into the language and need not be declared and coded into your program. These functions fall into two basic groups: Mathematical functions, which provide fundamental operations such as square and square root, absolute value, natural logarithms, and trig functions; and transfer functions, which define relationships between otherwise incompatible data types like **Integer** and **Char**.

Many books refer to the parameter passed to a standard function as its "argument." This borrows jargon from the world of mathematics and may be confusing, since some people end up wondering what the difference is between an argument and a parameter. There is no difference other than the term. To lessen the confusion, I will use the term parameter, which we have been using with respect to functions all along.

All of the standard functions described in this section may accept expressions as parameters, as long as those expressions evaluate to a value of the correct type. In other words, you may say **Sqrt(Sqr(X)+Sqr(Y))** as well as **Sqrt(16)**. Just make sure you don't try to extract the square root of a **Boolean** value, or of an enumerated type, and so on.

Turbo Pascal implements all the standard functions from ISO Pascal. In this section we'll discuss them in detail.

16.1 Round and Trunc

Round and **Trunc** are fence-sitters. They are both mathematical functions, in the sense that they provide a mathematical service, and they are also transfer functions, in that they provide a bridge between the incompatible types **Real** and **Integer**.

We have already seen, in Section 12.2, that any integer value may be assigned to a variable of type **Real**. The reverse is not true, however, since a **Real** value may have a decimal part, and there is no way to express a decimal part in type **Integer**. **Round** and **Trunc** give us our choice of two ways to "transfer" a **Real** value into an **Integer** value. **Round** and **Trunc** both accept parameters of type **Real** and return values that may be assigned to either type **Integer** or **Real**.

ROUND

In mathematics, "rounding" a number means moving its value to the nearest integer. This is the job done by **Round**. **Round(X)** returns an integer value that is the integer closest to **X**. The direction in which a real number with a fractional part is rounded is usually given as "up" or "down." This can be confusing when you start dealing with negative real numbers. I prefer to visualize a number line and speak of "toward zero" or "away from zero."

For **X** *greater than* 0: Rounds *away from zero* (up) for fractional parts greater than or equal to .5; rounds *toward zero* (down) for fractional parts less than .5.

For **X** *less than* 0: Rounds *away from zero* (down) for fractional parts greater than or equal to .5; rounds *toward zero* (up) for fractional parts less than .5.

Some examples:

```
Round(4.449)     { Returns 4  }
Round(-6.12)     { Returns -6 }
Round(0.6)       { Returns 1  }
Round(-3.5)      { Returns -4 }
Round(17.5)      { Returns 18 }
```

Because the way **Round** works is symmetric with respect to zero, **Round(−X)** is equal to −**Round(X)**.

Note that using **Round(X)** for **X > MaxInt** will generate runtime Error #92: Out of integer range.

TRUNC

Truncating a real number simply means removing its fractional part and dealing with what's left. **Trunc(X)** returns the closest integer value *toward* zero—and if you ponder that for a moment you'll see that it is equivalent to removing the fractional part and calling the whole number part an integer. Examples:

```
Trunc(17.667)      { Returns 17 }
Trunc(-3.14)       { Returns -3 }
Trunc(6.5)         { Returns 6  }
Trunc(-229.00884)  { Returns -229 }
```

As with **Round**, invoking **Trunc(X)** with **X > MaxInt** will generate runtime error #92: Out of integer range. Sadly, this prevents you from using **Round** and **Trunc** on large real numbers, even if you intend to assign the resulting value to type **Real**. Turbo Pascal's internal runtime code actually generates the rounded or truncated value as an integer, hence the range restriction. Real numbers may be rounded and truncated using the Turbo Pascal functions **Frac** and **Int** (see Section 16.8).

16.2   Sqr and Sqrt

Nothing complicated here. **Sqr(X)** squares **X**. It is completely equivalent to **X * X**, and Pascal includes it because squaring is done so frequently in mathematics, and also because (as we will discuss later) there is no exponentiation operator in Pascal and hence no clean notation for **X** raised to a power of two.

Sqr may operate on both integers and reals. If you square an integer with **Sqr**, the returned value is an integer. If you square a real with **Sqr**, the returned value is real.

Sqrt(X) may also operate on either an integer or real **X**, but the value returned is *always* type **Real**.

A few examples:

```
CONST
  PI = 3.14159;

VAR
  I : Integer;
  R : Real;

I := 64;
R := 6.077;

Sqrt(16)       { Returns 4.0; a real number! }
Sqrt(PI)       { Returns 1.77245 }
Sqrt(I)        { Returns 64; real number }
Sqr(2.4)       { Returns 4.8; again, real }
Sqr(7)         { Returns 49; integer or real }
Sqr(I)         { Returns 4096; integer }
Sqr(R)         { Returns 36.92993; real }
```

The following procedure calculates the length of the hypotenuse of a right triangle, given the other two sides:

```
FUNCTION Hypotenuse(Side1,Side2 : Real ) : Real;

BEGIN
  Hypotenuse := Sqrt(Sqr(Side1) + Sqr(Side2))
END;
```

The algorithm, of course, is the Pythagorean Theorem.

16.3 Trigonometric functions

There are three trigonometric functions among the standard functions of Pascal: **Sin**, **Cos**, and **ArcTan**. Where are **Tan**, **ArcSin**, and all the others? Well, given **Sin**, **Cos**, and **ArcTan**, all other trigonometric functions are easily derived. Insisting that they be built into the compiler would make the compiler more complex and prone to errors. It would also make the Pascal language more cluttered than it has to be.

Sin(X), **Cos(X)**, and **ArcTan(X)** all return real results. **X** may, however, be an integer or a real number. Note well that *X represents radians, not degrees*. A radian equals 57.29578 degrees. Radians, however, are usually thought of in terms of pi (3.14159) and fractions of pi. 360 degrees = 2pi radians; 180 degrees = pi radians, and so on.

Pascal's trigonometric functions behave as you would expect from textbook discussions of trigonometry.

DERIVING OTHER TRIG-ONOMETRIC FUNCTIONS

With **Sin**, **Cos**, and **ArcTan**, one can build functions returning all other trigonometric relationships. For example:

```
FUNCTION Tan(X : Real) : Real;

BEGIN
  Tan := Sin(X) / Cos(X)
END;

FUNCTION Cot(X : Real) : Real;

BEGIN
  Cot := Cos(X) / Sin(X)
END;

FUNCTION Sec(X : Real) : Real;

BEGIN
  Sec := 1 / Cos(X)
END;

FUNCTION Csc(X : Real) : Real;

BEGIN
  Csc := 1 / Sin(X)
END;
```

Note that even though the **X** parameter passed to these functions is declared as type **Real**, Turbo Pascal will allow you to pass an integer literal or variable in **X** without error, and will treat the value as a real number without a fractional part during the calculations.

16.4 Absolute value, natural logs, exponents

ABSOLUTE VALUE

Absolute value in mathematics is the distance of a number from zero. In practical terms, this means stripping the negative sign from a negative number and leaving a positive number alone. The Pascal function **Abs(X)** returns the absolute value of **X**. **X** may be type **Real** or **Integer**. The type of the returned value is the same as the type of **X**. For example:

```
Abs(-61)        { Returns 61; type Integer }
Abs(484)        { Returns 484; also Integer }
Abs(3.87)       { Returns 3.87; type Real }
Abs(-61.558)    { Returns 61.558; also Real }
```

The **Abs** function is actually a shorthand form of the following statement:

```
IF X < 0 THEN X := - X;
```

NATURAL LOGARITHMS

There are two Pascal standard functions that deal with natural logarithms. Natural logarithms are mathematical functions that turn on a remarkable irrational number named e, which, to six decimal places, is 2.718282. Explaining where e comes from, or explaining natural logarithms in detail, is somewhat outside the charter of this book. Do read up on them (in any senior high mathematics text) if the concept is strange to you.

Exp(X) returns the exponential function of **X**. **X** may be a real number or an integer, but the returned value is always real. The exponential function raises e to the **X** power. Therefore, when you evaluate **Exp(X)**, what you are actually evaluating is e^X.

Ln(X) returns the natural logarithm (logarithm to the base e) of **X**. **X** may be type **Integer** or **Real**, and the returned value, again, is always type **Real**. The sense of the **Ln(X)** function is the reverse of **Exp(X)**: Evaluating **Ln(X)** yields the exponent to which e must be raised to give **X**.

Natural logarithms are the most arcane of Pascal's mathematical standard functions. They are most used in mathematics that many of us would consider "heavy." However, there is one use for which natural logarithms fill an enormous hole in Pascal's definition: Exponentiation. Unlike most languages, Pascal contains no general function for raising X to the Yth power. (In FORTRAN the exponentiation operator is the double asterisk: **X**∗∗**Y** raises **X** to the Yth power.) **Exp** and **Ln** allow us to create a function that raises one number to a given power:

```
1          {<<<< Power >>>>}
2
3
4          { Described in section 16.4 -- Last mod 2/1/86    }
5
6          FUNCTION Power(Mantissa,Exponent : Real) : Real;
7
8          BEGIN
9            Power := Exp(Ln(Mantissa) * Exponent)
10         END;
```

This almost certainly looks like magic unless you really understand how natural logarithms work. Two cautions: The result returned is type **Real**, not **Integer**. Also, do not pass a zero or negative value to **Mantissa**. Runtime error #4: Ln argument error will result. Reason: **Ln(X)** for a negative **X** is undefined!

16.5   Ord and Chr

The functions **Ord** and **Chr** are true transfer functions, providing you with a well-documented "legal" pathway between the otherwise incompatible types **Integer** and **Char**. **Ord** actually provides the pathway between integers and *any* ordinal type—hence the name.

ORD

As its name suggests, **Ord(X)** deals with ordinal types. Ordinal types are those types that can be "enumerated"; that is, types with a fixed number of values in a well-defined order.

Ord(X) returns the ordinal position (an integer) of the value X in its ordinal type. The sixty-sixth character in the ASCII Character set is the capital letter 'A'. **Ord('A')** returns 65. The third color in our old friend type **Spectrum** is **Yellow**. **Ord(Yellow)** returns 2—remember (for both examples) that we start counting at 0!

CHR

Chr goes in the opposite direction from **Ord: Chr(X)** returns a character value corresponding to the **X**th character in the ASCII character set (**X** is an integer). **Chr(65)** returns the capital 'A', **Chr(66)** returns capital letter 'B', and so on. The most important use of **Chr(X)** is generating character values that are not expressed by any symbol that you can place between single quote marks. How do you put a line feed in quotes? Or worse yet, a bell character? You don't—you express them with **Chr**:

```
Chr(13)        { Returns ASCII carriage return (CR) }
Chr(7)         { Returns ASCII bell (BEL)     }
Chr(127)       { Returns ASCII delete (DEL) }
Chr(8)         { Returns ASCII backspace (BS) }
```

Chr allows you to return a character based on an integer expression. The procedure **CapsLock**, for example, uses **Ord** and **Chr** to translate a character into an integer, manipulate the integer, and then translate the integer back into a character:

```
PROCEDURE CapsLock(VAR Target : String);

VAR Lowercase : SET OF Char;
    I         : Integer;

BEGIN
  Lowercase := ['a'..'z'];
  FOR I := 1 TO Length(Target) DO
    IF Target[I] IN Lowercase THEN
      Target[I] := Chr(Ord(Target[I]) - 32)
END;
```

(Turbo Pascal has a built-in procedure, **UpCase**, which will accomplish the same thing as the expression

```
Chr(Ord(Target[I]) - 32)
```

but the procedure **CapsLock** as given above will compile under ISO Standard Pascal.)

Don't try to pass to **Chr** an integer value higher than 255. The results will be undefined, probably garbage.

16.7   Pred and Succ

We discussed these two standard functions informally in Section 13.4, in connection with **FOR** loops. Now it's time for a closer look.

One of the properties of an ordinal type is that its value exists in a fixed and well-defined order. In other words, for type **Integer**, 3 comes after 2, not before. For type **Char**, 'Q' follows 'P', which follows 'O', and so on. The order is always the same.

This order is called the "collating sequence" or "collating order" of an ordinal type. Given a value of an ordinal type, **Ord** tells you which position that value occupies in its collating sequence. Given a value of an ordinal type, **Pred** and **Succ** return the next value before that value or previous to that value, respectively.

```
Pred('Z')       { Returns 'Y' }
Succ('w')       { Returns 'x' }
Pred(43)        { Returns 42 }
Succ(19210)     { Returns 19211 }
Pred(Orange)    { Returns Red }
Succ(Green)     { Returns Blue }
Pred(Red)       { Undefined! }
```

This last example bears a closer look. The predecessor value of **Red** is undefined. Recall the definition of enumerated type **Spectrum**:

```
Spectrum = (Red,Orange,Yellow,Green,Blue,Indigo,Violet);
```

Red is the very first value in the type. There is nothing before it, so **Pred(Red)** makes no sense in the context of type **Spectrum**. Similarly, **Succ(Violet)** makes no sense, since there is no value in **Spectrum** after **Violet**.

Pred(<value>) of the first value of an ordinal type is undefined. **Succ(<value>)** of the last value of an ordinal type is undefined.

Pred and **Succ** provide a means of "stepping through" an ordinal type to do some repetitive manipulation on a range of the values in that ordinal type. For example, in printing out the names on a telephone/address list, we might want to put a little header before the list of names beginning with 'A', and then before the list of names beginning with 'B', and so on. Assuming that the names are stored in sorted order in an array, we might work it this way:

```
VAR
  Names      : ARRAY[1..200] OF String[35];
  NameCount : Integer;

PROCEDURE Header(Ch : Char);

BEGIN
  Write(LST,Chr(13),Chr(10));
  Writeln(LST,'[',Ch,']------------------------------')
END;

PROCEDURE PrintBook(NameCount : Integer);

VAR I    : Integer;
    Ch    : Char;
    AName : String[35];

BEGIN
  Ch := 'A';
  Header(Ch);
  FOR I := 1 TO NameCount DO
    BEGIN
```

(continues)

```
        AName :+ Names[I];
        IF AName[1] <> CH THEN
          REPEAT
            CH := Succ(CH);
            Header(Ch)
          UNTIL AName[1] = CH;
        Writeln(LST,AName)
      END
END;
```

(concluded)

Assume that the array **Names** has been filled somehow with names, and that the number of names has been placed in **NameCount**. The names must be in sorted order, last name first. When **PrintBook** is invoked, the list in **Names** is printed on the system printer, with a header for each letter of the alphabet:

```
          [A]-------------------------------
          Albert*Eddie
          Aldiss*Brian
          Anselm*Jo
          Anthony*Piers

          [B]-------------------------------
          Brooks*Bobbie
          Bentley*Mike

          [C]-------------------------------
          Chan*Charlie
          Charles*Ray
          Cabell*James Branch

          [D]-------------------------------

          [E]-------------------------------

          [F]-------------------------------
          Farmer*Philip Jose
          Foglio*Phil
          Flor*Donna
```

and so on. Letters for which no names exist in the list will still have a printed header on the list. The printed listing, if cut into memo book sized sheets, would make the core of a "little black book" for names and addresses.

Look at the listing of **PrintBook**. **Ch** is given an initial value of A. As the names are printed, the first letter of each name is compared to the letter stored in **Ch**. If they don't match, the loop

```
REPEAT
  Ch := Succ(Ch);
  Header(Ch)
UNTIL AName[1] = Ch;
```

is executed. The letter in **Ch** is "stepped" along the alphabet until it "catches up" to the first letter in **AName**. For each step along the alphabet, a header is printed.

We might have written **Ch := Chr(Ord(Ch)+1)** instead of **Ch := Succ(Ch)**. **Succ** provides a much crisper notation. And because **Chr** does not work with enumerated types, **Succ** is the only way to step along the values of a programmer-defined enumerated type like **Spectrum**.

16.7 Odd

The last of the standard functions from ISO Pascal is a transfer function: **Odd(X)**. **X** is an integer value. If **X** is an odd value, **Odd(X)** returns the Boolean value **True**. If **X** is an even value, **Odd(X)** returns **False**.

Odd is thus a way of expressing an integer value as a Boolean. Any even number can express the value **False**, and any odd number can express the value **True**. (0 is considered an even number by virtue of lying between two odd numbers, 1 and –1.)

Up to this point, all the functions described have been present in ISO Standard Pascal. Turbo Pascal provides a number of other built-in functions that ISO Standard Pascal does not.

16.8   Frac and Int

With these two functions you can "take apart" a real number into its whole number part and its fractional part.

Frac(R) returns the fractional part of real number **R**. In other words, **Frac(24.44789)** would return 0.44789.

Int(R) returns the whole number part of real number **R**. In other words, **Int(241.003)** would return 241.0.

Both **Frac** and **Int** return values of type **Real**.

16.9   Hi, Lo, and Swap

Type **Integer**, if you recall, is represented in memory as two bytes. There are times when it is necessary to obtain the value of each of the two bytes apart from its brother. Functions **Hi** and **Lo** allow you to do this:

Hi(I) returns the value of the high order byte of **I**. Technically, what happens is that the value of **I** is shifted eight bits to the right, so that the high order byte becomes the low order byte. The high order byte is filled with zero bits. For example:

Hi(256) returns 1. Why? Can you picture it happening?

Hi(17341) returns 67.

Hi(–10366) returns 215. How does the negative sign figure in?

Lo(I) returns the low order byte of **I**. All that happens here is that the high eight bits of **I** are forced to zero. For example:

Lo(256) returns 0.

Lo(17341) returns 189.

Lo(–10366) returns 130. Can **Lo** ever return a negative number?

Swap(I) *exchanges* the two bytes of integer **I**. The high order byte becomes the low order byte, and the low order byte becomes the high order byte. For example:

Swap(17341) returns –17085. Where does the negative sign come from?

Swap($66FF) returns $FF66. Hexadecimal notation makes things a good deal clearer!

Hi, **Lo**, and **Swap** find good use when you must move values into and out of CPU registers. Many Z80 and 8086 registers are two bytes wide and must be filled all at once; yet many operating system calls require that the two halves of a CPU register be filled with unrelated bytes of data. Furthermore, after a DOS call, the two bytes of a register may contain necessary but unrelated data and must be separated.

Suppose, for example, that you need to pass $01 to register AH and $06 to register AL. AH and AL are two halves of 8086 register AX, and AX must be passed to the operating system as a unit. Turbo Pascal treats AX as an integer, part of an important data structure called **RegPack** (see Section 20.6). How to load two separate numbers into one integer? Try this:

```
VAR
  AX,JMask,QBit : Integer;

JMask := $06;          { The high bytes of both these }
QBit  := $01;          { variables are zero! }
AX    := QBit;         { QBit goes into the low byte of AX; }
AX    := Swap(AX);     { then Swap flips low byte for high; }
AX    := AX + JMask;   { so that adding JMask to AX puts it }
                       { into AX's low byte. }
```

Hi and **Lo** comes into play when the operating system returns a value to your program in register **AX**. You want to extract **JMask** and **QBit** from **AX** again. Like so:

```
JMask := Lo(AX);       { JMask comes back in AX's low byte; }
QBit  := Hi(AX);       { and QBit in AX's high byte }
```

The need for **Hi**, **Lo**, and **Swap** will become more apparent after you understand what is involved in making DOS calls and software interrupts (see Section 20.6).

16.10   Random number functions

Built into Turbo Pascal are two functions that return pseudorandom numbers, **Random** and **Random(I)**. **Random** returns a real number, and **Random(I)** returns an integer.

Random returns a pseudorandom number of type **Real** that is greater than or equal to zero and less than 1. This statement:

```
FOR I := 1 TO 5 DO Writeln(Random);
```

might display:

```
7.0172090270E-01
7.3332131305E-01
8.0977424840E-01
6.7220290820E-01
9.2550002318E-01
```

The E–01 exponent makes all these numbers fall in the range 0.0 to 0.9999999999. All random numbers returned by the function **Random** fall within this range, but of course if you need random real numbers in another range, you need only shift the decimal point the required number of places to the right.

Random(I) returns random integers. The parameter is an integer that sets an upper bound for the random numbers returned by the function. **Random(I)** will return a number greater than or equal to zero and less than **I**. **I** may be any integer up to **MaxInt**. **I** may be negative; however, making **I** *any* negative value has the same effect as passing **MaxInt** to **Random(I)**. There is no way to make **Random(I)** return negative random numbers.

There is frequently a need for a random number in a particular range, say between 15 and 50 or between 100 and 500. The procedure **Pull** meets this need by extracting random integers until one falls in the range specified by **Low** and **High**.

```
1       {<<<< Pull >>>>}
2
3
4       { Described in section 16.10 -- Last mod 2/1/86  }
5
6       FUNCTION Pull(Low,High : Integer) : Integer;
7
8       VAR
9         I : Integer;
10
11      BEGIN
12        REPEAT                    { Keep requesting random integers until }
13          I := Random(High + 1); { one falls between Low and High }
14        UNTIL I >= Low;
15        Pull := I
16      END;
```

RANDOMIZE

The **Randomize** procedure exists because Turbo Pascal's random numbers, like all random numbers generated in software, are not random at all but only "pseudorandom," which means that a series of such numbers approximates randomness. The *series* of such numbers may well repeat itself each time the program is run, unless the random number generator is "reseeded" with a new seed value. This is the job of **Randomize**.

Randomize should be called at least once in every program, and to make your pseudorandom numbers more nearly random, it might be called each time you want a new random number or series of random numbers.

Randomize did not work correctly in Turbo Pascal releases 1 and 2. Release 3.0 **Randomize** appears to work correctly.

A DICE GAME

The following program shows one use of random numbers in a game situation. **Rollem** simulates the roll of one or more dice—up to as many as will fit across the screen. Procedure **Roll** may be placed in your function/procedure library and used in any game program that must roll dice in a visual manner. It will display a number of dice at location **X,Y** on the screen, where **X,Y** are the coordinates of the upper left corner of the first die. The **NumberOfDice** parameter tells **Roll** how many dice to roll; there is built-in protection against attempting to display more dice than space to the right of **X** will allow.

Rollem is also a good exercise in **REPEAT/UNTIL** loops. The **MakeBox** procedure was described in Section 14.1. In this version of **Rollem**, the values for the fields in the box-draw record **GrafChars** are filled via assignment statements. They could as well be read from a file. How would you go about making **GrafChars** a record constant, initialized with values correct for your computer?

```
1     {--------------------------------------------------------}
2     {                          Rollem                        }
3     {                                                        }
4     {   A dice game to demonstrate random numbers and box draws  }
5     {                                                        }
6     {                    by Jeff Duntemann                   }
7     {                    Turbo Pascal V3.0                   }
8     {                   Last update 1/22/86                  }
9     {                                                        }
10    {                                                        }
11    {                                                        }
12    {--------------------------------------------------------}
13
14
15    PROGRAM Rollem;
16
17    CONST DiceFaces : ARRAY[0..5,0..2] OF STRING[5] =
18                    (('     ',' o ','     '),   { 1 }
19                     ('o   ','     ','   o'),   { 2 }
20                     ('   o',' o ','o   '),     { 3 }
21                     ('o  o','     ','o  o'),    { 4 }
22                     ('o  o',' o ','o  o'),      { 5 }
23                     ('o o o','     ','o o o'));  { 6 }
24
25
```

(continues)

```
26          TYPE
27            GrafRec = RECORD
28                        ULCorner,
29                        URCorner,
30                        LLCorner,
31                        LRCorner,
32                        HBar,
33                        VBar,
34                        LineCross,
35                        TDown,
36                        TUp,
37                        TRight,
38                        TLeft : String[4]
39                      END;
40
41            String80 = String[80];
42
43
44          VAR
45            GrafChars    : GrafRec;
46            I,X,Y        : Integer;
47            Width,Height : Integer;
48            Quit         : Boolean;
49            Dice,Toss    : Integer;
50            DiceX        : Integer;
51            Ch           : Char;
52            Banner       : String80;
53
54
55          {$I BOXSTUFF.SRC}     { Described in Section 14.1 }
56
57
58          PROCEDURE Roll(X,Y          : Integer;
59                         NumberOfDice : Integer;
60                         VAR Toss     : Integer);
61
62          VAR I,J,Throw,XOffset : Integer;
63
```

(continues)

```
64          BEGIN
65            IF (NumberOfDice * 9)+X >= 80 THEN      { Too many dice horizontally    }
66              NumberOfDice := (80-X) DIV 9;         { will scramble the CRT display! }
67            FOR I := 1 TO NumberOfDice DO
68              BEGIN
69                XOffset := (I-1)*9;                 { Nine space offset for each die }
70                MakeBox(X+XOffset,Y,7,5,GrafChars); { Draw a die }
71                Throw := Random(6);                 { "Toss" it  }
72                FOR J := 0 TO 2 DO                  { and fill it with dots }
73                  BEGIN
74                    GotoXY(X+1+XOffset,Y+1+J);
75                    Write(DiceFaces[Throw,J])
76                  END
77              END
78          END;
79
80
81
82        BEGIN
83          Randomize;                    { Seed the pseudorandom number generator }
84          ClrScr;                       { Clear the entire screen }
85          Quit := False;                { Initialize the quit flag }
86          DefineChars(GrafChars);       { Go get box-draw characters for this machine }
87          Banner := 'GONNA Roll THE BONES!';
88          MakeBox(-1,1,Length(Banner)+4,3,GrafChars);            { Draw Banner box }
89          GotoXY((80-Length(Banner)) DIV 2,2); Write(Banner);  { Put Banner in it }
90          REPEAT
91            REPEAT
92              FOR I := 6 TO 18 DO       { Clear the game portion of screen }
93                BEGIN
94                  GotoXY(1,I);
95                  ClrEol
96                END;
97              GotoXY(1,6);
98              Write('>>How many dice will we Roll this game? (1-5, or 0 to exit): ');
99              Readln(Dice);
100             IF Dice = 0 THEN Quit := True ELSE  { Zero dice sets Quit flag }
101               IF (Dice < 1) OR (Dice > 5) THEN  { Show error for dice out of range }
```

(continues)

```
102              BEGIN
103                 GotoXY(0,23);
104                 Write('>>The legal range is 1-5 Dice!')
105              END
106           UNTIL (Dice >= 0) AND (Dice <= 5);
107           GotoXY(0,23); ClrEol;        { Get rid of any leftover error messages }
108           IF NOT Quit THEN             { Play the game! }
109             BEGIN
110               DiceX := (80-(9*Dice)) DIV 2;   { Calculate centered X for dice }
111               REPEAT
112                 GotoXY(1,16); ClrEol;
113                 Roll(DiceX,9,Dice,Toss);                    { Roll & draw dice }
114                 GotoXY(1,16); Write('>>Roll again? (Y/N): ');
115                 Readln(Ch);
116               UNTIL NOT (Ch IN ['Y','y']);
117               GotoXY(1,18); Write('>>Play another game? (Y/N): ');
118               Readln(Ch);
119               IF NOT (Ch IN ['Y','y']) THEN Quit := True
120             END
121        UNTIL Quit      { Quit flag set ends the game }
122     END.
```

(concluded)

16.11   Sound routines for the IBM PC

Turbo Pascal for the IBM PC contains two procedures that control sound production from the PC's speaker. These two procedures, **Sound** and **NoSound**, plus the more general built-in procedure **Delay** (found in all versions of Turbo Pascal) enable you to generate specified frequencies for specified periods of time.

Sound(Frequency) "turns on" a sound with a frequency given as Hertz (cycles per second) in **Frequency**. **Sound** says nothing about how long the sound will be generated; it will remain "on" until turned off by **NoSound**.

NoSound turns the speaker off again.

As a simplest-case example, to generate a 1 Khz (kilohertz) tone for one second, these three statements would be required:

```
Sound(1000);        { Initiate sound at 1000 Hertz }
Delay(1000);        { Delay for 1000 milliseconds }
NoSound;            { Turn sound off again }
```

Breaking away from the proverbial beep as a signal from your programs is easy enough, once you convince yourself that creative noise is not exclusively for video games. One simple signal I use is an audio "uh-uh" to signal that something is not right, especially character input from the keyboard:

```
1       {<<<< UhUh >>>>}
2
3
4       { Described in section 16.11 -- Last mod 2/1/86  }
5
6       PROCEDURE UhUh;
7
8       VAR
9          I : Integer;
10
11      BEGIN
12        FOR I := 1 TO 2 DO
13          BEGIN
14             Sound(50);
15             Delay(100);
16             NoSound;
17             Delay(50)
18          END
19      END;
```

Type this one in and try it—you'll get the idea.

One very serious problem with **Sound**, and especially with **Delay**, is that both procedures are highly dependent on CPU clock speed. Sounds produced with **Sound** will have a higher pitch on a machine with a faster clock, like the IBM PC/AT and the various "turbo" PC compatibles or ordinary PC's equipped with accelerator boards like Quadram's excellent QuadSprint.

Perception of tonal pitch is subjective enough to ignore in most cases, but the problem with **Delay** is objective: You specify delay duration in milliseconds, and on any machine but an IBM PC, the duration only approximately follows the milliseconds figure passed to **Delay**.

Accurately measuring duration in a CPU-independent fashion is complicated, and I will leave that subject for *Turbo Pascal Solutions*. For the time being, avoid using **Delay** for any application that requires an objective time delay—in fact, avoid it for almost anything but timing tones produced on the PC's speaker.

Controlling your CRT

Such a simple thing as controlling the placement of information on a CRT screen has been a thorn in the side of computer programmers as long as there have been computers. Each manufacturer of computers and terminals has considered his own set of screen control codes the best set possible, and the result has (predictably) been chaos. Most vendors of computer languages have simply given up and left CRT control as an exercise for the programmer.

Turbo Pascal is the only native code Pascal compiler for microcomputers that defines its own CRT interface standard. Its screen control procedures are not part of ISO Standard Pascal, but *someone* must set a standard if we are to have both portable Pascal code and full-screen Pascal applications; I suspect that given Turbo Pascal's outsized share of the Pascal market, other Pascal vendors will implement Turbo's screen control procedures in their own compilers before long.

Borland International preinstalls Turbo Pascal with full CRT control for a number of the most popular microcomputers, among them the IBM PC, Heath H89, Heath Z100, Xerox 820, and Victor 9000. Perhaps 80 per cent of all Turbo users can buy a preinstalled version of the compiler and not worry about which control codes do what to the screen. People with obscure CRT hardware will have to install their own screen control codes. See the *Turbo Pascal Reference Manual* for details.

I make a fuss about CRT control because it is *important*. The manner in which a program interfaces with its user is the most crucial attribute of that program. The days of the Mystical Order of the Computer Priesthood are over. A computer program that is hard to use will be left unused. In designing the concept of a computer program, lay out the face that the program presents to the user *first*. Your first allegiance as a programmer is to the needs of your user.

17.1   Built-in CRT functions and procedures

Turbo Pascal accomplishes its CRT control through a number of predefined functions and procedures. Some of them are fairly obvious and we have been using them in examples all along. In this section we will take a closer look at each.

CLRSCR This command blanks the CRT screen and returns the cursor to the upper left hand corner. Turbo Pascal considers the coordinates of the upper left corner of the screen to be 1,1, *not* 0,0 as many other programming environments (such as dBase II) do.

GOTOXY(X,Y) This command moves the cursor to position **X,Y** where **X** is the column (counting across from the left) and **Y** is the row (counting down from the top). **X** and **Y** may be type **Integer** or **Byte**, but not type **Real**. The upper left corner is position 1,1.

CLREOL The "EOL" in this command means "End Of Line." **ClrEOL** will clear the line containing the cursor from the cursor to the end of the line. Some older terminals are not capable of quite this sophistication and will clear the *entire* line containing the cursor. You should be aware of what your terminal can do before you plan any screen-intensive application.

DELLINE The cursor line is deleted, and lines are moved upward to fill in. An empty line is inserted at the bottom of the screen.

INSLINE An empty line is inserted at the cursor line. The line that previously contained the cursor is moved down beneath the inserted line, and all lines further down move down one line. The bottom screen line will be pushed off the bottom of the screen and lost.

LOWVIDEO

LowVideo sends a command to the CRT that sets a "video attribute" for all text sent to the screen after the command. Most CRT devices (the IBM PC and Victor 9000, for example) will interpret this attribute as the "dim" or "half-brightness" attribute. Characters sent to the screen after **LowVideo** is executed will show up as dimmer than normal character appearance.

Some terminals do not have a half-brightness attribute and may interpret **LowVideo**'s attribute as inverse (black on white) text or blinking text. The Xerox 820-II has a selectable attribute; your text may be highlighted as half-bright, inverse, or blinking, but only one of those three attributes may appear on the screen at any one time.

NORMVIDEO

What **LowVideo** does, **NormVideo** undoes. Text sent to the screen after **NormVideo** is executed will be displayed as normal characters without any special attribute.

Remember that there is nothing in Turbo Pascal's runtime code that will restore normal video if your program terminates after **LowVideo** has been executed. You will then find that all text typed to your screen will be displayed with the half-brightness (or whatever) attribute in force. If you use **LowVideo** in your program, it is good housekeeping to execute **NormVideo** before shutting down and returning to the operating system.

CRTINIT

If you defined a "terminal initialization string" during terminal installation this string will be sent to your terminal when **CRTInit** is executed. For the IBM PC and its close compatibles this command does nothing.

CRTEXIT

CRTExit sends the "terminal reset string" defined during terminal installation. With most terminals and computers, including the IBM PC, this command does nothing.

17.2 Useful screen control tactics

The previous nine routines are available from all versions of Turbo Pascal. Some of them (like **ClrEOL**) may work slightly differently on different terminal types. But the important thing is that, with a little care, a full-screen application program can work identically (from a user's perspective) on *all* machines capable of running Turbo Pascal. In this section we'll give you some tips on creating effective text displays from Turbo Pascal.

The **LowVideo** procedure provides a way to highlight (or lowlight, if you prefer) text as a way of setting it off from normal text. The problem is that making text dimmer than the bulk of the text on the screen is a backhanded way of calling attention to it. A better method to accent text is to execute **LowVideo** *immediately* at the start of your program so that half brightness is used for the bulk of the text displayed from your program. Then, when you want to highlight something, drop into normal video for a line or two and your text will stand out nicely:

```
NormVideo;
Writeln('Please call your service rep immediately!');
LowVideo;
```

You'll find after awhile that you'll be using familiar sequences of statements to do many display chores. For instance, to place a message at a particular place on the screen takes at least two statements:

```
IF ERROR THEN
  BEGIN
    GotoXY(10,24);
    Writeln('>>That file is missing or damaged!')
  END;
```

Highlighting your message with a video attribute (half-brightness or inverse video) adds two more statements to the compound statement:

```
IF ERROR THEN
  BEGIN
    LowVideo;
    GotoXY(10,24);
    Writeln('>>That file is missing or damaged!');
    NormVideo
  END;
```

If you want to center a message you will have to determine its length, subtract its length from 80 (the width of your typical screen), and divide the difference by two. All of this fooling around may be done inside a single text display procedure:

```
1          {<<<< WriteAt >>>>}
2
3
4          { Described in section 17.2 -- Last mod 2/1/86    }
5
6          PROCEDURE WriteAt(X,Y : Integer;
7                            Highlite : Boolean;
8                            UseCR    : Boolean;
9                            TheText  : String255);
10
11         BEGIN
12           IF Y < 0 THEN Y := 12;
13           IF X < 0 THEN X := (80-Length(TheText)) DIV 2;
14           GotoXY(X,Y);
15           IF Highlite THEN LowVideo;
16           IF UseCR THEN Writeln(TheText) ELSE Write(TheText);
17           NormVideo
18         END;
```

WriteAt will automatically center a line of text on your screen from side to side and from top to bottom, either or both as required. If you pass **WriteAt** a negative **X** parameter, your text line will be centered from side to side. If you pass it a negative **Y** value, the text line will be placed on line 12, which is centered on a 24- or 25-line screen.

In the constant declaration part of your program you should define a few Boolean constants for the use of **WriteAt**:

```
CONST
    Highlite : True;
    Normal   : False;
    CR       : True;
    NoCR     : False;
```

Rather than plugging the nondescript literals **True** and **False** into **WriteAt**'s parameter line, you can use the descriptive constants given above and make the intent of the parameters clear at a glance:

```
IF Error THEN WriteAt(-1,24,Highlite,NoCR,'<<DISK ERROR!>>');
```

This particular invocation of **WriteAt** will place a highlighted error message centered on line 24 of the screen. Since sending a carriage return to the screen after line 24 will scroll the screen up, the **UseCR** parameter is passed a **False** value by the Boolean constant **NoCR**.

WriteAt's purpose is actually to hide the details involved in centering a text line on the screen, highlighting it, and placing it at a particular X,Y position. These details add to the bulk of your code and may serve to obscure the real job of the program. When displaying an error message, the important thing to understand is why an error message must be displayed at that point, not how one highlights and centers a text line on the screen.

This is also a good place to point out that it is perfectly legal to break up a procedure call into several separate lines. This can make for less cluttered, easier-to-read source code. Pascal, which does not ordinarily respect the line structure of text files, does not care:

```
WriteAt(HPos + 6, YPos + Offset + 2,
        Highlite, NoCR,
        'This is a raid.  I repeat, this is a raid!');
```

The only thing you *can't* break out into more than one line is a text literal. You could not, in the line above, have written:

```
WriteAt(HPos + 6, YPos + Offset + 2,
        Highlite, NoCR,
        'This is a raid.
        I repeat, this is a raid!');
```

Turbo Pascal would stop with Error 55: String constant exceeds line. To pass **WriteAt** a string literal longer than will fit on a single line, you must concatenate two shorter string literals:

```
WriteAt(HPos + 6, YPos + Offset + 2,
        Highlite, NoCR,
        'This is a raid.  I said, son, this is a raid.' +
 ' Listen up in there!  Did you hear me? THIS IS A RAID!');
```

Unless the screen were wider than 80 characters, the above message would likely "wrap" around to the next line down when displayed on the screen.

A FUNCTION FOR YES/NO QUESTIONS

Perhaps the most common questions to occur during dialogs between a computer program and a user are simple yes/no questions. Coding such a question up involves something close to this:

```
Write('>>Do you want to add another record? (Y/N): ');
Read(Ch);
IF NOT (Ch IN ['Y','y']) THEN
  Quit := True ELSE Quit := False;
```

These lines of code (with a different prompt, of course) would have to be repeated for every yes/no question in the program. Everything except the prompt can be bundled into a single function called **Yes**:

```
 1      {<<<< Yes >>>>}
 2
 3
 4      { Described in section 17.2 -- Last mod 2/1/86   }
 5
 6      FUNCTION Yes : Boolean;
 7
 8      VAR
 9        Ch : Char;
10
11      BEGIN
12        Read(Ch);
13        IF Ch IN ['Y','y'] THEN Yes := True ELSE Yes := False
14      END;
```

Now you can do this instead:

```
Write('>>Do you want to add another record? (Y/N): ');
IF Yes THEN Quit := True ELSE Quit := False;
```

The details of getting a character from the keyboard and seeing what it is are hidden by function **Yes**. The dialog nature of the interchange remains the important and visible characteristic of this piece of code. It is a cleaner, more readable way of handling yes/no dialogs in your programs.

A DATA ENTRY ROUTINE FOR BOOLEAN VARIABLES

Lots of different types of data come in pairs. Human beings are male or female, alive or dead. Telephones are TouchTone or pulse dial. Cars are U.S. made or foreign. Such data can be conveniently expressed as Boolean values:

```
VAR
  TouchDial,Male,Deceased,USMade : Boolean;
```

Displaying and entering Boolean values within a data entry screen involves a certain amount of rigamarole. For example, one way of displaying the current value of a Boolean variable and entering a new value might be this:

```
REPEAT
  Quit := False;
  GotoXY(1,5); Write('>>TouchTone or Pulse dialing? ');
  IF TouchDial THEN Write('TouchTone')
    ELSE Write('Pulse dial');
  Write(' Change? (Y/N): ');
  IF Yes THEN TouchDial := NOT TouchDial ELSE Quit
UNTIL Quit
```

Yes is the yes/no question function described above. A cleaner and more self-explanatory method of getting a Boolean value from the keyboard is the following procedure:

```
1    {<<<< FlipField >>>>}
2
3
4    { Described in section 17.2 -- Last mod 2/1/86    }
5
6    PROCEDURE FlipField(X,Y         : Integer;
7                        VAR State   : Boolean;
8                        TrueString  : String30;
9                        FalseString : String30;
10                       VAR Escape  : Boolean);
11
```

(continues)

```
12          VAR Blanker   : String80;
13              KeyStroke : 0..255;
14              WorkState : Boolean;
15              Ch        : Char;
16
17
18
19          PROCEDURE ShowState(NowState : Boolean);
20
21          BEGIN
22            GotoXY(X,Y); Write(Blanker);   { Erase the old label }
23            IF NowState THEN
24              BEGIN
25                GotoXY(X,Y);
26                Write(TrueString)   { Write TrueString for NowState = True }
27              END
28            ELSE
29              BEGIN
30                GotoXY(X,Y);
31                Write(FalseString);  { Write FalseString for NowState = False }
32              END
33          END;
34
35
36          BEGIN
37            Escape := False; Ch := Chr(0);
38            LowVideo;                         { Use highlighting }
39            FillChar(Blanker,SizeOf(Blanker),' ');   { Set up Blanker String }
40            WorkState:=State;                 { Temporary Boolean }
41            IF Length(TrueString)>Length(FalseString) THEN   { Adjust Blanker }
42              Blanker[0] := Chr(Length(TrueString)) ELSE    { String for lengths }
43              Blanker[0] := Chr(Length(FalseString));       { of meaning labels }
44            ShowState(WorkState);             { Display initial label }
45            REPEAT
46              WHILE NOT KeyStat(Ch) DO BEGIN {NULL} END;  { Calls KeyStat... }
47              KeyStroke := Ord(Ch);
48              IF KeyStroke = 27 THEN Escape := True ELSE
```

(continues)

```
49              IF KeyStroke<>13 THEN WorkState := NOT WorkState;
50            ShowState(WorkState);
51          UNTIL (KeyStroke=13) OR Escape;          { ...until CR or ESC is pressed }
52          IF NOT Escape THEN State:=WorkState;     { Update State if CR }
53          NormVideo;
54          ShowState(State);      { Redisplay State in non-highlighted text }
55        END;
```

(concluded)

When you use a Boolean variable in a program, it probably has a distinct and important meaning connected with each of its two states, **True** and **False**. **FlipField** displays the meaning of variable **State** and allows you to flip between its two states by pressing any key that is neither the escape key nor carriage return.

FlipField is passed two text labels in its parameter line: **True-String** describes the meaning of **State** when **State** is **True**. **FalseString** describes the meaning of **State** when **State** is **False**. For example, if **State** were a Boolean variable called **PatientSex**, **TrueString** might hold the string "Male" and **FalseString** might hold the string "Female." When **FlipField** begins running, it displays at **X,Y** the label corresponding to the current state of **State** as passed in the parameter line.

FlipField then waits on the keyboard for keypresses. If an ESC is entered, **FlipField** returns without making any change to **State**. If CR is entered, **FlipField** updates **State** to reflect the currently selected meaning and returns. If any other key is pressed, **FlipField** flips to the other meaning for **State** and updates the screen display at **X,Y** to match. Going back to our example, by pressing a key (space bar works well) repeatedly, **FlipField** will rapidly display "Male" and "Female" at the same location until either ESC or CR is pressed.

All the user must do to pick one of two states for a Boolean value is press CR when the meaning he wants is displayed on the screen. All possible keypresses are accounted for and he doesn't have to type a string at the keyboard with the possibility of misspellings.

FlipField requires **KeyStat**, a function that performs non-echo keyboard I/O through an operating system call. This routine varies, depending on which operating system you use, and will be described fully in Section 20.6.

SUPPRESSING UNWANTED TEXT CURSORS

Most computers have a flashing hardware cursor of some sort that is used when the operating system echoes characters back to input routines. There are many occasions (**FlipField** is a good example) when you have no need for a flashing cursor and would just as soon not have one calling attention to itself. At other times you may have elected (with a routine like **GetString**) to handle cursor display yourself. Then you have *two* cursors, and things get confusing.

Most computers allow you to turn off the hardware cursor. Sadly, there are as many ways to do this as there are computers. Some snooping through your hardware documentation may turn up a method. A pair of routines for turning the cursor off and turning it back on again should be a part of every programmer's CRT toolkit. We'll show you how these routines are done for the IBM PC. For other machines, you'll have to build **CursorOn** and **CursorOff** on your own.

```
1        {<<<< Monochrome >>>>}
2
3
4        { Described in section 17.2 -- Last mod 2/1/86   }
5        { HIGHLY specific to the IBM PC! }
6
7        FUNCTION Monochrome : Boolean;
8
9        TYPE
10         RegPack = RECORD
11                      AX,BX,CX,DX,BP,SI,DI,DS,ES,FLAGS : Integer
12                  END;
13
14       VAR
15         Regs : RegPack;
16
17       BEGIN
18         INTR(17,Regs);
19         IF (Regs.AX AND $0030) = $30 THEN Monochrome := True
20           ELSE Monochrome := False
21       END;
```

```
1              {<<<< CursorOn >>>>}
2
3
4              { Described in section 17.2 -- Last mod 2/1/86    }
5              { HIGHLY specific to the IBM PC }
6
7              PROCEDURE CursorOn;
8
9              TYPE
10               RegPack = RECORD
11                             AX,BX,CX,DX,BP,SI,DI,DS,ES,FLAGS : Integer
12                         END;
13
14             VAR
15               Regs : RegPack;
16
17             BEGIN
18               WITH Regs DO
19                 BEGIN
20                   AX := $0100;
21                   IF Monochrome THEN CX := $0B0C ELSE CX := $0607;
22                 END;
23               INTR(16,Regs)
24             END;
```

```
1              {<<<< CursorOff >>>>}
2
3
4              { Described in section 17.2 -- Last mod 2/1/86    }
5              { HIGHLY specific to the IBM PC }
6
7              PROCEDURE CursorOff;
8
9              TYPE
10               RegPack = RECORD
```

(continues)

```
11                        AX,BX,CX,DX,BP,SI,DI,DS,ES,FLAGS : Integer
12                   END;
13
14         VAR
15            Regs : RegPack;
16
17         BEGIN
18            WITH Regs DO
19              BEGIN
20                AX := $0100;
21                CX := $2000;   { Set CH bit 5 hi to suppress cursor }
22              END;
23            INTR(16,Regs)
24         END;
```

(concluded)

On the IBM PC, changing the cursor is done by calling the VIDEO routines in the ROM BIOS via Turbo Pascal's **Intr** procedure (see Section 20.6). Routine 1 in VIDEO handles cursor size. Suppressing the cursor is done by setting bit five of **Ch** and then calling VIDEO routine 1. If this bit is left cleared (its default state), the size of the visible cursor can be changed by putting the start scanline of the cursor (within its character cell) in **Ch** and the end line in **CL**. The lines are counted from the top of the character cell, from 0.

This would be a simple matter except that the two different types of display adapters sold by IBM have two different sizes of character cells. The cursor exists in the bottom of each character cell, and hence at different scanline positions for the two different adapters. The monochrome display cursor exists at character cell scanlines 12 and 13. The color graphics adapter cursor exists at scanlines 6 and 7. So while turning the cursor *off* is done identically for either display, you must know which display is installed to turn the cursor back on again.

This is what function **Monochrome** does. It returns a Boolean value **True** if the monochrome display is installed, or **False** if the color graphics adapter is installed. It gets its information by using BIOS interrupt 17 (11 hex) to fetch the IBM PC equipment status word. This word is a 16-bit bitmap in which bits are set according to what peripherals are installed in the machine. Bits 4 and 5 (counting from 0) specify the installed display adapter. If both bits are set, the monochrome display is installed. If either bit is cleared, the color display is installed.

The equipment status word is useful for determining many other things about the machine configuration. You might wish to develop a whole suite of functions for determining how much RAM is installed in the system, how many communications ports are installed, and so on. The definition for the equipment status word bitmap is in the comment header for Interrupt 11H in the ROM BIOS listing in the *Technical Reference Manual.*

Depending on the value returned by **Monochrome**, the **CX** register is given a value of $0B0C (monochrome) or $0607 (color) before calling the BIOS VIDEO routine via **Intr** to make the cursor visible again.

To suppress the cursor on the Xerox 820 you need to change the entire cursor character to a space character; the 820's cursor is not defined as a set of scanlines as is the cursor on the IBM PC. This is done by issuing a CTRL-E followed by the character you wish to be the new cursor:

```
PROCEDURE CursorOff;    { For the Xerox 820 }

BEGIN
  Writeln(Chr(5),' ') { A space cursor is invisible! }
END;

PROCEDURE CursorOn;    { For the Xerox 820 }

BEGIN
  Writeln(Chr(5),Chr(2)) { 820's char 2 is a white block }
END;
```

17.3   IBM PC text colors and attributes

In the past few years, the IBM PC has established what must be the closest thing to a CRT display standard that now exists in the microcomputer industry. The implementation of Turbo Pascal for the IBM PC contains some features that cater specifically to some of the powers of the two IBM PC display adapters: the monochrome display adapter, and the color graphics adapter. A number of newer computers from other companies have emulated one or both of these adapters and may therefore be able to run these special features successfully. I have tested Turbo Pascal's IBM PC features on the Compaq and Heath/Zenith Z150. Presumably, most of the closer IBM PC compatibles should work as well.

In this section we'll discuss IBM PC Turbo's text mode features. In the next section we'll take a look at Turbo's graphics features.

TEXT MODES   There are several different variations in text mode for the color graphics adapter. The **TextMode** command will select among the variations. **TextMode** may be invoked without a parameter to select the current or last text mode selected, or it may be given one of four predefined constants as a parameter, specifying which form of text mode is desired:

```
TextMode;           { Selects current or last mode used }
TextMode(C40);      { Selects 40-column with color enabled }
TextMode(C80);      { Selects 80-column with color enabled }
TextMode(BW40);     { Selects 40-column with color disabled }
TextMode(BW80);     { Selects 80-column with color disabled }
```

Disabling color on the color graphics adapter means suppressing the color burst signal on the composite video output of the adapter board. This causes composite monitors and TV sets to display what would otherwise be a color signal in black and white. The color burst signal exists *only* on the composite output. *If you are using the RGB outputs of the color graphics adapter, you cannot disable color!*

On the monochrome display adapter, there is, of course, no color available. Neither is there really a 40-column mode as we know it on the color card; if you select the C40 or 40 parameters, text will be displayed on the left half of the screen only, with characters their normal size and width. IBM's monochrome card cannot display the double-width characters used by the color card in 40-column mode. There is no point, then, in using a parameter with **TextMode** when you have the monochrome card installed in your computer.

No matter which display adapter you are using nor what variation of text mode you select, **TextMode** *always* clears the screen. **TextMode** also resets the current window to the entire physical screen.

WINDOW

There are times when it would be very convenient to treat separate areas of the screen as though each were a separate screen. Writing an application that does two or more separate things comes to mind, as in a split-screen editor or a communications program that monitors both COM1: and COM2: at the same time.

The **Window** procedure exists for this purpose. It is predeclared this way:

```
PROCEDURE Window(X1,Y1,X2,Y2 : Integer);
```

Parameters **X1** and **Y1** define the column and row of the upper left corner of the window to be defined, and **X2** and **Y2** define the lower right corner. Once a window is defined with **Window**, it remains in force until another window is defined, or until you execute the **TextMode** statement.

On the IBM PC, all screen commands operate with respect to the current window, which is either the full screen default or the last window set via **Window**. In other words, if you define a window by

```
Window(10,10,70,20);
ClrScr;
```

only the screen in the rectangular region defined by the given coordinates will be cleared. Surrounding areas of the screen will not be affected.

Similarly, using **GotoXY** within a window *always* uses the upper left corner of the window as the coordinate origin. In other words, with the window mentioned above set at 10,10 and 70,20, performing a **GotoXY(1,1)**; will position the cursor at what appears to be screen location 10,10. Because the window was set, however, Turbo Pascal treats 10,10 as though it were the upper left corner of the entire screen. Physical screen position 10,10 becomes the logical screen position 1,1.

Window makes it possible to selectively clear rectangular areas of the IBM PC screen very quickly—more quickly, in fact, than you can follow by eye, and certainly more quickly than writing lines full of spaces. Using this procedure:

```
1       {<<<< ClearRegion >>>>}
2
3
4       { Described in section 17.2 -- Last mod 2/1/86   }
5
6       PROCEDURE ClearRegion(X1,Y1,X2,Y2 : Integer);
7
8       BEGIN
9         Window(X1,Y1,X2,Y2);
10        ClrScr;
11        Window(1,1,80,25)
12      END;
```

you can clear any rectangular area of the screen.

One caution in using **Window**—when you define a window, you *must* execute a **ClrScr** or a **GotoXY** before your first **Write** or **Writeln** into the new window. **ClrScr** and **GotoXY** serve to bring the cursor "into" the window; if you simply follow a **Window** statement with a **Write** or **Writeln**, the cursor will stay outside the window, usually hugging the last line on the screen, and the text you are trying to write into your new window will remain on the bottom screen line.

TEXT COLORS AND MONOCHROME ATTRIBUTES

If you're using the color graphics adapter, you have complete control over both the foreground and background colors for each individual character position on the screen. Furthermore, if you wish, you can make a character of any color blink. Two built-in procedures give you control of text colors: **TextColor** and **TextBack-ground**.

These same two procedures also work if you have the monochrome display adapter installed, but what they do is a great deal different. The monochrome display does not display colors, but it allows you to set attributes on a character-by-character basis. These attributes include underline, dim, and blink. Setting an attribute is done the same way you would set a text mode color on the color graphics adapter.

Setting character color or attribute is done by passing a parameter to **TextColor**. The parameter is an integer having a value from 0–31:

```
TextColor(4);      { Selects yellow on color card }
```

The meaning of the parameter for the two display cards and various values is summarized in the table below:

Text colors and attributes

| VALUE | CONSTANT | Adapter | |
		COLOR GRAPHICS	MONOCHROME
0	Black	Black	Off
1	Blue	Blue	Dim underline
2	Green	Green	Off
3	Cyan	Cyan	Dim
4	Red	Red	Dim
5	Magenta	Magenta	Dim
6	Brown	Brown	Dim
7	LightGrey	Light grey	Dim
8	DarkGrey	Dark grey	Off
9	LightBlue	Light blue	Normal underline
10	LightGreen	Light green	Off
11	LighCyan	Light cyan	Normal
12	LightRed	Light red	Normal
13	LightMagenta	Light magenta	Normal
14	Yellow	Yellow	Normal
15	White	White	Normal
16		Black	Off
17		Blue blink	Dim blink underline

| | | Adapter | |
| | | | |
VALUE	CONSTANT	COLOR GRAPHICS	MONOCHROME
		Text colors and attributes *(continued)*	
18		Green blink	Off
19		Cyan blink	Dim blink
20		Red blink	Dim blink
21		Magenta blink	Dim blink
22		Brown blink	Dim blink
23		Light grey blink	Dim blink
24		Dark grey blink	Off
25		Light blue blink	Normal blink underline
26		Light green blink	Off
27		Light cyan blink	Normal blink
28		Light red blink	Normal blink
29		Light magenta blink	Normal blink
30		Yellow blink	Normal blink
31		White blink	Normal blink

The "constants" column in the table lists the 16 integer constants predefined by Turbo Pascal for the values 0 to 15. By using these constants you can make your code a little more self-explanatory:

```
TextColor(LightGreen);
```

There is one additional predefined integer constant, **Blink**. **Blink**'s value is 16. If you add blink to a color constant, you will get that color character that blinks:

```
TextColor(Red + Blink);
```

Again, this is only to make your code clearer; you could just as easily have plugged the literal 20 into the parameter and the result would have been the same.

The difference between the normal colors and the "light" colors is the intensity signal in the color graphics adapter's RGB outputs.

Light red is actually red with the intensity signal on, and so on. Some low-cost color monitors do not make use of the intensity signal, and on those monitors your light colors will be identical to their corresponding normal colors.

On the monochrome display adapter, the color values select various combinations of the dim, underline, and blink attributes. To display underlined text, you would invoke **TextColor** with a value that selects the underline attribute, display the text, and then invoke **TextColor** again with the attribute value previously in force. Although there are no predefined constants for the various attributes, nothing would prevent you from defining constants of your own for that purpose:

```
CONST
   Blink       = 27;
   Dim         = 3;
   Normal      = 11;
   Underline   = 9;
   DimBlink    = 19;
   DimUnderline = 1;

TextColor(Underline);      { Select normal underline text }
Writeln('Be sure to back up your data!');
TextColor(Normal);         { Select normal text display }
```

The background color of a character is the color taken on by the rest of the little rectangular cell that contains the character itself. For the background color you have your choice of the seven normal colors 1 to 7 and of course, color 0, black:

```
TextBackground(Blue);
```

As we show here, the predefined color constants may be used for **TextBackground** as for **TextColor**.

On the monochrome adapter, the background color translates to a black background (colors 0 and 2) or a white background (colors

1,3,4,5,6,7). Inverse video is not itself an attribute, as it is on some computers like the Xerox 820 and the old SOL/VDM display board. To display in inverse video you must display text in color black on a white background:

```
TextColor(Black);
TextBackground(1);
Writeln('Use inverse video for emphasis.');
TextColor(Normal);
TextBackground(Black);
```

Although it is not mentioned in the Turbo Pascal documentation, the text border (overscan) color may be set by using the **GraphBackground** procedure. The border color may be any of the 16 text colors described in the table above. Passing one of those color numbers to **GraphBackground** will set the border color immediately, and the border will remain that color until set to something else. If you set the border color within a program, returning to the Turbo Pascal Environment or to your operating system will not reset the border color to what it was before.

```
GraphBackground(Green);  {Sets border to green in text mode}
```

SAVING THE CURSOR POSITION

The IBM PC implementation of Turbo Pascal includes two functions that return the current X and Y position of the cursor.

WhereX returns the X coordinate of the cursor. **WhereY** returns the Y coordinate. Both return values are integers.

What are **WhereX** and **WhereY** good for? One application lies in the saving of entire text screens. "Painting" a screen with **GotoXY** and **Write** statements takes a certain amount of time. If your application needs to switch frequently among a number of different screens, you'll find yourself spending a noticeable amount of time watching the screens regenerate themselves.

It is possible to save a screen after it is drawn by using the **Move** routine (see Section 20.3) to move a copy of the entire 4K text mode video buffer to another location in free RAM. Then you can bring in another screen in a fraction of a second (assuming it had been saved to RAM as well after being painted to the screen or loaded from a screen file). The problem with this is that the cursor position is *not* saved in the video refresh buffer but elsewhere in system RAM. If you need to save a cursor position along with a screen, you must save it yourself. **WhereX** and **WhereY** allow you to assign the current cursor position to a pair of integer variables. When bringing in a previously-saved screen, you can then restore the cursor position from those two variables with **GotoXY**.

17.4 IBM PC basic graphics

Turbo Pascal gives you three levels of color graphics capability on the IBM PC and close compatibles: Basic graphics, extended graphics, and turtle graphics. Basic graphics existed in Turbo Pascal 2.0. Extended and turtle graphics were added with Turbo Pascal 3.0.

Before you can work with graphics at any level, you have to be able to set and change the graphics modes on your PC. Turbo has a fairly complete suite of graphics mode control statements available. We'll cover those first.

GRAPHICS MODES

IBM's color graphics adapter has two modes: Medium resolution and high resolution. (There is a low-resolution mode that is not supported on the IBM PC/XT ROM BIOS, but that is supported by the PCjr. Turbo Pascal does not support low resolution graphics, even on the PCjr.) Turbo Pascal provides setup procedures for both these supported graphics modes.

The **GraphColorMode** procedure puts the color graphics adapter in medium resolution (320 × 200) graphics mode. Color is enabled.

GraphMode is similar to **GraphColorMode** except that the color burst signal is disabled on the composite video output. This will render color images on your screen as mottled shades of gray. Again, as with color in text mode, you cannot disable color on the RGB outputs. If you are using an RGB monitor, **GraphColorMode** and **GraphMode** produce the same effect.

To set up your screen for high resolution graphics, use the **Hires** procedure. This will clear the screen and allow use of the 640 × 200 graphics.

This is a good place to point out that **ClrScr** *does not work correctly in any graphics mode.* The *only* way to clear the screen in graphics mode is to invoke one of the mode-setting procedures **Hires**, **GraphMode**, or **GraphColorMode**. Calling **ClrScr** in a graphics mode will make your screen look peculiar indeed.

GRAPHICS COLOR CONTROL

High resolution graphics mode allows only one foreground color and one background color at a time. You have your choice of any one of the sixteen colors described in connection with color text (see Section 17.3.) The color is selected with the **HiresColor** procedure:

```
HiresColor(Red);
HiresColor(14);
```

Medium resolution is more complicated. Colors are available as sets of four, numbered 0 to 3, in groups called "palettes." There are four palettes to choose from. Table 17.2 summarizes the colors in each palette:

Color palette in Turbo Pascal			
		Color #	
PALETTE	0	1	2	3
0	Background	Green	Red	Brown
1	Background	Cyan	Magenta	Light grey
2	Background	Light green	Light red	Yellow
3	Background	Light cyan	Light magenta	White

Think of a palette as a rule that instructs the hardware how to interpret the four colors that may be displayed at any one time. Only one of the four palettes may be in force at a given time. Changing palettes means that all the colors already on the screen (even though painted under a previous palette) change *instantly* to keep in line with the new palette.

For example, if you had painted a box in color 1 with palette 0 in force, that box would appear as green. If you change to palette 3, that box will instantly change to light cyan.

You should think of color 0 as being the color of Saran Wrap, that is, transparent. It lets the background color show through. Don't fall into the trap of thinking that color 0 must be black. It is really no color at all, and will be whatever the background color is at that time.

Palettes are selected with the **Palette** procedure:

```
PROCEDURE Palette(PaletteNumber : Integer);
```

PaletteNumber must be an integer expression from 0 to 3.

The background color is selected via the **GraphBackground** procedure:

```
PROCEDURE GraphBackground(Color : Integer);
```

Color must be an integer expression from 0 to 15, and it represents the 16 colors listed in the text colors table. You may use the predefined color constants listed in the table.

Background color is uniform throughout the entire screen. Like palette, when you change the background color, all background color area on your screen will change to the new color instantly.

In high resolution graphics, the background color is always black, and **GraphBackground** has no effect. As we mentioned in Section 17.3, **GraphBackground** may also be used to set the border (overscan) color in text mode.

BASIC GRAPHICS STATEMENTS

Plot and Draw   Everything connected with graphics up to this point has been mode setup work and color control. Basic graphics can do relatively little actual drawing to the screen. You have two abilities with basic graphics: Plot points and draw lines.

The **Plot** routine sets individual pixels to a particular color:

```
PROCEDURE Plot(X,Y,Color : Integer);
```

Y must always fall into the range 0 to 199. In medium resolution mode, **X** must lie in the range 0 to 319. In high resolution mode, **X** may run from 0 to 639.

Legal values for **Color** also depend on the current graphics mode. For medium resolution mode (the modes put in force by **Graph-Mode** and **GraphColorMode**), **Color** must be in the range 0 to 3. The color values displayed for colors 0 to 3 depend on the palette that is currently in force; see Table 17.2. For high resolution mode, **Color** may be one of only two values: 0 and 1. **Color** = 1 will plot a point at **X,Y** in the current high resolution color. This color is set via the **HiresColor** procedure mentioned above. **Color** = 0 will clear the point at **X,Y** to black.

Unlike text mode, Turbo Pascal's graphics mode X/Y coordinates begin at 0,0 at the upper left corner of the screen. Text mode coordinates, by contrast, begin at 1,1.

If **Plot** is called with an **X,Y** position outside the legal bounds for the mode in force, nothing will be plotted, but no error will be triggered.

Creating lines on the screen is done with the **Draw** procedure:

```
PROCEDURE Draw(X1,Y1,X2,Y2,Color : Integer);
```

X1 and **Y1** are the coordinates of the starting end of the line. **X2** and **Y2** are the coordinates of the endpoint of the line. **Color** may be any color value legal for the mode in force. In medium resolution this would be a value from 0 to 3; in high resolution it must be either 0 or 1. Lines are clipped if they fall outside the legal coordinate bounds of the current graphics mode. No error will be generated.

One obvious use of **Draw** is to develop a rectangular box-drawing procedure for framing areas of the graphics screen. The procedure below will frame an area with a multiple-line frame as wide as you desire.

```
1          {<<<< GBox >>>>}
2
3
4          { Described in section 17.4 -- Last mod 2/1/86    }
5
6          PROCEDURE GBox(X,Y,W,H,Lines,Color : Integer);
7
8          VAR
9            I,Inc : Integer;
10
11         BEGIN
12           FOR I := 1 TO Lines DO
13             BEGIN
14               Inc := (I-1) * 2;
15               Draw(X+Inc,Y+Inc,X+W-Inc,Y+Inc,Color);
16               Draw(X+Inc,Y+H-Inc,X+W-Inc,Y+H-Inc,Color);
17               Draw(X+Inc,Y+Inc,X+Inc,Y+H-Inc,Color);
18               Draw(X+W-Inc,Y+Inc,X+W-Inc,Y+H-Inc,Color);
19             END;
20         END;
```

Gbox illustrates an important point in all graphics programs: Don't calculate any identical value more often than you must. Calculation slows things down, and IBM PC graphics are legendary for never being quite fast enough. The value stored in **Inc** is used several times in the **Draw** statements, so you can gain a little speed by calculating **Inc** once and using it repeatedly.

GraphWindow Basic graphics also include **GraphWindow**, which gives you very elementary graphics windowing. **GraphWindow** is predeclared this way:

```
PROCEDURE GraphWindow(X1,Y1,X2,Y2);
```

Ordinarily, Turbo Pascal uses the entire 320 × 200 or 640 × 200 graphics screen in drawing lines and plotting points. Using **Graph-Window**, however, you can isolate any rectangular subarea of the graphics screen as a graphics window. After defining a graphics window, *all* plotting and drawing will be limited to that window. Furthermore, the upper-left corner of the graphics window becomes the new 0,0 point.

The best way to understand this is to see it in action. Study program **Hatcher** carefully and then run it.

```
1        {---------------------------------------------------------}
2        {                        Hatcher                          }
3        {                                                         }
4        {         Graphics window demonstration program           }
5        {                                                         }
6        {                             by Jeff Duntemann           }
7        {                             Turbo Pascal V3.0           }
8        {                             Last update 3/7/86          }
9        {                                                         }
10       {                                                         }
11       {                                                         }
12       {---------------------------------------------------------}
13
14       PROGRAM Hatcher;
15
16       VAR
17          X,J : Integer;
18
19       PROCEDURE Border;
20
21       BEGIN
22         Draw(0,0,319,0,3); Draw(0,0,0,199,3);
23         Draw(319,0,319,199,3); Draw(0,199,319,199,3);
24       END;
25
26       BEGIN
```

(continues)

```
27          GraphColorMode;    { Use color graphics mode }
28          X := 0;            { Set initial X figures }
29          J := X-180;
30          { Note that in both cases we draw well outside the window area!}
31          WHILE (X < 319) OR (J < 319) DO   { Draw red full-screen hatch }
32            BEGIN
33              DRAW(X,0,J,199,2);
34              X := X+8; J := X-180
35            END;
36          Border;                      { Draw a border around the screen }
37          GraphWindow(80,40,240,160);  { Cut our window down to 160 X 120 }
38          X := 320; J := X+180;        { Set initial X figures }
39          WHILE (X > 0) OR (J > 0) DO  { Do window hatch in green }
40            BEGIN
41              Draw(X,0,J,199,1);
42              X := X-8; J := X+180
43            END;
44          Border;      { Draw a yellow border around the graphics window }
45          Readln;
46          TextMode;    { Don't leave us in text mode! }
47        END.
```

(concluded)

Hatcher first fills the screen with red diagonal lines. Notice that **J** starts off with a negative value—meaning that the **Draw** statement is "drawing" lines on areas of the screen that don't exist, off to the left of the leftmost screen margin. This is no problem—Turbo Pascal's runtime code ignores commands to draw outside of the current graphics window, which ordinarily means the entire screen. Microsoft BASIC for the IBM triggers an "illegal function call" error for drawing outside the screen. With Turbo Pascal you needn't be quite so careful about how you draw your lines. The easiest way to hatch the entire screen is by the brute force method of hatching an area *greater* than the entire screen, and let Turbo Pascal "clip" the hatching to the bounds of the visible screen. **X** and **J** always remain 180 pixels apart, and hatching continues until *both* **X** and **J** have passed through the "visible" range of 0 to 319 (see Figure 17.1).

Having hatched the entire screen in red, **Hatcher** now draws a border all the way around the screen, using the **Border** procedure.

Next, **Hatcher** creates a 160 × 120 pixel graphics window in the center of the screen using **GraphWindow**. It then hatches the new, smaller window in green, using a similar brute-force method identical to the first save that J is now 180 pixels *greater* than X at all times, so the hatch lines slope in the opposite direction.

Note that we're still using the coordinate limits of the full screen: 319 × 199. However, only the 160 × 120 graphics window we defined using **GraphWindow** actually gets hatched. The portions of the hatching lines that extended beyond the limits of the window were clipped and not drawn.

Finally, **Hatcher** draws a yellow border around the graphics window. But look what happens: Only the top and left edge of the window get the border. Procedure **Border** draws four lines to absolute coordinates, but the right and bottom lines fall outside the 160 × 120 bounds of the graphics window. They are clipped and not drawn. The important point to remember is that the upper-left corner of a graphics window is *always* at coordinates 0,0. The right and bottom bounds of the window depend on how large the window is.

Sadly, although Turbo Pascal graphics windows can clip, they do not scale. In other words, if you arrange a series of **Draw** statements to draw a figure on the full screen, setting up a smaller graphics window and executing the same **Draw** statements will not draw a smaller version of your figure scaled to fit completely in the smaller window. (There are some graphics packages that will do this.)

There is no way in basic graphics to clear a graphics window without disrupting the entire screen. Executing a **GraphColorMode**

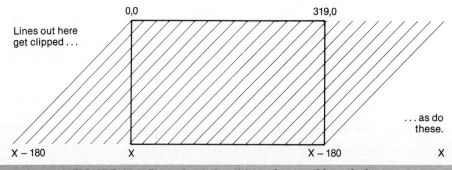

FIGURE 17.1 Brute-force hatching of a graphics window

or **Hires** statement will reset the current graphics window to the entire screen, and erase any graphics on the entire screen. The only way to clear a graphics window is to incorporate extended graphics (see Section 17.5) and use the **FillScreen** procedure. Filling a window with any color will overwrite any graphics within that window, and surrounding areas of the screen will not be affected.

Graphics windows are thus not especially useful, except as an aid to using certain "brute-force" methods of drawing figures that would ordinarily draw beyond the desired bounds of the window.

A SPIROGRAPH PROGRAM

You might think that Turbo Pascal's basic graphics aren't worth much, and to some extent that's true. **Plot** and **Draw** are much slower than they should be. In Section 20.10 we will provide an assembly-language hires-only replacement for **Plot** that is 2 to 3 times faster than Turbo Pascal's own routine. Using the assembly code **Plot** to plot a string of adjacent points, you can draw lines more quickly than **Draw**.

In the meantime, let's look at what can be done with basic graphics only. In practice, **Plot** isn't used very much. Mostly you would use it to create larger figures such as circles and curves. By being a little sneaky, however, it is possible to draw curves using nothing but the straight lines provided by **Draw**—and you'll find that plotting curves using lines is much faster than individually plotting every single dot via **Plot**.

There is a price to be paid, of course, and that is the complexity of the mathematics involved. Graphics work in general is math-intensive, and trigonometry-intensive in specific. If you're not up on your trig, the following program will seem rather magical, so you might crack that book you haven't opened since high school and review a little.

When I was twelve (and I am thirty-three at this writing) I had a gadget called a Spirograph that seemed pretty magical itself. A Spirograph is a large plastic gear with teeth on its inner circumference. It is mounted on a circular table of sorts to which you attach plain white paper. A set of smaller gears (which I'll call cogs to avoid confusion with the larger gear) with teeth on the outside comes with the set, along with some colored pencils.

The cogs, unlike the large gear, are solid disks with no large central hole. Instead, the cogs have small holes only large enough to pass a pencil point, at various points around their perimeter. The idea is to mesh a cog with the large gear, poke a pencil through one of the small holes in the cog, and run the cog around the inner perimeter of the larger gear. The pencil draws a smooth loop-de-loop curve on the paper as it rotates around the cog and revolves within the larger gear simultaneously. The sort of pattern drawn depends on the size relationship of the cog to the larger gear and to the distance of the pencil hole from the center of the cog. Some combinations produce elegantly simple four-lobed patterns; other combinations produce rosettes so dense they nearly cover the paper completely with colored lines. Figure 17.2 is a schematic drawing of my long departed plastic Spirograph.

Mysterious as it seemed to me then, the Spirograph is governed by well-known geometric principles. A fairly simple (if rather subtle) Turbo Pascal program can perform the same function as the Spirograph right on your high-resolution graphics screen. The most magical thing of all is that all the complex-seeming curves the Spirograph produces are all drawn with absolutely straight lines.

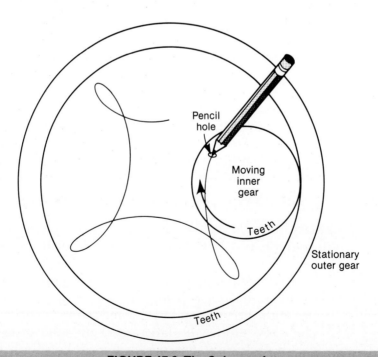

FIGURE 17.2 The Spirograph

```
1         {-------------------------------------------------------------}
2         {                      SpiroGraph                             }
3         {                                                             }
4         {    A fancy curve plotter using nothing but basic graphics   }
5         {                                                             }
6         {                             by Jeff Duntemann               }
7         {                             Turbo Pascal V3.0               }
8         {                             Last update 2/7/86              }
9         {                                                             }
10        {                                                             }
11        {                                                             }
12        {-------------------------------------------------------------}
13
14        PROGRAM SpiroGraph;
15
16        CONST
17          HighResolution   = True;
18          MediumResolution = False;
19
20        VAR
21          A,B,D,I : Integer;
22          Quit    : Boolean;
23
24
25        {$I YES.SRC}
26        {$I GBOX.SRC}
27
28
29        PROCEDURE Cross(X,Y,Size,Color : Integer; HiRes : Boolean);
30
31        VAR
32          YSize   : Integer;
33          YAdjust : Real;
34
35        BEGIN
36          IF HiRes THEN YAdjust := 0.583 ELSE YAdjust := 0.83;
37          YSize := Round(Size * YAdjust);
```

(continues)

```
38              Draw(X-(Size DIV 2),Y,X+(Size DIV 2),Y,Color);
39              Draw(X,Y-(YSize DIV 2),X,Y+(YSize DIV 2),Color)
40          END;
41
42
43
44          FUNCTION HighestCommonFactor(A,B : Integer) : Integer;
45
46          VAR
47            I,J,HCF : Integer;
48
49          BEGIN                 { Euclid's algorithm for finding the HCF }
50            IF A < B THEN       { of two integers A and B. }
51              BEGIN
52                HCF := A;
53                I   := B
54              END
55            ELSE
56              BEGIN
57                HCF := B;
58                I   := A
59              END;
60            REPEAT
61              J := I MOD HCF;
62              IF J <> 0 THEN
63                BEGIN
64                  I := HCF;
65                  HCF := J
66                END
67            UNTIL J = 0;
68            HighestCommonFactor := HCF
69          END;
70
71
72          PROCEDURE SpinWheels(A,B,D,XO,YO : Integer; HiRes : Boolean);
73
74          VAR
75            Rab,N,Lines,I,HCF : Integer;
```

(continues)

```
76          Alpha,Beta,ADif,AoverB : Real;
77          XOLD,YOLD,XPT,YPT : Real;          { Line endpoint coordinates }
78          YAdjust           : Real;
79
80       BEGIN
81          { Y must be adjusted for asymmetrical IBM PC pixels: }
82          IF HiRes THEN YAdjust := 0.583 ELSE YAdjust := 0.83;
83          RAB := A-B; Alpha := 0.0;
84          ADif := PI/50.0; AoverB := A/B;
85          HCF := HighestCommonFactor(A,B);
86          N := B DIV HCF; Lines := 100 * N;
87          XOLD := RAB + D; YOLD := 0.0;
88          FOR I := 1 TO Lines DO
89            BEGIN
90              Alpha := Alpha + Adif;
91              Beta := Alpha * AoverB;
92              XPT := RAB * COS(Alpha) + D * COS(Beta);
93              YPT := RAB * SIN(Alpha) - D * SIN(Beta);
94              DRAW
95              (Round(XOLD)+XO,Round(YOLD*YAdjust)+YO,
96                Round(XPT)+XO,Round(YPT*YAdjust)+YO,1);
97              XOLD := XPT; YOLD := YPT;
98            END
99
100      END;
101
102
103      BEGIN
104        Quit := False;
105        TextColor(7);
106        HiResColor(15);
107        HiRes;                         { Draw conceptual illustration: }
108        GBox(0,0,639,199,2,1);
109        GotoXY(20,2); Write('*Turbo SpiroGraph *** by Jeff Duntemann*');
110        SpinWheels(180,180,140,320,110,HighResolution);
111        SpinWheels(40,40,40,420,110,HighResolution);
112        Cross(320,110,15,1,HighResolution);
113        Cross(420,110,10,1,HighResolution);
```

(continues)

```
114        Cross(420,95,5,1,HighResolution);
115        Draw(180,70,180,100,1);
116        Draw(320,70,320,100,1);
117        Draw(180,75,240,75,1);
118        Draw(260,75,320,75,1);
119        GotoXY(32,10); Write('A');
120        Draw(380,116,380,150,1);
121        Draw(420,116,420,150,1);
122        GotoXY(51,19); Write('B');
123        Draw(432,86,480,86,1);
124        Draw(432,95,480,95,1);
125        GotoXY(62,12); Write('D');
126        Draw(383,70,418,93,1);
127        GotoXY(2,4);   Write('A small cog of radius B moves');
128        GotoXY(2,5);   Write(' about the rim of a toothed');
129        GotoXY(2,6);   Write(' circle of radius A.');
130        GotoXY(2,8);   Write('A pencil follows the');
131        GotoXY(2,9);   Write(' motion of the cog');
132        GotoXY(2,10); Write(' through a hole,');
133        GotoXY(2,11); Write(' distance D from the');
134        GotoXY(2,12); Write(' rim of the cog.');
135        GotoXY(2,14); Write('The pencil draws a');
136        GotoXY(2,15); Write(' curved pattern as it');
137        GotoXY(2,16); Write(' moves along.');
138        GotoXY(57,4); Write('You may vary the values');
139        GotoXY(57,5); Write(' of A, B, and D.');
140        GotoXY(57,7); Write('Try 180,100, and 50');
141        GotoXY(57,8); Write(' to start!');
142        GotoXY(57,24); Write('(CR) to play: ');Readln;
143        REPEAT
144          HiRes;
145          GBox(0,0,639,199,2,1);
146          GotoXY(2,2); Write('Enter A (Circle diameter ): '); Readln(A);
147            GotoXY(2,3); Write('Enter B (Cog diameter)    : '); Readln(B);
148            GotoXY(2,4); Write('Enter D (Pencil radius)   : '); Readln(D);
149          FOR I := 2 to 4 DO
150            BEGIN
151              GotoXY(2,I);
152              Writeln('                                ')
```

(continues)

```
153                END;
154            GotoXY(60,24); Write('A:',A,' B:',B,' D:',D);
155            SpinWheels(A,B,D,320,100,HighResolution);
156            GotoXY(2,24); Write('Try another one? (Y/N): ');
157            IF NOT Yes THEN Quit := True
158        UNTIL Quit;
159        TextMode
160    END.
```

(concluded)

The algorithm is from Ian Angell, the British computer scientist who has written several theoretical books about computer graphics. The first half of the program uses **GBox** and **Draw** to create a graphical "help screen" explaining in simplified terms how the mechanical Spirograph operates. The actual pattern-drawing code is fairly simple and is entirely contained within **SpinWheels**.

Giving a blow-by-blow of the mathematics behind the Spirograph principle is somewhat beyond the scope of this book; I recommend Ian Angell's *Advanced Graphics with the IBM Personal Computer*.[1] The relative complexity of the pattern produced depends on the relationship between the three numbers A,B, and D. In particular, if A and B have a high common factor (or if one is a low multiple of the other), the pattern will be relatively simple and draw fairly quickly. On the other hand, if A and B have a low highest common factor, or no common factor at all, the pattern will be complex and virtually fill the area within the circle.

If A and B are the same (which in the physical Spirograph isn't possible), the pattern will be a circle of diameter D. This makes the **SpinWheels** routine generally useful as a way of drawing circles with only a series of straight lines.

One interesting thing to do is add a **Readln** and a second **Draw** statement to **SpinWheels**, the **Draw** using color 0 to "erase" the line previously drawn in color 1. This allows you to "step through" the generation of a figure one line segment at a time as shown in the following snippet of code.

---

[1] I.O. Angell, *Advanced Graphics with the IBM Personal Computer* (New York: John Wiley & Sons, 1985).

```
Draw
(Round(XOLD)+XO,Round(YOLD*YAdjust)+YO,
 Round(XPT)+XO,Round(YPT*YAdjust)+YO,1);
Readln;
Draw
(Round(XOLD)+XO,Round(YOLD*YAdjust)+YO,
 Round(XPT)+XO,Round(YPT*YAdjust)+YO,0);
```

As you might expect, the line segments are short, but perhaps not as short as you might think necessary to produce such smooth-looking curves!

SpiroGraph provides an interesting example of a program that runs *enormously* more quickly with an 8087 math coprocessor installed than without. And to see those lines *really* move, run **SpiroGraph** on a PC/AT with an 80287.

17.5   IBM PC extended graphics

Turbo Pascal V3.0 for the IBM PC has additional graphics support not included with earlier versions. This support is referred to as "extended graphics."

Unlike everything else that we have studied so far, extended graphics support is not built into the Turbo Pascal compiler itself. Extended graphics reside in a single large external machine-code file (**GRAPH.BIN**) shipped with Turbo Pascal. Although only a little over 5K bytes in size, **GRAPH.BIN** contains 40 separate machine-language functions and procedures, all of which support PC graphics.

As with basic graphics, extended graphics are designed to work *only* with the IBM Color Graphics Adapter or equivalent third-party graphics card. There is no support in Turbo Pascal for Hercules, IBM EGA, or exotic third-party graphics boards like Tecmar's Graphics Master.

The routines in **GRAPH.BIN** are considered external machine-code routines, and to be used they must be declared as external (see Section 20.9). To make it easy, Borland supplies an include file containing all the correct external declarations for the routines contained in **GRAPH.BIN**. This file is called **GRAPH.P**. **GRAPH.P** is an ordinary text file that can be edited in the Turbo Editor. Include it as you would any include file:

```
{$I GRAPH.P}
```

With **GRAPH.P** included in your source program, all the extended graphics routines are declared, and you can use them just as though they were built in.

The structure of **GRAPH.P** bears some examination. After some constant declarations that support turtle graphics, the first line in **GRAPH.P** is:

```
procedure Graphics;            external 'GRAPH.BIN';
```

This line opens the file **GRAPH.BIN** and gives the file as a whole a name, **Graphics**. "Graphics" does not itself represent a routine, but a reference point from which its contained machine code routines are accessed.

A typical routine declaration from **GRAPH.P** looks like this:

```
PROCEDURE FillScreen(Color : Integer); external Graphics[45];
```

The notation **external Graphics[45]** is new to Turbo Pascal V3.0. It is possible to store many separate machine-code routines in an external file, and reference them separately using an offset figure into the machine-code file. The "45" indicates that the entry point for procedure **FillScreen** is at an offset of 45 bytes into the machine-code file that had been given the name **Graphics** previously.

Unless you intend to use Turbo Pascal's turtle graphics (which I consider a waste of time), fully half the routines declared in **GRAPH.P** are not used. Sadly, there's little advantage in editing unnecessary declarations out of **GRAPH.P**, as the entire machine-code file is loaded in and merged with your program during compilation, regardless of how many or how few of its entry points are declared in **GRAPH.P**. At best, you will gain a fraction of a second in compilation time. The size of your .COM file will be the same.

COLORTABLE   There are four available colors in medium resolution graphics mode on IBM's Color Graphics Adapter. (So long as you consider color 0—background—a color.) The Turbo Pascal runtime code maintains a "color translation table" that enables some special tricks to be played with colors. The color translation table is four values that default to 0,1,2,3. It gives you a new way of choosing colors for drawing to the screen. Ordinarily, you specify a color in the parameter line for drawing primitives like **Draw** and **Circle**, and the figure is drawn in that color. When you specify a color value of –1, however, the color translation table picks the color, based on the color already on the screen at the position you wish to draw.

If you think of the color translation table as an **ARRAY[0..3] OF Integer**, the logic can be informally expressed as, "If you draw over color X on the screen, you get color Y," where X is the index into the color table (0 to 3) and Y is the value stored in the color table at that index.

It's easier to express as a table (see Figure 17.3).

Default

Write:	0	1	2	3
and get:	0	1	2	3

ColorTable (3,2,1,0);

Write:	0	1	2	3
and get:	3	2	1	0

ColorTable (2,3,0,1);

Write:	0	1	2	3
and get:	2	3	0	1

FIGURE 17.3 Color translation tables

For the default table value 0,1,2,3, nothing out of the ordinary happens: You draw over color 0 and you get color 0; draw over color 1 and you get color 1, etc. Now consider the second table, 3,2,1,0. Here, if you draw over color 0 you get color 3, draw over color 1 and get color 2, draw over color 2 and get color 1...whatever color is on the screen when you draw on it gets "reversed."

The color translation table is changed with this routine:

```
PROCEDURE ColorTable(Color0,Color1,Color2,Color3 : Integer);
```

To change the color translation table to 3,0,1,2, for example, invoke it as **ColorTable(3,0,1,2)**.

In practice, **ColorTable** would be more useful if it weren't so slow. In the sample program I'll give a little later, I use a figure in an array to draw a bomb, and then another "black-out" figure in a second array to erase the bomb. By repeating this process while moving the location of the bomb figure each time I draw and erase it, the bomb moves smoothly down the screen. I could dispense with the need to use a "black-out" figure by changing the color translation table to 3,2,1,0 and drawing the bomb again. I would then have to change the color translation table *back* to 0,1,2,3 to draw the bomb "normally" in its new position. For each position on the screen (and the bomb has to move through more than 150 of them) I would have to change the color translation table twice. This slows the bomb down so badly that it looks more like a leaking blimp than a bomb, which is not the stuff of which exciting video games are made.

ARC

Extended graphics includes a primitive for drawing arcs:

```
Arc(OriginX,OriginY,Angle,Radius,Color : Integer);
```

Parameters **OriginX** and **OriginY** are the starting points for the arc itself, *not* the arc's center of radius. **Angle** is given in degrees and is the portion of a circle through which the arc will be drawn. Where **Angle** is positive, the arc is drawn clockwise from **OriginX,OriginY**; where **Angle** is negative, the arc is drawn counterclockwise.

There is something very seriously wrong with **Arc** (see Fig. 17.4). One use of arcs is to create graphics rectangles with rounded corners, which are very nice for graphics windowing schemes. As I quickly discovered, only two of the four necessary corner arcs can be drawn with **Arc**. Arcs are always drawn "up" from their origin points; there is no way to draw them "down" or to one side or the other. And while it is possible to draw a 270 degree arc in a color, followed immediately by a 180 degree arc in black with the same origin and radius to erase the unwanted parts of the arc and yield a 90 degree arc starting "down," speed is a problem, along with disrupting graphics falling along the path of the unwanted arc segment. It's not worth it. There are points at which I (as it were) draw the line.

CIRCLE Drawing circles (well, ellipses) is done with **Circle**:

```
PROCEDURE Circle(X,Y,Radius,Color : Integer);
```

The drawn circle's center will be at **X,Y** with radius **Radius**, drawn in **Color**. As with any **Color** parameter in a graphics primitive, a negative value will hand off color selection to the color translation table.

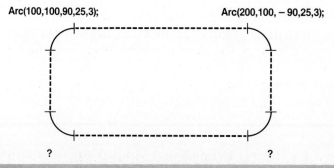

Arc(100,100,90,25,3); Arc(200,100, −90,25,3);

FIGURE 17.4 The trouble with ARC

Unlike the truly marvelous circle-draw routine in IBM BASICA, there is no way to set an "aspect ratio" with **Circle**. In other words, the proportions of your circle are dependent on the asymmetrical vertical and horizontal scales of the Color Graphics Adapter. In 320 × 200 your circles will be a little bit elliptical, and in 640 × 200 mode they will be a *lot* elliptical, with the long axis vertical.

Unalterable ellipses are creatures of extremely limited usefulness. If you need to draw circles, your best bet is to use the **SpinWheels** procedure from the Spirograph program in the previous section. **SpinWheels** is relatively slow, but it can draw a true circle or an ellipse of any reasonable aspect.

GETDOTCOLOR   The useful mirror-image function of setting points is finding out what color a particular screen point is. For that, use

```
FUNCTION GetDotColor(X,Y : Integer) : Integer;
```

Given a pixel's coordinates in **X,Y**, **GetDotColor** will return the color of that pixel as an integer value from 0 to 3.

One use of **GetDotColor** is in determining when an animated object has touched an area of color, perhaps representing a wall or a target. An animated object can "feel" a pixel or two ahead of itself and determine whether an area of a specified color is approaching. The bombs of program **Bomber** do this to determine when they have struck a target.

Note that early printings of the *Turbo Pascal Reference Manual* mistakenly print this function's name as **GetPoint**.

FILLSCREEN   The only way to clear a graphics window is to use **FillScreen**:

```
PROCEDURE FillScreen(FillColor : Integer);
```

If no graphics window has been defined with the **GraphWindow** procedure (see Section 17.5), **FillScreen** will fill the entire screen with the color specified by **FillColor**. If a window has been defined, only the area within the window will be filled. If you specify color 0, you will clear the screen or current graphics window to black.

Filling a window with **FillColor** equal to –1 will replace the colors of all graphics within the window with colors specified in the color translation table. If the color table is set to 0,1,2,3, nothing will happen. However, if the color table is set to 0,1,2,0, anything in color 3 will be set to color 0, effectively (and *quickly!*) erasing whatever was drawn in color 3 without affecting anything drawn in any other color. If the color table is set to 3,2,1,0, **FillScreen** will invert the colors of all graphics within the window. This is a fast and easy way to accomplish certain special effects.

FILLSHAPE

The technical term for a primitive of this type is "flood"; what it does is fill an enclosed area of any shape with a specified color:

```
PROCEDURE FillShape(X,Y,FillColor,BorderColor : Integer);
```

The shape to be flooded must be completely bounded by the color passed in **BorderColor**. The flood color is passed in **FillColor**. You specify the shape to be filled by specifying a point within the shape with coordinates **X,Y**.

Anything drawn within the shape will be overwritten by the flooding color. The color translation table is not operative here; negative values for the two color parameters will be ignored.

You have to be careful using **FillShape**. If there is even the tiniest "sneak path," one pixel in width out of the shape to be filled, the color will find it, and it will then spill out and perhaps destroy the rest of the graphics on the screen. (Unless, of course, the shape is enclosed within a larger shape that is itself fully closed.)

FILLPATTERN

This is a somewhat more disciplined and interesting routine:

```
PROCEDURE FillPattern(X1,Y1,X2,Y2,Color : Integer);
```

The idea here is to draw a rectangular area with a pattern instead of a color. The pattern is set with the **Pattern** procedure, which I will describe next. The rectangular region is specified by an upper-left corner at **X1,Y1** and a lower-right corner at **X2,Y2**. The pattern will be displayed in the color passed in **Color**; the color translation table is not operative here.

As this is not a flood primitive, there is no danger of the pattern "leaking" and filling the rest of the screen. Nothing will occur outside the rectangular area whose corners are passed in the parameter line.

PATTERN   The pattern used by **FillPattern** is defined by **Pattern**:

```
PROCEDURE Pattern(PatternStyle : PatternArray);
```

in which **PatternArray** is a user-defined type given as

```
ARRAY[0..7] OF Byte
```

The pattern is set up by the arrangement of bits within the numeric value stored in the eight bytes in **PatternStyle**. A 1-bit becomes a color point within the pattern. A 0-bit does not affect the underlying area, and will let existing color "shine through" it.

Designing a pattern is best done with square-ruled graph paper. Lay out an 8 × 8 pixel square and darken in the pixels you wish to be in your pattern. It takes some practice, because you tend to forget that the pattern is endlessly repeated through the filled rectangular area, and the edges of the pattern join up with themselves. The block you lay out may bear little resemblance to the actual pattern it produces in a filled rectangle. After some practice, you may get a feel for it, but I suspect trial and error will play an important part in the design of any pattern.

Figure 17.5 shows three pattern arrays and the blocks from which they were derived, along with screen dumps of the resultant patterns as they would appear on your graphics screen. Note especially the non-intuitive connection between the design block for the "squiggles" pattern and the pattern itself—it took some trial and error to get that one right, whereas "blocks" is a self-contained little figure and is very suggestive of the final result on the screen.

Pattern operates with some intelligence across the two graphics modes supported by extended graphics: In both high resolution and color graphics modes each bit in the array is one pixel rather than

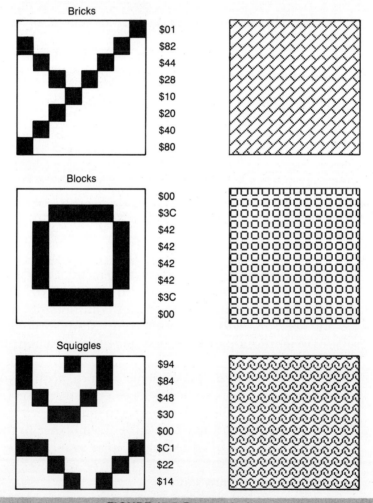

FIGURE 17.5 Pattern design

one bit in the display buffer. The difference is crucial in that, for color graphics, one bit in the display buffer is only one of two bits that define a colored pixel. If the bits in a **PatternArray** were simply "blitted" (a very appropriate bit of graphics jargon stemming from BLT'ed, or BLock Transferred) to the screen, false color problems would occur, and the pattern would be only four color graphics pixels wide.

The use of both **Pattern** and **FillPattern** is demonstrated by the following program, which includes definitions for six different patterns (including the three patterns defined in Figure 17.5), and fills six rectangular areas of the screen with the six patterns.

```
1    {------------------------------------------------------------}
2    {                        Patterns                            }
3    {                                                            }
4    {            Graphics pattern demonstration program          }
5    {                                                            }
6    {                        by Jeff Duntemann                   }
7    {                        Turbo Pascal V3.0                   }
8    {                        Last update 1/31/86                 }
9    {                                                            }
10   {                                                            }
11   {                                                            }
12   {------------------------------------------------------------}
13
14   PROGRAM Patterns;
15
16   TYPE
17      PatternArray = ARRAY[0..7] OF Byte;
18
19   CONST
20      Halftone1 : PatternArray =
21                  ($CC,$33,$CC,$33,$CC,$33,$CC,$33);
22      Halftone2 : PatternArray =
23                  ($AA,$55,$AA,$55,$AA,$55,$AA,$55);
24      Squiggles : PatternArray =
25                  ($94,$84,$48,$30,$00,$c1,$22,$14);
```

(continues)

```
26        Vertical  : PatternArray =
27                    ($CC,$CC,$CC,$CC,$CC,$CC,$CC,$CC);
28        Bricks    : PatternArray =
29                    ($01,$82,$44,$28,$10,$20,$40,$80);
30        Blocks    : PatternArray =
31                    ($00,$3C,$42,$42,$42,$42,$3C,$00);
32
33
34      {$I GRAPH.P}
35
36      BEGIN
37        GraphColorMode;
38        Pattern(Halftone1);
39        FillPattern(0,0,106,100,1);
40        Pattern(Halftone2);
41        FillPattern(107,0,213,100,2);
42        Pattern(Squiggles);
43        FillPattern(213,0,319,100,3);
44        Pattern(Vertical);
45        FillPattern(0,101,106,199,3);
46        Pattern(Bricks);
47        FillPattern(106,101,213,199,2);
48        Pattern(Blocks);
49        FillPattern(213,101,319,199,1);
50        Readln;
51        TextMode;
52      END.
```

(concluded)

GETPIC

The last two graphics routines we'll cover are inverses of one another: **GetPic** and **PutPic**. As their names imply, **GetPic** "lifts" a rectangular region of graphics from the screen into storage in an array, and **PutPic** puts a rectangular region of graphics from an array back down onto the screen. They are similar to, if not as powerful as, the graphics **GET** and **PUT** from IBM BASICA.

GetPic is defined this way:

```
PROCEDURE GetPic(VAR Buffer : <any type>; X1,Y1,X2,Y2 : Integer);
```

X1 and **Y1** define the upper left corner of the rectangular region to be lifted from the screen, with **X2** and **Y2** defining the lower right corner. Graphics information is lifted from this region into **Buffer**, which may be of any type large enough to hold the graphics image you want to lift. How much room you need in **Buffer** for a given rectangular region is given by these two equations:

For color graphics mode:

```
BytesRequired = ((Width + 3) DIV 4) * (Height * 2) + 6;
```

For high resolution mode:

```
BytesRequired := ((Width + 7) DIV 8) * Height + 6;
```

Buffer's type is not critical, but its usage implies a record structure incorporating a three-integer header followed by a data area:

```
CONST
  FigureSize = 400;

TYPE
  FigureType = RECORD
                 ModeCode : Integer;   { 2=color; 1=hires }
                 Width    : Integer;
                 Height   : Integer;
                 Pixels   : ARRAY[0..FigureSize] OF Byte
               END;
```

This record type could contain a figure requiring 400 bytes of space or less, which for a square figure in color graphics mode would be about 26 by 26 pixels. Making the size figure a constant means you could change the size for several record definitions for figures of the same size by altering only the one constant. Sadly, Pascal does not allow array variables to change size "on the fly" during execution. The size of any array must be set at compilation time.

When you invoke **GetPic**, it returns **Buffer** filled with not only the data from the screen but also the height, width, and mode code filled in correctly. **ModeCode** is 2 for color graphics mode and 1 for high resolution mode, and actually corresponds to the number of bits per pixel required in that mode. With the pattern stored in **Buffer**, you can alter the screen and put the pattern back down again by handing the filled **Buffer** to **PutPic**.

PUTPIC

As we mentioned earlier, **PutPic** is the inverse of **GetPic**. What **GetPic** "lifts" from the screen, **PutPic** "lays down" again. It is defined this way:

```
PROCEDURE PutPic(Buffer : <any type>; X,Y : Integer);
```

PutPic takes whatever data is in **Buffer** and lays it down as a rectangular pattern on the screen, with **X** and **Y** defining the lower left corner of the rectangle. You don't have to specify an opposite corner because the **Width** and **Height** fields in **Buffer** already determine how large the figure is. All you have to do is fix the lower left corner at some pixel position and **PutPic** will do the rest.

Most of the time you are likely to use **PutPic** to lay down an image picked up by **GetPic**—but you can also build an image from scratch in a buffer, and then use **PutPic** to lay the image down on the screen, even though it was never displayed initially.

The process is best approached as if designing a pattern for **FillPattern**: Draw a rectangular box the size of your figure on graph paper and blacken in the squares of the pixels you wish colored. Then you have to derive the hexadecimal numbers from the binary patterns represented by the blackened squares (for 1-bits) and the white squares (for 0-bits.)

This is fairly straightforward for high resolution mode, in which each bit in the data array represents one pixel on the screen. For color graphics mode, it takes *two* bits in the data array to represent one pixel on the screen. Two 1-bits side-by-side will represent a pixel in color 3; two 0-bits side-by-side will represent a pixel in color 0. The other two combinations of one bit on beside one bit off will represent colors 1 and 2. In practice, trying to design colored images from scratch is considerably more trouble than it is worth, especially for large figures.

Another consideration is that the pixels on the IBM PC's graphics screen are not symmetrical, whereas the squares on your graph paper probably are. An IBM high-resolution graphics pixel is more than twice as high as it is wide. A figure that looks nice on graph paper will look "squeezed" and narrow when displayed on the graphics screen. If you intend to do a lot of this, it might pay off in aggravation avoided to generate some graph paper with a T-square and triangle (or, if you're lucky, a laser printer and CAD package) reflecting the pixel proportions of the PC. Use a ratio of 5:12 for high resolution, and 5:6 for medium resolution color graphics.

You must remember that for some odd reason, **PutPic** lays down its array from the bottom upward. This is why you specify a *lower* left hand corner with **PutPic**'s **X** and **Y** parameters. You must take that orientation into account when you derive your array of binary data from the blackened squares on your graph paper. Instead of indexing your array from the top of the figure down, you must index it from the bottom up. If you index it from the top down, your figure will be displayed upside-down (see Figure 17.6).

AN EXTENDED GRAPHICS EXAMPLE

The program **Bomber** illustrates the use of many of the extended graphics primitives described in the last few pages. It is not a game in the sense that it can be played, but it illustrates many of the techniques contained in the design of games using PC graphics.

Very simply, **Bomber** displays a row of rectangular targets at various positions on the screen. Then animated bomb figures descend from the top of the screen, eventually colliding with the targets. When a bomb contacts a target, the target disappears. This continues until all the targets are gone.

The targets are simple rectangles, drawn by the **GBar** procedure. They are 40 pixels wide, and there are eight of them across the width of the screen. They are positioned at random vertical positions, and those random positions are stored in an array called **Targets**. **Targets** is an array of eight integers, one for each target on the screen. A value is stored into each integer by the random number generator routine called **Pull** (see Section 16.10). This is the Y-position for that target.

The bomb figure is defined as an array constant. This is a good way to define simple graphics figures, as all the work of loading graphics information into the array is handled by the compiler itself and need not be accomplished with assignment statements. A good idea (as I've done here) is to add a comment after each graphics row bitmap, displaying asterisks for each high bit in the bitmap. This gives the reader of your code (who may or may not be you, remember) a rough idea of what the figure is supposed to look like. Again, remember that in the source code it will appear upside-down relative to its orientation on the graphics screen.

A second bomb figure is defined, the same height and width as the first, this one filled with zeroes. To move the bomb down the screen, it must first be displayed with **PutPic** and then erased, by using **PutPic** to lay down the "blanker" bomb figure atop it. The visible bomb is then laid down one pixel lower, erased again, and so on. The bomb moves one pixel position down the screen with each cycle. This action is accomplished within the **DropBomb** procedure.

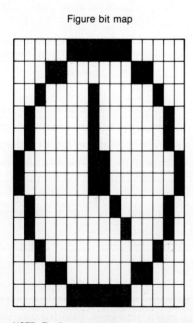

Figure bit map

Hexadecimal equivalent		Figure array element	
07	E0	22	23
18	18	20	21
21	04	18	19
41	02	16	17
41	02	14	15
81	81	12	13
81	81	10	11
40	42	8	9
40	22	6	7
20	04	4	5
18	18	2	3
07	E0	0	1

NOTE: The figure is stored in an array defined as: ARRAY[0..23] OF Byte.

FIGURE 17.6 Designing a high-resolution figure

```
1        {------------------------------------------------------}
2        {                      Bomber                          }
3        {                                                      }
4        {        Extended graphics demonstration program       }
5        {                                                      }
6        {                        by Jeff Duntemann             }
7        {                        Turbo Pascal V3.0             }
8        {                        Last update 4/13/86           }
9        {                                                      }
10       {    From the book, COMPLETE TURBO PASCAL, by Jeff Duntemann  }
11       {    Scott, Foresman & Co. (c) 1986,1987   ISBN 0-673-18600-8  }
12       {------------------------------------------------------}
13
14       PROGRAM Bomber;
15
16       {$I GRAPH.P}
17
18       CONST
19         MissileSize = 39;
20         Hatch       = True;
21         NoHatch     = False;
22
23       TYPE
24         PatternArray = ARRAY[0..7] OF Byte;
25
26         MissileRec = RECORD
27                        ModeCode,Width,Height : Integer;
28                        Pixels : ARRAY[0..MissileSize] OF Byte
29                      END;
30
31         TargetRec  = RECORD
32                        ModeCode,Width,Height : Integer;
33                        Pixels : ARRAY[0..511] OF Byte
34                      END;
35
36         TargetArray = ARRAY[0..7] OF INTEGER;
37
```

(continues)

```
38
39          CONST
40            Lines : PatternArray =
41                    ($44,$88,$11,$22,$44,$88,$11,$22);
42
43          { Note well that PutPic images are displayed "upside-down" }
44          { from the orientation in which you code them.  The bomb   }
45          { below points "up" in the listing but will be nose-down   }
46          { when PutPic shows it on the screen! }
47
48          Bomb : MissileRec =
49                  (ModeCode : 2;   { 2 = Color Graphics; 1 = HiRes }
50                   Width    : 8;   { Remember...2 bits per pixel!  }
51                   Height   : 20;
52                   Pixels   : ($0F,$F0,   {    ********    }
53                               $3F,$FC,   {  ************  }
54                               $FF,$FF,   {****************}
55                               $FF,$FF,   {****************}
56                               $FF,$FF,   {****************}
57                               $FF,$FF,   {****************}
58                               $FF,$FF,   {****************}
59                               $FF,$FF,   {****************}
60                               $FF,$FF,   {****************}
61                               $FF,$FF,   {****************}
62                               $FF,$FF,   {****************}
63                               $3F,$FC,   {  ************  }
64                               $0F,$F0,   {    ********    }
65                               $03,$C0,   {      ****      }
66                               $0F,$F0,   {    ********     }
67                               $3F,$FC,   {  ************  }
68                               $FC,$3F,   {******    ******}
69                               $FC,$3F,   {******    ******}
70                               $FC,$3F,   {******    ******}
71                               $FC,$3F)); {******    ******}
72
73          VAR
74            I                : Integer;
75            NoBomb           : MissileRec;    { "Black" bomb that erases visible bomb }
```

(continues)

```
76        X,XNose,YNose : Integer;
77        BombX           : Integer;       { Column from which bomb is dropped }
78        TargetFigure  : TargetRec;      { The target itself, replicated by PutPic }
79        Targets        : TargetArray;    { Array of flags showing which targets hit }
80        DetonateX,DetonateY : Integer; { Point at which bomb encountered target }
81
82
83     {$I PULL.SRC }   { Described in Section 16.10 }
84
85
86     PROCEDURE GBAR(X,Y,Width,Height,EdgeColor,FillerColor : Integer;
87                    Hatch : Boolean;
88                    HatchPattern : PatternArray);
89
90     BEGIN
91       Draw(X,Y,X+Width,Y,EdgeColor);
92       Draw(X,Y+Height,X+Width,Y+Height,EdgeColor);
93       Draw(X,Y,X,Y+Height,EdgeColor);
94       Draw(X+Width,Y,X+Width,Y+Height,EdgeColor);
95       IF Hatch THEN
96         BEGIN
97           Pattern(HatchPattern);
98           FillPattern(X+1,Y+1,X+Width-1,Y+Height-1,FillerColor)
99         END
100      ELSE
101        FillShape(X+1,Y+1,FillerColor,EdgeColor);
102    END;
103
104
105    FUNCTION AllClear(Targets : TargetArray) : Boolean;
106
107    VAR
108      I : Integer;
109
110    BEGIN
111      AllClear := True;   { Start by assuming all targets have been hit... }
112      FOR I := 0 TO 7 DO
113                          { ...but if any haven't, return FALSE }
```

(continues)

```
114              IF Targets[I] <> 0 THEN AllClear := False
115          END;
116
117
118          PROCEDURE ClearTarget(DetonateX,DetonateY : Integer;
119                                VAR Targets : TargetArray);
120
121          VAR
122            I : Integer;
123
124          BEGIN         { Erase the target by drawing a "black" bar over it }
125            GBar((DetonateX DIV 40)*40,DetonateY,40,10,0,0,NoHatch,Lines);
126            Targets[DetonateX DIV 40] := 0;
127          END;
128
129
130          PROCEDURE DropBomb(StartX,StartY : Integer;
131                             VAR DetonateX,DetonateY : Integer);
132
133          VAR
134            YNose : Integer;
135
136          BEGIN
137            YNose := StartY;
138            REPEAT
139              PutPic(Bomb,StartX,YNose);        { Draw the bomb }
140              PutPic(NoBomb,StartX,YNose);       { Erase the bomb }
141              YNose := Succ(YNose);              { Prepare to draw it one pixel down }
142            UNTIL (GetDotColor(StartX+4,YNose+1) <> 0) OR (YNose+1 >= 199);
143            { Bombs travel downward until they hit a target or hit the screen bottom }
144            DetonateX := StartX;  DetonateY := YNose + 1;
145          END;
146
147
148
149          BEGIN
150            Randomize;              { Randomization: the spice of life... }
151            FillChar(NoBomb,Sizeof(NoBomb),Chr(0)); { Blacken the bomb-blanker... }
```

(continues)

```
152        WITH NoBomb DO                            { ...and fill its header }
153          BEGIN
154            ModeCode := Bomb.ModeCode;
155            Height := Bomb.Height;
156            Width  := Bomb.Width
157          END;
158        GraphColorMode;
159                                { Pull random vertical positions for the targets }
160        FOR X := 0 TO 7 DO Targets[X] := Pull(85,180);
161                                { Draw a target for the intro and "lift" it }
162        GBar(140,120,40,10,1,2,NoHatch,Lines);
163        GetPic(TargetFigure,140,120,180,130);
164                                { Do the animated intro }
165        DropBomb(156,24,DetonateX,DetonateY);
166        GotoXY(16,18); Write('Bombs Away!');
167        GotoXY(12,19); Write('Press (CR) to begin:');
168        Readln;
169                                { Blank the screen again and begin }
170        GraphColorMode;
171
172        { Now we lay down the targets, each of which is 40 pixels wide.  The }
173        { vertical (Y) position of each target is stored in array Targets. }
174        { The elements of Targets also function as collision flags, which }
175        { are set to zero when a given target is struck by a bomb.  When all }
176        { elements in Targets are zeroed, the game is over. }
177        FOR I := 1 TO 8 DO PutPic(TargetFigure,(I-1)*40,Targets[I]);
178        YNose := 24;
179        XNose := Pull(5,300);
180        REPEAT                  { Drop bombs until all the targets are gone }
181          { The following statement ensures that bombs will not "graze" the next }
182          { target to the right by making sure each bomb is dropped from a point }
183          { at least eight pixels from the right edge of each target position }
184          REPEAT BombX := Pull(5,310) UNTIL (BombX MOD 40) < 32;
185          DropBomb(BombX,24,DetonateX,DetonateY);
186          ClearTarget(DetonateX,DetonateY,Targets);
187          IF KeyPressed THEN Halt    { To stop things early }
188        UNTIL AllClear(Targets);
189        GotoXY(1,23); Write('Press (CR) to continue: ');
```

(continues)

```
190          Readln;
191          TextMode;    { Don't ever leave the user in graphics mode! }
192          END.
```

(concluded)

Two things can happen when a bomb is dropped. It either strikes a target, or it travels on to the bottom of the screen. **DropBomb** determines whether or not the bomb contacts a target by testing the color of the pixel one pixel beneath the center of the bomb's nose. This is done with Turbo Pascal's **GetDotColor** function, which returns the color value of a given pixel at a given position. If that color is anything but black (0), the bomb is about to contact a target, and **DropBomb** returns with the X,Y position of the contact point in **DetonateX** and **DetonateY**. If, on the other hand, the Y position of the nose of the bomb reaches 199, then the bomb has missed all the targets and reached the bottom of the screen.

The procedure **ClearTarget** accepts **DetonateX** and **DetonateY** and determines which target (if any) has been struck. If a target has in fact been struck, the target is erased by drawing a "black" bar over the target with **GBar**. **ClearTarget** then stores a zero in the array element of **Targets** corresponding to the struck target. This indicates that that target has been struck and erased from the screen.

After each bomb is dropped, a function called **AllClear** checks array **Targets** to see if all the eight targets have been struck and their elements zeroed. When all elements are zero, **AllClear** returns **True** and the program ends. The program can be ended at any time by pressing any key.

As the bombs fall, you will notice bands rippling through the bomb image. This is due to a conflict between Turbo Pascal's writing the bomb image to graphics RAM and the PC reading graphics RAM in order to display what exists there. There is nothing much to be done about it without dropping into some rather arcane assembly-language tricks.

Aside from some rather simple games in which only a single object is in motion at one time ("pong"-type games) Turbo Pascal is not an ideal environment for developing real-time animated graphics. Good machine-code routines for time-critical functions can help tremendously, but they are not easy to write. I hope to fill in some of these gaps in my forthcoming book, *Turbo Pascal*

Solutions: Graphics. In the meantime, you might investigate third-party graphics libraries such as Metagraphics' excellent Metawindow (see Appendix A). Graphics are one of the most difficult of all computer applications to do well. The IBM PC's graphics cards are not good as graphics go (see the Atari ST for a cheap graphics engine of startling power), and the 8088 has a choke-point in its 8-bit data bus that severely restricts the speed of data flowing between RAM and the CPU. Future 32-bit machines based on the 80386 will be much better. Finally, I hope that someday, someone will realize that pixels are supposed to be as wide as they are high!

Console, printer, and disk I/O

A computer program is a universe unto itself. Within its bounds, data structures are created, changed, and deleted. Calculations are performed and the results used in still more calculations. Much occurs in a computer program's universe in the course of getting a job done.

However, it is out here in *our* universe that the job comes from and the finished work is needed. Somehow some of the critters living in a computer program have to cross the threshold between the program-universe and the real universe. The pathways between the computer program and the outside world are collectively called "input/output" or, more tersely, "I/O." In Pascal, all I/O is handled under the umbrella category of files.

18.1 Device files and disk files

To most people, the word "file" conjures images of filing cabinets and various other places to store things for future perusal and reuse. However, another connotation of the word "file" strikes closer to heart of the Pascal file: a long row of people or objects in a straight line, often in the process of moving from one place to another in an orderly fashion. Soldiers file from the parade ground to the mess hall, and so on.

A Pascal file is a stream of data, either coming or going. Not all "files" are data sorted on disk or tape. Your keyboard is a file: a stream of characters triggered by your fingers and sent inward to the waiting program. Your CRT screen is a file: a flat field painted with visible symbols by a stream of characters sent from the program inside the computer. Your printer is a file: a device that accepts a stream of characters from the program and places them somehow onto a piece of paper.

The last example contains an important word: "device." Your keyboard is a device, as are your CRT screen, your printer, and your modem. All are files that have one endpoint in the computer program and another endpoint in a physical gadget that absorbs or emits data (sometimes both). This kind of file we call a "device file."

The other kind of file is the most familiar kind: a collection of data recorded as little magnetic disturbances on a clean piece of magnetic plastic. These are "disk files." Files in Turbo Pascal are of one type or another, either device files or disk files.

DEVICE FILE NAMES

All files have names. You're certainly familiar with the list of file names that comes up when you use the DIR facility of your operating system. DIR displays a directory of disk file names on a given disk drive. Device files have names as well, if not such easily displayable ones.

Each operating system has its own means of getting information to and from devices. Most operating systems have a set of standard devices that are supported by function calls to the operating system BIOS (Basic Input/Output System.) Turbo Pascal recognizes names for all devices supported by the host operating system. These names are used by the Turbo Pascal file handling machinery just as names for disk files are used.

Table 18.1 summarizes Turbo Pascal's device file names.

Virtually all computers recognize CON:, KBD:, TRM:, and LST:. AUX: is a combination of RDR: and PUN:, which in turn harken back to the old days when paper tape was still in use. Many modern computers give Turbo Pascal no physical device to hook to RDR: and PUN:. Some associate the two devices with a serial port, or two parallel ports. You will have to look to your hardware/operating system documentation to find out where, if anywhere, the RDR: and PUN: devices lead to. Similarly, the USER device is not supported

Device file names in Turbo Pascal	
Name	Device definition
CON:	Buffered system console. Echoes input characters CR as CR/LF; BS as BS/SP/BS. As OUTPUT, echoes CR as CR/LF; LF alone is ignored. HT (horiz. tab) is expanded to every 8 columns. CAN (CRL-X) erases input line and returns cursor to its starting column.
KBD:	System console as INPUT only. No echo or interpretation.
TRM:	*Unbuffered* system console. No editing ability. Characters are echoed to the screen.
LST:	System list device, OUTPUT only. No interpretation done by Turbo Pascal; operating system may expand tabs. Virtually always represents the system printer.
AUX:	Output to operating system punch device; input from reader device. Your computer may not necessarily recognize this device. *There is no status call.*
USR:	Input and output via operating system USER device. Your computer may not necessarily recognize this device. *There is no status call.*

on all implementations of the MS DOS operating system, and is not supported at all under CP/M-80.

As though to add to the confusion, many CP/M-80 and CP/M-86 computers have a facility for connecting different physical devices to the several device files depending on the value of an "I/O byte." Again, you will need to go to your computer's documentation to see what options are available to you.

Even then, you should be careful. Both the Xerox 820 and the IBM PC, for example, connect RDR: and PUN: to the RS232 modem port. This might imply that RDR: and PUN: could be used to write a "dumb terminal" program to read characters from keyboard and send them to the modem, and read characters from the modem and send them to the screen. Unfortunately, there is no way to test RDR: to see if a character is ready to be read before you actually go in and read one. And if a character is *not* ready, the **Read** statement will wait until one is ready, effectively "hanging the system" until something comes in on the modem line. In practice, AUX: and USR: by themselves are not especially useful devices.

The CON: device should never be explicitly opened at the same time as the KBD: device. Trying to open both may lock up the system.

18.2 Logical and physical files

ISO Standard Pascal does not make a distinction between device and disk files. In ISO Pascal, a file is a file—a stream of data either coming or going. One end of the line is inside the Pascal program, and Pascal simply doesn't care what sort of thing is on the other end of the line.

Turbo Pascal has to modify this notion a little—for random files, as an example—but the "everything out there is a file" bias remains. By not getting involved in the downdeep details of how a character is printed or sent to the screen, Pascal can present a uniform front to many different operating systems. This makes for less work in translating a Pascal program from one operating system environment to another.

This separation between *what* a file does and *how* it does it is sharply drawn in Pascal, between the concepts of "logical" and "physical" files.

A logical file is a Pascal abstraction, beginning with the declaration of a file variable in the variable declaration part of a program:

```
StatData : FILE OF Integer;
```

This tells us that **StatData** is a file and contains integers, nothing more. It says nothing about whether or not the file exists on a disk, which disk, or how much data exists in the file.

That information falls under the realm of physical files. A physical file is an actual device (for device files) or an actual collection of data on some sort of storage medium. A physical disk file has a file name, a size, a record length, an access mode (read only, read/write, hidden, system, etc.), perhaps a timestamp for last access and an interleave factor, and other things as well. It is *not* an abstraction, and by not being an abstraction a physical file must pay attention to all those gritty little details that make storing and retrieving data on disk possible.

All these little details are very much hardware and operating system dependent. If Pascal had to take care of such details, it would be nearly an entirely separate language for each computer/operating system combo it runs on, as is very nearly the case these days with BASIC. (And it has always been the case with FORTH.)

So Pascal provides logical files, and the operating system provides physical files. When a logical file becomes associated with (or "assigned to" as is often said) a physical file, a path exists between the program's inner universe and the outside world. That file is then said to be "open."

INPUT AND OUTPUT

All Pascal programs are capable of accepting input from the keyboard and writing output to the CRT screen. Two standard device files are always open for this purpose: **Input** and **Output**.

In some Pascals you must explicitly name **Input** and **Output** when using them with **Read**, **Write**, **Readln**, and **Writeln**:

```
Writeln(Output,'Files do it sequentially...');
```

In Turbo Pascal, **Input** and **Output** are the default files for use with **Read**, **Write**, **Readln**, and **Writeln**. If you omit the name of a file in one of those statements, the compiler assumes **Input** for **Read** and **Readln**, and **Output** for **Write** and **Writeln**. You need only write:

```
Writeln('Files do it sequentially...');
```

and Turbo Pascal will know to send the text line to your CRT screen.

Similarly, to accept input from the **Input** logical file, which is always connected to your keyboard and always open, you need only write:

```
Readln(AString);
```

and the program will wait while you type text at the keyboard, going on only when it detects a carriage return, or when you have filled the string variable out to its maximum physical length. The text you typed will be immediately available in the variable **AString**.

There is no need to include the identifier **Input** in the **Readln** statement, although you may if you wish.

Input and **Output** are considered text files, which means that only printable ASCII characters and a few control characters may be read from them or written to them. *However,* **Read**, **Readln**, **Write**, and **Writeln** contain limited abilities to convert binary data types such as **Integer** to printable representations. It is, therefore, legal to **Write** an integer to **Output** because **Write** converts the integer to printable characters before **Output** ever sees it. (For a fuller discussion see Section 18.4, under "Using **Read** and **Write** with text files.")

OTHER PREDEFINED LOGICAL DEVICE FILES

Like most Pascals, Turbo Pascal predefines logical files **Input** and **Output** and keeps them open at all times. In Turbo Pascal there are a number of other predefined logical device files that you may use without having to open or close them. These logical devices are in fact "opened" forms of the physical device file names (like CON:, KBD: and so on) described above (see Table 18.2).

Input and **Output** normally default to device name CON:, but you can change that assignment to device name TRM: with the $B compiler directive (see Section 23.4). $B+ (the default) assigns them to CON:, and $B- assigns them to TRM:.

Turbo Pascal's predefined logical device files are always open and cannot be reassigned to other physical device names. Trying to use **Assign**, **Reset**, **Rewrite**, or **Close** on them will generate an error.

18.3 Declaring and assigning files

Declaring a file gives the file a name and a data type:

```
FileVariableName : FILE OF <type>;
```

<type> may be any valid data type except a file type. (A file of files makes no logical sense and is illegal.) <type> can be a standard type like **Integer** or **Boolean**, or it can be a type that you have defined, like records, sets, enumerated types, or arrays. A file can be a file of

Predefined logical and physical device files	
Input	assigned to CON: or TRM: re $B option
Output	assigned to CON: or TRM: re $B option
CON	assigned to CON:
TRM	assigned to TRM:
KBD	assigned to KBD:
LST	assigned to LST:
AUX	assigned to AUX:
USR	assigned to USR:

only one type, however; you cannot declare a file of **Integer** and then write records or sets to it.

Declaring a file creates a file buffer in your data area. This file buffer is a variable of the type the file is declared to be. It is a "window" into the file; the actual open end of the data pipe between the program and the outside world.

Unlike ISO Standard Pascal and most other commercial implementations of Pascal, Turbo Pascal does not allow direct access to the file window via **Get**, **Put**, or the caret notation:

```
VAR
   NumFile : FILE OF Integer;

NumFile^ := I;   { Illegal in Turbo; OK in Standard Pascal }
Put(NumFile);
```

CONNECTING LOGICAL FILES TO PHYSICAL FILES WITH ASSIGN

Opening a file involves, in part, creating a connection between a logical file that is declared in the program and a physical file that exists outside the program. Creating this connection is the job of the built-in procedure **Assign**.

Assign takes two parameters: a file variable that has been declared in the program, and a string variable or literal that names a physical file:

```
PROCEDURE Assign(A_FILE : <filetype>; FileName : String);
```

Assign creates the File Information Block (usually called a FIB) that each file must have to be used by the program. Once associated with a physical file, a logical file may be opened for write access or read access. This is done with **Reset** and **Rewrite**.

OPENING FILES WITH RESET AND REWRITE

The **Assign** procedure is *not* part of ISO Standard Pascal. Most commercial Pascal compilers use it as the means of connecting logical to physical files. However, **Assign** does only half the job of opening a file; its job is limited to linking a logical file with a physical file. Getting a logical file ready to be written to or read from involves two built-in procedures: **Reset** and **Rewrite**. These procedures are part of ISO Standard Pascal.

An open file has in its FIB what we call a "file pointer." This is not a pointer variable as we know it, but rather a logical marker indicating which element in the file will be read or written to next.

Reset opens a file for reading. Some device files allow both read access and write access at the same time; these files are opened with **Reset** also. When a file is to be opened for random file I/O using **Seek** (see Section 18.10), **Reset**, again, is used.

Reset does not disturb the previous contents of a disk file. The file pointer is positioned at the first data item in the file. If the file is empty when **Reset** is executed, the **EOF** function returns **True** for that file.

Some examples:

```
Assign(MyFile,'A:ADDRESS.TXT');
Reset(MyFile);

Assign(Keys,'KBD:');
Reset(Keys);
```

Reset can also be used on a file that is already open. For an open disk file, this will reposition the file pointer to the first record in the file. Performing a **Reset** on an open device file does nothing. If the device file is one of Turbo Pascal's predefined logical devices, **Reset** will generate an error.

Rewrite opens files that are *only* to be written to and not read from while they are currently open. When **Rewrite** is executed on a disk file, all previous contents of the disk file are overwritten and lost. Note that you may use either **Reset** or **Rewrite** on device files; the action on the device file is identical for both.

```
Assign(MyFile,'B:GRADES.DAT');    { Old grades are lost! }
Rewrite(MyFile);

Assign(Printer,'LST:');    { The pre-opened file LST may }
Rewrite(Printer);          { be used instead of doing this }
```

BINARY FILES VS. TEXT FILES

All disk files can eventually be seen as collections of bytes grouped somehow on a diskette or hard disk. Pascal makes a distinction between files that can contain absolutely any binary pattern in a stored byte, and those files that are allowed to contain only printable characters and certain (very few) control characters. Files that may contain any byte pattern at all are called "binary" or "non-text" files. Files that are limited to printable characters are called text files.

Text files are allowed to contain printable ASCII characters plus whitespace characters. Whitespace characters include carriage return (hex 0D), linefeed (hex 0A), formfeed (hex 0C), horizontal tab (hex 09), and backspace (hex 08). Although not technically a whitespace character, the bell character (hex 07) is also permitted in text files.

Text files may be "typed" (via the operating system **TYPE** command) directly from disk to the screen without sending the display controller into suicide fits.

An important consequence of allowing only printable characters is that text files in Pascal may contain an end-of-file (EOF) marker character. Binary files may *not* contain an EOF marker because binary files are allowed to have any 8-bit character pattern as valid data. Therefore, the operating system (and thus Turbo Pascal) could not tell an EOF marker character from just more legal binary data.

Text files in the CP/M and MS/PC DOS operating system families use CTRL-Z (hex 1A) as the EOF marker. When Pascal writes a text file to disk, it places one or more CTRL-Z characters after the last data character. In the CP/M family of operating

systems, Pascal fills any leftover characters in the last 128-byte block
of *any* file (not only text files) with CTRL-Z.

Text files in Turbo Pascal are declared this way:

```
VAR
  MyFile   : FILE OF Text;    { Both forms are legal }
  YourFile : Text;
```

Any file that is not declared to be a **FILE OF Text** or simply **Text** is
considered a binary file. The difference between the two becomes
critical when you need to detect where data ends in the file. We will
examine this problem in detail in connection with the EOF function in Section 18.5.

The normal file buffer size for a text file is 128 bytes. Turbo
Pascal 3.0 for PC/MS DOS allows you to specify a larger buffer size
when a text file is declared. The new size figure is given in brackets
after the identifier **Text**:

```
MyFile : FILE OF Text[$1000];   { 4K text file buffer }
```

The file buffer is a region of memory into which data is loaded from
disk. If your program does a lot of reading and writing to its text
files, you can minimize disk "thrashing" (movement of data to and
from the physical disk) by creating a larger buffer. I/O is done to
the buffer, in effect, until you flush or close the file or until you
move the file pointer outside the range of data currently in the
buffer. With a good sized buffer, you can do a lot without having to
go out to the physical disk drive.

The downside, of course, is that a 4K buffer is 4K less memory to
use for other things. In the PC/MS DOS world, memory is cheap.
Go for 640K, and your programs will benefit in many non-obvious
ways.

18.4   Reading from and writing to files

It is in the realm of file I/O where Turbo Pascal deviates most strongly from ISO Standard Pascal. Standard Pascal has a pair of file procedures called **Get** and **Put**. These work with a data structure called the "file window," which is a slice of the file to be read or written to. When you **Get** from a file, the next item in the file is placed in the file window, from which it may be accessed at leisure. Similarly, when you wish to write an item to a file, you place it in the file window and then **Put** the file window out to the disk.

Turbo Pascal does *not* implement **Get** and **Put**, nor does it make the file window directly available to the programmer. If you are porting Pascal code from another compiler, all **Get**s, **Put**s, and file window references will have to be edited to use **Read** and **Write** instead.

USING READ AND WRITE WITH NON-TEXT FILES

We won't say much more about **Get** and **Put**. They do nothing that can't be done with **Read** and **Write**. That, and their awkwardness, and the need to keep the size of the compiler down were the reasons Turbo Pascal does not implement **Get**, **Put**, and the file window concept of file I/O.

The following discussion deals with "typed" or binary files that are not files of **Text**. Text files are a special case and will be covered in the next section.

Once a file has been opened with **Reset**, data may be read from the file with the **Read** procedure. **Read** takes at least two parameters: a file variable and one or more variables with the same type as the file.

```
VAR
   StatRec,Rec1,Rec2,Rec3  : NameRec;
   MyFile : FILE OF NameRec;

Assign(MyFile,'B:Names.DAT');
Reset(MyFile);

Read(MyFile,StatRec);
Read(MyFile,Rec1,Rec2,Rec3);
```

Here, **NameRec** is a record type defined earlier in the program. In this example, the **Read** statement reads the *first* record from **MyFile** into the record variable **StatRec**. There is no mention of the file window variable, although the file window is involved beneath the surface in the code that handles the **Read** function. The second **Read** statement reads the next three elements of **MyFile** into **Rec1**, **Rec2**, and **Rec3**, all at one time. This is a convenient shorthand; there is no difference in doing this than in doing three distinct **Read** statements.

Write works just the same way, with the same parameters; the only difference being the direction the data is flowing:

```
Assign(MyFile,'B:Names.DAT');
Rewrite(MyFile);

Write(MyFile,StatRec);
Write(MyFile,Rec1,Rec2,Rec3);
```

Read and **Write** work *sequentially;* each time **Read** or **Write** is used, the file pointer is bumped to the next element down the file. The process never works backwards; you cannot begin at the end of the file and work your way back. (Again, for that sort of thing you need random file I/O—see Section 18.10.)

USING READ AND WRITE WITH TEXT FILES

A text file is a stream of printable characters between the program and a device file or disk file. The **Read** and **Write** statements are used to transfer a data item (or list of data items) to or from the text file character stream. The data items do not have to be of the same type. We've been doing things like this informally all through this book:

```
VAR
  Unit  : Char:
  Count : Integer;

Write('The number of files on disk ',Unit,' is ',Count);
```

Here, a list of four data items is being sent to device file **Output**. Two are string literals, one is a character, and one is an integer.

Text files, as we saw in the previous section, may contain only printable ASCII characters and certain control characters. Integer variables are not ASCII characters; they are two-byte binary numbers that are not necessarily printable to the screen.

Yet when you write

```
VAR
  I : Integer;

I := 42;
Write(I);
```

the two ASCII characters "4" and "2" appear on your screen. They are an ASCII representation of a 2-byte binary integer that could as well have been written in base 2 as 00000000 00101010. **Read** and **Write** contain the machinery for converting between numeric variables (which are stored in binary form) and printable ASCII numerals.

Write also has the ability to take Boolean values (which are actually binary numbers 0 or 1) and convert them to the words "TRUE" and "FALSE" before passing them to a text file. **Read**, however, does *not* convert the ASCII strings "TRUE" or "FALSE" to Boolean values!

Read and **Write**, when used with text files, can accept data types **Integer**, **Char**, and **Byte**, and subranges of those three types plus type **Real**. **Write** will also accept Boolean values; remember that **Read** will not. Enumerated types, pointers, sets, arrays, and record types will generate error 66 or 62 during compilation. Attempting to **Read** a Boolean value from a text file will generate error 66: I/O not allowed.

Although **Read** will accept a string variable, it's better practice to use **Readln** for reading strings (see below on **Readln**). The problem is that strings on a text file character stream carry no information about how long they are. If you **Read** from a text file stream into a string variable, the string variable will accept characters from the file until it is physically filled. If the file ends before the string is completely filled, the system may hang or fill the remainder of the string with garbage.

READLN AND WRITELN

Pascal includes a pair of I/O procedures that work only on text files: **Readln** and **Writeln**. They introduce a whole new concept: dividing a Pascal text file into "lines."

Ordinary text on a printed page is a series of lines. A Pascal text file is a one-dimensional stream of characters; it has none of the two-dimensional quality of a printed page. To model text as we see it in the real world, Pascal defines an end-of-line character (EOL) that is inserted into the character stream of a text file after each line of printable characters. The definition of the EOL character may vary from system to system. For most microcomputers, EOL is not one character but two: the sequence carriage return/line feed (hex 0D/0A). This is a holdover from teletype's heyday, when it took one control character to return the typehead to the left margin and another to index the paper up one line.

The **Writeln** procedure is exactly like **Write**, save that it follows the last item sent to the text file character stream with the EOL character. For our discussion, EOL will always be the pair CR/LF.

```
PROGRAM WriteInt;

VAR
  IntText : Text;
  I,J     : Integer;

BEGIN
  Assign(IntText,'B:INTEGERS.DAT');
  Rewrite(IntText);
  FOR I := 1 TO 25 DO Writeln(IntText,I);
  Close(IntText);
END.
```

This program writes the ASCII equivalent of the numbers from 1 to 25 to a text file. Each numeral is followed by a CR/LF pair. A hexdump of file INTEGERS.DAT will allow you to inspect the file character stream:

```
0000   31 0D 0A 32 0D 0A 33 0D   0A 34 0D 0A 35 0D 0A 36
0010   0D 0A 37 0D 0A 38 0D 0A   39 0D 0A 31 30 0D 0A 31
0020   31 0D 0A 31 32 0D 0A 31   33 0D 0A 31 34 0D 0A 31
0030   35 0D 0A 31 36 0D 0A 31   37 0D 0A 31 38 0D 0A 31
0040   39 0D 0A 32 30 0D 0A 32   31 0D 0A 32 32 0D 0A 32
0050   33 0D 0A 32 34 0D 0A 32   35 0D 0A 1A 1A 1A 1A 1A
0060   1A 1A 1A 1A 1A 1A 1A 1A   1A 1A 1A 1A 1A 1A 1A 1A
0070   1A 1A 1A 1A 1A 1A 1A 1A   1A 1A 1A 1A 1A 1A 1A 1A
```

If you know your ASCII well (or have a table handy) you can see the structure of the character stream in this file: ASCII numerals separated by 0D/0A pairs. Turbo Pascal fills out the 128-byte block after the end of data with CTRL-Z characters. In text files, the first CTRL-Z signals end of file; more on that shortly.

In a sense, **Writeln** writes only strings (minus length bytes) to its files. If you hand it a variable that is not a string, **Writeln** will convert it to a string before writing it to its file.

Readln reads one line from a text file. A line, again, is a series of characters up to the next EOL marker. If **Readln** is reading into a string variable, the number of characters read becomes the logical length of the string. Thus, unlike **Read** and **Write**, **Readln** and **Writeln** can in fact maintain information on string length in a file, since all strings written by **Writeln** are bounded by EOL markers.

FORMATTING WITH WRITE PARAMETERS

Write and **Writeln** allow certain formatting options when writing data to text files, including the screen (**Output**) and system printer. These options as given to the **Write** and **Writeln** statements are called "write parameters."

The simplest write parameter applies to any variable that may be written to a text file, and specifies the width of the field in which the variable is written.

```
<any Writeable variable> : <field width>
```

When written, data (if any) in the variable will be right justified within a field of spaces <field width> wide. For example:

```
CONST
  Bar = '|';

VAR
  I    : Integer;
  R    : Real;
  CH   : Char;
  OK   : Boolean;
  Txt  : String;

I := 727;
CH := 'Z';
R := 2577543.67;
OK := False;
Txt := 'Grimble';

Writeln(Bar,I:5,Bar);
Writeln(Bar,CH:2,Bar);
Writeln(Bar,R:12,Bar);
Writeln(Bar,OK:7,Bar);
Writeln(Bar,TXT:10,Bar);
Writeln(Bar,-R,Bar);
Writeln(Bar,R,Bar);
```

When run, this code snippet produces this output:

```
|  727 |
| Z|
| 2.577544E+06|
|  FALSE|
|   Grimble|
|-2.57754E+06|
| 2.57754E+06|
```

Note that the real numbers are always expressed in exponential (also called "scientific") notation; that is, as powers of 10, even though originally expressed with a decimal point and no exponent. To express a real number without the exponent, you must include a second write parameter for the width of the decimal part of the field:

```
<real value> : <field width> : <decimal width>
```

The value <decimal width> indicates how many decimal places are to be displayed. For example:

```
R := 7.775;
S := 0.123456789;
T := 7765;

Writeln(Bar,R:10:3,Bar);
Writeln(Bar,R:10:1,Bar);
Writeln(Bar,R:5:2,Bar);
Writeln(Bar,S:6:6,Bar);
Writeln(Bar,S:12:6,Bar);
Writeln(Bar,S:12:12,Bar);
Writeln(Bar,S:5,Bar);
Writeln(Bar,T:5:2,Bar);
Writeln(Bar,T:5,Bar);
Writeln(Bar,T:6:6,Bar);
```

This code produces the following output:

```
|     7.775|
|       7.8|
| 7.77|
|0.123457|
|      0.123457|
| 1.2345678E-01|
| 1.E-01|
|7765.00|
| 8.E+03|
| 7.7650003E+03|
```

A reminder here: You cannot begin a fractional real number (such as .123456789, above) with a decimal point. You *must* begin the number with a 0 as shown, or error 41: Unknown identifier or syntax error, will appear during compilation.

WRITING TO THE SYSTEM PRINTER

Your printer is a physical device that may be accessed as a text file. You have the option of assigning the file name LST: to a text file and **Reset**ing it, or using the preopened device file LST. Either way you set up a printer text file, writing any text to that text file will print the text on your printer:

```
VAR
  Printer : Text;

Assign(Printer,'LST:');          { Open a printer file }
Rewrite(Printer);

Writeln(Printer,'This text will now appear on the printer.');
Writeln(LST,'This will too, and it''s easier!');
```

Using **Writeln** to the printer will end each line with a carriage return/linefeed pair that will bring the printhead to the left margin of the next line. Using **Write** will leave the printhead where it is after printing the text:

```
Write(LST,'Active drive units now include: ');
FOR Drive := 'A' to 'P' DO
  IF CheckDrive(Drive) THEN Write(LST,Drive,' ');
Writeln(LST,' ');
```

This will print:

```
Active drive units now include: A B D M N
```

Even if you open a printer file yourself (rather than use preopened file LST), you need not close the file.

18.5 IOResult and EOF

IORESULT

Working with creatures like disk files that lie outside the borders of the program itself is risky business. You can build machinery into your program to make sure that the program never attempts to divide by zero, or never attempts to index past the bounds of an array. But how do you make sure that (when you want to open a disk file) the file is on the disk and the disk is in the proper disk drive?

The program does not have absolute control over disk files in the way it has absolute control over numbers, arrays, and other variables. The only way to be sure a file is on the disk is to go out and try to read it. If the file isn't out there, there must be some way to recover gracefully.

The runtime code that Turbo Pascal adds to every program it compiles guards against runtime errors such as an attempt to open (for reading) a file that does not exist. Such an attempt will generate an I/O error 01: File does not exist. Your program will terminate, and if you are running from within the Turbo Environment, Turbo will begin searching for the location of the **Reset** statement that tried to open the file.

Obviously, if there is a legal possibility of a file not existing on the disk, you cannot allow your program simply to crash. Better to determine that an error has happened *without* crashing, so that the program could do something about it, such as creating a new file or looking somewhere else for the old one. Turbo Pascal provides the **IOResult** function to let the program know how successful it has been in striking a path to the outside world. It is predeclared by Turbo Pascal this way:

```
FUNCTION IOResult : Integer
```

After each I/O statement is executed, a value is given to the **IOResult** function. This value can then be tested to determine whether the I/O statement completed successfully. A 0 value indicates that the I/O operation went normally; anything else constitutes an error code.

However, the runtime code error traps will still crash your program when an error is encountered, whether or not you use **IOResult**. To keep the program running in spite of the error, you must disable the error trap with the compiler command $I. This is done by surrounding the I/O statement with an {$I-} command (turn traps off) and an {$I+} command (turn traps on again.)

For example:

```
Assign(MyFile,'B:BOWLING.DAT');
{$I-} Reset(MyFile); {$I+}  { Suspend error traps during Reset }
IF IOResult <> 0 THEN
  BEGIN
    Beep;
    Writeln('>>The bowling scores file cannot be opened.');
    Writeln('  Make sure the scores disk is in the B: drive');
    Writeln('  and press (CR) again:')
  END;
```

This code snippet checks **IOResult** immediately after executing a **Reset** to open a file for read. If **IOResult** returns a non-zero value, the program displays a message to the operator.

IOResult is cleared to zero and refilled with a new value at the beginning of *all* I/O primitives. This includes **Readln** and **Writeln** when used (as we have been using them all along) to talk to the keyboard and the screen via device files **Input** and **Output**. This means you *cannot* directly write the value returned by **IOResult** to the screen or to a file!

```
{$I-} Reset(MyFile); {$I+}
Writeln('The result of that Reset is ',IOResult);  { No! }
```

No matter what happens when **Reset(MyFile)** is executed, the above snippet will *always* display:

```
The result of that Reset is 0
```

Given that restriction, it is probably good practice to assign the value of **IOResult** to an integer variable immediately after an I/O statement and work with the integer variable rather than the function itself.

EOF

Another uncertainty in dealing with disk files lies in knowing where the file ends. Most operating systems keep some sort of information on file size, but as with most hardware-dependent information there are no standards. MS DOS knows a file's size down to the byte; the CP/M operating systems cut it no closer than a 128-byte physical disk sector.

For CP/M this presents a serious problem: The operating system has no way of knowing where within the last 128-byte block in the file real data ends. For CP/M binary files, that is simply that; *there is no way to know from inspecting the physical file precisely where data in a binary file ends.* It's somewhere in the last 128-byte block assigned to that file, but the operating system literally can't tell you where it ends. And you can't mark it with a "special" character (like CTRL-Z, as in text files) because in a binary file *all* binary patterns are allowed and there can be no "special" characters.

Turbo Pascal deals with this problem in a unique manner that makes Turbo binary disk files incompatible with binary disk files produced by non-Turbo programs. When it creates a new binary file, it allocates a 4-byte header at the very start of the file. Two unsigned integer values are stored in this header: The first value (two bytes) gives the number of records. The second value (also two bytes) gives the size of each record in bytes. With these two values, Turbo Pascal can calculate precisely where the end of a binary file falls.

This file header is, however, a two-edged sword. Programs compiled by CP/M-80 Turbo Pascal have runtime code that assumes that the first four bytes of a file contain record count and record length. If a Turbo Pascal program tries to open and read a file produced by a non-Turbo program, it will interpret the first four bytes of the file as record count and record length, and possibly get very confused.

This problem applies only to CP/M-80 versions of Turbo Pascal. MS/PC DOS versions can obtain complete file information from the operating system, and thus MS/PC DOS files do *not* have any sort of header attached automatically by Turbo Pascal. MS/PC DOS Turbo Pascal programs can read files produced in other ways without any problem.

With that in mind, consider the **EOF** (End Of File) function, which is predeclared this way:

```
FUNCTION EOF(FileVar : <any file type>) : Boolean
```

FileVar can be any legal file type. The EOF function returns True as soon as the last item in the file has been read. At that point the file pointer points just past the end of data in the file, and *no further reads should be attempted.* I/O error 99 will occur if you try to read beyond the end of a file. This applies to both text files and binary files.

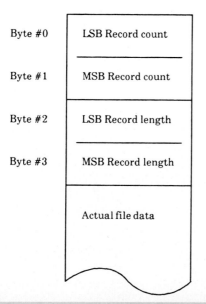

Byte #0 — LSB Record count

Byte #1 — MSB Record count

Byte #2 — LSB Record length

Byte #3 — MSB Record length

Actual file data

Both record count and record length are stored physically as integers, with the LSB *before* the MSB in the file.

FIGURE 18.1 CP/M file header format

Turbo Pascal's runtime code determines **EOF** in two different ways, separately for text and binary files. For binary files, Turbo compares the value of the file pointer to the record count field in the header. As soon as the file pointer has been incremented past the record count, **EOF** becomes true.

Text files, on the other hand, have no header and thus no such record count. An **EOF** marker character is placed at the end of the last item written. For both CP/M and MS DOS, this character is CTRL-Z, or hex 1A. As soon as the file pointer is found to be pointing at a CTRL-Z character, **EOF** becomes true. This happens as soon as the last item in the file is read.

The following program assumes a binary file of integers. It reads all the integers in the file, testing for **EOF** at each read. As it reads each integer, it keeps a running total and a running count, and then produces an average value for all the integers in the file. Note the use of the $I compiler command when opening the file:

```
1        {-------------------------------------------------------}
2        {                      Average                          }
3        {                                                       }
4        {          Binary file I/O demonstration program        }
5        {                                                       }
6        {                           by Jeff Duntemann           }
7        {                           Turbo Pascal V3.0            }
8        {                           Last update 5/1/86           }
9        {                                                       }
10       {                                                       }
11       {                                                       }
12       {-------------------------------------------------------}
13
14       PROGRAM Average;
15
16       VAR
17          IntFile      : FILE OF Integer;
18          I,J,Count    : Integer;
19          Average,Total : Real;
20
```

(continues)

```
21        BEGIN
22          Assign(IntFile,'INTEGERS.BIN');
23          {$I-} Reset(IntFile) {$I+}
24          I := IOResult;
25          IF I <> 0 THEN
26            BEGIN
27              Writeln('>>File INTEGERS.BIN is missing or damaged.');
28              Writeln('  Please investigate and run the program again.')
29            END
30          ELSE
31            BEGIN
32              Count := 0; Total := 0.0;
33              WHILE NOT EOF(IntFile) DO
34                BEGIN
35                  Read(IntFile,J);
36                  Count := Count + 1;
37                  Total := Total + J;
38                END;
39              Close(IntFile);
40              AVERAGE := Total / Count;
41              Writeln;
42              Writeln('>>There are ',Count,' integers in INTEGERS.BIN.');
43              Writeln('  Their average value is ',Average:10:6,'.');
44            END
45        END.
```

(concluded)

18.6   FileSize and FilePos

Turbo Pascal supplies two built-in functions for determining the size of a binary disk file and the position of the file pointer within a disk file. Note that **FileSize** and **FilePos** may *not* be used with text files!

FileSize is predeclared this way:

```
FUNCTION FileSize(FileVar : <binary filetype>) : Integer
```

The function **FileSize** returns an integer count of the number of items stored in the file. **FileVar** is an open binary file (*not* a text file). An empty file will return a zero value. Since the function returns an integer value, it can (theoretically) only return a value as large as 32,767. A larger number (up to 65,535) will be returned as a negative number. For example, for a file containing 48,000 items, **FileSize** would return a value of –17536. To calculate the true number of items you must then add the negative integer to 65,536. To do this in your program you must revert to real numbers:

```
VAR
  Size : Real;

IF FileSize(MyFile) < 0 THEN Size := FileSize(MyFile) +
65536.0;
```

The largest number of items that a binary file under CP/M-80 may legally contain under Turbo Pascal is 65,535.

Function **FilePos** is predeclared this way:

```
FUNCTION FilePos(FileVar : <binary filetype>) : Integer
```

A binary file's file pointer is a counter that indicates the next item to be read from the file. The **FilePos** function returns the current value of a file's file pointer. **FileVar** is an open binary file (*not* a text file). The first item in a file is item number 0. When a file is first opened, its file pointer is set to 0. Each **Read** operation will increment the file pointer by one. The **Seek** procedure (see Section 18.10) will put the file pointer at a particular value to enable random access to a binary file.

SUPPORT FOR MS DOS LARGE FILES

The MS DOS operating system allows binary files to have many more than 65,536 records. A 16-bit type such as **Integer** can only count to 65,536, even if the sign bit is used. For dealing with very large files under MS DOS, Turbo Pascal provides the **LongFileSize** and **LongFilePos** functions:

```
FUNCTION LongFileSize(VAR FileVar : <binary filetype>) : Real;

FUNCTION LongFilePos(VAR FileVar : <binary filetype>) : Real;
```

Note that the name of **LongFilePos** is erroneously given as **LongFile-Position** in the Turbo Pascal Reference Manual. The identifier **LongFilePosition** is *not* recognized by the compiler and will generate an error.

These two functions operate exactly the same way as **FileSize** and **FilePos**, save that the type of their return value is **Real**. Real numbers are the only way in Turbo Pascal to count beyond 65,536. Of course, you can use these functions on small files as well and should use them in any case where you expect a file might be called upon to contain more than 65,536 records. Now, that is a lot of records, and unless you have a hard disk system you are not likely to see a file that large without filling the disk first.

There is also a **LongSeek** procedure for random access support of large MS DOS files (see Section 18.10).

18.7   Miscellaneous file routines

The last group of Turbo Pascal file routines we'll discuss are all extensions to the ISO Standard Pascal definition. Most Pascals have routines like these, but sadly, their invocation syntax and parameters vary widely. Any time you use file I/O, you can be almost certain that your programs will be non-portable. (There is no way even to close a file in ISO Pascal!) This is yet another reason why I have not stressed adherence to the ISO Standard in this book. If file I/O cannot be made portable, you might as well hang it up.

FLUSH

Every file has a buffer in memory, and when you write to a file, the data you've written actually goes to the buffer rather than directly to the physical disk file. Periodically, based on decisions it makes on its own, the Turbo Pascal runtime code will flush the buffer to disk, actually transferring the data to the physical disk file. You can force such a flush to disk with the **Flush** procedure. It is predeclared this way:

```
PROCEDURE Flush(<filevar>);
```

<filevar> is any opened file variable. *Do not use* **Flush** *on a closed file!*

CLOSE

Closing a file that you have opened ensures that all data written to the file are physically transferred from the file buffer to disk. In Turbo Pascal the **Close** procedure does this job:

```
PROCEDURE Close(<filevar>);
```

As with **Flush**, <filevar> is any opened file. It is all right to close a file that has been closed already.

Closing files that had not been changed while open was previously optional. With Turbo Pascal 3.0, this is no longer the case. You *must* close all opened disk files to keep the operating system happy. Turbo Pascal 3.0 for PC/MS DOS uses file handles, of which there are only 16 available. File handles, once allocated by opening a file, will not be freed for further use until the file is closed. If you neglect to close a few temporary files, you may soon run out of file handles.

Of course, if you exit a program before closing a file that has been written to, the runtime code makes no guarantee that all records written to the file buffer will actually make it out to the physical disk file.

ERASE

Deleting a disk file from within a program is done with the **Erase** procedure:

```
PROCEDURE Erase(<filevar>);
```

<filevar> is any file variable that has been assigned to a physical file. In other words, if you try to **Erase** a file variable to which no physical file has yet been assigned, the runtime code has no way of knowing which file you want to delete:

```
VAR
   NumFile: FILE OF Integer;

Assign(NumFile,'VALUES.BIN');
Erase(NumFile);
```

Eraseing a file that is open (in other words, set up for use by **Reset** or **Rewrite**) may do no harm, but it is better practice to close a file before deleting it. Some operating systems, particularly multitasking ones, require that a file be unlocked before it is deleted.

RENAME

Turbo Pascal gives you the ability to change the name of a disk file from within a program with the **Rename** procedure:

```
PROCEDURE Rename(<filevar>; NewName : String80);
```

<filevar> is any file that has been assigned to a physical file with **Assign**. As with **Erase**, trying to rename a file without connecting it to a physical file is meaningless.

Use **Rename** with some caution. It is possible to rename a file to a name already used by another disk file. No error will result, but you will have two files with the same name, and getting the *right* one when you need one of the two files will be a problem indeed.

As with **Erase**, renaming an open file should not be done, largely because of file locking restrictions of some current (or future) operating systems.

APPEND

This routine is available for PC/MS DOS only. **Append** provides a way to quickly move the file pointer to the end of a text file without having to explicitly read the file and throw away the characters read up to EOF.

Append is used instead of **Rewrite:**

```
PROCEDURE Append(<filevar>);
```

<filevar> must be assigned to some physical text file before **Append** can be used. The contents of the file are not destroyed, as they are with **Rewrite**. The file is opened for output, however, at EOF. Adding text to the file with **Write** or **Writeln** will position the new text at and following EOF.

TRUNCATE

Like **Append**, **Truncate** is available only with PC/MS DOS versions of Turbo Pascal. **Truncate** is conceptually similar to **Append**. Both prepare a file for the adding of additional data via **Write** or (for text files) **Writeln**. **Truncate** is predeclared this way:

```
PROCEDURE Truncate(<filevar>);
```

When executed, **Truncate** chops a file off at the current position of the file pointer. In other words, if you have read part way down a file and execute **Truncate**, the remainder of the file will be thrown away. The file is then ready for output, even if you opened the file with **Reset**.

Truncate works with all kinds of files, not simply text files, as with **Append**.

Standard Pascal does not allow writing to a file that contains data. When a file is opened for output in Standard Pascal, all previous contents of the file are destroyed. This defies the logic of the real world, in which files are built by an ongoing process of reading, writing, updating, and deleting. **Append** and **Truncate** make real-world use of data files a great deal more convenient than in Standard Pascal.

18.8   Using text files

Given its variable-length string type, its built-in string functions and procedures, and Standard Pascal's **Readln** and **Writeln** procedures, Turbo Pascal is a natural choice for working with text files. In this section we'll show you a real-life example of a useful program for manipulating text files.

FILTER PROGRAMS

There is a whole class of programs that read a file in chunks, perform some manipulation on the chunks, and then write the transformed chunks back out to another file. This type of program is called a "filter" program, because it filters a file through some sort of processing. The data changes according to a set of rules as it passes through the processing part of the program.

A good example would be a program to force all lowercase characters in a file to uppercase. Turbo Pascal is not sensitive to character case, but some programs and language processors (particularly COBOL and APL) do not interpret lowercase characters correctly. To pass a text file between Pascal and APL, all lowercase characters in the file must be set to uppercase.

A filter program to accomplish this task would work this way:

```
Open the input file for read and create a new output file.

While not end-of-file keep doing this:
  Read a line from the input text file.

  Force all lowercase characters in the line to uppercase.
  Write the line out to the output text file.

Close both files.
```

This basic structure is the same for all text file filter programs, except for the processing that is actually done line-by-line. You could just as easily force all uppercase characters in the line to lowercase, count the words in the line, remove all BEL characters (CTRL-G) from the line, expand HT (tab; CTRL-I) characters to 8-space characters, and so on.

You could, in fact, combine two or more processes into one filter program; say, force lowercase to uppercase and count characters.

A TWO-WAY CASE FILTER PROGRAM

The following program can perform two distinct functions: It can force all lowercase characters in a text file to uppercase, or all uppercase characters to lowercase. Which of the two actions is taken depends on a parameter entered on the command line:

```
CASE UP B:COBOL.SRC          Forces lower to upper

CASE DOWN B:PASTEXT.SRC      Forces upper to lower
```

Note that the name of the program source *file* is "CASE.PAS," while the name of the *program* is "CASER." The reason is that **CASE** is a reserved word and may not be used in a program. However, you may *name* a program code file anything you like, and here **CASE** is the best name for the actual runnable program file on disk.

```
1      {------------------------------------------------------------}
2      {                          Case                              }
3      {                                                            }
4      { An upper/lower case conversion filter program for text files }
5      {                                                            }
6      {                    by Jeff Duntemann                       }
7      {                    Turbo Pascal V3.0                       }
8      {                    Last update 1/31/86                     }
9      {                                                            }
```

(continues)

```
10              {                                                    }
11              {                                                    }
12              {----------------------------------------------------}
13
14
15              PROGRAM Caser;              { "CASE" is a reserved word... }
16
17              CONST
18                Upper = True;
19                Lower = False;
20
21              TYPE
22                String40   = String[40];
23                String80   = String[80];
24                String255  = String[255];
25
26              VAR
27                I,J,K      : Integer;
28                Quit       : Boolean;
29                Ch         : Char;
30                WorkFile   : Text;
31                TempFile   : Text;
32                NewCase    : Boolean;
33                WorkLine   : String80;
34                WorkName   : String80;
35                TempName   : String80;
36                CaseTag    : String80;
37
38
39              {$I FRCECASE.SRC }     { Contains ForceCase }
40
41
42              {>>>>MakeTemp<<<<}
43
44              PROCEDURE MakeTemp(FileName : String80; VAR TempName : String80);
45
46              VAR
47                Point : Integer;
```

(continues)

```
48
49        BEGIN
50          Point := Pos('.',FileName);
51          IF Point > 0 THEN Delete(FileName,Point,(Length(FileName)-Point)+1);
52          TempName := Concat(FileName,'.$$$')
53        END;
54
55
56      { CASER MAIN }
57
58    BEGIN
59      Quit := False;
60      IF ParamCount < 2 THEN    { Missing parms error }
61        BEGIN
62          Writeln('<<Error!>> CASE requires two command line parameters:');
63          Writeln('          CASE UP B:FOOFILE.TXT or');
64          Writeln('          CASE DOWN B:FOOFILE.TXT');
65          Writeln('          Invoke CASE again with the proper parameters.')
66        END
67      ELSE
68        BEGIN
69          WorkName := ParamStr(2);
70          Assign(WorkFile,WorkName);  { Attempt to open the file }
71          {$I-} Reset(WorkFile); {$I+}
72          IF IOResult <>0 THEN
73            BEGIN
74              Writeln('<<Error!>> File ',WorkName,' does not exist.');
75              Writeln('          Invoke CASE again with an existing FileName.');
76            END
77          ELSE
78            BEGIN                { See if UP/DOWN parm was entered }
79              CaseTag := ParamStr(1);
80              CaseTag := ForceCase(Upper,CaseTag);
81              IF CaseTag = 'UP' THEN NewCase := Upper ELSE
82                IF CaseTag = 'DOWN' THEN NewCase := Lower ELSE
83                  Quit := True;
84              IF Quit THEN
85                BEGIN
```

(continues)

```
86                    Writeln
87                    ('<<Error!>> The case parameter must be "UP" or "DOWN."');
88                    Writeln
89                    ('          Invoke CASE again using either "UP" or "DOWN".');
90                  END
91                ELSE
92                  BEGIN
93                    Write('Forcing case ');
94                    IF NewCase THEN Write('up ') ELSE Write('down ');
95                    MakeTemp(WorkName,TempName);  { Generate temporary FileName }
96                    Assign(TempFile,TempName);    { Open temporary file }
97                    Rewrite(TempFile);
98                    WHILE NOT EOF(WorkFile) DO
99                      BEGIN
100                       Readln(WorkFile,WorkLine);
101                       Write('.');                { Dot shows it's working }
102                       WorkLine := ForceCase(NewCase,WorkLine);
103                       Writeln(TempFile,WorkLine)
104                     END;
105                   Close(TempFile);              { Close the temporary file }
106                   Close(WorkFile);              { Close original source file... }
107                   Erase(WorkFile);              { ...and delete it. }
108                   Rename(TempFile,WorkName);    { Temporary file becomes source }
109                 END
110             END
111           END
112       END.
```

(concluded)

Most of **CASER** is actually setup: making sure files exist, making sure valid commands were entered at the command line; and so on. The real meat of the program is simplicity itself:

```
WHILE NOT EOF(WorkFile) DO
   BEGIN
      Readln(WorkFile,WorkLine);
```

(continues)

```
   Write('.');                    { Dot shows it's working }
   SetCase(ForceCase,WorkLine);
   Writeln(TempFile,WorkLine);
END;
```

(concluded)

This loop executes repeatedly as long as there are lines to be read in **WorkFile**. A line is read, **SetCase** adjusts the case of the characters in the line, and then the line is written to **TempFile**. When **Readln** reads the last line in the text file, the **EOF** function will immediately return **True**. The text file is "filtered" through **SetCase** into a temporary file. When the original file has been read completely, it is erased with **Erase** and the temporary file is renamed to become the original file.

If you're nervous about deleting your original text file (and that is not a totally unhealthful feeling), you could close it with **Close** instead of **Erase** and then give **TempFile** a new file extension instead of .$$$. (I have used ".ZZZ" in the past.) If you're careless about backing up important files, this is a very good idea.

18.9   Using binary files

A text file is distinctive in being the *only* type of Pascal file that may contain records of varying lengths. Pascal treats text files specially in other ways, by limiting the range of characters that may legally reside in the file, and by the EOF character that accurately flags where written data ends. Binary files, by contrast, are given none of this special treatment.

A binary file is a file containing some number of data items of a given type:

```
TYPE
   KeyFile = FILE OF KeyRec;
   CfgFile = FILE OF CfgRec;
   IntFile = FILE OF Integer;
```

Only one data type may be stored in a binary file. You could not, for example, write a variable of type **KeyRec** and type **CfgRec** to the same logical file.

Each instance of a data item in a binary file is called a "record," whether the data item is a Pascal record type or not. One integer stored in an **IntFile** as defined above could be considered a record of the **IntFile**.

One common use of binary files puts only one record in the file: the "configuration file." Consider a complicated program that performs file maintenance and telecommunications. The program is used at a great many sites owned by a large corporation. The names of the files it works with change from site to site, as do the telephone numbers it must call to link with the host mainframe computer.

Rather than "hard-code" things such as telephone numbers into the Pascal source file, it makes more sense to store them out to a file. The easiest way is to define a record type containing fields for all the site-specific information:

```
TYPE
  CfgRec  = RECORD
                  SiteName    : String;
                  SiteCode    : Integer;
                  AuthOp      : String;
                  HostCode    : Integer;
                  PhoneNum    : String;
                  P1FileName  : String;
                  P2FileName  : String;
                  AXFileName  : String
                END;

  CfgFile = FILE OF CfgRec;

VAR
  SiteFile : CfgFile;
  CfgData  : CfgRec;
```

All the data items that change from site to site are present in one single record. When loaded with the correct site values for a particular site, the record can be easily written to disk:

```
Assign(SiteFile,'B:SITEDATA.CFG');
Rewrite(SiteFile);
Write(SiteFile,CfgData);
Close(SiteFile);
```

Here, once **SiteFile** is opened, the single **CfgRec** is written to disk with the **Write** statement.

18.10   Using random-access files

All file access methods we have discussed so far have been "sequential." That is, when you open a file you may access the first record, and then the second, and then the third, and so on until you run out of records. All records in the file are accessible, but only at the cost of always starting at the beginning and scanning past all records up to the one you need.

"Random access" of a file means the ability to open a file and simply—*zap!*—read record 241, without having to read anything else first. Then, without any further scanning, simply—*zap!*—write data to record 73. Turbo Pascal gives you this ability through the **Seek** procedure.

Random access is possible with all binary files. Text files may *not* be accessed randomly; for random access to work, all records in a file must be the same length. Binary files that were written sequentially with **Write** may be read or rewritten randomly by using **Seek**. Binary files written randomly by using **Seek** may be read sequentially with **Read**.

Seek is not part of ISO Standard Pascal, although several other Pascals, including UCSD Pascal, implement it much the same way. **Seek** is predeclared this way:

```
PROCEDURE Seek(FileVar : <binary filetype>; RecNum : Integer);
```

Seek manipulates the file pointer of opened binary file **FileVar**. **Seek** may *not* be used with text files! It sets the file pointer of **FileVar** to **RecNum**. The next **Read** done on **FileVar** will read the **RecNum**'th record from the file:

```
VAR
    Keys : KeyFile;
    AKey : KeyRec;

Assign(Keys,'NAMES.KEY');
Reset(Keys);

Seek(Keys,17);
Read(Keys,AKey)
```

In this example, record 17 of the file **NAMES.KEY** is read from disk and assigned to the variable **AKey**.

The **Seek** procedure can move the file pointer to any record up to record 65,535. The MS DOS operating system allows files with a great many more records than that—theoretically, up to more than 8 *billion* records. For random access of files with more than 65,535 records you must use **LongSeek**:

```
PROCEDURE LongSeek(FileVar : <binary filetype>; RecNum : Real);
```

LongSeek functions exactly the way **Seek** functions. One penalty for the extended range of **LongSeek** is that it will be slightly (but not noticeably) slower than **Seek**.

Note that **LongSeek** can be used on any binary file, even a small one. You should use **LongSeek** on any file that you expect will have more than 65,535 records in it. Along with **LongSeek**, Turbo Pascal provides the **LongFileSize** and **LongFilePos** functions for dealing with large MS DOS files. These functions are described in Section 18.6.

You should be careful not to **Seek** past the end of the file. I/O error 91: Seek beyond end-of-file will result. Testing **FileSize** before **Seek**ing is always a good idea.

A BINARY SEARCH PROCEDURE

Finding a particular record in a file is perhaps the central problem of all business-related computer science. If you know the record number there is no problem; you either go directly to the record with **Seek** or scan sequentially through the file with **Read**, counting records up to the desired number. In most cases, however, you want to locate a record *based on what's in the record.*

A sequential search is simple enough: You start reading at the beginning of the file and test each record to see if it's the one you want. If it's a big file, or if your search criteria are complicated enough, such a search can take minutes or even hours on hard disk–based systems. Since such a search ties up the computer completely while the search is under way, it can become a costly way to work.

There are many ways to approach the searching of files, but no method is as easy to understand and use as that of binary search.

Binary searches depend upon the file being sorted on the data you wish to search for. In other words, if you want to find a person's name in a file, the records in the file (each containing someone's name) must be in alphabetical order by the name field.

We presented a couple of very fast sorting methods in earlier sections. The shellsort and quicksort can both be modified to sort any type of data structure that can exist in an array. Sorting a file involves loading its records from disk into an array, sorting the array, and writing the sorted records back out to the file on disk. The file can then undergo a binary search.

Briefly, binary searching involves dividing a file in half repeatedly, making sure that the desired record is somewhere in the half that is retained at each division. In time the halves divide down to nothing, and if the record is not found at that point it does not exist in the file.

In detail:

The binary search procedure is passed a file to search (called a key file for reasons we'll explain shortly); the number of records in the file; and a data item (in our example, a string) containing the data we're searching for.

Starting out, a variable **Low** contains the record number of the first record in the file (1) and a variable **High** contains the record number of the last record in the file. **High** and **Low** are always the bounds of the region we will be searching. At the outset, they encompass the entire file.

The search begins: The procedure calculates a record number halfway between **High** and **Low** and stores that in **Mid**. The record at **Mid** is read and tested. If the data part of the record at **Mid** matches our "key," the search is over. It probably won't happen quite so quickly.

Because the file is sorted, we can state this: If our key is *greater* than the data at **Mid**, we must now search the half of the file above **Mid**. If our key is *less* than the data at **Mid**, we must search the half of the file below **Mid**.

The procedure thus sets up a new **High** and **Lo** for the half of the file in which our desired record must exist. The process begins again, now with only half of the file. A new **Mid** is calculated, and the record at the new **Mid** is read and tested. If **Mid** isn't the record we want, we have our choice of two new, smaller sections of the file to search. And so we continue, setting up **High** and **Low** as the bounds of a still smaller section of the file.

This continues until one of two things happens: (1) We find that the record we read at **Mid** is the record we want, or (2) **Mid** collides with either **High** or **Low**. If that happens, the search is over without finding what we want. Our key does not exist in the file.

(Of course, if the file is not fully sorted, our desired record may in fact exist in the file and yet the binary search may not find it. The file must be completely and correctly sorted or all bets are off!)

The actual Pascal code for such a binary search function follows. **KeySearch** requires the following type definitions prior to its own definition:

```
TYPE
  KeyRec = RECORD
             Ref     : Integer;
             KeyData : String[25]
           END;

  KeyFile = FILE OF KeyRec;
```

```
1          {<<<< KeySearch >>>>}
2
3
4          { Described in section 18.10 -- Last mod 2/1/86  }
5
6          FUNCTION KeySearch(VAR Keys    : KeyFile;
7                             VAR KeyRef  : Integer;
8                                 MatchIt : String80) : Boolean;
9
10         VAR High,Low,Mid : Integer;
11             SearchRec    : KeyRec;
12             Found        : Boolean;
13             Collided     : Boolean;
14             RecCount     : Integer;
15
16         BEGIN
17           KeyRef := 0;                { Initialize variables     }
18           RecCount := FileSize(Keys);
19           High := RecCount;
20           Low := 0;
21           KeySearch := False; Found := False; Collided := False;
22           Mid := (Low + High) DIV 2;  { Calc first midpoint       }
23
24           IF RecCount > 0 THEN         { Don't search if file empty}
25             REPEAT
26               Seek(Keys,Mid);             { Read midpoint record     }
27               Read(Keys,SearchRec);
28               { Collision between Mid & Low or Mid & High?   }
29               IF (Low = Mid) OR (High = Mid) THEN Collided := True;
30               IF MatchIt = SearchRec.KeyData THEN  { Found it! }
31                 BEGIN
32                   Found := True;           { Set found flag...    }
33                   KeySearch := True;       { ...function value... }
34                   KeyRef := SearchRec.Ref  { ...and file key      }
35                 END
36               ELSE             { No luck...divide & try again  }
```

(continues)

```
37              BEGIN
38                IF MatchIt > SearchRec.KeyData THEN Low := Mid
39                  ELSE High := Mid; { Halve the field }
40                Mid := (Low + High + 1) DIV 2;    { Recalc midpoint }
41                KeyRef := Mid { Save Mid in parm }
42              END
43            UNTIL Collided OR Found
44        END;
```

(concluded)

KEYED FILES   **KeySearch** has some machinery in it that goes beyond simply searching a file for a matching data string. **KeySearch** returns an integer parameter **KeyRef**, which it takes from the **KeyRec** record it locates. The **Ref** field of the **KeyRec** type allows us to build a "keyed" file system.

It is both difficult and hazardous to sort a large data file composed of large ("wide") records. Difficult because the entire file (or big chunks of it for a sort/merge system) must be in memory at one time; hazardous because sorting involves rewriting the entire file after every sort. Rewriting an entire file greatly increases vulnerability to disk errors that can corrupt data in the file, or even (worst case) make the file unreadable.

Furthermore, sorting a file involves swapping many large records around, even if the part of the record that is sorted (called the "key field") is a very small part of the entire record. A lot of that swapping time is simply wasted.

It would be better, faster, and safer to extract and sort only that part of the record that needs to be sorted. This is what a key file is for. The **KeyData** field is that data that is sorted. The **Ref** field is the record number of the record in the main data file from which the **KeyData** field was extracted. If we binary search a key file for a given string, **Ref** will give us the record number where we can find the rest of the data associated with that string. In other words, if we binary search a key file containing only names, **Ref** will allow us to read the record containing the address, phone number, and other information associated with the name we found (see Fig. 18.2).

The simple program beginning on page 365 assumes the existence of a data file and key file sorted on the data file's **Name** field. The program waits for a name to be entered, then searches the key file for the name. If the name is present in the key file, the program reads the data record for the rest of the data associated with that name, and displays that data.

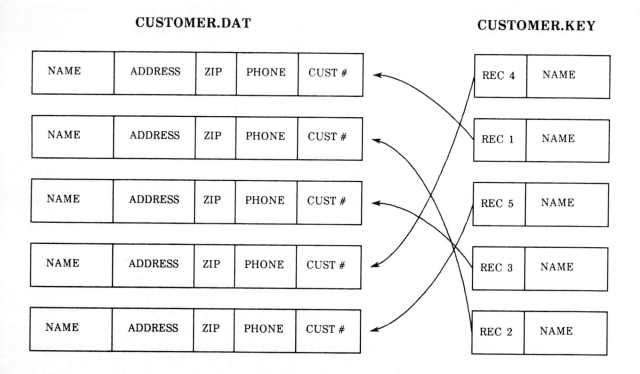

CUSTOMER.DAT   **CUSTOMER.KEY**

Records in the data file are stored in the order they were entered. The data file itself is never sorted. Instead, keys are extracted from the data file into a key file. Then the smaller key file is sorted. This also presents less risk of damaging the data file.

Key files contain fields extracted from the data file, plus pointers into the data file. Records are in sort order by the key field.

FIGURE 18.2 Keyed files

```
 1            {-------------------------------------------------------}
 2            {                        ShowName                       }
 3            {                                                       }
 4            {         Keyed file binary search demo program         }
 5            {                                                       }
 6            {                      by Jeff Duntemann                }
 7            {                      Turbo Pascal V3.0                }
 8            {                      Last update 2/1/86               }
 9            {                                                       }
10            {                                                       }
11            {                                                       }
12            {-------------------------------------------------------}
13
14            { Unlike most programs in this book, this program requires two }
15            { external files to operate: FRIENDS.NAP and FRIENDS.KEY.  The }
16            { two files will be included on the source listings diskette.  }
17            { FRIENDS.NAP is a file of NAPRec containing some number of     }
18            { name/address/phone records.  FRIENDS.KEY is a sorted key      }
19            { file containing keys extracted from FRIENDS.NAP.  You can     }
20            { Write a utility to extract keys from a .NAP file and sort     }
21            { them using either the SHELLSORT or QUIKSORT procedures given }
22            { in Section 14. }
23
24
25            PROGRAM ShowName;
26
27
28            TYPE
29                String3    = String[3];
30                String6    = String[6];
31                String30   = String[30];
32                String40   = String[40];
33                String80   = String[80];
34                String255  = String[255];
35
36            NAPRec = RECORD
```

continues)

```
37                    Name    : String30;
38                    Address : String30;
39                    City    : String30;
40                    State   : String3;
41                    Zip     : String6
42                 END;
43
44      NAPFile = FILE OF NAPRec;
45
46      KeyRec  = RECORD
47                   REF : Integer;
48                   KeyData : String30
49                END;
50
51      KeyFile = FILE OF KeyRec;
52
53
54      VAR I,J,K      : Integer;
55          RecNum     : Integer;
56          Parm       : String80;
57          WorkRec    : NAPRec;
58          WorkFile   : NAPFile;
59          WorkKey    : KeyFile;
60
61
62      {$I KSEARCH.SRC}   { Contains KeySearch }
63
64
65      { SHOWNAME MAIN }
66
67      BEGIN
68        ClrScr;
69        IF ParamCount < 1 THEN            { Missing parms error }
70          BEGIN
71            Writeln('<<Error!>> You must enter a name on the command line:');
72            Writeln('          A>SHOWNAME Duntemann*Jeff ')
73          END
74        ELSE
```

(continues)

```
75          BEGIN
76            Parm := ParamStr(1);
77            Assign(WorkFile,'FRIENDS.NAP');  { Open the names data file }
78            Reset(WorkFile);
79            Assign(WorkKey,'FRIENDS.KEY');   { Open the names key file }
80            Reset(WorkKey);
81            IF KeySearch(WorkKey,RecNum,Parm) THEN  { If key is found...}
82              BEGIN                          { We have record # into data file }
83                Seek(WorkFile,RecNum);       { Seek to record # in data file }
84                Read(WorkFile,WorkRec);      { Read data record from data file }
85                WITH WorkRec DO              { and display the name/address data }
86                  BEGIN
87                    Writeln('>>NAME    : ',Name);
88                    Writeln('  ADDRESS : ',Address);
89                    Writeln('  CITY    : ',City);
90                    Writeln('  STATE   : ',Zip);
91                  END
92              END
93            ELSE
94              Writeln('>>Sorry, ',Parm,' not found.');
95          END
96        END.
```

(concluded)

Records are added to the data file at end of file, and never rewritten unless the data must be changed somehow.

Another important advantage of a keyed file system is that your main data file can effectively be sorted on two or more of its fields at the same time. You can just as easily have a key file keyed on the **Address** or **Zipcode** field. There is the disk space overhead required for the additional key files, but that is nothing like the space it would take to hold the same data file duplicated in its entirety once for each field!

18.11   Using untyped files

All of the file access methods we've discussed so far make some kind of assumption about the structure of the file being read or written. A file is really nothing more than a collection of sectors on a disk

LEARNING THE LANGUAGE

containing bytes of information. Turbo Pascal allows you to treat a file as a series of blocks without any assumptions about what type of data the file contains.

Any disk file may be declared as untyped and accessed on a block-by-block basis. The declaration for an untyped file simply omits a type for the file:

```
WorkFile : FILE;
```

It doesn't matter how the file was originally written. Text files, binary files, program files, or any files, whether created by Turbo Pascal or any other program, may be declared and opened as an untyped file.

Untyped files have a default record length of 128 bytes. This means that whenever you perform a **BlockRead** or a **BlockWrite** on an untyped file (see below), 128 bytes of data are moved between the disk and the file buffer or vice versa.

This is handy for programs that need to process data in 128-byte chunks, such as the **HexDump** program we'll look at shortly. Often it is better to be able to move data in larger blocks. Turbo Pascal for PC/MS DOS allows you to set the block size for untyped files by an optional parameter on the **Reset** and **Rewrite** statements:

```
PROCEDURE Reset(FileName : String; BLockSize : Integer);
PROCEDURE Rewrite(FileName : String; BlockSize : Integer);
```

BlockSize must be at least 128 or a multiple of 128, up to **MaxInt**.

Note that using the optional bock size parameter with a typed file will generate **Error 5: ')' expected**. You can *only* use the block size parameter with untyped files!

Accessing untyped files is done with two routines: **BlockRead** and **BlockWrite**. They are virtually identical except for the direction data move:

```
PROCEDURE BlockRead(AFile : FILE;
                        Buffer : <any type>;
                        Blocks : Integer;
                        Result : Integer);

PROCEDURE BlockWrite(AFile : FILE;
                        Buffer : <any type>;
                        Blocks : Integer;
                        Result : Integer);
```

Parameter **AFile** is an untyped file. **Buffer** is a variable of any type that is at least 128 bytes or a multiple of 128 bytes in size. **Blocks** is the number of blocks to be read or written. These blocks will default to 128 bytes in size, or (for PC/MS DOS versions of Turbo Pascal) their size can be set with an optional parameter to **Reset** and **Rewrite**, as described above. **Result** indicates the number of blocks that were actually read or written. **Result** is an optional parameter; you may omit it if you like.

I/O on untyped files is very fast because the data need not be sorted out into lines or structures; it is simply moved *en masse* between the disk and **Buffer**. It is most useful for file moves and for those applications where data in a file are best treated as large lumps without interpretation.

One simple example is the saving and loading of graphics screens on the IBM PC Color Graphics Adapter. Graphics images exist in a 16384-byte RAM buffer on the adapter. Saving a graphics screen is as easy as saving a memory image of the buffer to disk:

```
PROCEDURE GSave(GName : String80; VAR IOR : Integer);

TYPE
  ScreenBuf = ARRAY[0..16383] OF Byte;

VAR
  GBuff : ScreenBuf ABSOLUTE $0B800 : $0;
  GFile : FILE;
```

(continues)

```
BEGIN
  Assign(GFile,GName);
  Rewrite(GFile,16384);
  BlockWrite(GFile,GBuff,1);
  IOR := IOResult;
  Close(GFile);
END;
```

(concluded)

GBuff is an *absolute* variable; that is, a variable that is explicitly created at a particular location in memory, usually outside the program's data area. (In this case at $B800 : $0, the address of the Color Graphics Adapter's video refresh buffer.) (See Section 20.1.)

Loading a saved graphics image from disk into the Color Graphics Adapter buffer is just as easy:

```
PROCEDURE GLoad(GName : String80; VAR IOR : Integer);

TYPE
  ScreenBuf = ARRAY[0..16383] OF Byte;

VAR
  GBuff : ScreenBuf ABSOLUTE $0B800 : $0;
  GFile : FILE;

BEGIN
  Assign(GFile,GName);
  {$I-} Reset(GFile,16384); {$I+}
  IOR := IOResult;
  IF IOR = 0 THEN
    BEGIN
      BlockRead(GFile,GBuff,1);
      IOR := IOResult;
      Close(GFile)
    END
END;
```

For both procedures, the **GName** parameter is a string containing the full file name of the graphics file to be read or written. **IOR** returns the **IOResult** I/O status code from the block I/O operation, which may be tested by the calling logic to determine how the operation went, and take action accordingly. Note that the block size is set to 16384, the size of a RAM buffer on the Color Graphics Adapter. This means that one block I/O operation will transfer an entire screen between disk and video buffer. This is the fastest way within Turbo Pascal of moving a graphics screen between disk and buffer.

The following program demonstrates the use of **GSave** and **GLoad**. Note that, like any graphics software, it requires a graphics adapter, and will not run on the Monochrome Display Adapter.

```
1     {--------------------------------------------------------------}
2     {                        GraphFiler                            }
3     {                                                              }
4     {          Graphics file I/O demonstration program             }
5     {                                                              }
6     {                              by Jeff Duntemann                }
7     {                              Turbo Pascal V3.0                }
8     {                              Last update 1/31/86              }
9     {                                                              }
10    {                                                              }
11    {--------------------------------------------------------------}
12
13    PROGRAM GraphFiler;
14
15    TYPE
16       String80 = String[80];
17
18    VAR
19       I        : Integer;
20       ErrorCode : Integer;
21
22
23    PROCEDURE GSave(GName : String80; VAR IOR : Integer);
24
```

(continues)

```
25        TYPE
26          ScreenBuff = ARRAY[0..16383] OF Byte;
27
28        VAR
29          GBuff : ScreenBuff ABSOLUTE $B800 : 0;
30          GFile : File;
31
32        BEGIN
33          Assign(GFile,GName);
34          Rewrite(GFile,16384);
35          BlockWrite(GFile,GBuff,1);
36          IOR := IOResult;
37          Close(GFile)
38        END;
39
40
41        PROCEDURE GLoad(GName : String80; VAR IOR : Integer);
42
43        TYPE
44          ScreenBuff = ARRAY[0..16383] OF Byte;
45
46        VAR
47          GBuff : ScreenBuff ABSOLUTE $B800 : 0;
48          GFile : File;
49
50        BEGIN
51          Assign(GFile,GName);
52          {$I-} Reset(GFile,16384); {$I+}
53          IOR := IOResult;
54          IF IOR = 0 THEN
55            BEGIN
56              BlockRead(GFile,GBuff,1);
57              Close(GFile)
58            END
59        END;
60
61
62        BEGIN  { GraphFiler MAIN }
```

(continues)

```
63              ClrScr;
64              HiResColor(15);                { Use white as foreground color }
65              HiRes;                         { Clears graphics screen }
66              TextColor(1);
67              FOR I := 0 TO 199 DO           { Draw lines }
68                IF I MOD 5 = 0 THEN Draw(0,0,640,I,1);
69              GSave('LINES.PIC',ErrorCode);    { Save graphics image to a file }
70              Write('Press RETURN to clear screeen and re-load image: ');
71              Readln;
72              HiRes;                         { Clears graphics screen }
73              GLoad('LINES.PIC',ErrorCode);    { Load saved file into display buffer }
74              Readln;
75              TextMode
76            END.
```

(concluded)

A HEX DUMP PROGRAM

GSave and **GLoad** treat an area of memory as one big block. Their whole purpose is to read and write a large memory image to or from disk as quickly as possible. Other applications may involve reading a file as many small blocks and working with the data one block at a time.

The following program displays a hex dump of any disk file:

```
1       {------------------------------------------------------------}
2       {                        HexDump                             }
3       {                                                            }
4       {            Hex dump program for all disk files             }
5       {                                                            }
6       {                             by Jeff Duntemann              }
7       {                             Turbo Pascal V3.0              }
8       {                             Last update 2/1/86             }
9       {                                                            }
10      {                                                            }
11      {                                                            }
12      {------------------------------------------------------------}
```

(continues)

```
13
14         PROGRAM HexDump;
15
16         {$V-}  { Relaxes String length type checking on VAR paramaters }
17
18         CONST
19           Up   = True;
20           Down = False;
21
22         TYPE
23           String255  = String[255];
24           String128  = String[128];
25           String80   = String[80];
26           String40   = String[40];
27           Block      = ARRAY[0..127] OF Byte;   { One disk sector   }
28           BlockArray = ARRAY[0..15] OF Block;   { BlockRead reads   }
29                                                 { 16 Blocks at once }
30
31
32         VAR
33           I,J,K       : Integer;
34           Parm        : String80;
35           Ch          : Char;
36           DumpFile    : FILE;
37           XBlock      : Block;
38           DiskData    : BlockArray;
39           Blocks      : Integer;        { Counts Blocks within }
40                                         { BlockArray }
41           BlockCount  : Integer;        { Tallies total # Blocks Read }
42           Buffers     : Integer;
43           Remains     : Integer;
44           Device      : Text;           { Will be either LST: or CON: }
45
46
47
48         {$I FRCECASE.SRC }   { Described in Section 15.3 }
49         {$I YES.SRC }        { Described in Section 17.2 }
50         {$I WRITEHEX.SRC }   { Described in Section 20.2 }
```

(continues)

```
51
52
53      {>>>>DumpBlock<<<<}
54
55      PROCEDURE DumpBlock(XBlock : Block; VAR Device : Text);
56
57      VAR
58        I,J,K : Integer;
59        Ch    : Char;
60
61      BEGIN
62        FOR I:=0 TO 7 DO        { Do a hexdump of 8 lines of 16 chars }
63          BEGIN
64            FOR J:=0 TO 15 DO    { Show hex values }
65              BEGIN
66                WriteHex(Device,Ord(XBlock[(I*16)+J]));
67                Write(Device,' ')
68              END;
69            Write(Device,'   |');    { Bar to separate hex & ASCII }
70            FOR J:=0 TO 15 DO        { Show printable chars or '.' }
71              BEGIN
72                Ch:=Chr(XBlock[(I*16)+J]);
73                IF ((Ord(Ch)<127) AND (Ord(Ch)>31))
74                THEN Write(Device,Ch) ELSE Write(Device,'.')
75              END;
76            Writeln(Device,'|')
77          END;
78        FOR I:=0 TO 1 DO Writeln(Device,'')
79      END;  { DumpBlock }
80
81
82      {<<<<ShowHelp>>>>}
83
84      PROCEDURE ShowHelp(HelpName : String80);
85
86      VAR
87        HelpFile : Text;
88        HelpLine : String80;
```

(continues)

```
89                I        : Integer;
90
91            BEGIN
92              Writeln;
93              Assign(HelpFile,HelpName);
94              {$I-} Reset(HelpFile); {$I+}
95              IF IOResult = 0 THEN
96                FOR I := 1 TO 20 DO
97                  BEGIN
98                    Readln(HelpFile,HelpLine);
99                    Writeln(HelpLine)
100                 END;
101             Close(HelpFile)
102           END;
103
104
105           BEGIN
106             CLRSCR;                          { Clear the CRT }
107             Parm := '';
108                                              { Caps lock printer parameter }
109             IF ParamCount > 1 THEN Parm := ForceCase(Up,ParamStr(2));
110             IF ParamCount < 1 THEN           { Error - no parms given }
111               BEGIN
112                 Writeln('<<Error!>> You must enter a filename after invoking');
113                 Write  ('          HexDump.COM.  Display help screen? (Y/N): ');
114                 IF Yes THEN ShowHelp('DUMPHELP.TXT')
115               END
116             ELSE
117               BEGIN
118                 Assign(DumpFile,ParamStr(1));  { Attempt to open the file }
119                 {$I-} Reset(DumpFile); {$I+}
120                 IF IOResult <> 0 THEN          { Error if file won't open }
121                   BEGIN
122                     Writeln('<<Error!>> File ',ParamStr(1),' does not exist.');
123                     Write  ('          Display help screen? (Y/N): ');
124                     IF Yes THEN ShowHelp('DUMPHELP.TXT');
125                   END
```

(continues)

```
126              ELSE
127                BEGIN                        { See if print Parm was entered; }
128                                             { and select output Device }
129                  IF (Pos('PRINT',Parm) = 1) OR (Pos('P',Parm) = 1) THEN
130                    Assign(Device,'LST:') ELSE Assign(Device,'CON:');
131                  Reset(Device);
132                  BlockCount := FileSize(DumpFile);  { FileSize in 128-Byte Blocks }
133                  IF BlockCount = 0 THEN
134                    Writeln('File ',ParamStr(1),' is empty.')
135                  ELSE
136                    BEGIN
137                      Buffers := BlockCount DIV 16;  { # of 16-Block Buffers }
138                      Remains := BlockCount MOD 16;  { # of Blocks in last buffer }
139                      FOR I := 1 TO Buffers DO       { Dump full 16-Block Buffers }
140                        BEGIN
141                          BlockRead(DumpFile,DiskData,16); { Read 16 disk Blocks }
142                          FOR J := 0 TO 15 DO
143                            DumpBlock(DiskData[J],Device)  { Dump 'em... }
144                        END;
145                      IF Remains > 0 THEN  { If fractional buffer Remains, dump it }
146                        BEGIN
147                          BlockRead(DumpFile,DiskData,Remains); { Read last buffer }
148                          FOR I := 0 TO Remains-1 DO
149                            DumpBlock(DiskData[I],Device)       { Dump it }
150                        END
151                    END;
152                  Close(DumpFile)
153                END
154            END
155        END.
```

(concluded)

As with the **CASE** program, parameters are extracted from the command line with **ParamCount** and **ParamStr**. The first parameter is the name of the file to be dumped; the second is optional: the word **PRINT** or the letter **P**, indicating that the dump is to be sent to the printer:

```
A>HEXDUMP B:MYFILE.TXT            or
A>HEXDUMP B:MYFILE.TXT PRINT      or
A>HEXDUMP B:MYFILE.TXT P
```

The program uses **BlockRead** to read the file 128 bytes at a time, and then display the 128-byte block in hexadecimal format using **WriteHex**. Another interesting feature of this program is a simple on-line help system using a small text file. When an error message is displayed, the user is asked if he or she would like to see the help file; if the answer is yes, the text file containing help information is opened and read line by line to the screen.

The text file may be produced on any text editor, and may be anything at all as long as it has no more than 23 lines of 79 or fewer characters. (Most CRT systems will linefeed when 80 characters are displayed on a single line, and if an 80-character line has a CR/LR pair at its end, your help screen will be double-spaced and scroll off the top of the screen.)

18.12 Using MS/PC DOS structured directories

Version 2.0 and later of MS/PC DOS supports "structured directories"; that is, directories that may contain not only files but also subsidiary directories called "subdirectories." These subdirectories are functionally identical to the "root" directory on a disk and may contain files or subdirectories of their own.

This is not the place to discuss the details of DOS structured directories. Peter Norton's *MS DOS and PC DOS User's Guide* (Robert W. Brady Co. 1984) provides one of the better treatments.

Versions 1 and 2 of Turbo Pascal did not contain support for structured directories. Beginning with Version 3.0, Turbo Pascal added support for DOS structured directories. This section describes that support.

GETDIR

This procedure allows Turbo Pascal programs to determine which directory is on any disk drive on the system. It is predeclared this way:

```
PROCEDURE GetDir(Drive : Integer; VAR CurrentDirectory : String);
```

The input to **GetDir** is **Drive**, an integer containing a value that specifies which disk drive is to be queried. The correspondence between integer values and physical drive specifiers runs like this:

```
0 = The logged drive
1 = A:
2 = B:
3 = C:
```

and so on. Some versions of the Turbo Pascal 3.0 manual are in error on this point, and claim that 0 = A:, and so on. *0 always indicates the logged drive,* regardless of what the manual says.

GetDir's output is **CurrentDirectory**, a string that returns the path of the current directory on the specified disk drive.

The following program will display the current directories for the logged drive and drives A through D:

```
1     {-----------------------------------------------------------}
2     {                       ShowDir                             }
3     {                                                           }
4     {             "GetDir" demonstration program                }
5     {                                                           }
6     {                             by Jeff Duntemann             }
7     {                             Turbo Pascal V3.0             }
8     {                             Last update 5/6/86            }
9     {                                                           }
10    {                                                           }
11    {                                                           }
12    {-----------------------------------------------------------}
13
```

(continues)

```
14        PROGRAM ShowDir;
15
16        VAR
17          I,Error : Integer;
18          CurrentDirectory : String[80];
19
20        BEGIN
21          FOR I := 0 TO 4 DO
22            BEGIN
23              GetDir(I,CurrentDirectory);
24              IF I = 0 THEN Write('Logged drive: ')
25                ELSE Write('Drive      ',Chr(64+I),': ');
26              Writeln(CurrentDirectory)
27            END
28        END.
```

(concluded)

One unfortunate weakness of **GetDir** is that it does not return any error condition for checking on a disk drive that doesn't exist. **IOResult** returns 0 in all cases. Determining what disk drives actually exist from within Turbo Pascal is not trivial. I present a routine for doing so in *Turbo Pascal Solutions*.

MKDIR

Creating a new subdirectory is the job of **MkDir**, predeclared this way:

```
PROCEDURE MkDir(NewDirectory : String);
```

When invoked, **MkDir** will create a new subdirectory with the path specified in **NewDirectory**.

When you use **MkDir**, *always* disable runtime error checking around it, as you should always do with **Reset** (see Section 18.5), followed by an invocation of the **IOResult** function. Trying to create a subdirectory that already exists, or a subdirectory on a volume that has been marked Read Only, or with an invalid path, will trigger a runtime error and terminate your program unless runtime error checking has been disabled. **IOResult** will return 1 for all ordinary errors, and 0 if the operation completed successfully.

RMDIR

Deleting a subdirectory is accomplished with **RmDir**:

```
PROCEDURE RmDir(TargetDirectory : String);
```

The path of the subdirectory to be removed is passed to **RmDir** in **TargetDirectory**. As with **MkDir**, runtime error checking should be disabled around the **RmDir** statement, as runtime errors can occur if the subdirectory does not already exist or if it still contains undeleted files. Again, the returned error code from **IOResult** will be 1. 0 indicates that the subdirectory was successfully removed.

You cannot delete the root directory, the current directory (often indicated by a single period in a pathname: ".") or the parent directory (often indicated in a pathname with two periods: ".."). If you try to delete what looks like an empty directory and still get an error, there may be files in the directory marked as "hidden" or "system" files, and therefore not displayed from the DOS DIR command. Inspect the subdirectory with a directory utility like **The Norton Utilities**, **WindowDOS**, or one of the many good public-domain directory utilities available from your user group. If there are files of any kind in a directory, you cannot delete it!

CHDIR

The "current directory" of a disk drive can be simply thought of as the directory named in the DOS prompt with the (essential, as far as I'm concerned) PROMPT PG command in force. In other words, if you're working on drive C: and the command prompt says

```
C:\TURBO\HACKS\GRAPHICS>
```

the current directory for drive C: is \TURBO\HACKS\GRAPHICS. The current directory is where DOS looks for programs and files when no pathname to a specific directory is given.

Even though you may execute a program from a particular directory (say, \TURBO) your program can change the current directory to something entirely different. When it finishes executing, the current directory will remain changed; nothing in Turbo Pascal's runtime code will automatically change it back. If you want to change the current directory back to what it was originally, you must first save the current directory path in a string variable by invoking **GetDir** (see above) and then changing back to the original directory by executing another **ChDir** just before your program terminates.

ChDir is predeclared this way:

```
PROCEDURE ChDir(TargetDirectory : String);
```

Just as with the other procedures that operate with subdirectories, **ChDir** can trigger runtime errors if the specified directory does not exist, or if the given path in **TargetDirectory** is somehow invalid. Turn runtime error checking off around **ChDir** and sample the error condition with **IOResult** after each invocation.

Dynamic variables and pointers

19.1   Managing the heap

Back in Chapter 10, we described dynamic variables and pointers in some detail but said very little about where dynamic variables actually exist. Like everything else in a computer program, they exist in electronic memory. What is important is how they are stored there and how remaining storage space is managed.

We have used the terms "heap" and "heapspace" informally without defining them. Heapspace is that region of memory set aside for allocation to dynamic variables. When you say

```
New(APtr);
```

you have created a brand new dynamic variable that did not exist before. It exists in heapspace, and it is accessed through the pointer variable **APtr**.

When a program begins running, it reserves some quantity of RAM for dynamic variables. In the Turbo Pascal Environment, all memory not needed by code, static data, and stack will be allocated to the heap.

MEMAVAIL AND MAXAVAIL

Knowing how much memory is actually available for dynamic variables can be critical. In a Turbo Pascal program, the stack grows downward from high memory, and the heap grows upward from low memory, beginning immediately above the static data. If the two collide, your system *will* crash.

The key is not to create a dynamic variable that is larger than the available heap memory. Turbo Pascal provides two functions for measuring available memory: **MemAvail** and **MaxAvail**. They are predeclared:

```
FUNCTION MemAvail : Integer;

FUNCTION MaxAvail : Integer;
```

MemAvail returns a value that indicates the total amount of memory available for dynamic variables. It works differently for Z80 and 8086 versions of Turbo Pascal. For Z80 versions, **MemAvail** returns the amount of heapspace in *bytes*. In 8086 versions, **MemAvail** returns the number of 16-byte paragraphs available on the heap. This difference occurs because, in an 8086 system, it is likely that the amount of heapspace is far larger than the largest value an integer variable can contain.

MaxAvail returns a value that is the size of the largest single block of free memory in the heap. Like **MemAvail**, it returns bytes for Z80 versions of Turbo Pascal and 16-byte paragraphs for 8086 versions.

Regardless of the CPU, if either **MemAvail** or **MaxAvail** returns a value larger than **MaxInt**, it will be expressed as a negative number. *This is true even if you assign the value of **MemAvail** or **MaxAvail** to a real number.* This is because Turbo Pascal's runtime code treats such values as unsigned integers, and does not interpret the high bit as a negative sign. This allows numbers as large as 65,535 to be returned from **MemAvail** and **MaxAvail**. As the Z80 cannot address more than 65,536 bytes of memory and the 8086 cannot address more than 65,536 paragraphs of memory, using the high bit this way covers all situations in both the Z80 and 8086.

To deal with such a value properly, you must convert it to a positive real number by adding 65536 to it. This is best done as a pair of functions:

```
1     {<<<< RealMemAvail >>>>}
2
3
4     { Described in section 19.1 -- Last mod 2/1/86   }
5
6     FUNCTION RealMemAvail : Real;
7
8     VAR
9       R : Real;
10
11    BEGIN
12      R := MemAvail;
13      IF R < 0 THEN R := R + 65536.0;
14      R := R * 16;          { DELETE THIS LINE FOR Z80 TURBO!! }
15      RealMemAvail := R
16    END;
```

```
1     {<<<< RealMaxAvail >>>>}
2
3
4     { Described in section 19.1 -- Last mod 2/1/86   }
5
6     FUNCTION RealMaxAvail : Real;
7
8     VAR
9       R : Real;
10
11    BEGIN
12      R := MaxAvail;
```

(continues)

```
13          IF R < 0 THEN R := R + 65536.0;
14          R := R * 16;            { DELETE THIS LINE FOR Z80 TURBO!! }
15          RealMaxAvail := R
16        END;
```

(concluded)

The functions as given are for 8086 versions of Turbo Pascal; to use them on Z80 versions you must delete the R := R * 16 statements. On the 8086, **MemAvail** and **MaxAvail** return paragraphs, not bytes, so to convert their values to bytes you must multiply by 16.

The difference between **MemAvail** and **MaxAvail** has to do with how the heap works. Dynamic variables are created with **New** (see Section 10.3). When you're finished with a dynamic variable, you can erase it with **Dispose** (see Section 10.5). **Dispose** frees the memory formerly occupied by the dynamic variable. The problem is that, unlike the stack, which holds data items in strict order and releases them in strict order, the heap holds dynamic variables anywhere it has room. Disposing of them at random tends to cut the heap into small slices of free memory, each where a disposed dynamic variable used to exist.

This means that it is possible to have 16K of heap space according to **MemAvail** and *still* not be able to create a new dynamic variable. If there is no single free block of memory large enough to hold a dynamic variable of a given type, you cannot safely invoke **New** and create that variable. To do so could create a dynamic variable that overlaps an existing (and possibly important) dynamic variable.

Thus, the function of **MaxAvail** is to determine whether it is possible to safely create any given dynamic variable:

```
IF MaxAvail < SizeOf(MyType)     { For 8080/Z80 only! }
   THEN Writeln('Not enough room!');
```

This example calculates the size that a dynamic variable will be by invoking **SizeOf** on the *type* of the dynamic variable. If that size figure is greater than the value returned by **MaxAvail**, then no single block of memory exists that is large enough to hold another dynamic variable of that type.

What can you do if you find you have no spot large enough to create a new dynamic variable? Nothing automatic; there is no facility in Turbo Pascal that can shuffle the heap around, gathering free memory together into a single contiguous block. (This is sometimes called "garbage collection" and it is *very* hard to do.) All you can do is start disposing of existing dynamic variables until a large enough block opens up somewhere.

The real answer, of course, is to anticipate this problem and not keep large dynamic variables or structures (such as linked lists or trees; see below) hanging around in the heap when they are not needed. Create them. Use them. Then *immediately* throw them away!

19.2   Linked lists

The whole point of having dynamic variables is to be able to create and destroy them as needed without having to predeclare them at compile time. For single variables, this hardly seems worth the bother. Dynamic variables really come into their own when you begin building entire structures of variables in heapspace—structures whose size and shape may not be known at compile time, and that may change drastically from execution to execution of the program, depending on the job required.

The subject of data structures is a large and difficult one. It encompasses structures such as circular buffers, linked lists, doubly linked lists, and trees. Space will not allow us to go deeply into dynamic data structures; that subject can itself do justice to an entire book. As an example of what dynamic variables can do, we will look at simple linked lists.

When we first looked at dynamic variables, in Chapter 10, we saw that a dynamic variable is tethered to its program's static data area by a pointer variable. Dynamic variables have no names, so the only way to use them is to work from the pointer variable, which does have a name.

Consider a record type that includes, as one of its fields, a pointer variable to another record like itself:

```
TYPE
  NADPtr = ^NADRec;

  NADRec = RECORD
              Name    : String80;
              Address : String80;
              City    : String80;
              State   : String80;
              Zip     : String80;
              Next    : NADPtr
           END;
```

One of these records, once created in heapspace and tethered to the static data area, could be made to point to another such record in heapspace, and it to another, and so on. We could have an entire string of records, each one pointing to the next, with the whole tied to our program by just a single pointer variable.

Such a collection of dynamic records linked by pointers is called a "linked list" (see Figure 19.1). The very last record in the list contains a pointer whose value is **Nil**—again, remember that **Nil** only means a pointer that points to nothing. The **Nil** pointer signals the end of the linked list.

TRAVERSING A LINKED LIST

As with any dynamic variable, the list has no name. Its tether to reality is a pointer variable with a name, but neither the records themselves nor the pointers that link them have names. The pointer that tethers the list to static data is often called the "root."

How do we access the records in a linked list? The first record, rather obviously, is **Root^**, since the pointer variable **Root** points to it. But how about the record pointed to by the pointer buried in **Root^**? You can, in fact, say **Root^.Next^**, which can be read (somewhat awkwardly) as "the record pointed to by the **Next** pointer contained in the record pointed to by **Root**." Obviously, it gets still worse for the third record in the list, **Root^.Next^.Next^**. Subject to certain limits of the compiler, you can go on this way for many levels: **Root^.Next^.Next^.Next^.Next^ .Next^** and so on.

But that won't work. Why? *It assumes we know how many records are in the linked list at compile time.* Recall, the reason to use dynamic variables is to create structures whose size and shape may *not* be known at compile time.

No—the way to deal with dynamic structures is to be dynamic. We must move along the linked list, looking at one record at a time, until we detect the end of the list. This process is called "traversing" a linked list.

Traversing a list requires a little extra machinery. Specifically, we need a new pointer to help us, in addition to the root pointer. Look over the following code, which displays data from records of a linked list pointed to by **Root**:

```
Current := Root;     { Current and Root both point to list }

WHILE Current <> Nil DO
   BEGIN
      ShowRecord(Current^);  { Displays data in record Current^ }
      Current := Current^.Next   { Points Current to next record }
   END;
```

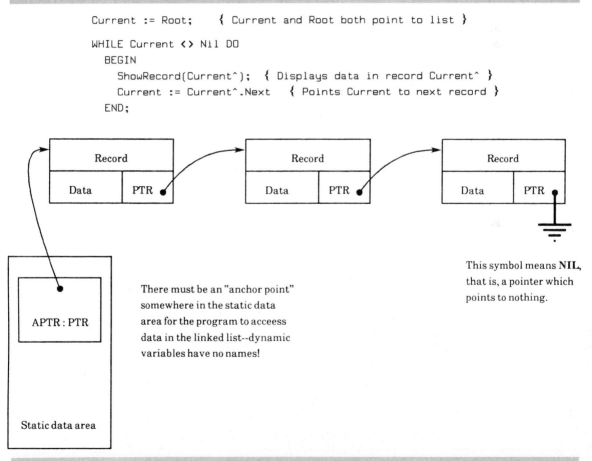

There must be an "anchor point" somewhere in the static data area for the program to acceess data in the linked list--dynamic variables have no names!

This symbol means **NIL,** that is, a pointer which points to nothing.

FIGURE 19.1 A linked list

Assigning one pointer to another, you'll recall, means that both pointers now point to the same item. **Current** and **Root** both point to the first record in the list. **Root** is the list's anchor into reality; we must *not* change it without good reason.

However, we can make **Current** "travel" along the list by assigning to it the value of the **Next** field in the record it currently points to. Eventually **Current** is pointing to the last record in the list. The **Next** field inside that last record has a value of **Nil**. When **Current** is assigned **Current^.Next**, then **Current** takes on the value **Nil**. The **WHILE** loop is thus satisfied and the loop terminates.

BUILDING LINKED LISTS

We covered traversing a linked list before explaining how a linked list is built, because traversing the list can be part of the process of building the list. How the list is built depends upon your needs.

Linked lists are either "ordered" or not. An ordered list is built so that when you traverse the list, you will encounter the items in the list in some sort of order according to the data carried in the items. If, as you traverse a list, you find that all the items are in alphabetical order by one of the item's data fields, then that is an ordered list.

Building a list that is not ordered is simplicity itself. Given **GetRec**, a procedure that supplies filled records (of type **NADRec** as given above), this code will construct a linked list:

```
VAR
   WorkRec      : NADRec;
   Root,Holder  : NADPtr;

Root := Nil;
Holder := Root;
FOR I := 1 TO 10 DO
   BEGIN
      GetRec(WorkRec);        { Fill the (static) work record    }
      New(Root);              { Create empty dynamic record      }
      WorkRec.Next := Holder; { Copy root pointer into WorkRec    }
      Root^ := WorkRec;       { Copy work record into Root^       }
      Holder := Root          { Point Holder to list root again   }
   END;
```

The critical point here is that new records are inserted at the *beginning* of the list rather than at the end. The very first record loaded into the list becomes the "tail" of the list, pushed further from the root by each new record returned by **GetRec**.

A short list may not have to be ordered, because even a beginning-to-end sequential search on a short list (less than 100 to 200 items) is so fast that ordering it is not worth the small amount of time saved in searches.

There are other reasons to order a list: We may want to *use* the data in some order in addition to searching it for matching data. For example, searching for names in an unordered list may be acceptably fast, but you wouldn't want to print out the names (say, for an address book) in random order.

Building an ordered list involves some traversing. Briefly, to add an item to an ordered list you must traverse the list until you find the place in the list where the new item must be inserted to keep the list in order. Once you find the proper spot, you insert the item. The following procedure builds an ordered list of records by adding a record in proper order to a list pointed to by **Root**:

```
1    {<<<< Builder >>>>}
2
3
4    { Described in section 19.2 -- Last mod 2/1/86   }
5
6    PROCEDURE Builder(VAR Root : NADPtr; WorkRec : NADRec);
7
8    VAR
9      Current,Last : NADPtr;
10
11   BEGIN
12     IF Root = Nil THEN        { List is empty! }
13       BEGIN
14         New(Root);
15         WorkRec.Next := Nil;
```

(continues)

```
16                    Root^ := WorkRec
17                 END
18              ELSE                         { List already contains some records }
19                BEGIN
20                  Current := Root;
21                  REPEAT                    { Traverse list to find correct spot }
22                     Last := Current;
23                     Current := Current^.Next
24                  UNTIL (Current = Nil) OR (Current^.Name > WorkRec.Name)
25                                           { Found spot--now insert new record  }
26                  IF Root^.Name > WorkRec.Name THEN   { Record becomes new }
27                     BEGIN                            { first item on list }
28                       New(Root);              { Create new record for Root }
29                       WorkRec.Next := Last;   { Copy root pointer to Next  }
30                       Root^ := WorkRec        { Copy WorkRec to new record }
31                     END
32                  ELSE                               { Record belongs in  }
33                     BEGIN                           { mid-list somewhere }
34                       New(Last^.Next);       { Create new record for Last}
35                       WorkRec.Next := Current; { Point new rec to Current  }
36                       Last^.Next := WorkRec;   { Copy WorkRec to new record}
37                     END
38                END
39           END;
```

(concluded)

There are three possibilities that must be dealt with separately:

1. The list is empty. **Root** is equal to **Nil**. The record passed to **Builder** becomes the first record in the list. No traversing is necessary at all.
2. Testing the first record in the list (**Root^**) shows that the new record must be inserted *before* **Root^**. This new record must then become **Root^**, and its **Next** field must be made to point to the old **Root^**.
3. Traversing the list shows that the record must be inserted somewhere within the list or at its end. The record must be inserted between two existing records or between the last record and **Nil**.

It is to cater to possibility 3 that the pointer **Last** was created (see Figure 19.2). **Last**, as its name implies, points to the last record

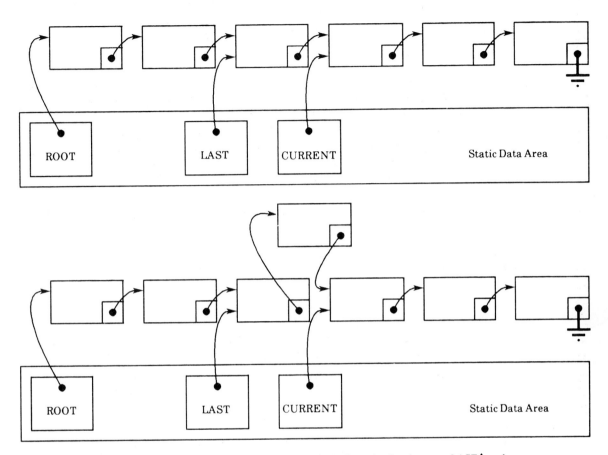

After finding the proper insertion point by traversing the list, the list is broken between LAST^ and CURRENT^. A new record is created at LAST^.NEXT. The record to be inserted is copied into the new record. Then the new record's NEXT field is set equal to CURRENT, which "heals" the break in the list.

FIGURE 19.2 Inserting a record into a linked list

pointed to by **Current**. **Last** is always one record behind **Current**, once **Current** moves off "home base." Having **Last** right behind **Current** makes it easy to insert a record into the list. With **Current** safely pointing to the rest of the list, the list is broken at **Last^.Next** and a new dynamic record is created for **Last^.Next** to point to:

```
New(Last^.Next);
```

Now to "heal" the break in the list: **WorkRec**'s **Next** field is pointed to by **Current^**. **WorkRec** is now part of the second fragment of the list. Finally, **WorkRec** is assigned to **Last^.Next**. The list is whole once again, with **WorkRec** inserted between **Last^** and **Current^**.

DISPOSING OF A LINKED LIST

We have emphasized that you don't throw away a linked list by cutting the list free of its root pointer. The space in memory is still occupied, albeit by unreachable and now useless records. A linked list must be disposed of in an orderly manner. In some respects it is

HOLDER is first set equal to ROOT↑.NEXT. This keeps a "tether" on the list while ROOT↑ is disposed of.

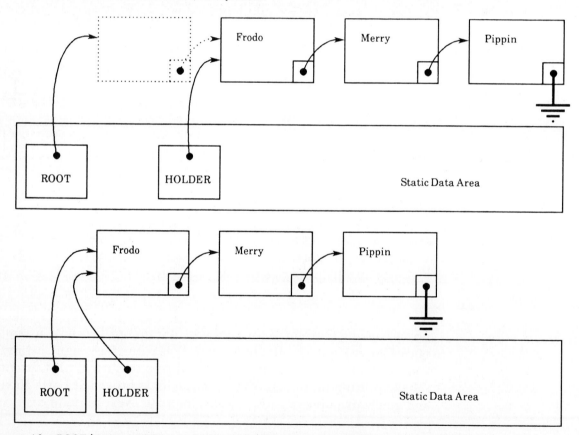

After ROOT↑ is gone, ROOT is set equal to HOLDER, so that HOLDER may once again be set to the record ROOT↑.NEXT↑, and the process continued until the entire list has been disposed of.

FIGURE 19.3 Disposing of a linked list

a mirror image of the method used to create an unordered linked list. Since the order of the records doesn't matter when you're disposing of them, the same method is used to dispose of ordered and unordered lists (see Figure 19.3).

Pointer **Root** anchors the list to be disposed of. A second pointer, **Holder**, is also needed. With **Root** pointing to the first record in the list, **Holder** is made to point to the second record. Now **Holder** is anchoring the list from one record further on than **Root**. **Root^** can thus be safely disposed of.

Root is then pointed to **Holder^**. With **Root** now also at the new beginning of the list, **Holder** may be moved up to the second record in the list, allowing **Root^** to be disposed of. The loop continues until no more records remain.

```
1      {<<<< ListDispose >>>>}
2
3
4      { Described in section 19.2 -- Last mod 2/1/86   }
5
6      PROCEDURE ListDispose(VAR Root : NADPtr);
7
8      VAR
9        Holder : NADPtr;
10
11     BEGIN
12       IF Root <> Nil THEN        { Can't dispose if no list!  }
13         REPEAT
14           Holder := Root^.Next;  { Grab the next record...     }
15           Dispose(Root);         { ...dispose of the first... }
16           Root := Holder         { and make the next the first }
17         UNTIL Root = Nil
18     END;
```

19.3 A simple list manager program

To reinforce all the various ways of manipulating linked lists, in this section we'll present a simple list manager program. **ListMan** is the skeleton of a "personal address book" to contain names, addresses, and (if you add another field to the **NADRec** record type) phone numbers. **ListMan** is more than just a demonstration of linked list handling, it is your chance to show your stuff by building on it.

ListMan creates and adds records to ordered lists, saves them to disk, loads them from disk, and disposes of them gracefully when they are no longer needed. After each change to the size of the list, the number of records that may be added is displayed at the top of the screen.

The **AddRecords** procedure in **ListMan** is an expansion of the **Builder** procedure given above. **AddRecords** performs an additional service: It looks for duplicate names. There may be two John Browns in your Christmas card list, but you may also have accidentally typed his name in twice. **AddRecords** shows you both duplicate records on the screen at once and allows you to throw away the most recently entered one if it is, in fact, a duplicate.

CheckSpace shows how **MemAvail** is used. **MaxAvail** is not used because records are not deleted at random. Lists are deleted all at once, so no heapspace fragmentation will occur. If you were to expand **ListMan** to allow the deletion of records from the list at random (a good idea—what if you don't get a Christmas card from John Brown this year?) you will have to begin using **MaxAvail**.

Another function lacking in **ListMan** is search-and-edit. In other words, if John Brown moves, you will need to search the list for his name and change the address data stored in his record. The code to do this could be cribbed from **AddRecords**, which already searches the list for duplicates of the record to be inserted. You might, in fact, "break out" the search-for-duplicate code into a separate procedure that may be called by both **AddRecords** and your hypothetical search-and-edit procedure. In the same way, you could use the **GetString** procedure given in Section 15.2 to write a more general data entry/edit procedure, replacing the sequence of **Readlns** in **AddRecords**. Both **AddRecords** and your search-and-edit procedure could call the new data entry/edit procedure.

This is much of the magic of Pascal: The building of "toolkit" routines that may be called by two or more procedures in a program. In this way, the richness of function of a program may be increased tremendously without turning the program into something of Godzillan size.

```
 1         {----------------------------------------------------}
 2         {                       ListMan                      }
 3         {                                                    }
 4         {    Mailing list manager demo using dynamic (heap) storage  }
 5         {                                                    }
 6         {                            by Jeff Duntemann       }
 7         {                            Turbo Pascal V3.0        }
 8         {                            Last update 2/1/86       }
 9         {                                                    }
10         {                                                    }
11         {                                                    }
12         {----------------------------------------------------}
13
14         PROGRAM ListMan;
15
16         TYPE
17           String30 = String[30];      { Using derived string types }
18           String6  = String[6];       { makes type NAPRec smaller }
19           String3  = String[3];
20
21           NAPPtr = ^NAPRec;
22           NAPRec = RECORD
23                      Name    : String30;
24                      Address : String30;
25                      City    : String30;
26                      State   : String3;
27                      Zip     : String6;
28                      Next    : NAPPtr      { Points to next NAPRec }
29                    END;                    { in a linked list }
30
31           NAPFile = FILE OF NAPRec;
32
33
34         VAR
35           Ch     : Char;
36           Root   : NAPPtr;
```

(continues)

```
37        Quit     : Boolean;
38
39
40
41     {$I YES.SRC }       { Contains Yes }
42
43
44     PROCEDURE ClearLines(First,Last : Integer);
45
46     VAR
47       I : Integer;
48
49     BEGIN
50       FOR I := First TO Last DO
51         BEGIN
52           GotoXY(1,I);
53           ClrEOL
54         END
55     END;
56
57
58
59     PROCEDURE ShowRecord(WorkRec : NAPRec);
60
61     VAR
62       I : Integer;
63
64     BEGIN
65       ClearLines(17,22);  { Clear away anything in that spot before }
66       GotoXY(1,17);
67       WITH WorkRec DO
68         BEGIN
69           Writeln('>>Name:      ',Name);
70           Writeln('>>Address:   ',Address);
71           Writeln('>>City:      ',City);
72           Writeln('>>State:     ',State);
73           Writeln('>>Zip:       ',Zip)
74         END
```

(continues)

```
75          END;
76
77
78          PROCEDURE CheckSpace;
79
80          VAR
81            Space      : Integer;
82            RealRoom   : Real;
83            RecordRoom : Real;
84
85          BEGIN
86            Space := MemAvail;      { MemAvail returns negative Integer for   }
87                                    { space larger than 32,767.  Convert }
88                                    { (to a real) by adding 65536 if negative }
89            IF Space < 0 THEN RealRoom := 65536.0 + Space ELSE RealRoom := Space;
90
91            RealRoom := RealRoom * 16;   { Delete this line for Z80 versions! }
92                                        { MemAvail for 8086 returns 16-byte  }
93                                        { paragraphs, not bytes!! }
94
95            RecordRoom := RealRoom / SizeOf(NAPRec);
96            ClearLines(2,3);
97            Writeln('>>There is now room for ',RecordRoom:6:0,' records in your list.');
98          END;
99
100
101         PROCEDURE ListDispose(VAR Root : NAPPtr);
102
103         VAR
104           Holder : NAPPtr;
105
106         BEGIN
107           GotoXY(27,10); Write('>>Are you SURE? (Y/N): ');
108           IF YES THEN
109             IF Root <> Nil THEN
110               REPEAT
111                 Holder := Root^.Next;   { First grab the next record...      }
112                 Dispose(Root);          { ...then dispose of the first one... }
```

(continues)

```
113              Root := Holder              { ...then make the next one the first }
114           UNTIL Root = Nil;
115        ClearLines(10,10);
116        CheckSpace
117     END;
118
119
120     PROCEDURE AddRecords(VAR Root : NAPPtr);
121
122     VAR
123        I       : Integer;
124        Abandon : Boolean;
125        WorkRec : NAPRec;
126        Last    : NAPPtr;
127        Current : NAPPtr;
128
129     BEGIN
130        GotoXY(27,7); Write('<<Adding Records>>');
131        REPEAT                { Until user answers 'N' to "MORE?" question... }
132           ClearLines(24,24);
133           FillChar(WorkRec,SizeOf(WorkRec),CHR(0));  { Zero the record }
134           ClearLines(9,15);
135           GotoXY(1,9);
136           WITH WorkRec DO        { Fill the record with good data }
137             BEGIN
138               Write('>>Name:     '); Readln(Name);
139               Write('>>Address:  '); Readln(Address);
140               Write('>>City:     '); Readln(City);
141               Write('>>State:    '); Readln(State);
142               Write('>>Zip:      '); Readln(Zip)
143             END;
144           Abandon := False;
145                              { Here we traverse list to spot duplicates: }
146
147           IF Root = Nil THEN    { If list is empty point Root to record }
148             BEGIN
149               New(Root);
150               WorkRec.Next := Nil;  { Make sure list is terminated by Nil }
```

(continues)

```
151                    Root^ := WorkRec;
152                END
153              ELSE                         { ...if there's something in list already   }
154                BEGIN
155                  Current := Root;       { Start traverse at Root of list }
156                  REPEAT
157                    IF Current^.Name = WorkRec.Name THEN { If duplicate found }
158                      BEGIN
159                        ShowRecord(Current^);
160                        GotoXY(1,15);
161                        Write
162 ('>>The record below duplicates the above entry''s Name.  Toss entry? (Y/N): ');
163                        IF Yes THEN Abandon := True ELSE Abandon := False;
164                        ClearLines(15,22)
165                      END;
166                    Last := Current;
167                    Current := Current^.Next
168                  UNTIL (Current = Nil) OR Abandon OR (Current^.Name > WorkRec.Name);
169
170                  IF NOT Abandon THEN            { Add WorkRec to the linked list  }
171                    IF Root^.Name > WorkRec.Name THEN { New Root item!      }
172                      BEGIN
173                        New(Root);              { Create a new dynamic NAPRec  }
174                        WorkRec.Next := Last;   { Point new record at old Root }
175                        Root^ := WorkRec        { Point new Root at WorkRec     }
176                      END
177                    ELSE
178                      BEGIN
179                        NEW(Last^.Next);        { Create a new dynamic NAPRec, }
180                        WorkRec.Next := Current; { Points its Next to Current  }
181                        Last^.Next^ := WorkRec; { and assign WorkRec to it     }
182                        CheckSpace              { Display remaining heapspace }
183                      END;
184                END;
185            GotoXY(1,24); Write('>>Add another record to the list? (Y/N): ');
186          UNTIL NOT Yes;
187        END;
188
```

(continues)

```
189
190        PROCEDURE LoadList(VAR Root : NAPPtr);
191
192        VAR
193          WorkName : String30;
194          WorkFile : NAPFile;
195          Current  : NAPPtr;
196          I        : Integer;
197          OK       : Boolean;
198
199        BEGIN
200          Quit := False;
201          REPEAT
202            ClearLines(10,10);
203            Write('>>Enter the Name of the file you wish to load: ');
204            Readln(WorkName);
205            IF Length(WorkName) = 0 THEN    { Hit (CR) only to abort LOAD }
206              BEGIN
207                ClearLines(10,12);
208                Quit := True
209              END
210            ELSE
211              BEGIN
212                Assign(WorkFile,WorkName);
213                {$I-} Reset(WorkFile); {$I+}
214                IF IOResult <> 0 THEN           { 0 = OK; 255 = File Not Found }
215                  BEGIN
216                    GotoXY(1,12);
217                    Write('>>That file does not exist.  Please enter another.');
218                    OK := False
219                  END
220                ELSE OK := True                 { OK means File Is open }
221              END
222          UNTIL OK OR Quit;
223          IF NOT Quit THEN
224            BEGIN
225              ClearLines(10,12);
226              Current := Root;
```

(continues)

```
227            IF Root = Nil THEN                  { If list is currently empty }
228              BEGIN
229                NEW(Root);                       { Load first record to Root^ }
230                Read(WorkFile,Root^);
231                Current := Root
232              END                                { If list is not empty, find the end: }
233            ELSE WHILE Current^.Next <> Nil DO Current := Current^.Next;
234            IF Root^.Next <> Nil THEN { If file contains more than 1 record }
235            REPEAT
236              NEW(Current^.Next);                { Read and add records to list }
237              Current := Current^.Next;    { until a record's Next field  }
238              Read(WorkFile,Current^)      { comes up Nil    }
239            UNTIL Current^.Next = Nil;
240            CheckSpace;
241            Close(WorkFile)
242          END
243      END;
244
245
246      PROCEDURE ViewList(Root : NAPPtr);
247
248      VAR
249        I        : Integer;
250        WorkFile : NAPFile;
251        Current  : NAPPtr;
252
253      BEGIN
254        IF Root = Nil THEN                      { Nothing is now in the list }
255          BEGIN
256            GotoXY(27,18);
257            Writeln('<<Your list is empty!>>');
258            GotoXY(26,20);
259            Write('>>Press (CR) to continue: ');
260            Readln
261          END
262        ELSE
263          BEGIN
264            GotoXY(31,7); Write('<<Viewing Records>>');
```

(continues)

```
265              Current := Root;
266              WHILE Current <> Nil DO    { Traverse and display until Nil found }
267                BEGIN
268                  ShowRecord(Current^);
269                  GotoXY(1,23);
270                  Write('>>Press (CR) to view Next record in the list: ');
271                  Readln;
272                  Current := Current^.Next
273                END;
274              ClearLines(19,22)
275            END
276      END;
277
278
279      PROCEDURE SaveList(Root : NAPPtr);
280
281      VAR
282        WorkName : String30;
283        WorkFile : NAPFile;
284        Current  : NAPPtr;
285        I        : Integer;
286
287      BEGIN
288        GotoXY(1,10);
289        Write('>>Enter the filename for saving out your list: ');
290        Readln(WorkName);
291        Assign(WorkFile,WorkName);    { Open the file for write access }
292        Rewrite(WorkFile);
293        Current := Root;
294        WHILE Current <> Nil DO        { Traverse and write }
295          BEGIN
296            Write(WorkFile,Current^);
297            Current := Current^.Next
298          END;
299        Close(WorkFile)
300      END;
301
302
```

(continues)

```
303
304          BEGIN        { MAIN }
305             ClrScr;
306             GotoXY(28,1); Write('<<Linked List Maker>>');
307             CheckSpace;
308             GotoXY(17,8);  Write('--------------------------------------------');
309             Root := Nil; Quit := False;
310             REPEAT
311                ClearLines(5,7);
312                ClearLines(9,24);
313                GotoXY(1,5);
314                Write
315                ('>>[L]oad, [A]dd record, [V]iew, [S]ave, [C]lear list, or [Q]uit: ');
316                Readln(Ch);                  { Get a command }
317                CASE Ch OF
318                 'A','a' : AddRecords(Root);  { Parse the command & perform it }
319                 'C','c' : ListDispose(Root);
320                 'L','l' : LoadList(Root);
321                 'S','s' : SaveList(Root);
322                 'V','v' : ViewList(Root);
323                 'Q','q' : Quit := True;
324                END; { CASE }
325             UNTIL Quit
326          END.
```

(concluded)

Low level machine hooks

Programs written in ISO Standard Pascal are reasonably portable from one machine to another, largely because ISO Standard Pascal ignores the details of each machine. Programs written under Standard Pascal are akin to batch programs running on mainframe machines—no interaction with the user and no interaction with peripherals other than **Input** and **Output**. Nothing in the Pascal standard allows the connection of a logical to any physical file, so technically, ISO Standard Pascal can't handle disk file I/O at all—therefore making portability a myth in any event.

In the real world, you cannot ignore the machine. To be useful, programs must be able to work with all available resources the hardware can offer, or else the hardware is simply wasted. To avoid wasting hardware features, Turbo Pascal provides a number of low level "machine hooks" not defined in Standard Pascal.

All the features mentioned in this section are specific to Turbo Pascal. Other Pascals (Pascal/MT+, for example) may have similar low level extensions, but they work just differently enough in practice to make "drop-in" portability a myth. Before attempting to compile Pascal code from other compiler environments, spend a little time reading it closely with red pen in hand—details count!

20.1 Absolute variables

Many computers locate certain functions at certain specific addresses in memory. The IBM PC's Color Graphics Adapter, for example, locates its screen buffer at segment B800 hex. If a program wishes to read from or write to a graphics buffer, it needs to take the absolute memory location of the buffer into account.

Turbo Pascal allows you to declare variables at specific places in memory. These are called "absolute variables." They are declared as ordinary variables are, with the addition of the reserved word **ABSOLUTE** followed by the machine address of the first byte of the variable. In the Z80 world, an absolute variable might be declared this way:

```
VAR
    IOByte : Byte ABSOLUTE $03
```

The CP/M IO byte is located at address 3 in the Z80 address space. The address could have been given as simply "3" but it is good practice to display addresses in hex (by way of the dollar sign prefix) with a leading zero.

In the 8086 world a machine address has a 16-bit segment and a 16-bit offset, so the address format is a little different:

```
TYPE
   CGABuff = ARRAY[0..16383] OF Byte;

VAR
   GraphBuff : CGABuff ABSOLUTE $0B800 : $00
```

IBM's Color Graphics Adapter board keeps its display buffer at segment $B800 offset 0. The segment address is given first, separated from the offset with a colon.

Defining an absolute variable allocates nothing in your data space. When the program needs to read or write to the variable, it goes directly to the physical address that you gave it in the source code. *No protection exists for overwriting critical system resources.* If you gave it the wrong address, the compiled code will freely write to that address, even if to do so will crash the system bloodily.

The address given in an absolute variable declaration need not be a numeric literal. Named constants are also legal:

```
CONST
   RefreshBase = $0B000 : $0;

VAR
   GraphBuff : CGABuff ABSOLUTE RefreshBase;
```

You may give the address in one additional way: By specifying a variable name. The address of that variable becomes the address of the absolute variable. It is important to understand what this does: It maps an absolute variable *on top of* a variable declared previously. *The contents of the previously declared variable have nothing to do with where Turbo Pascal locates the absolute variable.*

An example may make this clearer:

```
VAR
   InChar   : Char;
   BuffByte : Byte ABSOLUTE InChar;
```

What we have here are two variables, each 1 byte in size, occupying the *same* location in memory. At compile time Turbo Pascal simply replaces the name of the variable **InChar** with **InChar**'s address in the static data area. **InChar** and **BuffByte** have incompatible types, but by placing a value in one the same value may be placed in both.

This may look familiar to you. It is, in effect, the same thing as a free union variant record (see Section 9.4), described a little more tersely and considerably less portably. In both cases, two (or more) data items occupy the same physical memory, so that accessing one will access the other, regardless of data type. It is used mostly to cheat on Pascal's strong typing restrictions. The same warnings that apply to free union variant records apply here: Know what you're doing.

Without saying much about it, we offered a pair of examples of the use of absolute variables in Section 18.11, while discussing **BlockRead** and **BlockWrite**. **GLoad** and **GSave** declare an array of 16,384 bytes at an absolute location corresponding to the IBM PC Color Graphics Adapter graphics refresh buffer. This allows the Pascal code to read and write graphics data between disk and the refresh buffer.

20.2   Absolute address functions

Turbo Pascal has extended the Standard Pascal language definition with a number of functions that deal in actual physical machine addresses. Some of these functions work different in the Z80 and 8086 versions of the compiler; some are present only in the 8086 versions. Use them with care. Like most Turbo Pascal features found in this section, they are guaranteed non-portable, and can wreak havoc on your system if used incorrectly.

ADDR

Knowing where an entity is in memory allows a lot of power to deal with non-standard machine hardware. Turbo Pascal includes the **Addr** function for returning a machine address pointer to any instantiated variable, function, or procedure. **Addr** is predeclared this way:

```
FUNCTION Addr (<variable or function or procedure>) : Pointer;
```

The pointer returned by **Addr** is compatible with any pointer type. In other words, the type of pointer returned by **Addr** is a pointer to whatever variable type the parameter to **Addr** happens to be. Since Pascal does not allow the creation of pointers to procedures or functions, the pointer that **Addr** returns to a procedure or function has no type but must be considered a pure machine address. Note that for Z80 versions of the compiler, **Addr** returns a

16-bit machine address, and for 8086 versions returns a 32-bit machine address.

```
PROGRAM Pointers;

TYPE
  PChar = ^Char;

VAR
  CH      : Char;
  B       : Byte;
  CharPtr : PChar;

BEGIN
  CH := 'Z';
  B := 65;
  CharPtr := Addr(B);
  CH := CharPtr^;
  Writeln('CH=',CH);
END.
```

when run, displays:

```
CH=A
```

In this example, **Addr** is used to create a pointer to a variable of type **Byte** *and assign that pointer to a pointer-to-character pointer variable.* What this means is that **CharPtr** now points to **B**, a variable of type **Byte**, and the value stored in **B** can thus be assigned to character **CH** without running afoul of Pascal's strong type checking.

To be fair, the same effect could (and should!) have been done with the **Chr(X)** transfer function. We used the **Char** and **Byte** types in the example program because they are simple and easy to understand. Tricky type conversion like this is usually done with larger and more complicated data types, typically records, arrays, or structured buffers dictated by your hardware or foreign software. *It should be obvious that you can get into trouble this way,* normally by using pointers to assign between data types that are of different physical sizes. If you assign a value in a record variable that is 200 bytes long to a record variable of a different type that is only 150 bytes long, 50 bytes worth of adjacent variables and code could be overwritten, with unpredictable (but predictably unpleasant) consequences. Do what you want, but *know what you're doing.*

Addr can only return a pointer to a unique, named entity that currently exists in memory somewhere. **Addr** cannot be used to regenerate a pointer to a "lost" dynamic variable. Nor can **Addr** reach "down into" a procedure or function from outside and return a pointer to a local variable, function, or procedure. Local entities cannot be accessed until they are instantiated; in other words, a procedure's local variables literally do not exist until that procedure is invoked. Finally, **Addr** cannot return the address of a constant, because there is no single location for a constant value. The compiler builds constants into the code wherever the constant is named. There are as many copies of a constant in a program as there are uses of the constant's identifier, so no single address exists for **Addr** to return.

In the 8080/Z80 world, pointers are 16-bit machine addresses. In the 8086 world, pointers must be 32-bit creatures, because an 8086 machine address includes a 16-bit segment and a 16-bit offset. Some compilers from the 8-bit world (particularly C compilers) allow free interchange of integers and pointers; obviously, this would not be meaningful in an 8086 environment. Type checking is indeed good for something!

THE 8086 SEGMENT FUNCTIONS

The 8086 versions of Turbo Pascal (CP/M-86, MS DOS, and PC DOS) include several built-in functions for returning important 8086 segment register values. All machine addresses in an 8086 computer have two 16-bit portions: the segment and offset. The segment portion of an address is one of 65,536 overlapping 64K regions of memory that begin every 16 bytes in the 8086 address space. The offset is a distance in bytes into one of those segments. Together, the segment and offset can specify each one of 1,048,576 separate memory locations.

Several registers within the 8086 specify which of those 65,536 segments are to be used for certain purposes. There is a *code segment,* which specifies the segment in which currently executing code must exist; a *data segment,* in which data items must reside to be accessible to certain CPU manipulations; and the *stack segment,* in which the CPU sets up its system stack.

There are times when you may want to examine or use the values in these registers. Turbo Pascal for the 8086 provides three functions to return segment register values:

CSeg returns the current value of the Code Segment register.
DSeg returns the current value of the Data Segment register.
SSeg returns the current value of the Stack Segment register.

All of these functions return a value of type **Integer**.

SEG AND OFS

These two functions are used to return the segment and offset of a data item, procedure, or function:

```
FUNCTION Seg(<data item/procedure/function>) : Integer

FUNCTION Ofs(<data item/procedure/function>) : Integer
```

<Data item> may be one element of an array or a field in the middle of a record. It may not be a file.

NOTE: A recognized bug in Turbo Pascal 2.0 prevents **Seg** from compiling with a function or procedure name as its parameter. The way around this is to use the **CSeg** function (see above) to extract the segment portion of a procedure's or function's address, since such creatures always reside in the current code segment. Borland International may correct this bug in a future release.

PTR

The **Ptr** function does a job similar to **Addr**. It takes a machine address and turns it into a pointer that may be assigned to any pointer type. **Ptr** is useful for generating a pointer to machine resources that exist at a fixed location in its memory space.

```
FUNCTION Ptr(<machine address>) : Pointer
```

In a Z80 environment, <machine address> must be type **Integer**. For 8086 machines, however, a machine address is a 32-bit quantity, and must be expressed as two integers separated by a comma. The first integer is the segment part of the machine address. The second integer is the offset:

```
1          {------------------------------------------------------------}
2          {                           WHICH                            }
3          {                                                            }
4          {        Display adpater detction demonstration program      }
5          {                                                            }
6          {                               by Jeff Duntemann            }
7          {                               Turbo Pascal V3.0            }
8          {                               Last update 1/31/86          }
9          {                                                            }
10         {                                                            }
11         {                                                            }
12         {------------------------------------------------------------}
13
14         PROGRAM WhichDisplay;  { For the IBM PC! }
15
16         TYPE
17           BytePtr = ^Byte;
18
19         VAR
20           BP : BytePtr;
21           B  : Byte;
22
23         BEGIN
24           BP := Ptr($0030,$0410); { Address of equipment flag byte }
25           B  := BP^;
26           IF (B AND $30) = $30 THEN Writeln('Monochrome display installed!')
27             ELSE Writeln('Color graphics adapter installed!')
28         END.
```

In the IBM PC, there is a byte at $0030:$0410 that stores information on which of several hardware options are installed on that particular machine. By examining two of the bits in that byte you can tell whether the Monochrome Display Adapter or the Color Graphics Adapter is installed. The example program above creates a pointer to this equipment flag byte by passing the byte's segment and offset addresses to **Ptr**, which bundles them together into a pointer and assigns them to pointer variable **BP**.

PEEKING AND POKING WITH THE MEM ARRAY

Actually, using the **Ptr** function to access an absolute location in machine memory (as we just did in the preceding section) is more work than you need to go through simply to do that. Turbo Pascal gives you direct read/write access to *all* of your computer's memory space by way of the **Mem** (all versions) and **MemW** (8086 only) arrays.

Z80 versions   For Z80 versions of Turbo Pascal, **Mem** is an array of byte, predeclared this way:

```
Mem : ARRAY[0..$FFFF] OF Byte;
```

The index type is **Integer**. Note that for the "top half" of the Z80's 64K address space you must express a literal address as a hexadecimal value rather than a decimal value. Turbo only recognizes literal decimal values up to **MaxInt**, 32,767. Of course, you can assign a hexadecimal literal larger than **MaxInt** (up to $FFFF) to an integer value, and **Mem** will recognize it as a positive value, even though it would print to your screen as a negative value.

Mem allows you to perform "peak" and "poke" operations similar to those in BASIC. Reading CP/M's I/O byte at absolute location $03 is done this way:

```
IOByte := Mem[3];
```

You can write to **Mem** just as easily:

```
Mem[3] := IOByte;
```

There is no real speed or code advantage to using **Mem** for this purpose over declaring an absolute **Byte** at address 3.

8086 versions   Machine addresses on 8086 systems have two parts, a segment and an offset. **Mem** works much the same way on an 8086 machine as it does on a Z80 machine, save that both parts of the address must be given, separated by a colon:

```
HardwareFlag := Mem[$0030:$0410];
```

This is another way of allowing you access to the IBM PC's hardware configuration flag byte at $0030:$0410. It is somewhat terser than using the **Ptr** function to build a pointer to it but has no other advantages. The easiest and (in my opinion) the best way to access absolute locations in machine memory is to define absolute variables at those locations. That done, there is no need to assign pointers or peek at memory in the **Mem** array; whatever lies at that absolute memory location is already in your variable with no further action on your part.

In 8086 versions of Turbo Pascal you also have **MemW**, an array whose items are integers rather than bytes. Otherwise it is identical to **Mem** in terms of operation. Both the segment and the offset part of the address must be present in the index, separated by a colon:

```
DeviceCount := MemW[$F000:$34A6]
```

USING UNTYPED VAR PARAMETERS

This is a feature of Turbo Pascal that is completely unique, as far as I know. It will probably seem extremely peculiar to you. I have included it in this section because it is, in a sense, yet another absolute address function built into the way Turbo passes parameters to procedures and functions.

You might remember from Section 14.1 that all function and procedure parameters must have a type. In Turbo Pascal this is only half true; **VAR** parameters do *not* have to have a type. This, for example, is a completely legitimate procedure header:

```
PROCEDURE VarDump(VAR Target; ItSize : Integer);
```

Any variable at all, regardless of its size or type, may be passed to **VarDump** in its parameter **Target**. This is what untyped **VAR** parameters are for: to allow you to sneak around Pascal's strict type checking and pass any variable to a function or procedure, in cases where the type of the variable is not important.

To explore the concept, let's build a debugging tool. Procedure **VarDump** is a handy thing to have in your toolkit: It will accept any variable in **Target** and give a hex dump of the contents of that variable on your screen or printer. Inserting invocations of **Var-Dump** into your program will allow you to "peek" at the contents of critical variables while your program runs.

You may have already inserted **Writeln** statements in your programs to display the values of printable data items such as integers, reals, and characters. **VarDump** will show you what's in data items that are incompatible with **Writeln** (sets, records, etc.) or that contain unprintable binary data.

```
1        {<<<< VarDump >>>>}
2
3
4        { Described in section 20.2 -- Last mod 2/1/86   }
5
6        PROCEDURE VarDump(VAR Device : Text; VAR Target; ItSize : Integer);
7
```

(continues)

```
8        CONST
9          Printables : SET OF Char = [' '..'}'];
10
11       VAR
12         I,J        : Integer;
13         Full,Left : Integer;
14         DumpIt    : ARRAY[0..MAXINT] OF Byte ABSOLUTE Target;
15
16       PROCEDURE DumpLine(Offset,ByteCount : Integer);
17
18       VAR
19         I : Integer;
20
21       BEGIN
22         FOR I := 0 TO ByteCount-1 DO                { Hex dump the data }
23           BEGIN
24             WriteHex(Device,DumpIt[(Offset*16)+I]);
25             Write(Device,' ')
26           END;
27         FOR I := 0 TO 56 - (ByteCount*3) DO Write(Device,' ');  { Space interval }
28           Write(Device,'|');                        { Show first boundary bar }
29         FOR I := 0 TO ByteCount-1 DO                { Show printable equivalents }
30           IF Chr(DumpIt[(Offset*16)+I]) IN Printables THEN
31             Write(Device,Chr(DumpIt[(Offset*16)+I]))
32           ELSE Write(Device,'.');
33         Writeln(Device,'|')                         { Final boundary bar }
34       END;
35
36
37       BEGIN
38         Full := ItSize DIV 16;   { Number of 16-byte chunks in Target }
39         Left := ItSize MOD 16;   { 'Leftover' bytes after last 16-byte chunk }
40         FOR I := 0 TO Full-1 DO  { Not executed if less than 16 bytes in Target }
41           DumpLine(I,16);
42         IF Left > 0 THEN         { Not executed if size of Target divides by 16 }
43           DumpLine(Full,Left);
44         Writeln(Device)         { Space down one line after dump }
45       END;  { VARDUMP }
```

(concluded)

Before you look too closely at the actual code making up **Var-Dump**, look at its parameter line and variable declarations. **Target** has no type. The identifier **Target** is followed immediately by a semicolon.

If it has no type, what can be done with it? Not many things; it is incompatible with *all* other data types. You cannot assign either to **Target** or from **Target**. Neither can **Target** take part in any sort of expression. Without a data type, Pascal's runtime code cannot determine what sort of data exists in **Target** nor even how large it is. About all the information an untyped **VAR** parameter carries with it into a procedure is the address at which the actual variable being passed to the parameter begins.

That, however, can be a lot.

The declaration of the local variable **DumpIt** is the key:

```
DumpIt : ARRAY[0..MaxInt] OF Byte ABSOLUTE Target;
```

In Turbo Pascal, a variable declared as **ABSOLUTE** exists at a specific location in machine memory given by the address after the keyword **ABSOLUTE**. In this case, the address is not an address but **Target**, the untyped **VAR** parameter.

Target provides the absolute starting address for **DumpIt**, as large an array of bytes as Turbo Pascal can declare. **DumpIt** begins at the same address as **Target**, and since **DumpIt** is *very* large, it will most likely be larger than any variable you pass in **Target**. By addressing bytes in **DumpIt** you can access any data that exist in the variable passed in **Target**, regardless of what data type that variable happens to be. **DumpIt** is "mapped onto" whatever variable is passed in **Target**. We've already seen how one variable may be mapped onto another via **ABSOLUTE**. Here, a *parameter* is mapped onto a variable, allowing any parameter to become a simple array of bytes.

You might worry a little about mapping a 32,767-byte variable over an actual parameter that may only be 2 or 3 bytes long. Nothing will happen to data or code beyond the end of your actual parameter *if* you know the actual parameter's size and avoid disturbing bytes beyond that size boundary. This is what the **ItSize** parameter does. Since nothing in **Target** tells the code how large its actual parameter is, **ItSize** must be passed separately. Of course, if you pass a value larger than the value of the actual parameter and then alter the actual parameter, you run the risk of disturbing other code and data with unknown (but probably unpleasant) effects.

The **Device** parameter allows you to send the output of **VarDump** to your console, printer, or a text file. The predeclared text file **CON** will send output to your console. **LST** sends it to your printer. Pass the name of an open text file in **Device**, and output will be written to that text file.

Any time you need to pass several different data types to a procedure in a single parameter, this is the way to do it. This is *not* an ISO Standard Pascal feature, nor does it exist (to my knowledge) in any other implementation of Pascal. More examples of its use will arise in the bit manipulation procedures described in Section 20.4.

20.3   High-speed block moves and fills

Certain operations are very easy and fast in assembly code, yet very ponderous and slow when done in Pascal. Moving large blocks of data from one place to another can take a lot of time, often when time is critical: for example, when swapping entire CRT screen buffers in and out of display RAM. Turbo Pascal provides a number of built-in routines to do this sort of work nearly as quickly as it could be done in pure assembly language.

MOVE

Move provides a very fast, general-purpose block move function for use on a byte level. **Move** is predeclared this way:

```
PROCEDURE Move(<source>,<destination>,Count : Integer);
```

Both <source> and <destination> may be any type at all, and need not be the same type. This leniency allows you to move data wholesale from records into screen buffers, etc. **Count** is the number of bytes of data you wish to move.

Ordinarily, data are moved from the first (leftmost) byte of <source> to the first (leftmost) byte of <destination>. (The exception is when <source> and <destination> overlap; see below.) <Destination> may also be an element in an array, allowing you to move data into the middle of an array, rather than just to the beginning of an array. **Count** bytes are moved. If we had this situation:

```
VAR
  MyBuff, YourBuff : ARRAY[1.255] OF Byte;

Move(MyBuff,YourBuff,128);
```

MyBuff[1] would first be moved to **YourBuff[1]**. Then **MyBuff[2]** would be moved to **YourBuff[2]**, and so on. This works *very* quickly compared with using a **FOR** loop to do the move. Also, a **FOR** loop would not be able to move data between different data types.

The most obvious application of **Move** is in tossing screen and other buffers around. A graphics screen buffer on the IBM PC is 16,384 bytes long. A graphics generator program with an on-line help facility might wish to "stuff away" the working graphics screen so it can bring up a help screen. Later, when the operator is finished reading the help screen, the graphics workscreen can be restored. **Move** can accomplish this with great ease:

```
TYPE
  GBuff = ARRAY[0..16383] OF Byte;

VAR
  Display : ABSOLUTE [$0B800 : $00] GBuff;
  Cachel  : ABSOLUTE [$09000 : $00] GBuff;

Move(Display, Cachel,16384);

<perform help screen manipulations here>

Move(Cachel,Display,16384);
```

Move can also be used to move data from one part of a data structure to another area within the *same* data structure. The source and destination areas may overlap; the **Move** procedure is smart enough to determine how to perform the move so that data does not overwrite itself during the move.

(Pascal/MT+ uses a separate procedure, **MoveRight**, to handle this problem. Turbo Pascal's **Move** procedure is somewhat "smarter" than Pascal/MT+'s **Move** and **MoveRight** procedures. **Move** in Turbo Pascal is slightly slower, but only slightly.)

Move is a low level byte-oriented procedure. It is very fast, but rather "dumb"; it does not recognize data types nor the boundaries of variables. **Move** will obediently move a 200-byte variable into a 100-byte variable—but in the process you will overwrite 100 bytes of adjacent storage, with possibly disastrous consequences. One good idea is to use **SizeOf** (see below) to supply the **Count** parameter when moving one variable into another. That way, even if you change the physical size of the variable to be moved, the **Count** figure will always automatically be exactly right.

FILLCHAR

Turbo Pascal provides a way to fill an area of memory with some byte value. **FillChar** should be considered a high speed buffer-blanker. It is predeclared this way:

```
PROCEDURE FillChar(<destination>; Count : Integer; Ch : Char);
```

As with **Move**, <destination> may be any data type. **Count** indicates how many bytes are to be filled. **Ch** is the byte value with which **FillChar** will fill <destination> from its beginning to **Count** bytes past its beginning. If <destination> is an array, you may also specify an element of the array as a starting point to enable you to begin filling in the middle of <destination> if you need to:

```
VAR
  TBuff : ScreenBuff;

FillChar(TBuff,SizeOf(TBuff),Chr(0));
FillChar(TBuff[4096],2048,Chr(7));
```

As with the block move procedures, **FillChar** does not respect boundaries of variables or code segments. If **Count** takes the fill beyond the edge of <destination>, whatever lies beyond will be obliterated by the fill. Use **FillChar** with care.

SIZEOF

The **SizeOf** function allows your program code to "know" how large a variable or data type is. Within the bounds of ISO Pascal there is no need for this; but certain Turbo Pascal extensions need to know the size, in bytes, of the creatures they act upon. **SizeOf** is predeclared this way:

```
FUNCTION SizeOf(<data type or variable>) : Integer;
```

The parameter may only be a data type or a variable; **SizeOf** cannot determine the sizes of functions, procedures, or constants.

The **FillChar** procedure (see above) is the simplest example of this. **FillChar** fills a variable with a given byte-size value. It needs to know how large the variable is to do this:

```
FillChar(MyRec,SizeOf(MyRec),Chr(0));
```

This statement takes the record **MyRec** and fills it with binary 0. The middle parameter tells **FillChar** how large a region of memory must be filled with 0's.

You could, of course, simply fill in the size parameter with a literal constant:

```
FillChar(MyRec,144,Chr(0))
```

Assuming that **MyRec** is a record type that is 144 bytes in size, this will work handily. *But* . . . if you ever change the definition of

MyRec's record type (and thus its size) you could be in serious trouble. **FillChar** does not recognize the boundaries of data items; it starts at the beginning of the destination variable and lays down as many filler bytes as the size parameter calls for. If you pare down **MyRec** to occupy only 120 bytes, **FillChar** will still lay down 144 binary 0's, overwriting adjacent code or data.

Using **SizeOf** with **FillChar** ensures that **FillChar** will always *exactly* fill the destination variable, neither a byte more nor a byte less, regardless of how often you change the definition of the destination variable's type.

With care, of course, you don't need **SizeOf**. But you might as well allow the compiler to take as much work and worry off your hands as it can. Bugs proceeding from hard-coded size parameters are insidious, inconsistent, and completely avoidable. Use **SizeOf** with all the move and fill built-ins: **FillChar**, **Move**, and also with **BlockRead** and **BlockWrite**.

20.4   Bit manipulation

Dealing with numbers and characters has been the traditional task of Pascal. Dealing with the computer itself, on its very low levels, or dealing with machinery existing in the outside world demands more precision than the ability to grasp 8 or 16 bits at a time. In systems programming, where memory is usually at a premium, important information is often stored in a single bit. Often, 8 information bits are placed together in a byte (often called a "flag byte," since it contains eight 1-bit flags.) Though the computer reads and writes the flag byte as a unit, it must be able to set, clear, and individually interpret each 1-bit flag in the byte.

Flag bytes like this are frequently used to control peripheral chips like serial port controllers, parallel port controllers, and baud rate generators. These chips are generally accessed as machine I/O ports. Because of the way our computers work, speaking of reading I/O ports and working with bits is best done together.

SETTING, CLEARING, AND TESTING BITS

Unlike Pascal/MT+, Turbo Pascal has no built-in facilities for testing, setting, or clearing bits. To manipulate bits you must deal with whole bytes or integers and use Turbo Pascal's bitwise logical operators to "mask" out the bits you wish to leave alone. We looked at these bitwise operators in Section 11.4. Do refer to that section if their operation is unclear to you.

WORKING WITH ONE BIT AT A TIME

In situations where you need to isolate one single bit from an 8- or 16-bit variable, it's quite easy to create a set of bit manipulation functions that will work on any such variable, regardless of type. In this section we'll show you how such functions work.

TestBit First of the three is a function that tests whether a particular bit is 1 ("set") or 0 ("cleared"). **TestBit** returns **True** if the selected bit is set and false if it is cleared.

The **BitNum** parameter specifies that bit you wish to test. The bits within an 8-bit variable are numbered 0 to 7. In a 16-bit variable they run from 0 to 15. Bit 0 is the least significant bit; in the pure binary representation of a number it represents 2 to the 0th power, or 1. Bit 1 represents 2 to the first power, or 2; and so on.

The following demonstration program contains the **TestBit** function. The program prompts you for an integer, and then prints the binary equivalent of the integer you enter. It does this by testing each bit of the integer and printing a '1' if the bit is set and '0' if the bit is cleared. To exit the program enter 0:

```
 1          {-------------------------------------------------------------}
 2          {                        BINARY                               }
 3          {                                                             }
 4          {             Bit test demonstration program                  }
 5          {                                                             }
 6          {                             by Jeff Duntemann               }
 7          {                             Turbo Pascal V3.0                }
 8          {                             Last update 1/31/86              }
 9          {                                                             }
10          {                                                             }
11          {                                                             }
12          {-------------------------------------------------------------}
13
14          PROGRAM BinaryDemo;
```

(continues)

```
15
16          VAR
17            I,J : Integer;
18
19
20          FUNCTION TestBit(VAR Target; BitNum : Integer) : Boolean;
21
22          VAR
23            Subject : Integer ABSOLUTE Target;
24            Dummy   : Integer;
25
26          BEGIN
27            Dummy := Subject;
28            Dummy := Dummy SHR BitNum;
29            IF Odd(Dummy) THEN TestBit := True
30              ELSE TestBit := False
31          END;
32
33
34          BEGIN
35            REPEAT
36              Write('>>Enter an integer (0 to exit): ');
37              Readln(I);
38              FOR J := 15 DOWNTO 0 DO
39                IF TestBit(I,J) THEN Write('1') ELSE Write('0');
40              Writeln; Writeln
41            UNTIL I = 0
42          END.
```

(concluded)

TestBit tests bit **BitNum** in **Target**. If the bit is set, the function returns **True**. If the bit is cleared, the function returns **False**. **Target** is an untyped **VAR** parameter, as we described in the previous section. Using an untyped **VAR** parameter allows us to pass any 8- or 16-bit variable to **TestBit**, regardless of its type. A larger variable will, in fact, be accepted by **TestBit** in its **Target** parameter; however, **TestBit** will ignore any bytes after the first two.

BinaryDemo produces output like this:

```
>>Enter an integer (0 to quit): 17367
0100001111010111

>>Enter an integer (0 to quit): 16
0000000000010000

>>Enter an integer (0 to quit): 0
0000000000000000
```

How does this work? You only want to examine one bit out of the 8 or 16 in **Target**. There is already a standard Pascal procedure that tests a single bit in an 8- or 16-bit variable, although it may not be the bit you want: **Odd(X)** tests bit 0 of X. If that bit is set, **Odd** returns a Boolean value of **True**. If the bit is cleared, **Odd** returns **False**.

Odd works this way because all odd numbers, expressed as binary bit patterns, will have bit 0 set to 1. To test a bit other than bit 0 you must move your desired bit down into the 0 position. This is done with the **SHR** (SHift Right) operator. **SHR** shifts the desired bit from its position down to bit 0. **Odd** then tests to see if that bit is set or cleared.

SetBit Turning on one single bit of an 8- or 16-bit variable is the job of **SetBit**:

```
1        {<<<< SetBit >>>>}
2
3
4        { Described in section 20.4 -- Last mod 2/1/86    }
5
6        PROCEDURE SetBit(VAR Target; BitNum : Integer);
7
8        VAR
9          Subject : Integer ABSOLUTE Target;
10         Mask    : Integer;
11
```

(continues)

```
12        BEGIN
13          Mask := 1 SHL BitNum;
14          Subject := Subject OR Mask
15        END;
```

(concluded)

SetBit sets bit **BitNum** in **Target**. How? This time we're setting up an actual bitmask. **Mask** starts out with a single set bit in bit 0, the least significant (and rightmost) bit in an integer. If we wanted to set bit 0, this would be sufficient. To set the other bits, we have to move that single set bit "over" to the bit position we wish to set. This is done by shifting **Mask**'s single set bit leftward with Turbo Pascal's **SHL** operator. The number of bits it must be shifted is the same number of bits as the bit number we wish to set. For an example, say we wish to set bit 6 of a variable. Here's **Mask** before and after the shift:

```
       Mask containing the integer value 1:

              0000000000000001

       Mask after shifting 6 bits leftward:

              0000000000100000
```

Now we have a proper bitmask. To use it, apply the mask against the target variable (say, a value of 129) with the bitwise logical operator **OR**:

```
              0000000010000001
                     OR
              0000000001000000
                   yields
              0000000011000001
```

Follow each bit column down, applying the **OR** operator between each bit in the value (top) with the mask (middle) to produce the result (bottom). If bit 6 of the value was cleared, the OR with bit 6 in the mask will set it. If bit 6 in the value was already set, the operation will have no effect.

For an example of **SetBit** in use we can turn once again to CRT business. The ASCII character set uses only seven of the eight bits in an 8-bit **Char** variable. The eighth bit is an "extra" bit that has found some interesting uses. The IBM PC uses the "high bit" to define a completely distinct 128-character set, which includes foreign language characters, form-drawing characters, and mathematical symbols. Many (especially older) computers display the familiar ASCII characters in reverse video if bit 7 is set in those characters. This allows us to write a procedure for displaying a character string in reverse video:

```
1        {<<<< WriteHi >>>>}
2
3
4        { Described in section 20.4 -- Last mod 2/1/86    }
5        { For use on Sol/20, Xerox 820, and others. }
6        { NOT for use on the IBM PC! }
7
8        PROCEDURE WriteHi(MyText : String255; CRLF : Boolean);
9
10       VAR
11         I : Integer;
12
13       BEGIN
14         FOR I := 1 TO Length(MyText) DO SetBit(MyText[I],7);
15         IF CRLF THEN Writeln(MyText) ELSE Write(MyText)
16       END;
```

WriteHi assumes that you have defined a type **String255** previously in the program.

Of course, **WriteHi** only works correctly on computers whose hardware supports reverse video when bit 7 is high. This includes the Xerox 820-II, Processor Tech SOL-20, and numerous S100 video boards. The IBM PC, as previously mentioned, uses the high bit for the alternate character set and has other means for generating reverse video.

ClearBit   The flipside of setting bits is clearing them, and we can define a procedure **ClearBit** to do that job:

```
1       {<<<< ClearBit >>>>}
2
3
4       { Described in section 20.4 -- Last mod 2/1/86    }
5
6       PROCEDURE ClearBit(VAR Target; BitNum : Integer);
7
8       VAR
9         Subject : Integer ABSOLUTE Target;
10        Mask    : Integer;
11
12      BEGIN
13        Mask := NOT(1 SHL BitNum);
14        Subject := Subject AND Mask
15      END;
```

ClearBit clears bit **BitNum** in **Target**. **Target**, as with **TestBit** and **SetBit**, may be any 8- or 16-bit variable (types **Char**, **Byte**, **Integer**, or **Boolean**). **Target** may be larger than two bytes, but any bytes after the second will be ignored. Remember that setting a bit puts that bit to a binary 1; and clearing a bit puts that bit to a binary 0. The mechanism here is almost identical to that of **SetBit**, save that we have inverted the mask and are using the **AND** bitwise operator rather than **OR**:

```
0000000011000001
       AND
1111111110111111
     yields
0000000010000001
```

Again, follow each bit column down, applying the top bit (the value) upon the middle bit (the mask) to yield the result on the bottom. If you are still a little fuzzy on how bitwise **AND** and **OR** work, refer to Section 11.4.

ClearBit will be used in the interrupt-driven terminal program in Section 20.8.

WORKING WITH SEVERAL BITS AT A TIME

The three procedures just presented work only with one bit at a time. The general method of creating a mask and using the bitwise logical operators works as well for several bits as it does for one, since each bit is operated upon separately.

A good example is the **WriteHex** procedure we have used in the **HexDump** program and **VarDump** procedure described previously:

```
1     {<<<< WriteHex >>>>}
2
3
4     { Described in section 20.4 -- Last mod 2/1/86   }
5
6
7     PROCEDURE WriteHex(VAR Device : Text; BT : Byte);
8
9     CONST
10       HexDigits : ARRAY[0..15] OF Char = '0123456789ABCDEF';
11
12     VAR
13       BZ : Byte;
14
```

(continues)

```
15          BEGIN
16            BZ := BT AND $0F;
17            BT := BT SHR 4;
18            Write(Device,HexDigits[BT],HexDigits[BZ])
19          END;
```

(concluded)

WriteHex prints a byte in hexadecimal notation. In hexadecimal notation, each 4-bit half of a byte (a ''nybble'') has its own base 16 digit from 0 to F. The first line of code in **WriteHex** isolates the low nybble of the byte by masking out the high nybble. If the byte happened to be 122 (hex 7A) the mask operation would look like this:

```
          01111010    ($7A)
            AND
          00001111    ($0F)
            yields
          00001010    ($0A)
```

The **AND** operation forces all the 1-bits in the high nybble to 0-bits, while retaining the low nybble without change.

Isolating the high nybble is done in a slightly different way. We need the high nybble, but if we simply mask out the low nybble we will have not $7 but $70—which is far outside the range of the array **HexDigits**. We must change $70 to $07. It's done by shifting the $7A value four bits to the right. The low nybble gets ''bumped off the edge'' into oblivion, and 0-bits are fed into the byte from the high side to take their place:

```
Before shifting:    01111010      ($7A)

After shifting:     00000111      ($07)
```

Not only does this bring the high nybble down to the low nybble where we need it; it zeroes out the high nybble to keep it out of mischief.

BT and **BZ** now contain $07 and $0A respectively. By indexing into **HexDigits** with those values ($0A is equivalent to decimal 10, recall) we come up with the characters '7' and 'A'. Voila! Hex on the half byte!

If the working of **SHL** and **SHR** still puzzles you, review their introduction in Section 11.2.

20.5   Dealing with I/O ports

Most Z80 and 8086 peripheral devices are "I/O mapped"; that is, they are reached through special I/O instruction opcodes rather than mapped onto RAM memory. An "I/O port" is actually a code number that is sent onto the address bus, along with some sort of signal (usually a special pin on the CPU chip itself) indicating that an I/O operation is under way. If a physical device exists on the address bus that responds to that code number, data will be sent or received between the CPU and the peripheral device.

The Z80 CPU has 256 such I/O ports; the 8086, by using two bytes for the code number, has 65,536.

Turbo Pascal accesses I/O ports through a pair of predeclared arrays: **Port** (all versions) and **PortW** (8086 versions only). **Port** sends or receives one byte at a time. **PortW** sends or receives an integer quantity, which contains two bytes. Legal indices for **Port** in Z80 versions of Turbo Pascal are 0 to 255. **Port** for the 8086 and **PortW** may be indexed from 0 to $FFFF. (Since Turbo Pascal does not have an "unsigned integer," integer values higher than 32767 must be expressed in hexadecimal.) **Port** and **PortW** may be considered as predeclared arrays as follows:

```
Port : ARRAY[0.255] OF Byte;        { For the Z80 }

Port : ARRAY[0..$FFFF] OF Byte;     { For the 8086 }

PortW : ARRAY[0..$FFFF] OF Integer; { 8086 ONLY! }
```

PORT

When you read a byte from the **Port** array, you are actually reading a byte from the port whose number is the subscript of the element read:

```
StatByte := Port[4];
```

This statement reads from I/O port 4 by reading element 4 of the array **Port**.

In a similar fashion, writing a byte to an element of **Port** actually writes a byte to the I/O port whose number is the subscript of the element written to:

```
Port[$10] := SIOSetup;
```

Here the byte **SIOSetup** is written to I/O port 16 (hex 10) by assigning the byte to element 16 of **Port**.

As far as your code is concerned, **Port** is treated no differently from an array of **Byte** with two exceptions:

1. You may not reference the entire array as the identifier **Port** without a subscript. Whenever **Port** is used it *must* have a subscript!

2. Individual elements of **Port** may not be passed to procedures in reference (**VAR**) parameters.

Port may be indexed by constants, variables, or expressions.

PORTW

In 8086 versions of the compiler you may also use the array **PortW**. **PortW** is, in essence, a 16-bit version of **Port**. Its index type is **Integer** and its elements are also type **Integer**.

PortW should be used *only* when you must transfer 16 bits at a time between your program and an I/O port. We're accustomed to calling the IBM PC a 16-bit machine, but that's questionable, since the 8088 CPU chip presents a very definite 8-bit bus to the outside world. Attempting to read 16 bits from a single I/O port on an 8-bit bus may actually do a number of different things, depending on the electrical nature of the device that responds to the requested I/O port number. You may get garbage in the high byte of the returned integer. You may get a duplication of the low byte in the high byte. You may also read the next higher I/O port number (if one has been implemented in the system) into the high byte. Whatever happens is not likely to be meaningful for all 16 bits.

The same cautions apply when attempting to *write* 16 bits to an I/O port in the PC or XT using **PortW**. Use **Port** instead, for the PC and XT. **PortW** should work correctly on the PC/AT (since the AT is a true 16-bit machine with a 16-bit bus) and on most machines incorporating an 8086 (rather than 8088) CPU.

The declaration of **PortW** was given in a novel fashion:

```
PortW : ARRAY[0..$FFFF] OF Integer;
```

There are 65,536 ports in **PortW** but only 32,767 positive integers. Unlike most Pascals, Turbo Pascal lacks an unsigned integer type (called **Word** in most other Pascals) that would serve here. So the trick of stating the index in hex is necessary whenever you need to address a port whose address is greater than **MaxInt**.

Note that **PortW** returns integers rather than bytes. Both the port numbers and the values passed between port and machine are 16-bit quantities.

The same two restrictions that apply to **Port** also apply to **PortW**. And don't forget that **PortW** is not present in Z80 versions of the compiler!

The following statement will fire the one-shots in the IBM PC Game Controller Adapter:

```
Port[$201] := 0; { Anything out to port $201 fires oneshots }
```

20.6   DOS calls and 8086 software interrupts

Every disk operating system (generally referred to as a "DOS") has a list of primitive functions that perform necessary operations like disk and console I/O. These functions are informally referred to as "DOS calls."

Each implementation of Turbo Pascal has a function that makes DOS calls. Because the calling procedure for each operating system is different, it (sadly) must be a different routine for each DOS.

CP/M-80

CP/M-80 versions of Turbo Pascal give you four routines with which to make DOS calls:

```
PROCEDURE BDOS(Func : Integer; Parm : Integer);

FUNCTION BDOS(Func : Integer; Parm : Integer) : Integer;

PROCEDURE BDOSHL(Func : Integer; Parm : Integer);

FUNCTION BDOSHL(Func : Integer; Parm : Integer) : Integer;
```

For all four routines: **Func** is the number of the function you wish to call. **Parm** is a 16-bit parameter that some DOS calls require. You may omit the **Parm** parameter if the DOS call you wish to make does not require it. **Func** is placed in the Z80 C register.

BDOS and **BDOSHL** are available as both functions and procedures. Some DOS calls return a value to the calling logic and some do not. The procedure and function form work identically, save that the functions should be used to make those DOS calls that return a value.

The difference between **BDOS** and **BDOSHL** lies in the register pair from which the function return value is taken. BDOS returns the value it finds in Z80 register pair DE after the call is made. **BDOSHL** returns the value found in Z80 register pair HL.

A simple example is direct console I/O. It is possible to read and write to the console without CP/M interpreting control characters like CTRL-S and CTRL-P, especially. If you need total control of keyboard input or screen output, direct I/O is a necessity.

The following function tests console input to see if a character is ready. If one is ready, the function value returns as **True** and the character is returned in **Ch**. If no character is ready, the function value returns as **False**.

```
1       {<<<< KeyStat >>>>}
2
3
4       { Described in section 20.6 -- Last mod 2/1/86   }
5       { This KeyStat specific to CP/M-80 }
6
7       FUNCTION KeyStat(VAR Ch : Char) : Boolean;
8
9       BEGIN
10        Ch := Chr(BDOS(6,255));
11        KeyStat := Ch <> Chr(0)
12      END;
```

CP/M-86
For CP/M-86, the DOS call function is simpler, thanks to a more versatile way of passing parameters to and from the DOS call. The syntax for the CP/M-86 **BDOS** procedure is simple:

```
PROCEDURE BDOS(VAR Registers : RegPack);
```

The type **RegPack** is a record consisting of integers to hold values for each one of the 8086's internal registers:

```
TYPE
  RegPack = RECORD
              AX,BX,CX,DX,BP,SI,DI,DS,ES,FLAGS : Integer
            END;
```

This data type is *not* predeclared and you must include the above declaration in the type declaration part of each program that calls **BDOS**. If you know your 8086 specifics, you'll recognize the names of the fields within **RegPack**.

To use CP/M-86's BDOS, assign necessary input values to the appropriate registers in **Registers**. Then make the call.

As an example, the **KeyStat** function given above for CP/M-80 can be translated easily to work under CP/M-86. The parameters are identical:

```
1        {<<<< KeyStat >>>>}
2
3
4        { Described in section 20.6 -- Last mod 2/1/86  }
5        { This KeyStat specific to CP/M-86 }
6
7        FUNCTION KeyStat(VAR Ch : Char) : Boolean;
8
9        TYPE
10         RegPack = RECORD
11                     AX,BX,CX,DX,BP,SI,DI,DS,ES,FLAGS : Integer
12                   END;
13
14       VAR
15         Registers : RegPack;
16
17       BEGIN
18         Registers.AX := $0600;   { DOS call 6: Direct Console I/O }
19         Registers.DX := 255;     { Selects non-echo read function }
20         BDOS(Registers);         { Make the CP/M-86 DOS call }
21         Ch := CHR(Registers.AX); { The character is returned in AX }
22         KeyStat := Ch <> Chr(0)
23       END;
```

I do not have a great deal of experience with CP/M-86. It is not a widely-used operating system and is far inferior to MS DOS. There are a lot more available DOS call functions under CP/M-86 than under CP/M-80, and you will have to read the CP/M-86 documentation for more details.

**MS DOS AND
PC DOS**

Virtually all popular 8086 microcomputers use MS DOS or the IBM PC version of MS DOS, PC DOS. Although there are major differences between the PC DOS and MS DOS versions of Turbo Pascal, the differences are not important in terms of DOS calls. The **MSDOS** procedure will work well with either operating system.

As with the CP/M-86 version of BDOS, the **MSDOS** procedure uses the **RegPack** structure to pass values back and forth between your program and the operating system. As many of the simpler calls of **MS DOS** were modeled after CP/M-80 and CP/M-86, the direct console I/O function for **MS DOS** is almost identical to the one for CP/M-86:

```
1        {<<<< KeyStat >>>>}
2
3.
4        { Described in section 20.6 -- Last mod 2/1/86   }
5        { This version specific to PC/MS DOS             }
6
7        FUNCTION KeyStat(VAR Ch : Char) : Boolean;
8
9        TYPE
10         RegPack = RECORD
11                     AX,BX,CX,DX,BP,SI,DI,DS,ES,Flags : Integer
12                   END;
13
14       VAR
15         Registers : RegPack;
16
17       BEGIN
18         Registers.AX := $0600;    { DOS call 6: Direct Console I/O }
19         Registers.DX := 255;      { Selects non-echo read function }
20         MSDOS(Registers);         { Make the DOS call }
```

(continues)

```
21          Ch := Chr(Registers.AX); { The character is returned in AX }
22          KeyStat := Ch <> Chr(0)
23        END;
```

(concluded)

The *only* difference here, as you'll see, is the name of the procedure that actually does the DOS call.

KeyStat is used in situations where you want to "poll" the keyboard without sitting and waiting for someone to type something. If a key has been pressed, fine; go process it; otherwise, there are other things to be done. **KeyStat** does the work of both a **KeyPressed** function (that simply tells whether or not a key has been pressed) and a function for actually reading the character from the keyboard. You might use it this way:

```
Quit := False;
REPEAT
  IF KeyStat(Ch) THEN
    CASE Ch OF
      'D' : DisconnectLine;
      'E' : MopUpAndExit;
      'Q' : Quit := True;
      'R' : Restart;
    ELSE Beep;
    END;  { CASE }
  SendAChar
UNTIL Quit;
```

Here, you have code that is sending characters down a communications line on a continuing basis. It must, however, monitor the keyboard to see if a command is typed at any point during the transmission. In the loop, it sends a character, checks the keyboard, sends another character, checks the keyboard again, and so on.

The CP/M-80 version of **KeyStat** is used in the interrupt-driven dumb terminal program **Iterm** in the next section.

Another good example of an MS DOS call is the "free disk space call," call $36. This call is present in MS DOS version 2.0 and later; don't try to use it under MS DOS 1.1:

```
1      {<<<< FreeBytes >>>>}
2
3
4      { Described in section 20.6 -- Last mod 2/1/86   }
5      { Specific to MS/PC DOS }
6
7      FUNCTION FreeBytes(Unit : Char) : Real;
8
9      TYPE
10       RegPack = RECORD
11                    AX,BX,CX,DX,BP,SI,DI,DS,ES,Flags : Integer
12                 END;
13
14     VAR
15       Registers : RegPack;
16       UnitByte  : Byte;
17       R,A,B,C   : Real;
18
19     BEGIN
20       Unit := UpCase(Unit);
21       IF Unit IN ['A'..'D'] THEN    { A=1; B=2; C=3; D=4 else 0 }
22          UnitByte := Ord(Unit)-64
23       ELSE UnitByte := 0;
24       Registers.DX := UnitByte;
25       Registers.AX := $36 * 256;  { Call # must go in high byte}
26       MSDOS(Registers);
27       { Call $36 returns # of bytes per sector in CX; }
28       { # of sectors per cluster in AX, and # of free }
29       { clusters in BX, so free space in bytes is      }
30       { AX * BX * CX.  This must be done in reals to   }
31       { avoid integer overflow. }
32       A := Registers.AX; B := Registers.BX; C := Registers.CX;
```

(continues)

```
33              R := A * B * C;
34              FreeBytes := R
35           END;
```

(concluded)

FreeBytes returns the number of free bytes on the disk drive whose unit is passed in **Unit**. Passing a character *not* in the set A..D (legal MS DOS disk drive specifiers) will check for space on the currently-logged disk drive:

```
Space := FreeBytes('*');   { Checks logged disk drive }
```

The function returns a real value because disk drives hold orders of magnitude more bytes than an integer value can express. Counting objects with real numbers is not considered good practice but Turbo Pascal's lack of a long integer type makes it necessary.

8086 SOFTWARE INTERRUPTS

Accessing peripheral devices that are not recognized by DOS calls is frequently done on 8086 computers via the concept of a "software interrupt." A hardware interrupt is a signal sent to a physical pin on the CPU integrated circuit; when that signal is detected the CPU saves what it's doing and immediately executes what is called an "interrupt service routine" somewhere else in memory. As soon as the service routine has been completed, the CPU picks up what it was doing before the interrupt.

A software interrupt is much the same thing, except that it is triggered, not by an electrical signal on a CPU input line, but by a machine instruction within the program that is running. The CPU saves its current task, jumps to the software interrupt service routine, does what it must, and then resumes its current task.

This might sound like nothing more than calling a machine-language subroutine, and in most ways it is. The critical difference is that *the calling logic need not know where the subroutine is located.*

The lowest 4K of 8086 memory is reserved for interrupt vectors. An interrupt vector is simply the address of an interrupt service routine. Each vector occupies four bytes: two for the segment and two for the offset. Interrupts are numbered starting from 0, and their vectors are placed in memory such that interrupt 0's vector is in the first four bytes of memory; interrupt 1's vector is in the next four bytes, and so on. To call an interrupt service routine, a program need not have the address of the routine built into its code. If it knows the number of the interrupt, the 8086 chip will itself look up the address of the service routine in low memory, pass control to the service routine, and return control to the calling program when the service routine is finished.

This allows the computer's manufacturer a lot of leeway in dealing with updates of ROM utility and BIOS routines. If BIOS routines are maintained as software interrupt service routines, they can literally be anywhere in memory, and their actual locations can change with new releases of the BIOS. The location of a routine's *address* will always be the same, however, down in the vector table in low memory. Regardless of where the actual code for the routine may be, the calling logic can use it.

The ROM BIOS routines in the IBM PC are set up as software interrupt service routines. The video control routines are accessed via software interrupt $10. A print screen operation is initiated via software interrupt $05.

There are lots of available software interrupts, literally hundreds, in fact. Some third-party vendors have begun writing driver routines for their peripheral devices as software interrupts. The best example of this is the Microsoft Mouse.

The mouse has a driver routine that keeps track of where the mouse pointer should be, monitors the buttons for presses, changes the shape of the mouse cursor, and so on. This driver routine loads itself atop DOS and stores its location in the vector for software interrupt 51. By issuing a software interrupt 51 (in hex, $33), a program can access the mouse driver without actually knowing where the driver code is.

Turbo Pascal provides a generalized routine for making software interrupts:

```
PROCEDURE Intr(IntNum : Integer; VAR Registers : RegPack);
```

The interrupt number is passed in **IntNum**, and **Registers** is our old friend **RegPack**, whom we met in connection with DOS calls. Passing values to and from software interrupts is almost always done through values placed in machine registers through **RegPack**. Accessing the Microsoft Mouse driver routine is easy using **Intr**:

```
1     {<<<< Mouse >>>>}
2
3
4     { Described in section 20.6 -- Last mod 5/3/86    }
5     { Specific to the Microsoft Mouse driver }
6
7     PROCEDURE Mouse(VAR M1,M2,M3,M4 : Integer);
8
9     VAR
10      Registers : RegPack;
11
12    BEGIN
13      WITH Registers DO
14        BEGIN
15          AX := M1; BX := M2; CX := M3; DX := M4
16        END;
17      Intr(51,Registers);
18      WITH Registers DO
19        BEGIN
20          M1 := AX; M2 := BX; M3 := CX; M4 := DX
21        END
22    END;
```

All that happens here is the loading of the four parameters into registers **AX**, **BX**, **CX**, and **DX**, the invocation of the software interrupt via **Intr**, and unload the registers back into the four parameters. The same procedure could be used to invoke nearly any software interrupt that did not require other registers. All you would need do is change the interrupt number literal passed to **Intr**.

Of course, if you need more parameters, you can add them easily enough, loading them into other register fields within **Registers**.

Procedure **Mouse** will be used in the **FatPad** graphics program at the end of this section.

20.7 Using machine code with Turbo Pascal

There are many things that the Pascal language simply can't do, and the closer to the hardware you work, the more of them you find. There are other things (real-time graphics and animation come to mind) that you simply can't do fast enough, no matter how you do them, so you need to do them as fast as you possibly can.

You may at some point decide to write portions of your programs in pure machine code and interface them to code written in Pascal. Turbo Pascal provides a number of different ways to do this, and in this section we'll describe them all. The last two portions of Section 20 involve two relatively ambitious example programs: One, for the Z80, is an interrupt driven dumb terminal program. The other, for the IBM PC and close compatibles, is a graphics scratchpad program that provides a 640 × 200 pixel "window" into a virtual pad 400 × 1280 pixels in extent. Both of these programs involve interface to machine code, DOS calls, absolute variables, and most of the other low level machine hooks we've been describing.

Machine code is the lowest level language that a CPU understands. It consists of the minute instructions built right into the silicon of the microprocessor chip, and deals only with registers, pure binary numbers, and locations in memory. Variables, data structures, files, and expressions simply don't exist in machine code. Each tiny step that serves to accomplish some task is completely under your control.

It is *very* difficult work, compared with the relative ease of arranging high level statements in a language such as Pascal. The bugs that arise in connection with machine code work are often subtler, harder to find, and more catastrophic than those arising from work in Pascal. Machine code allows you complete freedom to tell the computer what to do, and, unlike Pascal, it also allows you complete freedom to blow your program session into the Twilight Zone.

You should think long and hard before committing any portion of your program to machine code. The first question you must ask yourself is: Can Pascal do it? Turbo Pascal provides an unusually rich repertoire of extensions, many of which provide "sneaky" means of getting at machine resources. There may be a way to do what you must do by using the high level statements that Turbo Pascal already provides.

The other question is harder to answer and has to do with the question of speed: Is the higher speed I might gain by programming in machine code going to be worth the trouble I will probably go through to accomplish that gain in speed?

Almost anything you can do in Pascal can, in fact, be done faster in machine code. How much faster is questionable, but as mentioned above, there are a few areas, such as graphics, in which any important speed gain is worth a great deal in terms of satisfaction with the final product.

If you decide that something is to be done in machine code, then do it, but work smart. Keep a log of bugs you find and solve, and take notes on your techniques. Comment the living daylights out of your code, both on the Pascal end and on the machine code end. Don't be ashamed to have more lines of comments than lines of code. Text is cheap. Time is not. You and your friends will stand to profit by your record-keeping in months and years ahead when it keeps you from reinventing the same old wheels and falling into the same old traps.

There are two methods of dropping into machine code from within a Turbo Pascal program. One method is called "inline" code. Inline code is machine code actually coded into the body of your program. The other method is to assemble separately a machine code subroutine and interface the subroutine to your Pascal program as an "external" subroutine. Relatively small and simple machine code routines are best done as inline code; larger and more ambitious routines are best done with the help of an assembler and interfaced to your program as externals.

INLINE MACHINE CODE VIA INLINE

From your computer's perspective, your entire program is nothing more than a line of machine instructions. You don't write those individual machine instructions. You provide Turbo Pascal a set of instructions (your source code file) and Turbo Pascal writes the machine instructions.

To do peculiar things (or ordinary things more quickly) you may need to write some of those machine instructions yourself. Turbo Pascal provides a feature called **INLINE** to give you this ability.

Machine instructions take the form of binary numbers. **INLINE** is a statement that allows you to insert machine instructions in the middle of a program body, function, or procedure, in the form of binary numbers:

```
INLINE(<number>/<number>/<number>/...<number>);
```

These numbers can be expressed as decimal or hexadecimal literals (things like 17, 244, or $FA) or named constants. They are enclosed in parentheses after the keyword **INLINE** and separated by slashes ("/"). Like all of Pascal's syntax **INLINE**'s is free-form. The numbers do not have to be on the same line. In fact, it is best to keep them on separate lines so each machine instruction can have its own comment to the side, indicating its equivalent mnemonic and purpose.

Numeric literals generate one byte of code if they fall in the range 0 to 255. Larger literals generate two bytes of code within **INLINE**. Named constants, variable references, function references, and program counter references *always* generate two bytes of code no matter what their value. These two rules can be overridden by the use of symbols "<" and ">". Preceding a number or reference with "<" forces it to occupy only one byte, even if it represents a 2-byte quantity. The higher order byte is discarded and the lower order byte retained. A number or reference preceded by ">" forces it to occupy two bytes. A 1-byte quantity will be expanded with a higher order byte of zero.

For example, this **INLINE** statement:

```
INLINE(>$77 / <$8899);
```

would actually generate three bytes of code: $77 $00 $99. Note that the > symbol forces the $88 to be discarded.

An asterisk (∗) may be an argument to **INLINE**, with or without a signed offset. An asterisk alone is replaced with the current program counter. (For the 8086 this is an offset into code segment CS; for the Z80 is a 2-byte absolute address.) If the asterisk is followed by an offset, the compiler adds the offset to the program counter before being placed in the code file. A jump "backwards" is done by giving the offset a negative value which, when added to the program counter, will decrement it.

Because of the considerable differences between the Z80 and 8086 processor instructions sets, the actual machine codes used for the two processors will be utterly different. You will have to become familiar with each processor separately through the various books devoted to assembly language programming.

Z80 INLINE Variable identifiers may be arguments to **INLINE**. The compiler replaces a variable identifier with its 2-byte absolute address.

All Z80 registers may be used, subject to the restrictions of your own hardware. (Some Z80 machines forbid user programming of certain registers connected with the interrupt system.) However, the stack pointer SP should be the same on exit from **INLINE** as it was on entry.

INLINE code is frequently placed within a procedure having the **INLINE** statement as its only statement. The procedure may have parameters and local variables. For a simple example, consider the following procedure, which accepts two integer parameters and swaps their values:

```
PROCEDURE Swap(VAR X,Y : Integer);

BEGIN
   INLINE($ED4B/X/          { LD BC,(X) }
          $ED5B/Y/          { LD DE,(Y) }
          $ED53/X/          { LD (X),DE }
          $ED43/Y)          { LD (Y),BC }
END;
```

The 'X' and 'Y' identifiers in the **INLINE** statement are replaced at compile time with the addresses of X and Y from the program's data area. The comments to the right contain the assembly language mnemonics that would produce the code contained in **INLINE**, were you to feed the comment lines through an assembler.

It's good practice to write **INLINE** procedures exactly as though they were assembly language source code, only with the mnemonics bracketed as comments. The compiler (obviously) ignores the mnemonics, but they will help you understand what would otherwise be pure hexadecimal machine code. Since the instruction set of the Z80 is a superset of the 8080 instruction set, you may write machine code as though Turbo Pascal were executing on an 8080 processor.

A more practical application of **INLINE** lies in the calling of utility routines in system ROM. Most modern microcomputers have a ROM in their memory space somewhere that contains utility routines for reading the serial ports and parallel ports, manipulating a system clock, and other tasks closely related to the hardware. The Xerox 820-II has a routine in its ROM that can move a video refresh buffer back and forth between the special video RAM segment and normal RAM space. This allows you to save screens and bring them back in an instant rather than painting them every time you need them.

Turbo Pascal has no primitive such as **CALL** in BASIC that allows you to jump to an arbitrary machine language location. The only way to set up machine registers and make such a jump into ROM is through **INLINE**:

```
{-------------------------------------------------------------}
{ >>>>CRT IMAGE SAVE AND RESTORE<<<<<                          }
{                                                             }
{       >Hardware-specific to the Xerox 820-II computer!<     }
{                                                             }
{ There is a routine in ROM (jump table address $F033) that   }
{ performs memory block moves between the alternate memory    }
{ block (which includes ROM and CRT RAM) and main RAM. These  }
{ two procedures use that routine to stash an entire screen   }
{ up to high memory (typically $B000) and bring it back again.}
{ This is used for help screens when we don't want to disrupt  }
{ what's on the screen but need the whole screen to work.      }
{-------------------------------------------------------------}
```

(continues)

```
PROCEDURE CRTSave;

BEGIN
   INLINE($3E / 1      /    { 1 means CRT RAM -> MAIN RAM }
         $21 / $3000 /      { Source address in CRT RAM   }
         $11 / $B000 /      { Dest. address in MAIN RAM   }
         $01 / $0FFF /      { # of bytes to move (4K-1)   }
         $C3 / $F033 );     { Jump into ROM to do it...   }
END;

PROCEDURE CRTRestore;

BEGIN
   INLINE($3E / $FF    /    { -1 means MAIN RAM -> CRT RAM }
         $21 / $B000 /      { Source address in MAIN RAM  }
         $11 / $3000 /      { Dest. address in CRT RAM    }
         $01 / $0FFF /      { # of bytes to move (4K-1)   }
         $C3 / $F033 );     { Jump into ROM to do it...   }
END;
```

(concluded)

8086 INLINE   The main difference between Z80 **INLINE** and 8086 **INLINE** lies in the way variable references are handled. Z80 **INLINE** simply replaces a variable reference with the 2-byte absolute address of the variable. In the 8086 world, variable and typed constant references are given as 2-byte offsets relative to some particular 8086 register:

Global variables are replaced by the offset of the variable with respect to the DS register, since they exist in the program's data segment.

Local variables and procedure parameters are instantiated on the stack when the procedure containing **INLINE** is called, so a local variable reference is replaced by its offset relative to the base pointer, BP. More on this later.

Typed constants are generated in the code segment, so a typed constant reference is replaced by its offset relative to the CS register.

You may use all machine registers within **INLINE**, but you must preserve the entry values of BP, SP, DS, and SS if you want to change them, and you must then restore them before leaving **INLINE**.

The simplest useful example of 8086 **INLINE** I know of is the invocation of screen prints through the IBM PC's ROM BIOS print screen utility, accessed through software interrupt 5:

```
INLINE($CD / $05);   { Triggers screen print through INT 5 }
```

Executing this statement will initiate a screen print. You could also have invoked the print screen ROM routine using Turbo's **Intr** procedure (see Section 20.6), but that also means defining the **RegPack** type and a variable of that type, even though print screen takes no parameters nor returns any.

I do not favor using **INLINE** for machine code sequences longer than a dozen or so bytes. Beyond that it makes a lot more sense to construct your assembly code routines as separate assembly language source files and assemble them with an assembler such as Microsoft's superb MASM. The assembled machine code file is then included in your Turbo Pascal program during the compile process by the reserved word **EXTERNAL**. I'll show how to do this along with the discussion of the **FatPad** program in Section 20.9.

One further step that I favor in some instances is taking a proven external machine code routine and turning it into an **INLINE** statement. If you keep your machine code files as externals, they are separate files that must be kept track of, and without which you cannot recompile their intended host programs. Having machine code routines built into your Pascal source code through the **INLINE** statement keeps things tidy and allow you to include better documentation of the machine code routine in your Pascal source file itself. I'll explain how to turn an external machine code routine into an **INLINE** statement in Section 20.10.

20.8   A Z80 interrupt-driven terminal program

There are variations on the **INLINE** concept. One problem with **INLINE** is that you can't control where an individual statement within a program or procedure will actually reside in terms of machine address. If there is a reason why an **INLINE** routine may not reside at a particular spot in memory, you should not use **INLINE**.

A perfect case study of some of the bizarre "gotchas" that will befall you while doing low level machine work lies in the problem of interrupt-driving the serial port on the Xerox 820-II.

The 820 has a memory bank switching system that moves a RAM bank containing the video refresh memory in and out of the main Z80 memory map. Whenever the CPU needs to update the screen, it must move the video memory bank into the main memory map, make the change, and move it back out again. When "swapped in," the video memory bank begins at $3000—right where a good chunk of your program code might reside.

Ordinarily, this is no problem. When the video bank is swapped in, the processor ROM has control, and the ROM is way up in high memory above $F000. *However,* if the code executing in ROM is interrupted, and the interrupt vector points to a location within the swapped-in video buffer, the system will crash hard, as the CPU attempts to execute video information as though it were code. Moral: Interrupt routines *must* be placed well away from $3000 and kept away.

This makes **INLINE** inadvisable for writing 820 interrupt code. **INLINE** makes no promises about where in machine memory it will end up. The solution is a sort of pseudo-**INLINE**: Fill an integer array with code and make sure the array is defined with an **ABSOLUTE** location well out of harm's way. Load the interrupt vector table with the address of the first byte of the array, and when an interrupt is tripped for that vector, the interrupt service routine may be executed whether or not the video buffer is swapped in.

The **ITerm** program is a tour-de-force of low level techniques for Z80 Turbo Pascal. If you understand its operation fully, you will be quite capable of squeezing the last drop of performance out of your Z80 CP/M computer. The Xerox 820 is very similar in many ways to other single-board CP/M systems like the Big Board, Little Board, and Mega Board. Some of the port mapping and interrupt jump table locations may differ, but the underlying operation of the Z80 SIO chip and its internal registers will be the same.

```
1
2
3        {----------------------------------------------------------------}
4        {                             ITERM                              }
5        {                                                                }
6        {      Interrupt-driven terminal program for the Xerox 820-II    }
7        {                                                                }
8        {                                   By Jeff Duntemann            }
9        {                                   CP/M Turbo Pascal V2.0        }
10       {                                   Last Update 12/6/84           }
11       {                                                                }
12       {                                                                }
13       {                                                                }
14       {----------------------------------------------------------------}
15
16       PROGRAM ITERM;
17
18
19       CONST  BAUD_PORT = $00;        { SIO Baud rate control port on 820-II }
20              CTRL_PORT = $06;        { SIO control port on 820-II }
21              DATA_PORT = $04;        { SIO data port on 820-II }
22              INT_LOC  = $F800;       { Address of SIO interrupt routine  }
23              INT_BASE = $FF00;       { Base of mode 2 interrupt vector table }
24
25                    { RING BUFFER INTERRUPT SERVICE ROUTINE }
26       { This routine is an interrupt routine for incoming serial port data.   }
27       { This routine executes each time the SIO chip fills up with a complete }
28       { data character from the RS232 line.  The character is put in a ring   }
29       { buffer and a buffer pointer incremented.  The buffer and pointer are  }
30       { absolute variables that were previously defined at a particular place }
31       { in high memory. }
32
33              ROUTINE : ARRAY[0..29] OF BYTE =
34                 ($F5,          { PUSH AF       Save accumulator   }
35                  $E5,          { PUSH HL       Save HL register   }
36                  $F3,          { DI            Disable interrupts }
```

(continues)

```
37              $2A,$19,$F8,     { LD   HL,(LAST_SAVED)   Get current count  }
38              $DB,$04,         { IN   A,(04H)         Get the incoming character }
39              $77,             { LD   HL,A            Store it in the buffer      }
40              $23,             { INC  HL              Bump insertion pointer      }
41              $CB,$64,         { BIT  4,H             Make ring                   }
42              $28,$03,         { JR   Z,SIOINTL       Relative jump 3 forward     }
43              $21,$00,$C3,     { LD   HL,$C300        over reload of buffer head }
44              $22,$19,$F8,     { LD   (LAST_SAVED),HL   SIOINTL: Save counter    }
45              $E1,             { POP  HL              Restore HL register         }
46              $F1,             { POP  AL              Restore accumulator         }
47              $FB,             { EI                   Re-enable interrupts        }
48              $ED,$4D,         { RETI                 Return from routine         }
49              $00,$C3,         { DW $C300             LAST_SAVED                  }
50              $00,$C3,         { DW $C300             LAST_READ                   }
51              $00);

52
53      TYPE
54
55          STRING80 = STRING[80];
56          CODE_BLOCK = ARRAY[0..63] OF BYTE;
57          VECT_ARRAY = ARRAY[0..7] OF INTEGER;
58
59      VAR I,J,K    : INTEGER;
60          CH       : CHAR;
61          NOSHOW   : SET OF BYTE;
62          PARITY   : INTEGER;   { 0=no parity; 1=odd parity; 2=even parity }
63          PARITAG  : ARRAY[0..2] OF STRING[8];       { Holds parity tags  }
64          OK       : BOOLEAN;
65          HIBAUD   : BOOLEAN;   { TRUE = using 1200 baud, else 300 baud    }
66          QUIT     : BOOLEAN;   { Flag for exiting the terminal loop       }
67          DUMMY    : STRING80;
68
69          { The following variables all support the interrupt-driven ring buffer: }
70
71          INT_CODE : CODE_BLOCK ABSOLUTE INT_LOC; { Holds ring buffer serv. routine }
72          INT_VECT   : INTEGER ABSOLUTE $FF02;
73          LAST_READ  : INTEGER ABSOLUTE $F81B;   { Offset of last char. read   }
```

(continues)

```
74        LAST_SAVED  : INTEGER ABSOLUTE $F819;   { Offset of last char. saved  }
75        RINGPTR     : ^CHAR   ABSOLUTE $F81B;   { ON TOP OF LAST_READ! }
76        VECT_TBL    : VECT_ARRAY ABSOLUTE $FF00;  { SIO interrupt jump tbl   }
77
78
79    {<<<INCHAR>>>}
80    { This function is called AFTER function INSTAT has determined that a char   }
81    { is ready to be read from the ring buffer.  The char at LAST_READ/RINGPTR   }
82    { (the two are the same) is assigned to INCHAR's function value.  Then the    }
83    { value of LAST_READ is bumped by one via SUCC.  If the value of LAST_READ    }
84    { is found to have gone over the high ring buffer boundary of $CFFF to $D000  }
85    { then LAST_READ is "rolled over" to become $C300 (the low boundary of the    }
86    { buffer) again.  When LAST_READ "catches up to" LAST_SAVED (by being =) the  }
87    { ring buffer is considered empty. }
88
89    FUNCTION INCHAR : CHAR;
90
91    BEGIN
92      INCHAR := RINGPTR^;                 { Grab a character from the ring buffer }
93      LAST_READ := SUCC(LAST_READ);       { Increment the pointer; check bounds:  }
94      IF LAST_READ >= $D000 THEN LAST_READ := $C300  { Correct if it hits $D000   }
95    END;
96
97
98    {<<<INSTAT>>>}
99    { This function determines if there is a new character to be read from the    }
100   { ring buffer.  There are two pointers into the ring buffer: LAST_SAVED,       }
101   { and LAST_READ.  LAST_SAVED is the address of the last character placed       }
102   { into the buffer by the SIO interrupt service routine.  LAST_READ is the      }
103   { address of the last character read from the ring buffer.  When the two are   }
104   { equal, the last character read was the last character saved, so we know we   }
105   { have read all the characters that have been placed into the buffer.  Only    }
106   { when LAST_SAVED gets "ahead" of LAST_READ must we read characters from the   }
107   { ring buffer again.  These two pointers chase each other around and around    }
108   { the ring.  As the ring buffer is just a hair over 3300 bytes long,           }
109   { LAST_SAVED can get WAAAAY ahead of LAST_READ before there's trouble in       }
110   { River City.  On the other hand, if this ever happens, there will be no       }
111   { warning.  Just trouble.                                                      }
```

(continues)

```
112
113          FUNCTION INSTAT : BOOLEAN;
114
115          BEGIN
116            IF LAST_SAVED <> LAST_READ THEN INSTAT := TRUE
117              ELSE INSTAT := FALSE
118          END;
119
120
121          PROCEDURE OUTCHR(CH : CHAR);
122
123          BEGIN                           { Loop until TBMT goes high }
124            REPEAT I := PORT[CTRL_PORT] UNTIL (I AND $04) <> 0;
125            PORT[DATA_PORT]:=ORD(CH)       { Then send char out the port }
126          END;
127
128
129          PROCEDURE SET_7_BITS;
130
131          BEGIN
132            PORT[CTRL_PORT]:=$13;              { Select write register 3 }
133            PORT[CTRL_PORT]:=$41;              { 7 bits per RX char, enable RX}
134            PORT[CTRL_PORT]:=$15;              { Select write register 5 }
135            PORT[CTRL_PORT]:=$AA               { 7 bits per TX char, enable TX}
136          END;
137
138
139          PROCEDURE SET_8_BITS;
140
141          BEGIN
142            PORT[CTRL_PORT]:=$13;              { Select write register 3 }
143            PORT[CTRL_PORT]:=$C1;              { 8 bits per RX char, enable RX}
144            PORT[CTRL_PORT]:=$15;              { Select write register 5 }
145            PORT[CTRL_PORT]:=$EA               { 8 bits per TX char, enable TX}
146          END;
147
148
149
```

(continues)

```
150        PROCEDURE SET_PARITY(PARITY : INTEGER);
151
152    BEGIN
153      PORT[CTRL_PORT]:=$14;                  { Select SIO Register 4 }
154      CASE PARITY OF                         { All 3: 16X clock, 1 stop }
155         0 : PORT[CTRL_PORT]:=$44;           { 0=No parity }
156         1 : PORT[CTRL_PORT]:=$45;           { 1=Odd parity }
157         2 : PORT[CTRL_PORT]:=$47;           { 2=Even parity }
158        ELSE PORT[CTRL_PORT]:=$47;           { Defaults to even parity }
159      END; { CASE }
160    END;
161
162
163    PROCEDURE INT_ENABLE;
164
165    BEGIN
166      PORT[CTRL_PORT] := $11;                { Select write register 1 }
167      PORT[CTRL_PORT] := $18                 { and turn interrupts on  }
168    END;
169
170
171    PROCEDURE INT_DISABLE;
172
173    BEGIN
174      PORT[CTRL_PORT] := $01;                { Select write register 1 }
175      PORT[CTRL_PORT] := $00                 { and disable interrupts  }
176    END;
177
178
179    {<<<INT_SETUP>>>}
180
181    PROCEDURE INT_SETUP;
182
183    BEGIN
184      FILLCHAR(INT_CODE,SIZEOF(INT_CODE),CHR(0));  { Zero array to hold routine  }
185      FOR I := 0 TO 29 DO                          { Move the routine out of the }
186        INT_CODE[I] := ROUTINE[I];                 { constant into the array.    }
187      FOR I := 0 TO 7 DO VECT_TBL[I] := ADDR(INT_CODE);
```

(continues)

```
188        INT_ENABLE;                          { Finally, enable SIO interrupts.  }
189      END;
190
191
192      {>>>>INITSIO<<<<<}
193
194      PROCEDURE INITSIO(HIBAUD : BOOLEAN; PARITY : INTEGER);
195
196      BEGIN
197        SET_PARITY(PARITY);            { Set parity }
198        SET_7_BITS;                    { Set SIO to 7 bits RX/TX }
199        IF HIBAUD THEN                 { Set baud rate: }
200          PORT[BAUD_PORT]:=$07         { 1200 baud code to baud port  }
201        ELSE PORT[BAUD_PORT]:=$05;     { 300 baud code to baud port   }
202        WRITE('<Changing to ');
203        IF HIBAUD THEN WRITELN('1200 baud>') ELSE WRITELN('300 baud>')
204      END;  { INITSIO }
205
206
207      FUNCTION GET_KEY : CHAR;
208
209      BEGIN
210        GET_KEY := CHR(BDOS(6,255))
211      END;
212
213
214      {>>>>CLEAR_BIT<<<<<<}
215
216      PROCEDURE CLEAR_BIT(VAR CH : CHAR; BIT : INTEGER);
217
218      VAR I,J : INTEGER;
219
220      BEGIN
221        I := NOT(1 SHL BIT);               { Create a bit mask }
222        J := ORD(CH) AND I;
223        CH := CHR(J)
224      END;
225
```

(continues)

```
226
227
228         {>>>>INIT_ITERM<<<<}
229
230         PROCEDURE INIT_ITERM;
231
232         BEGIN
233           NOSHOW:=[0,127];                     { Don't display these! }
234           PARITY:=2;                           { Defaults to even parity }
235           PARITAG[0]:='No'; PARITAG[1]:='Odd'; PARITAG[2]:='Even';
236           HIBAUD := TRUE;                      { Defaults to 1200 baud }
237           INITSIO(HIBAUD,PARITY);              { Do init on serial port A }
238           INT_SETUP                            { Init interrupt system }
239         END;  { INIT_TERM }
240
241
242
243         BEGIN                 {**** ITERM MAIN ****}
244           LOWVIDEO;
245           INIT_ITERM;         { Do inits on variables & hardware }
246           CLRSCR;             { Clear screen }
247
248           QUIT:=FALSE;        { Init flag for terminal exit  }
249
250           REPEAT              { Can only be exited by CTRL/E }
251
252             IF INSTAT THEN                    { If a char has come }
253               BEGIN                           { from the serial port }
254                 CH := INCHAR;                 { Go get it from the port; }
255                 CLEAR_BIT(CH,7);              { Scuttle the parity bit; }
256                 IF NOT (ORD(CH) IN NOSHOW) THEN WRITE(CH);  { Write CH to the CRT   }
257               END;     { Incoming character handling }
258
259             CH:=GET_KEY;                { See if a char was typed }
260             IF ORD(CH)<>0 THEN          { If non-zero, char was typed  }
261
262               CASE ORD(CH) OF           { Parse the typed character   }
263
264                   5 : QUIT:=TRUE;       { CTRL-E: Raise flag to exit }
```

(continues)

```
265
266          17 : BEGIN                { CTRL-Q: Step through parity  }
267              IF PARITY=2 THEN PARITY:=0 ELSE PARITY:=PARITY+1;
268              INITSIO(HIBAUD,PARITY);
269              WRITELN('<NOW USING ',PARITAG[PARITY],' PARITY>')
270          END;
271
272          18 : BEGIN                { CTRL-R: Toggle baud rate     }
273              HIBAUD:=NOT HIBAUD;
274              INITSIO(HIBAUD,PARITY)
275          END;
276
277          26 : CLRSCR;              { CTRL-Z: Clear CRT }
278
279          ELSE OUTCHR(CH);          { Send all others to modem,    }
280      END   { CASE }
281
282    UNTIL QUIT;
283    INT_DISABLE;                    { Turn off SIO interrupts...   }
284  END.  { ITERM }                   { ...and blow this crazyhouse...}
```

(concluded)

ITerm is a "dumb terminal" program. It does no file uploading or downloading. Its purpose is mediate among three devices: Your keyboard, your CRT, and your serial port, which is typically connected to a modem. Data coming from the serial port is sent to your screen; data coming from your keyboard is sent to the serial port. In concept, it is simplicity itself.

Why the need for interrupts? You can sit in a loop and "poll" the serial port (SIO) chip to see if it has data for you, or poll the keyboard to see if anything was typed, taking action only when data appears from one device or the other. Such polled terminal programs are common and very easy to write. The problem is one of speed.

If too much time elapses between one polling of the SIO and the next, an entire character can come in from the modem and be lost. The SIO chip doesn't wait for you to poll it; it puts a received character up on the rack and expects you to grab it. If another character comes in before the first has been grabbed, the new character will take the place of the old, and the old will simply disappear.

At 300 baud, characters are coming in so slowly that the computer has plenty of time between incoming characters to do what it has to do: clear its screen, move the cursor, and so on. At 1200 baud it can usually keep up, but not always—if the remote system is sending a large number of CRT control commands, the CPU can be so busy executing the commands that it will be unable to poll the SIO often enough. Lost characters are the result.

Interrupts provide the answer.

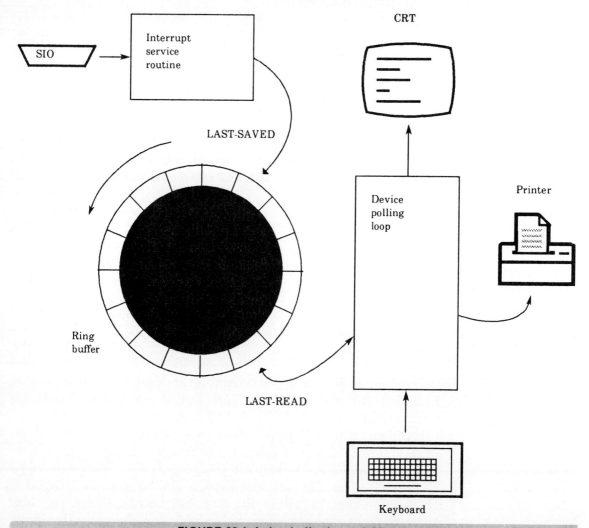

FIGURE 20.1 A ring buffer for serial input

Refer to Figure 20.1 during the following discussion. This is difficult stuff—you should know how the SIO works before attempting to understand **ITerm**.

Central to **ITerm**'s operation is something called a "ring buffer." Physically, a ring buffer is nothing more than an area of memory. Two pointers are set up to point to locations in the buffer. One, **LastSaved**, points to the last character placed in the buffer. The other, **LastRead**, points to the last character *read* from the buffer. The two pointers are incremented along the buffer as they do their jobs, as we'll describe below. What makes the buffer a ring buffer is that there is code that repoints both pointers back to the low end of the buffer once they are incremented off the high end. Metaphorically, this "wraps" the two ends of the buffer around until they meet, so that the two pointers can be incremented around and around the buffer without running off the end.

Now, how it works: The interrupt service routine (**Routine**) is executed whenever the SIO chip receives a complete character from the remote system. All the routine does is read a character from the SIO and write it into the buffer at the location pointed to by **LastSaved**. **LastSaved** is then incremented by one. This happens regardless of whatever else the CPU was doing at the time the interrupt occurred. If the terminal program isn't quite ready to accept another character from the SIO yet, that's all right. The character is safely stored in the ring buffer, waiting.

That's what **Routine**, the interrupt service routine, does. Now look down at the main program code for **ITerm**. It's a relatively simple polling loop. When simplified, the logic works like this:

```
REPEAT
    If an incoming character is waiting,
      go read it from the ring buffer and display it.
    If a character was typed at the keyboard,
      execute it if it was a command,
      else send it to the SIO.
UNTIL we decide to stop.
```

This, in essence, is all **ITerm** does. Let's look at the code more closely:

How does **ITerm** know if a character is waiting in the ring buffer?

The function **InStat** tests to see if **LastSaved** is equal to **LastRead**. If the last character saved was the last character read (think about that) nothing is waiting to be read, and **InStat** returns false. If the two pointers are *not* equal, it means that **LastSaved** has gotten ahead of **LastRead** in the ring buffer, and more characters have been saved than have been read. The terminal loop thus reads another character and displays it to the screen. **LastRead** is incremented by **InChar**, the function that actually reads characters from the ring buffer. The next time through the loop, **InStat** will again see if **LastSaved** is ahead of **LastRead**, and if it is, another character will be read until the two pointers are equal. *Whenever* **LastSaved** *and* **LastRead** *are equal, the ring buffer is considered empty.*

If the terminal loop is busy because it is executing keyboard commands, **LastSaved** can get considerably ahead of **LastRead**. That's all right, because in the long run, the terminal loop will get its work done and have plenty of time to grab and display incoming characters from the ring buffer.

Procedure **IntSetup** loads the interrupt service routine from the array constant **Routine** to the array variable **IntCode**. If Turbo Pascal allowed the definition of typed constants as **ABSOLUTE** (it does not), we could simply put **Routine** at the interrupt vector address and execute it directly. Consequently, we have to load **Routine** into an array that can be declared at the proper absolute location in memory.

The bulk of the rest of **ITerm** is code to support the Z80 SIO chip. Most of the routines like **OutChr**, **Set7Bits**, and **SetParity** are *not* specific to the Xerox 820 but are specific to the Z80 SIO. The constant **CtrlPort** may have to be changed for another machine, but the SIO internal register codes will be the same. What is likely to be specific to the 820 are the location of the interrupt routine array **Routine**, the interrupt vector location, and the port assignments for the SIO chip.

ITerm gives you all the "rough stuff" for the core of a good interrupt-driven smart terminal program. To add additional commands you need only add new options to the **CASE** statement in the main program loop. The distant descendent of **ITerm** that I use has **XMODEM** file transfer capability, data capture, line-by-line text file transmission with WordStar high bit/control character removal, an autodialer, and a simple command interpreter for command files, all in Turbo Pascal. As that program runs to about 1600 lines, it will have to wait for another book. But there is nothing there that you cannot do yourself, with a little planning and some low down machine level smarts.

20.9   A 400 X 1280 IBM PC graphics scratchpad

The ultimate in Turbo Pascal machine code interface is the external routine. An external routine is a .COM file (or .CMD in CP/M-86) generated by a compiler or assembler other than Turbo Pascal. Linking a routine generated by another compiler (C or another Pascal, for example) is usually more trouble than it's worth; I tend to think that you could just as effectively code anything you need to code in a high level language directly in Turbo Pascal itself. Where externals really come into their own is in code files generated by an assembler. Writing in assembler allows you the speed and power not available in a compiler like Turbo Pascal. Since hand-assembling bytes of code for **INLINE** is brutal work for anything larger than 50 bytes or so, external assembly code routines are often the only way to do any kind of ambitious machine code work from Turbo Pascal.

As with **INLINE**, there are important differences between the ways external routines are handled for Z80 computers and for 8086 computers.

Z80 EXTERNAL ROUTINES

Although the Turbo Pascal Reference Manual briefly mentions external routines for Z80 versions of the compiler, it is extremely awkward and I have never been able to make one work.

In theory, you must manipulate the compiler's memory use parameters to compile a "hole" in your .COM file of a size that will contain your external routine. You must then compile the program to disk with its hole. Then, you must load the compiled program with DDT, and use DDT to load the external routine into the hole. Once done, you then save the entire code/data area as a memory image to disk.

You also have the option of reading your assembly code file at runtime and loading it into the "hole" as though it were just more data. This is conceptually easier, but it requires that the .COM file containing the machine code always reside on disk with the program file itself. If the program file ever fails to locate its machine code file, it will have to abort.

The declaration for a Z80 external routine gives the compiler only the absolute location where the code begins:

```
PROCEDURE Plot(X,Y : Integer); EXTERNAL $E000;
```

When invoked, the code will jump to that location in memory—obviously, if there is nothing there but garbage, your system will come down hard.

I suspect that this feature (which exists so cleanly in the 8086 version of Turbo Pascal) was sacrificed to make the compiler smaller in the more RAM-limited Z80 environment.

For these reasons I do not recommend attempting external assembly code routines for Z80 versions of the compiler unless you are willing to spend a considerable amount of time and trouble experimenting. Copying raw opcodes from the left margin of an assembler .PRN listing into an **INLINE** statement works much better.

One can hope a future release of Z80 Turbo Pascal will provide an easier way to interface external assembly code routines to Pascal programs.

8086 EXTERNAL ROUTINES

The mechanism for linking to external routines from 8086 Turbo Pascal is a good deal more straightforward. Assembled code files are read from disk by the compiler at compile time and added to the code buffer of the program being compiled. All the loading and positioning of the external code is done by the compiler itself.

Your external routines must be declared in your Pascal program in a particular way:

```
PROCEDURE ScrnBLT(MovDir,PadX,PadY : Integer; VAR Pad : PadArray);
          EXTERNAL 'SCRNBLT';
```

The first line of the declaration is an ordinary procedure parameter line exactly as it would appear if the routine were written in Turbo Pascal. It has no procedure body nor any declarations, however, and beneath it must appear the **EXTERNAL** reserved word along with the name of the external code file in quotes.

Unlike Z80 machine code, external 8086 routines *must* be relocatable. You cannot specify where in memory the external is going to run. Neither can an external routine make any references to the data segment. The external routine is loaded at compile time and placed in the code segment. If you are compiling to a .COM file, the external routine becomes part of the .COM file at compile time.

Assuming you know your assembly language well (and you should know it well before you even *begin* to think of interfacing external routines to a Turbo Pascal program) the tricky part of external routines lies wholly in the passing of parameters between the external routine and your Pascal program.

Parameters and function results are passed on the stack. Before giving control to the external routine, the Pascal program pushes space for the function result (if the external routine is a function), the parameters, and finally, the return address onto the stack.

If the external routine has parameters, you will need to use the 8086 base pointer (BP) register to access the parameters on the stack. The very first thing your external routine should do is save the current value of BP (that the Pascal program has been using for other things) and copy the stack pointer (SP) into BP. The base pointer now acts as a fixed base for accessing your parameters, regardless of what else you do with the stack. If you keep on using the stack, and the stack pointer keeps moving up and down, you will have a terrible time trying to keep track of where your parameters are on the stack.

Our real world example is a graphics program called **FatPad**, with an external assembly code routine called **ScrnBLT**. We'll explain what they do in a moment—for now, look at the listing of **ScrnBLT** while we try to explain what the stack will look like when **FatPad** gives control to **ScrnBLT**.

```
1        {------------------------------------------------------------}
2        {                          FatPad                            }
3        {                                                            }
4        { EXTERNAL machine code interface demonstration for the IBM PC }
5        {                                                            }
```

(continues)

```
6      {                          by Jeff Duntemann              }
7      {                          Turbo Pascal V3.0              }
8      {                          Last update 1/31/86            }
9      {                                                         }
10     {                                                         }
11     {                                                         }
12     {---------------------------------------------------------}
13
14     PROGRAM FatPad;
15
16     { NOTE!  FATPAD REQUIRES THE MICROSOFT MOUSE AND 256K OR NO GO!!!   }
17
18     { Why limit yourself to drawing on a puny 640 X 200 screen?  FatPad  }
19     { sets up a "virtual pad" of double the normal hires resolution in   }
20     { both X & Y, giving you the equivalent of four whole screens to Draw }
21     { on.  Your normal 640 X 200 screen is a "window" into the virtual    }
22     { pad that may be "dragged" around the pad to let you view the whole  }
23     { virtual pad, albeit one 640 X 200 screen at a time.  1280 X 400!    }
24     { Now THAT's elbow room...                                           }
25
26     { It's not done with mirrors, but with SCRNBLT: SCReeN BLock Transfer.}
27     { SCRNBLT moves an entire 600 X 200 screen to and from the 1280 X 400 }
28     { virtual pad.  You start out with a blank pad.  (Keep in mind that a }
29     { "pad" and a "screen" are two specific and distinct entities here!)  }
30     { You Draw on the screen by holding down the left mouse button and    }
31     { moving the mouse.  You drag the window around the pad by holding    }
32     { down the right mouse button and moving the mouse.  Before actually  }
33     { dragging the window, SCRNBLT saves out whatever lines you have      }
34     { drawn on the window to the pad--and then moves in a new window from }
35     { the pad at the new X,Y.                                            }
36
37     { Press any key to exit the program.  This is strictly a demo of the }
38     { concept, and no facility is present to save a pad to a disk...so    }
39     { you might not want to get TOO fancy in your artwork...             }
40
41     { If you can't get FatPad to run, you might add some more RAM to your }
42     { system and try again.  Pad^ is 64K in size...and RAM is cheap!      }
43
```

(continues)

```
44                        { *    *   * }
45
46       { This type definition is ahead of the constants because we are      }
47       { using typed constants below (the mouse Cursor definitions)         }
48       { and when you use a typed constant you must define the type before  }
49       { you define the constant.  Typed constants are a feature specific to }
50       { Turbo Pascal and are not possible in most Pascal compilers.        }
51
52       TYPE
53          Cursorray = ARRAY[0..33] OF Integer;
54
55       CONST
56          GBase = $B800;                    { Base of PC graphics RAM   }
57
58          Fred : Cursorray =                { Our "mouse" Cursor... }
59
60             (8,8,                              { Fred's nose (8,8) is Cursor hotspot }
61             $0000,      {----------------}  { Screen Mask: }
62             $0000,      {----------------}
63             $0000,      {----------------}
64             $0000,      {----------------}
65             $0000,      {----------------}
66             $0000,      {----------------}
67             $0000,      {----------------}
68             $0000,      {----------------}
69             $0000,      {----------------}
70             $0000,      {----------------}
71             $0000,      {----------------}
72             $0000,      {----------------}
73             $0000,      {----------------}
74             $FFFF,      {****************}
75             $FFFF,      {****************}
76             $FFFF,      {****************}
77
78             $700E,      {-***--------***-}  { Cursor Mask: }
79             $F81F,      {*****------*****}
80             $77EE,      {-***-******-***-}
81             $1FF8,      {---**********---}
```

(continues)

```
82          $318C,          {--**---**---**--}
83          $2C34,          {--*-**----**-*--}
84          $2DB4,          {--*-**-**-**-*--}
85          $6DB6,          {-**-**-**-**-**-}
86          $FE7F,          {*******--*******}
87          $9819,          {*--**------**--*}
88          $4FF2,          {-*--********--*-}
89          $2004,          {--*----------*--}
90          $1FF8,          {---**********---}
91          $0000,          {----------------}
92          $0000,          {----------------}
93          $0000);         {----------------}
94
95
96          Dot : Cursorray =                   { Our Dot Cursor... }
97
98          (7,4,                               { The Dot's hotspot's at 7,4 }
99          $FFFF,          {****************}  { Screen Mask }
100         $FFFF,          {****************}
101         $FFFF,          {****************}
102         $F00F,          {****--------****}
103         $F00F,          {****--------****}
104         $F00F,          {****--------****}
105         $FFFF,          {****************}
106         $FFFF,          {****************}
107         $FFFF,          {****************}
108         $FFFF,          {****************}
109         $FFFF,          {****************}
110         $FFFF,          {****************}
111         $FFFF,          {****************}
112         $FFFF,          {****************}
113         $FFFF,          {****************}
114         $FFFF,          {****************}
115
116         $0000,          {----------------}  { Cursor Mask }
117         $0000,          {----------------}
118         $0000,          {----------------}
119         $0000,          {----------------}
```

(continues)

```
120                $0180,        {-------**-------}
121                $0000,        {---------------}
122                $0000,        {---------------}
123                $0000,        {---------------}
124                $0000,        {---------------}
125                $0000,        {---------------}
126                $0000,        {---------------}
127                $0000,        {---------------}
128                $0000,        {---------------}
129                $0000,        {---------------}
130                $0000,        {---------------}
131                $0000);       {---------------}
132
133
134
135                              { RegPack type is used in DOS and INTR calls }
136        TYPE
137          RegPack = RECORD
138                      AX,BX,CX,DX,BP,SI,DI,DS,ES,FLAGS : Integer
139                    END;
140
141          GBuff   = ARRAY[0..16191] OF BYTE;   { PC Graphics buffer }
142
143          PadType = ARRAY [0..159, 0..399] OF BYTE;  { A "fat Pad;" }
144                                                     { 1280 X 400   }
145          PadPtr  = ^PadType;
146
147
148        VAR
149          OldX,OldY,X,Y : Integer;      { Storage for Cursor X/Y positions }
150          M1,M2,M3,M4   : Integer;      { These are the parms for mouse calls }
151          I,J           : Integer;
152          R             : Real;         { For holding free space count }
153          Registers     : RegPack;      { Register structure for INTR calls }
154
155          VisiBuf       : GBuff ABSOLUTE GBase : $0000;  { Graphics buffer }
156          Pad           : PadPtr;       { Pointer to the virtual Pad }
157          PadX,PadY     : Integer;      { X and Y on virtual Pad }
```

(continues)

```
158       DX              : Integer;      { Delta X: Change in X coordinate  }
159       ArtFile         : File;         { Holds a 640 X 200 graphics image }
160
161
162       { This is a good example of how a fairly complicated external routine }
163       { is declared within Turbo.  See the SCRNBLT source for more info on  }
164       { parameter passing within the assembly code itself.                  }
165
166       PROCEDURE SCRNBLT(MOVDIR,PadX,PadY : Integer; VAR Pad : PadType );
167       EXTERNAL 'SCRNBLT';
168
169
170
171       {$I MOUSE.SRC}      { Described in Section 20.6 }
172
173
174
175       {<<<PadClear>>>}
176
177       PROCEDURE PadClear(VAR ThisPad : PadType);
178
179       BEGIN
180         FILLCHAR(ThisPad,Sizeof(ThisPad),CHR(0))
181       END;
182
183
184
185       PROCEDURE LoadCursor(Cursor : Cursorray);
186
187       VAR
188         Registers : RegPack;
189         CVar    : ARRAY[0..31] OF Integer;
190         I       : Integer;
191
192       BEGIN
193         FOR I := 0 TO 31 DO CVar[I] := Cursor[I+2];   { Copy cursor }
194         WITH Registers DO
```

(continues)

```
195               BEGIN
196                 AX := 9;
197                 BX := Cursor[0];      { Hotspot X }
198                 CX := Cursor[1];      { Hotspot Y }
199                 DX := OFS(CVar);      { Offset of cursor array  }
200                 ES := SEG(CVar);      { Segment of cursor array }
201               END;
202             INTR(51,Registers)        { Invoke mouse interrupt 51 }
203         END;
204
205
206         PROCEDURE ShowCursor;
207
208         BEGIN
209           M1 := 1; Mouse(M1,M2,M3,M4)  { Turn mouse cursor on }
210         END;
211
212
213         PROCEDURE HideCursor;
214
215         BEGIN
216           M1 := 2; Mouse(M1,M2,M3,M4)  { Turn mouse cursor off }
217         END;
218
219
220         PROCEDURE InitMouse;
221
222         BEGIN
223           M1 := 0; Mouse(M1,M2,M3,M4)
224         END;
225
226
227
228         BEGIN     { FatPad MAIN }
229           HiRes;                          { Choose graphics mode & color }
230           HiResColor(Yellow);
231           R := MemAvail;                  { MemAvail returns a negative qty }
```

(continues)

```
232    IF R < 0 THEN R := R + 65536.0; { for paragraphs over MaxInt       }
233    IF R < 16384.0 THEN
234      BEGIN
235        Writeln('>>Sorry, but you don''t have enough memory to run FatPad.');
236        Writeln('  Generally, 256K is the minimum amount required, but that');
237        Writeln('  may be affected by how many DOS extensions and device');
238        Writeln('  drivers are resident in your system.  64K of RAM is needed');
239        Writeln('  by the fat Pad buffer itself.  Returning to DOS...');
240        Halt
241      END;
242    New(Pad);                        { Create the fat pad }
243    Assign(ArtFile,'SNAPSHOT.PIC'); { Load in a sample picture to show   }
244    Reset(ArtFile);                  { how inadequite 640 X 200 is...     }
245    BlockRead(ArtFile,VisiBuf,128);
246    Close(ArtFile);
247    InitMouse;                       { Init mouse driver via mouse call 0 }
248    LoadCursor(Dot);                 { Pour Dot cursor into mouse cursor block  }
249    ShowCursor;                      { Turn mouse cursor on }
250
251    M1 := 3; PadX := 0; PadY :=0; OldX := 0; OldY := 0;  { Init variables }
252    PadClear(Pad^);                                     { & clear Pad    }
253
254    WHILE NOT KeyPressed DO       { Exit FatPad when any key pressed }
255      BEGIN
256        M1 := 3; Mouse(M1,M2,M3,M4);    { Poll mouse position and buttons }
257        IF (M2 AND 1) <> 0 THEN          { Left button draws }
258          BEGIN
259            HideCursor;                  { Hide mouse cursor before Draw   }
260            Draw(OldX,OldY,M3,M4,1);     { Draw line between old X,Y }
261            ShowCursor;                  { and new X,Y }
262            M1:=3;
263            OldX := M3;                  { Update old X & Y }
264            OldY := M4;
265          END
266        ELSE IF (M2 AND 2) <> 0 THEN     { Right button drags }
267          BEGIN
268            LoadCursor(Fred);
```

(continues)

```
269              DX := M3-OldX;              { Calc delta-X }
270
271                                { Now...we drag ONLY if Y has changed OR }
272                                { if X has changed by more than 16 bits: }
273          IF (Abs(DX) >= 16) OR (OldY <> M4) THEN
274            BEGIN
275              HideCursor;       { Hide mouse cursor before saving }
276                                { screen to the virtual pad       }
277              SCRNBLT(0,PadX,PadY,Pad^);      { save out screen at  }
278                                             { PadX,PadY to Pad     }
279              PadY := PadY - (M4-OldY);       { Apply deltas to new }
280              PadX := PadX - (M3-OldX);       { pad positions       }
281
282              IF PadY < 0   THEN PadY := 0;   { limit drag ranges    }
283              IF PadY > 200 THEN PadY := 200; { to meaningful values }
284              IF PadX < 0   THEN PadX := 0;
285              IF PadX > 640 THEN PadX := 640;
286
287              SCRNBLT(1,PadX,PadY,Pad^);      { "bring back" window's }
288                                             { worth of graphics from}
289                                             { new PadX,PadY in pad  }
290              ShowCursor;          { It's now safe to reshow cursor }
291              M1 := 3;
292              OldX := M3;          { Update old X/Y values }
293              OldY := M4;
294            END;
295          LoadCursor(Dot)          { BLT's over; bring back Dot cursor }
296        END
297      ELSE
298        BEGIN
299          OldX := M3;   { Must update old X,Y even if nothing is done }
300          OldY := M4;
301          END;
302        END;  { WHILE }
303      TextMode
304    END.
```

(concluded)

```
 1    ;==============================================================================
 2    ;
 3    ;     S C R N B L T  -  Graphics Screen Block Transfer for Turbo Pascal
 4    ;
 5    ;==============================================================================
 6    ;
 7    ;      by Larry Stone      21-Jul-84
 8    ;
 9    ; SCRNBLT is written to be called from Turbo Pascal V2.0 using the
10    ; EXTERNAL procedure convention.  It will copy the contents of the
11    ; video graphics display buffer (either low or high resolution) to
12    ; a designated memory location on a virtual "pad" of set dimensions.
13    ;
14    ; To use SCRNBLT, the following lines must be included in your Turbo
15    ; Pascal program.  The type "padtype" demonstrates how a PAD data type
16    ; may be declared. When the PAD type is declared, the dimensions of
17    ; the array must be as shown here.  It should also be specified ABSOLUTE
18    ; with the initial offset 0, so that all of a 64K segment is available
19    ; to it.
20    ;
21    ;  PROCEDURE SCRNBLT( MOVDIR, PADX, PADY : INTEGER; VAR PAD : PADARRAY );
22    ;     EXTERN 'SCRNBLT';
23    ;
24    ;  TYPE
25    ;     padtype = ARRAY [0..159, 0..399] OF BYTE;
26    ;  VAR
27    ;     pad : padtype ABSOLUTE $BA00 : $0000;    (* sample declaration *)
28    ;
29    ;  SCRNBLT(0, x, y, pad);   (* sample call; saves screen on pad(x,y) *)
30    ;
31    ; The parameters PADX and PAXY are specified as absolute coordinates
32    ; on the pad, exactly as screen coordinates would be specified.  The
33    ; X-coordinates correspond to the bits on the pad, not the bytes.
34    ;
35    ; The first parameter, "MOVDIR", determines the direction of the transfer.
36    ; If 0 is specified, the contents of the screen are transferred to the
37    ; designated area of the pad; if a nonzero number is specified,
```

(continues)

```
38          ; the designated area of the pad is transferred to the screen buffer.
39          ;
40          ; SCRNBLT transfers the contents of the screen as a rectangular block,
41          ; 80 bytes wide by 200 bytes high, to a rectangular area of the pad
42          ; at the designated x,y coordinates.  The pad area is not organized
43          ; exactly like the display buffer; odd and even lines are interleaved
44          ; in a more straightforward fashion to allow the offset of an x,y location
45          ; in the pad to be calculated as  (y * padwidth) + x.
46          ;
47          ; To use SCRNBLT with a Turbo Program:
48          ;------------------------------------
49          ; 1. Assemble this file with MASM.  "A> MASM SCRNBLT;"
50          ; 2. Link it into a .EXE file.      "A> LINK SCRNBLT;"
51          ; 3. Use EXE2BIN to make a .COM file. "A> EXE2BIN SCRNBLT.EXE SCRNBLT.COM"
52          ; 4. Declare as shown in your Turbo Pascal program.
53          ; 5. Ignore any minor diagnostic messages that may be generated when
54          ;    this file is assembled and linked.  EXE2BIN is supplied with the
55          ;    supplemental programs for PC-DOS; see the DOS manual.
56          ;
57
58          ;
59          ; EQUATES TO DEFINE GRAPHICS CONSTANTS
60          ;
61          PADWD   EQU     160                 ; WIDTH OF VIRTUAL PAD, BYTES
62          SCRNWD  EQU     80                  ; WIDTH OF REAL SCREEN
63          SCRNWD2 EQU     40                  ; HALF OF SCREEN WIDTH
64          HALFSC  EQU     100                 ; LINES FOR HALF OF SCREEN
65          EVENSC  EQU     0B800H              ; ADDRESS OF EVEN HALF OF SCREEN
66          ODDSC   EQU     02000H              ; OFFSET OF ODD HALF OF SCREEN
67
68          CODE    SEGMENT PUBLIC
69                  ASSUME  CS:CODE
70                  PUBLIC  SCRNBLT
71          ;
72          ; EQUATES FOR ARGUMENTS TO SCRNBLT
73          ;
74          PADOFS  EQU     4[BP]               ; OFFSET OF PAD ORIGIN
75          PADSEG  EQU     6[BP]               ; SEGMENT OF PAD
```

(continues)

```
76        PADY    EQU     8[BP]                  ; Y-COORD IN PAD
77        PADX    EQU     10[BP]                 ; X-COORD IN PAD
78        MOVDIR  EQU     12[BP]                 ; MOVE DIRECTION (0 = TO SCREEN)
79
80        SCRNBLT PROC    NEAR
81                PUSH    BP
82                MOV     BP,SP                  ; CALLING CONVENTION
83                PUSH    DS                     ; SAVE DS
84        ;
85        ; COMPUTE THE ADDRESS OF THE ORIGIN OF THE PAD AREA DESIGNATED BY
86        ; PADX, PADY.  LOC = PAD_OFFSET + (PADY * PADWD) + (PADX / 8)
87        ;
88                MOV     AX,PADY                ; PREPARE PADY * PADX
89                MOV     BX,PADWD
90                MUL     BX                     ; AX = PADY * PADX (DX TRASHED)
91                MOV     BX,PADX                ; ADD IN X COMPONENT:
92                MOV     CL,3                   ; (PREPARE TO SHIFT BY 3)
93                SHR     BX,CL                  ;  DIV BY 8 SO WE MOVE BY BYTE
94                ADD     AX,BX                  ;  ADD IT IN.
95                ADD     AX,PADOFS
96                CMP     WORD PTR MOVDIR,0      ; IS MOVDIR 0?
97                JE      BACKWRD                ; IF SO, DO BACKWARDS MOVE.
98        ;------------------------------------------------
99        ; MOVE "FORWARD" : FROM PAD TO REAL SCREEN
100       ;------------------------------------------------
101       ;  MOVE THE EVEN LINES OF THE SCREEN. THE LOOP IS CONTROLLED BY
102       ;  THE HALFSC VALUE IN DX; A REP MOVSW IS USED TO MOVE THE SCREEN
103       ;  LINES A WORD AT A TIME (PROBABLY NO MORE EFFICIENT ON AN 8088..)
104       ;
105               CLD                            ; BE SURE DIR. FLAG IS 0
106               MOV     BX,PADSEG              ; SOURCE IS PAD, SO SET DS TO
107               MOV     DS,BX                  ;  PAD SEGMENT
108               MOV     SI,AX                  ;  AND DI TO OFFSET IN PAD
109               MOV     BX,EVENSC              ; DEST IS SCREEN, SET ES TO SCREEN
110               MOV     ES,BX                  ;  SEGMENT.
111               MOV     DI,0                   ;  AND INDEX OF 0
112       ;
113       ; LOOP TO COPY EVEN LINES
```

(continues)

```
114             ;
115                     MOV     CX,HALFSC               ; PREPARE LOOP COUNTER
116     EVEN:   MOV     DX,CX                   ; RECORD LOOP COUNTER
117                     MOV     CX,SCRNWD2              ; SET UP COUNTER
118                     REP     MOVSW                   ; DO THE MOVE
119                     ADD     SI,PADWD+PADWD-SCRNWD   ; MOVE SI TO NEXT SCREEN LINE
120                     MOV     CX,DX
121                     LOOP    EVEN
122             ;
123             ; NOW SET UP FOR ODD LINES AND COPY THOSE
124             ;
125                     MOV     DI,ODDSC                ; SET DI TO ODD SCREEN OFFSET
126                     MOV     SI,AX
127                     ADD     SI,PADWD                ; SET SI TO FIRST ODD LINE
128             ;
129             ; COPY ODD LINES
130             ;
131                     MOV     CX,HALFSC               ; LOAD COUNTER
132     ODD:    MOV     DX,CX                   ; SAVE COUNTER
133                     MOV     CX,SCRNWD2              ; SET UP LINE COUNTER
134                     REP     MOVSW
135                     ADD     SI,PADWD+PADWD-SCRNWD   ; MOVE SI TO NEXT SCREEN LINE
136                     MOV     CX,DX                   ; GET LOOP COUNTER
137                     LOOP    ODD
138                     JMP     BYE                     ; LEAVE
139             ;----------------------------------------------------
140             ; MOVE "BACKWARD" : FROM REAL SCREEN TO PAD
141             ;----------------------------------------------------
142             ;   THIS IS ALMOST EXACTLY LIKE THE CODE ABOVE THAT MOVES
143             ;   FROM THE VIRTUAL SCREEN TO THE DISPLAY BUFFER
144             ;
145     BACKWRD:
146                     CLD                             ; BE SURE DIR. FLAG IS 0
147                     MOV     BX,PADSEG               ; DEST IS PAD, SO SET ES TO
148                     MOV     ES,BX                   ;  PAD SEGMENT
149                     MOV     DI,AX                   ; SET UP SOURCE INDEX
150                     MOV     BX,EVENSC               ; SET DS TO SCREEN SEGMENT
151                     MOV     DS,BX                   ;  FOR EVEN LINES OF SCREEN
```

(continues)

```
152                 MOV    SI,0                      ;  AND SOURCE INDEX
153          ;
154          ; LOOP TO COPY EVEN LINES
155          ;
156                 MOV    CX,HALFSC                 ; PREPARE LOOP COUNTER
157        BEVEN:   MOV    DX,CX                     ; RECORD LOOP COUNTER
158                 MOV    CX,SCRNWD2                ; SET UP COUNTER
159                 REP    MOVSW                     ; DO THE MOVE
160                 ADD    DI,PADWD+PADWD-SCRNWD     ; MOVE SI TO NEXT SCREEN LINE
161                 MOV    CX,DX
162                 LOOP   BEVEN
163          ;
164          ; NOW SET UP FOR ODD LINES AND COPY THOSE
165          ;
166                 MOV    SI,ODDSC                  ; SET DI TO ODD SCREEN OFFSET
167                 MOV    DI,AX
168                 ADD    DI,PADWD                  ; SET SI TO FIRST ODD LINE
169          ;
170          ; COPY ODD LINES
171          ;
172                 MOV    CX,HALFSC                 ; LOAD COUNTER
173        BODD:    MOV    DX,CX                     ; SAVE COUNTER
174                 MOV    CX,SCRNWD2                ; SET UP LINE COUNTER
175                 REP    MOVSW
176                 ADD    DI,PADWD+PADWD-SCRNWD     ; MOVE SI TO NEXT SCREEN LINE
177                 MOV    CX,DX                     ; GET LOOP COUNTER
178                 LOOP   BODD
179          ;
180          ; DONE.. CLEAN UP THE STACK AND LEAVE
181          ;
182        BYE:     POP    DS                        ; RESTORE DS
183                 MOV    SP,BP
184                 POP    BP                        ; CONVENTIONAL RETURN
185                 RET    10                        ; TRASH 10 BYTES FOR PARMS
186
187        SCRNBLT ENDP
188        CODE    ENDS
189                END
```

(concluded)

When the runtime code finishes allocating **ScrnBLT**'s parameters on the stack, the stack looks like this:

```
                    HIGH MEMORY

            |MSB MOVDIR         |
            |LSB MOVDIR         |
            |MSB PADX           |
            |LSB PADX           |
            |MSB PADY           |
            |LSB PADY           |
            |MSB PAD SEGMENT    |
            |LSB PAD SEGMENT    |
            |MSB PAD OFFSET     |
            |LSB PAD OFFSET     |
            |MSB RETURN SEGMENT |
            |LSB RETURN SEGMENT |
            |MSB RETURN OFFSET  |
            |LSB RETURN OFFSET  |  <-- SP

                    LOW MEMORY
```

By copying SP into BP at this point, BP can be used to access the parameters and SP is free to act as a stack pointer for the external routine. The equates within **ScrnBLT**, for the parameters specify the locations of the parameters relative to BP:

```
            MOVDIR  EQU    12[BP]
```

This means that **MovDir** is located 12 bytes higher than BP. Relate this to the stack diagram above until it makes sense. It is a good idea to get a few books on 8086/8088 assembly language before attempting your own external routines.

The Turbo Pascal Reference Manual explains in detail how each data type is represented in memory so that you will know how to interpret the raw bytes on the stack from within your external machine code routine.

Like **ITerm**, **FatPad** is a skeleton of a useful program with the hard work done for you: in this case, the interface between **FatPad** and the external assembly code routine **ScrnBLT**. It includes the interface routine to the Microsoft Mouse that was described in Section 20.6. **FatPad** is a "paint" program that allows you to draw freehand lines on the screen by moving the mouse with the left button pressed. If the right button is pressed, you can move the mouse and "drag" the visible window around the 400 × 1280 virtual pad. The virtual pad is as large as four ordinary high-resolution graphics screens.

ScrnBLT is short for SCReeN BLock Transfer. It moves a screen-sized chunk of graphics memory from the 400 × 1280 virtual pad to the video refresh buffer and back again. It is *not* a **BitBLT** (Bit BLock Transfer) routine, because it works only on word boundaries for speed's (and simplicity's) sake. On the other hand, the transfer is so fast you don't really notice it happening. The illusion of moving a window around a larger pad is quite complete.

Unlike **ITerm**, the operation of **FatPad** is not especially subtle, and it illustrates a good number of the low level machine hooks we have been describing in this section. The virtual pad is a dynamic variable in the heap. At 64K, it is as large as any single dynamic variable can be. **FatPad** opens and loads a saved 200 × 640 high resolution graphics image so you can plainly see the movement of the window about **Pad** with the graphics image in the upper left corner of **Pad**. **PadClear** uses **FillChar** to blank out the virtual pad, so **FatPad** will not attempt to display whatever electronic debris happened to exist in the 64K RAM segment where it allocated **Pad**. **LoadCursor** shows you how to change the mouse cursor pattern for the Microsoft Mouse. One of the two mouse cursors, **Fred**, really is a "mouse" cursor—try it and see! (**Fred** strongly resembles another well-known mouse, but using that name would be trademark infringement, wouldn't it?)

FatPad's main loop waits for any keypress to end the program. Within the loop, **FatPad** checks the position of the mouse and whether or not either button is pressed. If the left button is pressed, it draws a line between the last reported position of the mouse and the current position of the mouse. If this seems strange, consider that you can move the mouse faster than **FatPad** can poll the mouse (shades of **ITerm**) and if we only plotted a dot at each polled mouse position, we would be drawing a dotted line when the mouse was moved quickly. In most cases the line segments drawn are only two or three pixels long, and if you move the mouse slowly they will in fact be only a single pixel long, but the illusion of drawing a continuous, dot-by-dot line is very good.

Pressing the right button activates **ScrnBLT**. First **FatPad** **ScrnBLT**s the current screen out to **Pad** to make sure any lines you've drawn on the current screen will be present in **Pad**. Then **FatPad** allows the mouse to move freely while the right button remains depressed, and **ScrnBLT**s a screen's worth of graphics back from **Pad** whenever the mouse has moved up or down by a single pixel, or right or left by at least 16 pixels. As soon as the right button is released, **FatPad** assumes its simple polling loop again, waiting for a command to draw or drag.

The program is as simple as that. There are no commands for saving screens, drawing circles, or magnifying part of the image as "fatbits" à la Macintosh. On the other hand, you may be able to add some or most of these things yourself, especially with the help of a third-party graphics utility library like Metawindow (see Appendix C).

20.10 Converting external routines to INLINE statements

Once a machine code routine has been thoroughly shaken out and proven, you might want to convert it into an **INLINE** statement to make it a more easily readable part of your Pascal source code file. This is not outrageously difficult once you understand the difference between an **INLINE** call and an **EXTERNAL** call.

As we saw with **ScrnBLT**, an external machine code routine must push the old BP onto the stack, then save the current value of the stack pointer into BP. Then, when your external routine finishes executing, it must restore the old stack pointer from BP back into SP, pop the old base pointer into BP, and clear any parameters off the stack.

With **INLINE**, none of this needs to be done within the **INLINE** statement. An external routine is actually a Pascal procedure call, with its own instantiation on the stack. An **INLINE** statement, by contrast, is just a statement existing within a procedure, a function, or the main program body. If an **INLINE** statement exists within a function or procedure, the BP register is already available to act as an addressing base for parameters and local variables. All you need do is name the parameter or local variable, and the name will be replaced by its offset from the BP register. You need not (indeed, you *must* not) load the stack pointer into BP, nor must you clear parameters from the stack with a RET n opcode at the end of the **INLINE** code.

This is best shown by an example. Here is a machine code routine to replace Turbo Pascal's own rather lethargic **Plot** statement with something a little quicker:

```
 1    ;======================================================================
 2    ;
 3    ;     P L O T  -  Assembly language point plot for Turbo Pascal
 4    ;
 5    ;======================================================================
 6    ;
 7    ;     by Jeff Duntemann     6-Feb-86
 8    ;
 9    ; PLOT is a high-speed replacement for Turbo Pascal's rather slow
10    ; point-plotting routine of the same name.  This PLOT takes the same
11    ; parameters as Turbo's own PLOT but CAN ONLY BE USED IN HIGH
12    ; RESOLUTION GRAPHICS MODE.  It won't crash you in medium res but it
13    ; won't plot colors correctly either.
14    ;
15    ; This .ASM file is intended to be assembled with Microsoft's MASM,
16    ; and was developed under MASM V4.0.  Nothing fancy is going on here
17    ; so presumably it will assemble correctly using earlier versions of
18    ; MASM.  Once assembled, link it, EXE2BIN it, and then include it
19    ; into your Turbo Pascal programs by calling it as External:
20    ;
21    ;     PROCEDURE Plot(X,Y,Color : Integer); External('PLOT.COM');
22    ;
23    ; In COMPLETE TURBO PASCAL, there are also instructions for turning
24    ; the PLOT.COM file into an INLINE statement so that you no longer
```

(continues)

```
25          ; need to have PLOT.COM on your source code disk as a separate file.
26          ;
27          ; This is by no means the fastest possible point plot routine for
28          ; the IBM PC.  Certainly you patient clock-cycle pinchers could
29          ; squeeze a little more performance out of it.  Do try, and let me
30          ; know how well you do!
31          ;
32          ;
33          ;
34          ;
35          ;
36
37          BUFBASE   EQU      0B800H              ; BASE OF VIDEO RAM
38
39          CODE      SEGMENT PUBLIC
40                    ASSUME  CS:CODE
41                    PUBLIC  PLOT
42          ;
43          ;
44          ;   EQUATES FOR ARGUMENTS TO PLOT
45          ;
46          COLOR     EQU      4[BP]               ; OFFSET OF COLOR PARM
47          Y         EQU      6[BP]               ; OFFSET OF Y COORDINATE
48          X         EQU      8[BP]               ; OFFSET OF X COORDINATE
49
50          PLOT      PROC     NEAR
51                    PUSH     BP
52                    MOV      BP,SP
53                    PUSH     DS
54
55          ;
56          ;   FIRST WE CALCULATE THE Y OFFSET INTO THE VIDEO BUFFER
57          ;
58          BEGIN:    MOV      AX,Y                ; PUT Y IN AX REGISTER
59                    MOV      AH,AL               ;   AND LOW BYTE IN AH TOO
60                    AND      AX,01FEH            ; MASK AX WITH $01FE
61                    MOV      CL,3                ; MULTIPLY AX BY 8 VIA SHIFT
62                    SHL      AX,CL
```

(continues)

```
63                  MOV     BX,AX           ; COPY NEW VALUE INTO BX
64                  AND     BH,7            ; ZERO OUT HIGH 5 BITS OF BH
65                  MOV     CL,2            ; BY NOW AX HAS BEEN MULTIPLIED
66                  SHL     AX,CL           ;     BY 32...
67                  ADD     BX,AX           ; ADD AX TO BX; BX NOW CONTAINS
68                                          ;     Y VALUE MUTIPLIED BY 40
69
70          ;
71          ;   NOW WE CALCULATE THE X OFFSET INTO THE VIDEO BUFFER
72          ;
73                  MOV     AX,X            ; PUT X IN AX REGISTER
74                  MOV     CX,AX           ;     AND IN THE CX REGISTER
75                  SHR     AX,1            ; WE CAN'T USE CL TO SHIFT HERE
76                  SHR     AX,1            ;     SO WE SHIFT BY 1 THREE TIMES
77                  SHR     AX,1            ;     TO DIVIDE AX BY 8
78                                          ;     WHICH IS THE X OFFSET
79                  ADD     BX,AX           ; ADD X AND Y OFFSETS INTO BUFFER
80
81          ;
82          ;   HERE WE FETCH THE VIDEO BUFFER BYTE AND MODIFY THE DESIRED PIXEL
83          ;
84                  AND     CX,7            ; LOW 3 BITS OF CX CONTAIN BIT #
85                                          ;     OF DESIRED PIXEL
86                  MOV     AL,080H         ; STORE SINGLE BIT INTO AL BIT 7
87                  SHR     AL,CL           ; SHIFT BIT DOWN BY PIXEL NUMBER
88                  MOV     DX,BUFBASE      ; SET DS TO SEGMENT OF VIDEO BUFFER
89                  MOV     DS,DX
90                  MOV     CL,[DS:BX]      ; BRING BYTE IN FROM BUFFER
91                  MOV     DX,COLOR        ; PUT COLOR PARM INTO DX
92                  CMP     DL,0            ; IS COLOR=0?
93                  JE      PRESET
94
95      PSET:       OR      CL,AL           ; OR IN THE NEW PIXEL
96                  MOV     [DS:BX],CL      ; AND PUT IT BACK IN THE BUFFER
97                  JMP     BYE
98
99      PRESET:     XOR     AL,OFFH         ; INVERT THE PIXEL MASK
100                 AND     CL,AL           ; AND THE MASK AGAINST THE BYTE
```

(continues)

```
101                 MOV     [DS:BX],CL              ; AND PUT IT BACK IN THE BUFFER
102         ;
103         ;  DONE...CLEAN UP THE STACK AND LEAVE
104         ;
105         BYE:    POP     DS                      ; RESTORE DS
106                 MOV     SP,BP                   ; CLEAN UP STACK AND LEAVE
107                 POP     BP                      ; RESTORE BP
108
109                 RET     6                       ; TRASH 6 BYTES FOR PARMS
110
111        PLOT     ENDP
112        CODE     ENDS
113                 END
114
```

(concluded)

This routine, as coded, will assemble and link into a complete assembly language subroutine ready to include as an external, exactly as we did with **ScrnBLT**. You can call **Plot** as an external by declaring it this way:

```
PROCEDURE Plot(X,Y,Color : Integer); EXTERNAL 'PLOT.COM';
```

Converting it to an **INLINE** statement is best done by hand. All you need is a hexdump of **PLOT.COM**, generated, perhaps, by the **HexDump** program from Section 18.11. **Plot** is quite small; its hexdump is shown below:

```
0100   55 8B EC 1E 8B 46 06 8A-E0 25 FE 01 B1 03 D3 E0    U....F...%......
0110   8B D8 80 E7 07 B1 02 D3-E0 03 D8 8B 46 08 8B C8    ............F...
0120   D1 E8 D1 E8 D1 E8 03 D8-81 E1 07 00 B0 80 D2 E8    ................
0130   BA 00 B8 8E DA 8A 0F 8B-56 04 80 FA 00 74 07 0A    ........V....t..
```

(continues)

```
0140   C8 88 OF EB 07 90 34 FF-22 C8 88 OF 1F 8B E5 5D    ......4."......]
0150   C2 06 00 00 00 00 00 00-00 00 00 00 00 00 00 00    ................
0160   00 00 00 00 00 00 00 00-00 00 00 00 00 00 00 00    ................
0170   00 00 00 00 00 00 00 00-00 00 00 00 00 00 00 00    ................
```

(concluded)

Transcribe it from the hexdump to **INLINE** byte-by-byte, triple checking the accuracy of each number. If you're ambitious you'll add comments with assembly language mnemonics beside each line of code.

Note that the beginning and end of your routine should look something like this:

```
INLINE
  ($55 /              { PUSH BP }
   $8B / $EC /        { MOV BP,SP }

        .  .  .

   $8B / $E5 /        { MOV SP,BP }
   $5D /              { POP BP }
   $C2 / $06);        { RET 6 (or some other figure) }
```

These are the instructions that you must remove to turn your external routine to an **INLINE** statement.

Finally, you must melt in references to parameters or other data items from the main program. Typically, if you're converting an external routine it will only have parameter references, and these are fairly straightforward.

The easiest way to do it, in fact, is to convert the **INLINE** statement to a one-statement procedure. Then you don't need to add named parameter references, assuming that the declaration of the procedure matches the declaration of the original external routine. In that case, the assembler coded the offsets from BP correctly and you can leave them as is.

If there are any local variables in the block, however, you must let Turbo Pascal recalculate the offsets from BP for each named parameter reference in the **INLINE** statement. Go to your assembler source and spot each reference to a parameter. Then, find each instruction opcode that references a parameter (with the help of an instruction encoding table) in the hexdump, and find the offset value by which the instruction references the parameter from BP. The important question you must answer is: is the offset a 1-byte value or a 2-byte value?

For small external routines, the offset will be smaller than 256, and thus will fit in a single byte. *However,* named parameter references always generate 2-byte values within **INLINE** unless the 2-byte size is overridden with the "<" prefix. *You must precede any reference that generated a 1-byte offset with a "<" symbol.* Take a look at the little test program below and you'll soon see what I mean:

```
 1       {-------------------------------------------------------}
 2       {                        PlotTest                       }
 3       {                                                       }
 4       {         INLINE-from-EXTERNAL demonstration program     }
 5       {                                                       }
 6       {                     by Jeff Duntemann                 }
 7       {                     Turbo Pascal V3.0                 }
 8       {                     Last update 6/19/86               }
 9       {                                                       }
10       {                                                       }
11       {                                                       }
12       {-------------------------------------------------------}
13
14       PROGRAM PlotTest;
15
16       VAR
17         I : Integer;
18
19       PROCEDURE Plot(X,Y,Color : INTEGER);
20
21       BEGIN
```

(continues)

```
22
23          INLINE
24            ($1E /                    { PUSH DS }
25
26          { First we calculate the Y offset into the video buffer: }
27
28          $8B / $46 / <Y /    { MOV AX,Y        ; Put Y in AL.. }
29          $8A / $E0 /         { MOV AH,AL       ; ..and AH too }
30          $25 / $FE / $01 /   { AND AX,01FEH    ; Mask AX with $01FE }
31          $B1 / $03 /         { MOV CL,3        ; Multiply AX by 8.. }
32          $D3 / $E0 /         { SHL AX,CL       ; ..by shifting left 3X }
33          $8B / $D8 /         { MOV BX,AX       ; Copy new value into BX }
34          $80 / $E7 / $07 /   { AND BH,7        ; Zero out hi 5 bits of BH }
35          $B1 / $02 /         { MOV CL,2        ; By now AX has been }
36          $D3 / $E0 /         { SHL AX,CL       ; multiplied by 32; add AX }
37          $03 / $D8 /         { ADD BX,AX       ; to BX; BX now contains Y }
38                                               { ; multiplied by 40 }
39
40          { Now we calculate the X offset into the video buffer: }
41
42          $8B / $46 / <X /    { MOV AX,X        ; Put X in AX.. }
43          $8B / $C8 /         { MOV CX,AX       ; ..and CX too }
44          $D1 / $E8 /         { SHR AX,1        ; Divide AX by 8 by shifting }
45          $D1 / $E8 /         { SHR AX,1        ; right 3X...can't use CX! }
46          $D1 / $E8 /         { SHR AX,1        ; To get byte offset we add }
47          $03 / $D8 /         { ADD BX,AX       ; X offset to Y offset. }
48                                               { ; Now DS:BX contains the byte }
49                                               { ; that contains our pixel! }
50
51          { Here we fetch the video buffer byte and modify the }
52          { appropriate pixel: }
53
54          $81 / $E1 / $07 / $00 /  { AND CX,7     ; Lo 3 bits of CX are bit # }
55                                                  { ; of desired pixel }
56          $B0 / $80 /         { MOV AL,080H     ; Store hi bit into AL bit 7 }
57          $D2 / $E8 /         { SHR AL,CL       ; Shift bit down by pixel # }
58          $BA / $00 / $B8 /   { MOV DX,B800H    ; Set DS to video segment }
59          $8E / $DA /         { MOV DS,DX }
60          $8A / $0F /         { MOV CL,[DS:BX] ; Bring byte in from buffer }
```

(continues)

```
61      $8B / $56 / <Color /        { MOV DX,Color   ; Color parm in DX for test }
62      $80 / $FA / $00 /           { CMP DL,0       ; Is color parm = 0? }
63      $74 / $07 /                 { JE PRESET      ; If so, jump to clr pixel }
64                                        { PSET: }
65      $0A / $C8 /                 { OR CL,AL       ; OR new pixel into byte }
66      $88 / $0F /                 { MOV [DS:BX],CL ; put it back into buffer }
67      $EB / $07 / $90 /           { JMP BYE        ; and go home }
68                                        { PRESET: }
69      $34 / $FF /                 { XOR AL,0FFH    ; Invert the pixel mask }
70      $22 / $C8 /                 { AND CL,AL      ; AND mask against byte }
71      $88 / $0F /                 { MOV [DS:BX],CL ; put it back into buffer }
72
73      { Pop DS off the stack and go home: }
74
75                                  { BYE: }
76      $1F )                       { POP DS }
77
78      END;
79
80
81
82
83      BEGIN
84        HiResColor(15);
85        HiRes;
86        Readln;
87        FOR I := 0 TO 639 DO PLOT(I,0,1);  { Draw a line }
88        Readln;
89        FOR I := 0 TO 639 DO PLOT(I,0,0);  { and erase it again }
90        Readln;
91        TextMode
92      END.
```

(concluded)

All references to **Plot**'s three parameters **X,Y**, and **Color** are within
256 bytes of BP, thus generating 1-byte offsets, and therefore, they
must be preceded with "<".

In 99 per cent of cases, this is all you will need to do. However, if
you are embedding an **INLINE** routine within a much larger

procedure with lots of parameters and lots of local variables, you might have some 1-byte offsets mixed with some 2-byte offsets. A 1-byte offset within your proven external routine might need to be changed to a 2-byte offset, which carries a different machine code instruction. You will need to do some grimbling with a binary machine code chart and may end up losing more than a little hair in the process.

This is the reason I recommend writing externals and leaving them as externals. Writing machine code with **INLINE** looks like it ought to be much easier, but in fact it's considerably tougher. Let your assembler do the rough work. Stick with external routines whenever you can.

Having worked your way entirely through Part II, you should now have a pretty good feel for all of what Turbo Pascal can do. However, there's a big difference between knowing what it can do and using what it can do in structured innovative programs. That takes ongoing study, and most of all *practice*. The only way to become an expert programmer is to get down and program; often, intensely, and well.

At first, you will do well to take some of the simple programs presented here and enhance them. Adding code to save and restore virtual pads from **FatPad** is an excellent exercise in **BlockRead** and **BlockWrite**. Adding text file transmit ability to **ITerm** is another "easy" project and useful, as well.

In time you'll be designing your own programs. Start with small ones, keep program readability as a necessary value, and build on your experience.

You'll be writing thousand-liners in no time at all.

PART III

USING YOUR COMPILER

Introduction

In the same way that Part II of this book was an instruction manual for the Pascal language (as implemented in Turbo Pascal), Part III is an instruction manual for the Turbo Pascal compiler program itself. Rather than telling you how to write a Pascal program, Part III will tell you how to get the most from the Turbo Pascal Environment. There are numerous commands and options that make Turbo Pascal do different things in different ways, and this is the part of the book where we look at these options in detail.

This part of the book should not be considered a replacement for the Turbo Pascal Reference Manual. Much of the purely technical information about the environment in the reference manual has been left out—memory maps, for example. This part of the book is a tutorial on using the Turbo Pascal Environment, so that when you need to understand the more technical details in the Reference Manual, all the groundwork will have been laid.

The Turbo Pascal environment

Most traditional compiler programs are a special variant of the type of program known as a "filter." We looked at a very simple text file filter for changing the case of characters in the file in Section 18.8. Traditional filter programs (and most compilers) work this way: You begin from the operating system prompt (the archetypal "A>") and type the name of the program, along with a few parameters telling the program which files to work on and perhaps specify some instructions on how to do the work itself. The program then opens the input file, creates the output file, and begins reading the input file. Based on what it reads in the input file, the filter program writes something to the output file. In the case of a compiler program, the program reads lines of source code from the input file and outputs binary opcodes to the output file.

All other native-code Pascal compilers that I have tested use this system: MS Pascal, Professional Pascal, Pascal/MT+, Pascal/Z, Utah Pascal, and SBB Pascal. Turbo Pascal is an entirely different breed. Rather than a filter program, Turbo Pascal is an *environment,* within which you edit, compile, test, and debug programs.

In computer terms, an environment may be thought of as a place to stand with access to a set of tools. PC DOS and CP/M are environments. From your place to stand (that venerable "A>" prompt) you can pick up and use specific tools such as PIP and STAT (for CP/M) and CHKDSK and COPY (for PC DOS). The tools available from within an operating system environment are designed to let you manipulate the resources of the machine: the disk subsystem, printer, and display.

Turbo Pascal is a program that may be run from either CP/M or PC/MS DOS. It provides you with a different looking place to stand and a whole new set of tools. These tools are designed to let you edit and compile Pascal programs.

THE TURBO MAIN MENU: YOUR PLACE TO STAND

Turbo pascal is a program just like any other program. For CP/M-80 and PC/MS DOS it is called TURBO.COM; for CP/M-86 it is called TURBO.CMD. You start it running from the operating system prompt by naming it:

```
A>TURBO
```

Once Turbo loads from disk it takes control of your machine, clears your screen, and asks you a question:

```
----------------------------------------
TURBO Pascal system          Version 3.01A
                                 PC DOS

Copyright (C) 1983,84,85    BORLAND Inc.
----------------------------------------

Color display 80 x 25

Include error messages (Y/N)?
```

Turbo Pascal's error messages are kept in a separate file, and you have the option of *not* loading them into memory when the rest of the program comes in. If it seems like madness not to have error messages handy when using a compiler, you're at least partly right. Turbo Pascal always gives you an error message *number* when it discovers an error in your program, but it will also print out a human-readable error message—unless you choose not to load the error messages at the question shown above.

Omitting the error messages will save you about 1500 bytes of memory. This can be very important in memory-starved Z80 CP/M computers, where every byte counts. Unless you are *very* good at Turbo Pascal, however, not having error messages will force you to do a lot of thumbing through the manual or through this book looking for the error messages. In short, answer "Y" and load the error messages.

What appears on your screen next will be your place to stand: The Turbo Pascal main menu. On Z80 CP/M computers, the main menu will look like this:

```
Logged drive: A

Work file:
Main file:

Edit      Compile  Run   Save

eXecute   Dir      Quit  compiler Options

Text:      0 bytes (802A-802A)
Free: 22491 bytes (802B-D806)
```

For PC/MS DOS the main menu is a little bit different:

```
Logged drive: A
Active directory: \

Work file:
Main file:

Edit      Compile  Run   Save

Dir       Quit  compiler Options

Text:      0 bytes
Free: 62635 bytes

>
```

Perhaps the most important difference to the programmer is the amount of free space you have to work in—almost three times as much in an 8086-based computer. Whether the Z80 is a better processor than the 8086 is relatively unimportant—what counts in this game (as you'll come to see eventually) is elbow room.

Although you can't see it here on the printed page, on most computers the capital letter in each menu command is displayed in a different color or highlighted in some other way. These are your tools—and each one may be used by pressing a single letter, the letter that is highlighted within that command name.

The ">" mark is your command prompt. Beside it will be your cursor, waiting for a single-character command. From this prompt you can strike off on your own to accomplish various tasks within the Turbo Pascal Environment. When each task is complete, it will send you back to the ">" prompt, ready to do something else.

Your tools are all around you. What, then, can you do from within the Turbo Pascal Environment?

Several things:

1. You can tell Turbo Pascal what files you want to work with and what disk drives to find them on.
2. You can edit those files with the Turbo Editor and save edited files to disk.
3. You can compile a Pascal source file into a runnable Pascal program with the Turbo Pascal compiler.
4. You can run a Pascal program that has compiled correctly.
5. You can list the files on any disk drive.
6. You can enter a secondary menu, which sets up certain controls to modify the way various Turbo Pascal functions operate.

After completing each task, the Turbo Pascal Environment will give you the ">" prompt again. When you're through working with Turbo Pascal, you can press "Q" for "Quit" and control will return to your operating system.

This has been a quick overview of what to expect when running Turbo Pascal for the first time. Before running the program, read any READ.ME files on the distribution disk. These contain up-to-the-minute details on changes to the compiler. You may also have to install Turbo Pascal for your terminal or video driver if your machine is not one of the many supported by an off-the-shelf version.

Using the Turbo Pascal Editor

Creating a Pascal program involves editing a text file of Pascal statements that the compiler will translate into pure machine code. The Turbo Pascal environment includes a fairly powerful screen editor, which allows you to create and alter program text files and save them to disk. The editor uses commands, which are a subset of those offered by the popular WordStar word processing program. You can, however, redefine the keystrokes for each command to any different set of keystrokes you prefer. We will not describe this process here; the TINST program will do this for you. Read up on the process in Part 1.6.3 of the Turbo Pascal Reference Manual.

22.1 The work file

Unlike most text editors, the Turbo text editor requires that all of a file exist in RAM memory during editing. This sets an upper limit on the size of the files you can edit. For the Z80 version of Turbo Pascal you will probably have less than 13,000 bytes worth of editing space. For PC/MS DOS you will probably have a great deal more, perhaps as much as 55,000 bytes, depending on the amount of RAM in your machine and what other resident software is using RAM.

All editing is done on what is called the "work file." Setting the name of the work file is done with the W command from the Turbo Pascal environment prompt. Pressing W brings up this message:

```
Work file name:
```

You can then type in the name of the file you wish to edit. The file must conform to the file naming conventions of the operating system you are using on your machine. For most operating systems this means a name of no more than eight characters, with an optional file name extension of up to three characters, with a period separating the two parts of the name. Most operating systems prohibit certain characters within file names. Be familiar with what you can use as a file name and what you can't! If the file you name is not on the currently logged disk drive (the current disk drive is displayed at the top of the main menu) you must precede the file name by the letter of the unit where the file exists, followed by a colon:

```
Work file name: B:MYPROG.SRC
```

Once you have pressed return after the file name, the Turbo Pascal environment will attempt to open the file and load it into memory. If the file already exists on disk the entire file will be loaded into memory. If the file does *not* exist, the Turbo Editor will create the file under the name you entered. If you misspell the name of the file you want to load, the Turbo Editor will gladly go out and create a brand new empty file for you with the misspelled name. Watch your typing!

If the file is too large to fit in available memory, you will see this message:

```
File too big. Press <ESC>
```

Pressing the Escape key will bring back the Turbo Pascal environment prompt ">".

Assuming that your text file was small enough to fit comfortably into memory, you are now ready to go in and edit the file. The E command (one touch of the "E" key without pressing Return) will clear the screen and display either a blank screen (for a new file) or the first 25 lines of the file you requested.

22.2   Moving the cursor

When you first enter a file for editing, the cursor will be at the upper left corner of the screen. If you are working on a brand new file, you can begin typing text right there. In most cases, you will be editing an existing file, and you will have to move the cursor to where work needs to be done.

All commands within the Turbo Editor are control keystrokes; that is, you must hold the control (Ctrl) key down while pressing another key or two keys. All the keys that control cursor movement are grouped together for you in a cluster toward the left hand side of the keyboard:

```
    W   E   R
  A   S   D   F
    Z   X   C
```

ONE CHARACTER AT A TIME

Moving the cursor one character at a time can be done in all four directions:

CTRL-E moves the cursor **Up** one character.
CTRL-X moves the cursor **Down** one character.
CTRL-S moves the cursor **Left** one character.
CTRL-D moves the cursor **Right** one character.

The position of these four keys (E, X, S, and D) provides a hint as to which way they move the cursor. Look at how they are arranged on the keyboard:

```
        E
     S    D
        X
```

Until the directions become automatic to your fingers (as they will, if you do enough editing!), thinking of the "magic diamond" will remind you which way the cursor will move for which keypress.

When you move the cursor to the bottom of the screen and press CTRL-X one more time, the screen will "scroll." All the lines on the screen will jump up by one, and the top line will disappear. As long as the cursor is on the bottom line of the screen and you continue to press CTRL-X, the screen will scroll upward. If use CTRL-E to move the cursor back in the opposite direction (upward) until it hits the top of the screen, further CTRL-E's will scroll the screen downward one line per CTRL-E.

ONE WORD AT A TIME

The Turbo Editor will also move the cursor one word at a time to the left or right:

> **CTRL-A** moves the cursor **Left** one word.
> **CTRL-F** moves the cursor **Right** one word.

More hints are given here, since the A key is on the left side of the magic diamond, and the F key is on the right side of the magic diamond.

ONE SCREEN AT A TIME

It is also possible to move the cursor upward or downward through the file one whole screen at a time. "Upward" in this sense means toward the beginning of the file; "downward" means toward the end of the file. A screen is the height of your CRT display (usually 24 or 25 lines) minus one line of overlap.

> **CTRL-R** moves the cursor **Up** one screen.
> **CTRL-C** moves the cursor **Down** one screen.

MOVING THE CURSOR BY SCROLLING THE SCREEN

We described how the screen will scroll when you use the one-character-at-a-time commands to move upward (CTRL-E) from the top line of the screen or downward (CTRL-X) from the bottom line of the screen. You can scroll the screen upward or downward no matter where the cursor happens to be by using the scrolling commands:

CTRL-W scrolls the screen **Down** one line.
CTRL-Z scrolls the screen **Up** one line.

When you scroll the screen with these commands, the cursor "rides" with the screen as it scrolls upward or downward, *until* the cursor hits the top or bottom of the screen. Then further scrolling will make the screen "slip past" the cursor. The cursor will always remain visible.

These are all of the cursor movement commands that can be invoked by one-control keystroke. A few others are accomplished by holding the Control key down and pressing *two* keys in succession. *You must hold the Control key down through both keypresses!*

MOVING TO THE ENDS OF THE LINE

No matter where your cursor is on the screen, it is always within a line, even if that line happens to be empty of characters. Two commands will move the cursor either to the beginning (left end) of the line (screen column 1) or to the end of the line, which is the position following the last visible character on the line:

CTRL-Q/S sends the cursor to the **Beginning** of the line.
CTRL-Q/D sends the cursor to the **End** of the line.

MOVING TO THE ENDS OF THE FILE

The last set of cursor movement commands we'll describe takes the cursor to the beginning of the file or to the end of the file. If the file you are editing is more than a few screens long, it can save you a great deal of pounding on the keyboard to move one screen at a time.

CTRL-Q/R sends the cursor to the **Beginning** of the file.
CTRL-Q/C sends the cursor to the **End** of the line.

Because all of your file is in memory all the time, moving between the ends of the file can be done *very* quickly.

22.3 The editor status line

If you did any practicing at all in moving the cursor around a test file, you may have noticed the line at the very top of the screen, which did not move no matter where you sent the cursor. This is the editor status line, and it provides you with some important information while you are editing.

A typical instance of the status line looks like this:

```
Line 1    Col 1    Insert    Indent   A:MY_PROG.PAS
```

While you were moving the cursor around, the line and column numbers were continually changing to reflect where the cursor was in the file. The column number reflects the position of the cursor within its line; the line number indicates which line in the file contains the cursor, counting from the beginning of the file, *not* from the top of the screen.

At the other end of the status line is the name of the current work file, which is the name of the file you are editing.

The other two words (Insert and Indent) shown as part of the status line merit some explaining. Insert and Indent are the names of two "toggles." A toggle is a condition that may exist in one of two different states. A toggle is like a switch controlling the lights in a room; the switch may be either on or off.

Insert determines how newly typed characters are added to your work file. When Insert is on (that is, when the word Insert appears in the status line), characters that you type are *inserted* into the file. The characters appear over the cursor and immediately push the cursor and the rest of the line to the right to make room for themselves. The line becomes one character longer for each character that you type. If you press Return, the cursor moves down one line, carrying with it the part of the line lying to its right.

When Insert is off (if the word Insert is *not* displayed in the status line), characters that you type will *overwrite* characters that already exist in the file. No new characters are added to the file unless you move the cursor to the end of the line or the end of the file and keep typing. If you press Return, the cursor will move down to the first character of the next line down, but nothing else will change. A line will only be added to the file if you press Return with the cursor on the last line of the file.

Turning Insert on and off is done with a single control keypress:

```
CTRL-V toggles Insert on and off.
```

Indent is also a toggle. It indicates whether the Turbo Editor's auto-indent feature is on or off. When indent is on, the cursor will automatically move beneath the first visible character on a new line when you press Return. In other words (assuming that Indent is on), given this little bit of text on your screen:

```
FOR I := 1 TO 10 DO
  BEGIN
    Total := Total + I;
    Count := Succ(Count);_ <--Before pressing Return
    _

  ↑ After pressing Return
```

the cursor is at the end of the last line of text. When you press Return, the cursor will move down one line, but it will also space over automatically until it is beneath the C in COUNT. This allows you to begin typing the next line of code without having to space the cursor over so that it is beneath the start of the previous line.

The Turbo Editor's Indent feature allows easy "prettyprinting" of your Pascal source code files. This makes for easier reading of your source code files, and easier entry when you go to type them in.

Like Insert, Indent can be toggled on and off. It takes a double control keystroke to do it:

```
CTRL-Q/I toggles Indent on and off.
```

Indent is considered on when the word Indent appears in the status line.

22.4 Inserts and deletes

We've already seen how to insert characters into a text file: You make sure Insert is on, and type away. Each typed character will be inserted into the file at the cursor position.

It is also possible to insert entire blank lines. One way, of course, is to move the cursor to the beginning of a line and press Return (Insert must be on). A new blank line will be inserted above the line with the cursor, and the rest of the file will be pushed downward. The cursor will ride down with the text pushed downward.

The other way to insert a line is independent of the Insert toggle. Move the cursor to the beginning of a line and press CTRL-N. A new line will appear, pushing the rest of the file downward, *but the cursor will not move down with the other text.*

CTRL-N inserts a **New line** at the cursor position.

There are also a number of different ways to *delete* text as well. The simplest is to use the Delete key:

Delete deletes one **Character** to the **Left** of the cursor.

The cursor moves one character position to the left with each press of the Delete key. Notice that the Backspace key does not delete anything; it merely moves the cursor leftward, just as CTRL-S moves the cursor leftward.

Deleting characters to the right of the cursor is done a little differently:

CTRL-G deletes one **Character** to the **Right** of the cursor.

The cursor does not move. It "swallows" the character to its right, and the rest of the line to its right moves over to fill in the position left by the deleted character.

You can also (to save a few keystrokes) delete one word to the right of the cursor:

CTRL-T deletes one **Word** to the **Right** of the cursor.

When you press CTRL-T, all characters from the cursor position rightward to the end of the current word will be deleted. If the cursor happens to be on a space or group of spaces between words, that space or spaces will be deleted up to the beginning of the next word.

It is possible to delete from the cursor position to the end of the cursor line:

CTRL-Q/Y deletes from the cursor to **The end of the line.**

And finally, it is possible to delete the entire cursor line with a single control keystroke:

CTRL-Y deletes the entire **Line** containing the cursor.

The line beneath the cursor moves up to take the place of the deleted line, pulling up the rest of the file behind it.

22.5   Markers and blocks

There is no such thing as a page number in a Turbo Editor file. You can move the cursor to the beginning or end of the file with a single command, but to move to a specific place in the file is harder. The best way is to remember a distinctive title, procedure name, or something like that and search for it (see below). You might also make use of the Turbo Editor's two markers.

The Turbo Editor allows you to place two separate markers anywhere within your file, either alone or together. Alone, a marker defines a specific place within the file to which you can move the cursor with one command; together, the space between the two markers is identified as a *block* and may be manipulated in several different ways.

The two markers are invisible and do not appear on your screen in any way. If both are present in a file, however, all the text between them (the currently marked block) is shown as highlighted text.

The markers are named B and K, after the commands that position them in your file. Placing each marker is a two-character control keystroke:

CTRL-K/B places the **B** marker.
CTRL-K/K places the **K** marker.

A marker is placed at the cursor position and remains there until you move it elsewhere. You cannot delete or remove a marker once placed, although you can "hide" the block of text that lies between the markers.

MOVING THE CURSOR TO A MARKER

Perhaps you are working on a program source file and decide to use a particular variable. You don't remember, however, whether you declared the variable up in the variable declaration part of the program. Rather than just use the variable and perhaps forget to declare it later, you want to CTRL-Q/R to the beginning of the file, declare the variable, and then jump right back and pick up what you were doing. The fastest way is to set one of the markers to your current position, move to the beginning of the file, declare your variable, and then move the cursor to the marker that you placed back down where the real work is going on:

CTRL-Q/B moves the cursor to the **B** marker.
CTRL-Q/K moves the cursor to the **K** marker.

If you find yourself doing a lot of jumping back and forth between two widely separated parts of your program file, you might drop one of the markers at each place. Then you can jump from one to the other instantly, with a single command.

HIDING AND UNHIDING BLOCKS OF TEXT

The major use of markers, however, lies in their ability to define a block of text. There are a number of commands available in the Turbo Editor that manipulate the text that lies between the B and K markers.

You probably noticed while experimenting with setting markers that as soon as you positioned *both* the B and K markers in a file, the text between them became highlighted. The highlighted text is a marked text block. As we mentioned before, there is no way to remove a marker completely from a file once it has been set. You can, however, suppress the highlighting of text between the two markers. This is called "hiding" a block:

CTRL-K/H will **Hide** a **Block** of text.

Remember that the markers are still there. CTRL-K/H is a toggle. You invoke it once to hide a block, and you can invoke it a second time to "unhide" the block and bring out the highlighting again on the text between the two blocks.

Something else to keep in mind: The other block commands we'll be looking at below work *only* on highlighted blocks. Once a block is hidden, it is hidden from the block commands as well as from your eyes.

BLOCK COMMANDS

The simplest block command to understand is delete block. Getting rid of big chunks of text that are no longer needed is easy: Mark the text as a block with the two markers, and issue the delete block command:

CTRL-K/Y will **Delete** a **Block** of text.

The markers do not vanish with the block of text. They "close up" and occupy the same cursor position, but they are still there.

Copy block is useful when you have some standard text construction (a standard boilerplate comment header for procedures, perhaps) that you need to use several times within the same text file. Rather than type it in each time, you type it once, mark it as a block, and then copy it from the original into each position where you need it. Simply put the cursor where the first character of the copied text must go, and issue copy block:

CTRL-K/C will **Copy** a **Block** of text to the cursor position.

Moving a block of text is similar to copying a block of text. The difference, of course, is that the original block of text, which you marked, vanishes from its original position and reappears at the cursor position. You must first mark the text you wish to move as a block. Then put the cursor where you wish the marked text to go, and issue the move block command:

CTRL-K/V will **Move** a **Block** of text to the cursor position.

The last two block commands allow you to write a block of text to disk, or to read a text file from disk into your work file. Writing a block to disk begins by marking the block you want saved as a separate text file. Then, issue the write block command:

CTRL-K/W will **Write** a **Block** of text to disk.

The Turbo Editor needs to know the name of the disk file into which you want to write the marked block of text. It prompts you for the file name this way:

Write block to file:

You must type the name of the file, within the limitations your operating system sets on file names. Once the name is typed and you have pressed Return, the block is written to disk. The block remains highlighted, and the cursor does not move.

Reading a text file from disk into your work file is also easy. You position the cursor to where the first character of the text from the file should go, and issue the read block command:

CTRL-K/R will **Read** a **Block** of text from disk to the cursor position.

Just as with the write block command, the editor will prompt you for the name of the file that you wish to read from disk:

```
Read block from file:
```

There is one small "gotcha" of which you must be aware in connection with file names. If you enter a file name *without* a period or file extension (that is, a file name like FOO rather than FOO.PAS) the Turbo Editor will first look for a file named FOO. If it does not find one, it will then look for a file named FOO.PAS. If it cannot find a file with the entered name plus the .PAS file extension, it will issue this error message:

```
File FOO.PAS not found. Press <ESC>
```

After you press Escape, the file name prompt will again appear. You can cancel the command by pressing Return or by pressing CTRL-U.

The text file will be read and inserted into your work file at the cursor position. It will come in as a marked block, and you will have to issue the hide block command to remove the highlighting. Remember also that reading a block of text from disk will effectively move your two markers from elsewhere in your file and place them around the text that was read in.

The Turbo Editor is not especially picky about the type of files you read from disk. Text files need not have been generated by the Turbo Editor. Files need not be text files at all, in fact; but remember that reading raw binary data into a text file can cause the file to appear foreshortened: The first binary 26 (CTRL-Z) encountered in a text file is assumed to signal the end of the file. Data after that first CTRL-Z may or may not be accessible. Furthermore, the Turbo Editor will attempt to display the binary characters as is, and various computers may react to the attempted display of binary data in various ways. Many computers have screen drivers that automatically consider certain binary codes as display commands, and they may do unexpected things, such as clear the screen, bring up screen windows, add lines, send the cursor skittering around, and generally make a mess. *Be careful what you read into your work files.*

22.6   Searching and replacing

Much of the power of electronic text editing lies in its ability to search for a particular character pattern in a text file. Furthermore, once found, it is a logical extension of the search concept to replace the found text string with a different text string. For example, if you decide to change the name of a variable to something else to avoid conflict with another identifier in a program, you might wish to have the text editor locate every instance of the old variable name in a program and replace each one with the new variable name.

The Turbo Editor can do both search and search/replace operations with great ease. Simply locating a given text string in a program is often better than having page numbering (which the Turbo Editor does not). If you wish to work on the part of a program that contains a particular procedure, all you need do is search for that procedure's name and you will move the cursor right to the spot you want:

CTRL-Q/F will **Find** a given text string.

When you issue the find command, the Turbo Editor prompts you with a single word:

```
Find:
```

You must then type the text string you wish found, ending it with Return. The Turbo Editor then prompts you for command options:

```
Options:
```

Several command options may be given to both the find and find/replace commands. These are single letters (or numbers) and may be grouped together in any order without spaces in between:

```
Options: BWU
```

for example. We'll be discussing each option in detail shortly. Once you press Return after entering the options (if any), the Turbo Editor executes the command. For the find command, the cursor will move to the first character of the found text string. If the Turbo Editor cannot find any instance of the requested text string in the work file, it displays this message:

```
Search string not found. Press <ESC>
```

You must then press Escape to continue editing.

FIND/REPLACE   Find/replace goes that extra step further. Once the search text is found, it will replace the search text with a replacement text. The options mean everything here; you can replace only the first instance of the search text or all instances, and you can have the editor ask permission before replacing or simply go ahead and do the deed in as many instances of the search text as it finds. (This last operation is especially beloved of programmers, who call it a "search and destroy.")

As with find, the Turbo Editor prompts for the search text and options. It must also (for find/replace) prompt for the replacement string:

```
Replace with:
```

If no options are in force, the Turbo Editor will locate the first instance of the search string, place the cursor beneath it, and give you the permission prompt:

```
Replace (Y/N):
```

If you type a Y here (no Return required) the editor will perform the replacement. If you type an N, nothing will change.

SEARCH/   The Turbo Editor's find/replace options allow you to "fine-tune" a
REPLACE   find or find/replace command to cater to specific needs. For ex-
OPTIONS   ample, without any options the find command is case-sensitive. In other words, FOO, foo, and Foo are three distinct text strings, and searching for FOO will not discover instances of foo. With the U option in force, however, FOO, foo, and Foo are considered identical, and searching for any of the three forms will turn up instances of any of the three present. Several such options exist within the Turbo Editor. In general, they are the same find/replace options used by WordStar.

B is the **Search Backwards** option. Ordinarily, a search will proceed from the cursor position toward the end of the file. If the object of the search is closer to the beginning of the file than the cursor, the search will not find it. With the B option in force, the search proceeds *backwards* through the file, toward the beginning.

G is the **Global Search** option. As mentioned above, searches normally begin at the cursor position and proceed toward one end of the file or the other, depending on whether or not the B option is in force. With the G option in force, searches begin at the beginning of the file and proceed to the end, irrespective of the cursor position. The G option overrides the B option.

N is the **Replace Without Asking** option. Without this option, the editor (during a find/replace) will prompt you for a yes/no response each time it locates an instance of the search text. With N in force, it simply does the replacement. Combining the G and N options means that the editor will search the entire file and replace every instance of the search text with the replacement text, without asking. *Make sure you set it up right,* or you can cause wholesale damage to your work file. In general, *don't use G and N together without W.* (See below for details on the W option.)

U is the **Ignore Case** option. Without this option, searches are case-sensitive. FOO and foo are considered distinct and searching for one will not find the other. With the U option in force, corresponding lower and upper case characters are considered identical. FOO and foo will both be found on a search for either.

W is the **Whole Words** option. Without this option, the search text will be found even when it is embedded in a larger word. For example, searching for LOCK will find both BLOCK and CLOCK. With W in force, the search text must be bounded by spaces to be found. This option is especially important for global search/replace commands, when (if you omit W) replacing all instances of LOCK with SECURE will change all instances of BLOCK to BSECURE and all instances of CLOCK to CSECURE.

You may also give a number as one of the options. For the find command, this tells the editor to find the nth instance of the search text. For find/replace, a number tells the editor to find and replace text n times.

FIND OR FIND/REPLACE AGAIN

The Turbo Editor remembers what the last find or find/replace command was—search text, replacement text, options, and all. You can execute that last find or find/replace command again simply by issuing the find or find/replace again command:

CTRL-L will perform the last find or find/replace command **Again**.

CTRL-L can save you some considerable keystroking. Suppose, for example, you wanted to examine the header line of every procedure in a large (perhaps 1000 line) program with 30 or 40 procedures. The way to do it is to search for the string PROCEDURE with the G, U, and W options in effect. The first invocation of this command will find the first procedure in your program file. To find the next one, simply press CTRL-L. You need not reenter the search text PROCEDURE or the options. Each time you press CTRL-L, the editor will find the next instance of the reserved word PROCEDURE until it runs out of file, or until you issue a new and different find or find/replace command.

22.7 Saving your work

It is *very* important to keep in mind what is happening while you edit text files with the Turbo Editor. *You are editing entirely within memory*. Nothing goes out to disk while you are actually doing the edit. You can work on a file for hours, and one power failure will throw it all away. You must develop the discipline of saving your work every so often.

There is no way to save a file to disk from within the Turbo Editor. You must exit the editor and save it using the Save command from the Turbo main menu. Exiting the Turbo Editor is done with this command:

CTRL-K/D ends the edit and **Exits** to the Main Menu.

This command will bring up the main menu prompt ">" but it will *not* clear the screen. To clear the screen and display the menu itself you must press Return without entering any other command. Then the screen will clear and the familiar menu will be redisplayed.

From the main menu you need only press S. The work file will be saved to disk with this message:

```
Saving A:FOO.PAS
```

To continue editing, you need only press E again, and you will be back into the Turbo Editor. It is a small effort to save hours of work against the unexpected failure of power or machine.

Using the Turbo Pascal Compiler

Compared with the Turbo Editor, with its two-dozen-odd commands, there is very little that needs to be remembered about running the Turbo Pascal Compiler, aside from what you need to know about the Pascal language itself. Once you have a work file loaded into memory, you press C and let 'er rip. In this section we'll look closely at everything you need to know about the compiler, its commands, and the options it recognizes. In addition, we'll discuss some of the Main Menu commands that do not fit comfortably under the category of either editor or compiler.

23.1   What the compiler does

The central purpose of the entire Turbo Pascal environment, of course, is to create Pascal programs. Turbo Pascal compiles your work file to pure native code, which runs without the assistance of an intermediate code interpreter à la UCSD or JRT/Utah Pascal. For most program development you can compile your work file (which already exists in RAM) directly to native code in RAM, a process that happens with such speed as to astonish any programmer who has previously worked only with disk-to-disk filter-type compilers.

Once your program has compiled to RAM, it can be run from the Turbo Pascal environment, and when the program terminates, control passes back to the environment's main menu. It is thus possible to develop programs without any disk access at all—which is both dizzyingly fast and somewhat dangerous. A frantic session of edit/compile/run, edit/compile/run, can load your RAM memory with irreplaceable code existing nowhere else—perhaps not on paper, in your notes, or (at 3 A.M. after 10 hours at the tube) even in your head. Working with Turbo Pascal is undeniably intoxicating, and the tendency to work without ever saving to disk is strong.

Avoid that temptation.

One power glitch, one blown fuse, one little brother tripping over your machine's power cord and yanking it out of the wall will send all your hard work into the mystical bit bucket in the sky. Be wise. Save your program source work file to disk after each modification. And back up your disk after every session.

COMPILING TO DISK

By setting an option in the Options Menu (see Section 23.3), you can make the compiler write your program code to a disk file rather than to RAM. This is considerably slower than direct RAM-to-RAM compilation (though still amazingly fast compared with most other compilers), but it has its advantages.

Certain language features and development practices cannot be used when compiling from RAM to RAM. For example:

You cannot use **Chain** *or* **Execute**. These transfer control completely out of the currently-running program into another program, and since the Turbo Pascal Environment is just another program, it cannot allow control to leave it entirely.

You cannot use **DDT** *or* **DEBUG**. Trying to use DDT or DEBUG on the entire Turbo Pascal Environment while using it to develop a program is a short trip to insanity—it is not always clear whether the environment or your compiled program has control.

Your program may be just too big to compile into RAM. This problem comes up very frequently in Z80 versions of Turbo Pascal. In a 64K Z80 computer, your total free RAM for source *and* object code is about 22K. You needn't be a case-hardened Pascal expert to write programs that require 22K of RAM for object code alone. Once you latch onto an important Turbo Pascal development project, the day will soon come when you have no choice but to compile to disk.

In MS/PC DOS environments, the Turbo Compiler produces only .COM files rather than .EXE files. This limits an object code file to

64K (.COM files may be no larger than 64K) but allows for some-what quicker loading and easier debugging using DEBUG (DEBUG will not load an .EXE file without some sneakiness).

If you have selected compilation to .CHN files (see Section 23.3), the destination disk file will be a special kind of .COM file called a .CHN file, which is like a .COM file in all respects save that it does not contain the Turbo Pascal runtime library. This is one way of saving disk space in large program systems that consist of many independently compiled program files that pass control to one another by chaining via the **Chain** statement.

23.2 Main Menu commands

COMPILATION AND ERROR LOCATION

Assuming that the Pascal source code in your work file has no errors, compilation by the Turbo Pascal Compiler is a remarkably simple thing. The C command from the Main Menu begins com-pilation on the work file, if no main file has been specified, or on the main file, if you have specified a main file. (More on the main file below in connection with the M command.)

While compilation is under way, the compiler displays line num-bers on the screen to give you some flavor for how far along it is (and, not coincidentally, how fast it is going.) If you have selected compilation to a .COM or .CHN file (see Section 23.3), the compiler will also display the name of the disk file to which it is compiling your code:

```
Compiling --> A:ART.COM
        71 lines
```

If the compilation completes without any errors, the compiler will print out a summary of how large your code, data, and heap areas are. It will then display the ">" prompt once more and wait for another Main Menu command.

No matter how good a programmer you become, you will write programs with errors. Turbo Pascal is quite helpful in spotting errors in your programs. When the compiler discovers an error in your source code, it will stop the compilation and print a message like this:

```
Error 1: ';' expected. Press <ESC>
```

When you press Escape, the Turbo Editor will automatically take over, displaying your source code file with the cursor at the location where it noticed the error. This may not necessarily be where the problem exists, but it is always where the compiler first suspects that something is wrong.

For example, if you leave out a **BEGIN** in the middle of the program, the compiler will not necessarily notice that a **BEGIN** is missing until further down in the file, when something else doesn't add up. It may be that it finds, at the bottom of the program, that it has one too many **END**s. There are a fair number of other ways in which a missing **BEGIN** will make itself known to the compiler; which one eventually tips off the compiler will depend on how your program is laid out.

The point of all this is that while the compiler will give you a good hint when it passes the baton to the editor and places the cursor where it noticed a problem, you may have to hunt further to find the real cause of the problem.

RUNNING YOUR COMPILED PROGRAMS FROM MEMORY

If you have enough room to compile your programs directly into memory, the Turbo Environment will allow you to run your program with just one keypress. The R command transfers control to your compiled code.

On all machines, the computer prints the word "Running . . ." and then runs the program. On some machines (notably the IBM PC) the runtime portion of the code (for Turbo Pascal releases 1 and 2 *only*) clears the screen immediately after printing the word "Running . . ." This can be a problem if you take a program compiled on the IBM PC and try to run it on a machine that does not recognize the IBM PC's screen control interrupt 10H. For example, interrupt 10H sends the Zenith Z100 into absolute fits. Even in programs that do *no* screen control at all, that initial PC-compatible screen clear will send the Z100 off the deep end. There is no way to suppress that initial screen clear. *Releases 1 and 2 for the IBM PC are tightly tied to computers that correctly interpret interrupt 10H as PC video control.* This problem does not exist in Turbo Pascal 3.0.

When your program stops running (when the code executes a HALT statement or when execution runs off the bottom end of the program), control will return to the ">" prompt. Of course, if your program does something drastic or sneaky to system resources, the Turbo Pascal Environment may not be able to take control back, and you may have to reboot.

RUNNING PROGRAMS FROM DISK

In many cases you will compile programs to disk files. To run those you will have to exit the Turbo Pascal Environment completely and invoke the program from the operating system prompt, just as you would invoke any other program.

The Q command exits the Turbo Pascal Environment to the operating system prompt. Now, you may have a source file in memory that you have been editing and compiling. If you have not saved a copy to disk, exiting the Turbo Pascal Environment would throw the program away completely. The Turbo Environment is watching out for you, however: It sets a flag whenever you make any changes to your work file, and clears the flag only when you save your work file to disk with the S command. If you try to exit the Turbo Pascal Environment with the flag still set, you will see this message:

```
Workfile A:FOO.PAS not saved. Save (Y/N)?
```

If you press Y here, the Turbo Environment will save your work file to disk just as though you had invoked the S command from the Main Menu. Then (and only then) will it cease execution and hand control back to the operating system.

When you run a program from a disk file, of course, it will not pass control to the Turbo Pascal Environment when it is through running. The Turbo Pascal Environment is not involved in any way when you run a Turbo-compiled .COM or .CMD file from disk.

LOCATING RUNTIME ERRORS

We've already mentioned how the compiler will locate errors in your source code during compilation. Errors also occur while a program is running. These are called runtime errors, and include a subclass of runtime errors called I/O errors.

Runtime errors are errors that come about because a condition has arisen (usually in a data item) that the Turbo Pascal runtime code is unable to handle. Divide-by-zero is one of these. A perfectly valid division expression like 17 DIV X will cause a runtime error if X ever takes on a value of 0. Another and probably more frequent cause of runtime errors is file I/O problems, most notably attempting to open a disk file to read when the file does not exist on disk.

Turbo Pascal has a means of locating a runtime error in your source code that always seems magical the first time you see it work. For example, perhaps you're running a file management program from within the Turbo Pascal Environment. One of the required files is missing, however, because you forgot to create it before running the program. (This is terrible program design, but you'll probably commit this mistake once or twice while you're learning the Pascal ropes.) As soon as you attempt to **Reset** the nonexistent file, the Turbo Pascal Environment will capture the error and display this message:

```
I/O error 01, PC=28BC

Program aborted

Searching
  244 lines

Run-time error position found. Press <ESC>
```

Just after it displayed the word "searching," it had counted up lines of code just as it does when it is compiling. Once the error is found, if you press Escape, the Turbo Editor will take over and show you your source code with the cursor at the position where the error was noticed.

How does this work? It's not so great a trick as you might think at first. In every program there is a "program counter," which is a register that keeps track of which Z80 or 8086 opcode is being executed at any given time. When a runtime error occurs, the Turbo Pascal Environment copies down the value of the program counter at the moment the error is noticed, just before it takes over and displays the error message.

It then begins to compile your program source all over again. The Turbo Pascal compiler is a one-pass compiler, which means it generates machine code opcodes directly from your program source. As it generates the opcodes, it counts them, and after it counts them it throws the opcodes away. (It already has a compiled version of your program in memory and doesn't need another one.) Eventually, the opcode count matches the number of the opcode that was executing when the runtime error occurred. The recompilation stops right there, and the compiler marks the place in the source code where it stopped recompiling. When the Turbo Editor shows you the source code, it places the cursor where the compiler marked the location of the error.

Slick, no?

You'll have to look the runtime or I/O error number up in the back of this book or in your Turbo Pascal Reference Manual to determine the nature of the error. Locating the line of code causing the trouble is easier: You'll find that the marked error location for runtime errors is considerably closer to the true source of the trouble than the marked location for compile time errors.

Locating runtime errors that occur in programs run from disk (that is, without the Turbo Pascal Environment waiting in the background to capture the error and locate it in your source code for you) is a little more difficult. When a runtime error occurs in a Turbo Pascal program that was compiled to disk, you'll see this simple (and not so helpful) message:

```
I/O error 01, PC=2BB4

Program aborted
```

The compiled program does not contain the machinery to search the source code and find the error for you, even if the source code were somewhere close by in memory. What to do? Notice that the error message gives you that important, if cryptic, message PC=2BB4.

The runtime code within your compiled program is smart enough to capture and display the program counter at the time the fatal runtime error occurred. And while it hasn't the machinery to find the error, you have the power to jot the program counter value down on paper, bring up the Turbo Pascal Environment, load the source code from which the errant program was compiled, and put the Environment to work on it.

The Turbo Pascal Environment gives you access to the program recompiler, which finds the errors so handily in programs running under the direct control of the Environment. All you need is the program counter value and the source code from which you compiled the copy of the program that generated the runtime error.

First, load the source code by way of the W command. *Make sure the source code you load is the same as the source code from which you compiled the program.* If the object program did not compile from the source you load, the process will be misleading or meaningless.

You must press O from the Main Menu and enter the Options Menu. (More on the Options Menu in Section 23.3; this is the only part of the Options Menu we'll be discussing at this time.) One of the commands available within the Options Menu is F, Find Runtime Error. When you press F from the Options Menu, you'll get this prompt:

```
        Enter PC:
```

Type in the hexadecimal value that you copied from the screen. The search will begin immediately:

```
    Searching
     86 lines

  Run-time error position found. Press <ESC>
```

and the editor will take over, just like the last time. The recompiler will have marked your source code with the position at which the recompiled program counter matched the program counter where the runtime error occurred. The editor, once again, will place the cursor at the marked position. There's your error!

THE WORK FILE AND THE MAIN FILE

We discussed the work file in connection with creating and editing source programs with the Turbo Editor. *The work file is the file the editor edits.* I make this distinction because there is another file that the editor does *not* edit, and that is the main file. The main file is set with the M command from the Main Menu.

Like the work file, the main file is generally a Pascal source file. The main file is the Turbo Pascal Compiler's first choice. *If a main file has been defined, the compiler will compile it when the C command is given.* If no main file has been defined, the compiler will compile the work file instead.

This may seem peculiar, to edit one file and compile another. The Turbo Pascal Environment was set up this way to make it easy to edit and compile programs that are separated into chunks of source code. In computers with small amounts of memory (largely Z80 machines limited to 64K RAM overall), there is only about 22K of RAM available for both source and object code once the Turbo Pascal Environment is loaded into RAM. Large programs must then be cut up into "include files" (see Section 23.4) that remain on disk until they are called into memory by a special type of command embedded in the main source code file.

The work file/main file division allows you to edit and debug an include file while compiling the main file. If the compiler only compiled the work file, you would have to load the include file from disk, make changes to it, save it out to disk again, load the main file, and compile it by executing the C command. In fact, you can edit the include file, save it to disk, and compile the main file without having to load anything at all.

We'll have more to say about include files when we discuss compiler directives in Section 23.4.

DISPLAYING A DIRECTORY FROM THE MAIN MENU

There is a disadvantage in working within the Turbo Pascal Environment: the facilities of your operating system are not available. You cannot, for example, rename or delete files from the Main Menu. You *can,* however, display a directory listing for any disk device in your system by using the Main Menu D command.

Pressing D brings up this prompt:

```
Dir mask:
```

A "directory mask" is a means of specifying which files in a directory you wish to list. Simply pressing Return will display all files on the currently logged-in disk device. This is the same as entering "*.*". You may enter a disk drive specifier or pathname and list all the files on another disk drive or within a subdirectory:

```
C:

\turbolib\*.*
```

You may also enter file names containing wildcards, using both the * and ? wildcard characters. The asterisk wildcard character stands for an entire file name or file extension, or the part of a file name or file extension from the asterisk character until the end of the file name or file extension. The question mark wildcard stands for one character only.

*.PAS	would list all .PAS files;
PRINT*.PAS	might list files like PRINT01.PAS, PRINT02.PAS, PRINT820.PAS, and so on.
PRINTER.*	would list files like PRINTER.PAS, PRINTER.BAK, and PRINTER.COM.
PRINTER.00?	might list all overlay files (see Chapter 24) for program PRINTER.

CHANGING THE LOGGED DISK DRIVE

Up at the top of the Main Menu is a display of the logged disk drive:

```
Logged drive: A
```

The logged drive is the drive on which the Turbo Pascal Environment will look for all requested files for which a drive is not explicitly specified. In other words, if you specify a work file as C:MYPROG.PAS the Turbo Pascal Environment will look for MYPROG.PAS on the C: drive, no matter what. If you specify a work file as MYPROG.PAS, the Turbo Pascal Environment will look on the drive displayed as the logged drive.

The L command allows you to change the logged drive. Simply press L and then type in a letter from A to P followed by a colon. (Of course, if there is no drive P on your system you ought not type P:.) If you change your mind about logging in a different disk drive or simply need to reset the disk system after changing a disk under CP/M (see below) you simply press return without typing anything else.

For Turbo Pascal versions running under the CP/M operating system, the L command also serves the purpose of "logging in" a disk drive after you have changed disks in one of the drives. Whenever you change a work disk under CP/M you *must* execute the L command even if you do not specify a different drive. This resets the disk system and informs CP/M that a new disk is present in one of the drives. Without taking this step, CP/M will mark the drive with the changed disk as "read only" and will crash the Turbo Pascal Environment with an unrecoverable BDOS error the first time you attempt to write to the changed disk.

CHANGING THE ACTIVE DIRECTORY (PC/MS DOS ONLY)

At the top of the Main Menu for PC/MS DOS is the line

```
Active directory : \
```

This line will *not* appear for CP/M versions of Turbo Pascal. The active directory depends on a feature of PC/MS DOS V2.0 and later: subdirectories. If you have divided your floppy or hard disk into subdirectories, the A command is used to specify which subdirectory the Turbo Pascal Environment will search for a requested file. On my hard disk, for example, I have a subdirectory called **TURBO** within which I do all my programming in Turbo Pascal. There are literally hundreds of files on my hard disk, broadly separated into several categories. Each category has its own major subdirectory, and some of the larger subdirectories have subdirectories within them.

Before I run the Turbo Pascal Environment, I set the current directory with the DOS CD command. Then, after the Main Menu is displayed, the current directory reads:

```
Active directory: \TURBO
```

If you do not use subdirectories, or if you invoke Turbo Pascal from the root directory on a disk, the active directory will be shown as a single backslash "\".

You can change the active directory by pressing A and entering any legal subdirectory path.

EXECUTING AN EXTERNAL PROGRAM FILE (CP/M ONLY)

On the CP/M version of the Main Menu there is a command named eXecute. The X is capitalized because X is the letter by which you invoke the command. (Note that E is already taken for the Turbo Editor.) The eXecute command allows you to execute a program outside of the Turbo Pascal Environment, and return to the Environment when the program is finished running. When you press X, this prompt will appear:

```
Command:
```

You simply type the name of any program you could ordinarily run from the CP/M operating system prompt. The program will run, and when it finishes, the Turbo Pascal Environment will take control again.

23.3   Options Menu

In the previous section we covered all the commands in the Main Menu in detail except one: O, for compiler Options. The O command is actually a gateway to a separate menu of yet more commands for the Turbo Pascal Environment. Pressing O clears the screen and brings up an entirely new menu. In comparison with the Main Menu, the Options Menu is fairly simple:

```
compile -> Memory
           Com-file
           cHn-file

command line Parameters:

Find run-time error  Quit
```

We have already discussed the use of the F command of the Options Menu in connection with compilation and error location. The Options Menu Quit command exits the Options Menu and brings back the Main Menu. It does *not* take you out of the Turbo Pascal Environment entirely!

OBJECT CODE FORMAT

The top portion of the Options Menu is concerned with the way the compiler generates object code. You have three options here: You can generate object directly into memory; create a .COM file (.CMD for CP/M-86), which is a standalone program file that you run from outside the Turbo Pascal Environment; or you can generate a .CHN file, which is similar to a .COM file, save that it lacks the Turbo Pascal runtime library code.

The default is for the compiler to compile its code directly into RAM. Pressing C instructs the compiler to compile to a .COM file on disk. Pressing H instructs the compiler to compile to a .CHN file on disk. Pressing M will instruct the compiler to compile to RAM if you have previously changed the option to C or H.

Using .CHN files is a way of saving disk space. It is possible to pass control from one Turbo Pascal program to another. If you have a large number of .COM files chaining from one to another, you must realize that there is much duplication of standard runtime code among them. All .COM files, for example, contain the code that writes characters and numbers to the system console. (**Write** and **Writeln** are how your program accesses that code.) If only one program file contained that runtime code and the other program files shared it, you could save a considerable amount of disk space.

This is why .CHN files were created. The system works like this: You compile a "main" or "root" program to disk as a .COM file. This file contains the entire Turbo Pascal runtime library. It must be executed first, in order to get the runtime code into memory. It can, however, pass control to .CHN files with the **Chain** statement (see Section 13.10); .CHN files can also pass control to other .CHN files.

.CHN files are smaller than .COM files, and therefore load from disk more quickly. The other advantage in using chaining with .CHN files, then, is that when one passes control to another there is minimal time spent waiting for the programs to load from disk. On a hard disk system the transfer of control seems all but instantaneous.

There are two important disadvantages to splitting large programs into one .COM file and several .CHN files. First, passing variables from one program to another is tricky and tends to create hard-to-locate bugs, which involve one variable overlapping another and destroying data (see Section 13.10).

Second, **Chain** and **Execute** do not alter the amount of memory allocated to code and data by the .COM program that loaded first. This means that if your .COM file is small (a simple master menu, for example) and passes control to a large .CHN file (an accounts payable subsystem, perhaps) your program will crash in attempting to load more program code or data than there was room originally allocated. You must "twiddle" memory allocations via the S and E commands in Z80 systems and the O, D, I, and A in 8086 systems to give as much room to the .COM program as any .CHN program will require. This is harder than it should be, and I consider it a serious failing in the Turbo Pascal Environment's design.

Overlays, on balance, are a much better way to split a large system into manageable chunks. (See Chapter 24 for a full discussion of overlays and how to use them.)

If you select compilation to either .COM or .CHN files, a new set of commands will suddenly appear at the bottom of the Options

Menu. This set of commands is very different for Z80 computers and 8086 computers. We won't describe them in complete detail here; they are used to control the way the Turbo Pascal runtime code arranges program code and data in memory. They default to perfectly useable values, so for all but the most particular (or peculiar) applications you need not bother changing them.

For Z80 versions of the Turbo Pascal Environment, these are the Start address command and the End address command. The S and E commands control where in memory your program will be loaded and run, and how high in memory variables will be stored. Ordinarily, the Turbo Pascal runtime code positions variables as high in memory as it can. If you have something special (interrupt drivers and buffers are a good example; see the **Iterm** program in Section 20.8) you want kept in high memory and not disturbed by Turbo Pascal program data, you have to lower the "ceiling" to make room for your special constructions above the program data area. The E command sets the highest address the runtime code is allowed to use for variables. Anything above that will not be touched by anything in your compiled Turbo Pascal program.

Similarly, the S command sets the "floor" for the *compiled code* portion of your program. The Turbo Pascal runtime library always begins at $100 for Z80 systems, and the S command defaults to the highest address of the runtime library plus one. You can use the S command to allocate a "hole" between the runtime library and the start of your compiled code. This is a good place for the adventurous among you to load external machine code routines at runtime—but you should be warned that it is a difficult business.

The most common use of S and E is to adjust allocation of memory in systems that use **Chain** and **Execute**. Again, I recommend overlays over **Chain** and **Execute** in nearly all cases. If you are content to use overlays, except for very special systems type applications, you should leave the default values for S and E alone.

In 8086 systems, you have four commands here: O, D, I, and A, for Minimum cOde segment size, Minimum Data segment size, MInimum free dynamic memory, and MAximum free dynamic memory. Again, these adjust the way the Turbo Pascal runtime code allocates memory to code, data, and the heap. Unless you need to adjust allocations for **Chain** or **Execute** or to make way for some special structure in memory, the default values will serve you very well.

If you wish to know more about memory allocation in the various Turbo Pascal implementations, read the appendices of the Turbo Pascal Reference Manual carefully.

COMMAND LINE PARAMETERS IN MEMORY MODE

Finally, the Options Menu includes a command that allows you to enter command line parameters. This allows you to test programs that make use of the command line tail (see Section 15.3) without creating a .COM file and leaving the Turbo Pascal Environment entirely to test the program from the operating system command prompt.

When you press P in the Options Menu, this prompt appears beneath the ">" symbol:

```
Parameters:
```

At this point you type whatever would ordinarily be the command line tail after invoking your program at the operating system command prompt. Remember that this is for the tail *only;* you *don't* enter the name of the program itself! In other words, if you wanted to simulate the following command line:

```
A>HEXDUMP MYFILE.PAS PRINT
```

You would type only

```
MYFILE.PAS PRINT
```

and then press Return. Nothing will happen at that point; the Environment merely accepts your parameters and stores them either at CSEG : $80 (PC/MS DOS) or $80 (CP/M-80), where **ParamCount** and **ParamStr** can find them when invoked. The same restrictions on the use of **ParamCount** and **ParamStr** apply when using parameters entered from the Options Menu; you *must* access the parameters *before* opening your first disk file.

Also note that older methods of going directly to CSEG : $80 or to $80 via absolute variables (as outlined in the first edition of this book) will still work, because the Options Menu "pokes" your entered parameters into memory precisely as the operating system would have.

23.4   Compiler directives

In the previous section we looked at a number of commands in the Main Menu and Options Menu that determine how the compiler creates machine code. There are some other controls that direct the compiler's work, but rather than being menu commands, these are commands that you place directly into your source code as you edit it. They are called "compiler directives."

Most of the compiler directives have the advantage of being changeable during the course of program compilation. The most common example is the turning on and off of runtime error trapping. There are times when you will want the compiler to trap serious computational errors, and other times when you will prefer to be notified of them (via **IOResult**, for example) and take action on your own. The $I+/– compiler directive lets you turn off error trapping for a statement or two and then turn it back on again.

In this section we'll summarize the compiler directives recognized by the Turbo Pascal compiler. Those directives followed by "+/–" are toggles, which are either on "+" or off "–". You must pick only one in practice; in other words, a directive like "$I+/–" is not valid in your source code but is used here as a typographical device only to indicate that the $I toggle has two states, specified by plus and minus symbols.

Compiler directives are special-purpose comments. If the first character in a comment is a dollar sign ($) that comment will be interpreted by the compiler as a compiler directive. *There can be no space or other characters between the left comment delimiter (either "(*" or "{") and the dollar sign.*

Several compiler directives may be included in a single comment as a list separated by commas. In this case only the first directive need be preceded by a dollar sign. Here are some valid example compiler directives:

```
{$I-}
{$I A:MOUSELIB.SRC}
{$C-,R-}
(*$B-}
(*$U-,V-,C-*)
```

$B+/-:
I/O MODE
SELECTION

The $B+/- directive determines whether the CON device or the TRM device is mapped onto the standard files **Input** and **Output**. $B+ (the default) assigns CON to **Input** and **Output**. $B- assigns TRM to **Input** and **Output**. Unlike most of the other compiler directives, you are allowed to set $B only once in a program, before the reserved word **PROGRAM**, and cannot set it again.

$C+/-: CTRL-C
& CTRL-S
INTERPRETA-
TION

The runtime code has the ability to interpret CTRL-C and CTRL-S characters specially. The $C+/- toggle turns this ability off and on. When set to $C+ (the default) CTRL-C entered during a **Read** or **Readln** statement will terminate program execution; CTRL-S will toggle output to the screen on and off. If you include a $C- directive in your program file, neither character will be recognized in this fashion. Like $B+/-, this directive may be set only once, before the word **PROGRAM** at the top of your source file.

Using $C- will noticeably speed output to the screen.

$I+/-:
I/O ERROR
TRAPPING

This toggle determines whether I/O errors are trapped or simply reported. With $I+ in force (the default), the Turbo Pascal runtime code traps I/O errors with an error message and a program counter display, and then brings the program to a halt. With $I- in force, trapping is turned off. Errors will still be *reported* by the IOResult function (see Section 18.5), but it will be up to you to test **IOResult** for errors and take appropriate action.

It's generally good practice to turn trapping off only around the single statement that would generate a trappable I/O error, for example, **Reset** or **Rewrite**. Trapping should be left on ($I+) at all other times to capture the unexpected.

$I
‹FILENAME›:
INCLUDE FILE

I think it was a bad idea to have two different forms of the $I directive for two different functions, so take special note that $I ‹filename› has *nothing* to do with $I+/– as described above.

$I ‹filename› allows you to "include" a file during compilation. You'll recall that ordinarily *all* of your program source code must reside in memory to be compiled. Especially in Z80 systems where 64K is all the memory you can have, large source code files quickly outgrow available space.

The $I ‹filename› directive allows you to cut your source code up into chunks. When the compiler encounters the $I ‹filename› directive, it opens the disk file ‹filename› and begins compiling it. The file ‹filename› is not actually read into memory as a whole; the compiler simply reads it line by line, compiles the line to machine code, then throws the line away and reads the next line.

The best way to use $I ‹filename› is to keep the main program in your work file but farm most (or all) of your functions and procedures out to include files. This allows you to build source code libraries of routines grouped together around specific purposes. For example, I have an include file named **MOUSELIB.SRC**, which contains various routines for controlling the Microsoft Mouse. Rather than physically copying **MOUSELIB.SRC** into every source program that uses the mouse, I simply include **MOUSELIB.SRC** into the compilation with $I ‹filename›:

```
{$I C:MOUSELIB.SRC}
```

By setting the work file to your include file and the main file to your main program file, you can develop a routine library without having to change the work file from the library file to the main program source file every time you want to compile and test. (See Section 23.2 under the heading "The work file and the main file.")

Note that include files may *not* include any other files. In other words, you cannot nest include files. Only the main program source file can contain $I ‹filename› directives. The main file can, however, contain any number of $I ‹filename› directives.

$O
‹DRIVESPEC›:
OVERLAY FILE
DRIVE
SPECIFIER

IMPORTANT NOTE: This compiler directive is ONLY available with Turbo Pascal V2.0. Neither V1.0 nor V3.0 support it. For Turbo Pascal V3.0, this function is replaced by the **OvrPath** (PC/MS-DOS) and **OvrDrive** (CP/M) procedures, which will be discussed in Section 24.3.

As we will explain in Section 24.3, overlay files are ordinarily searched for at runtime on the default disk drive. You have the option of placing those overlay files on any valid disk unit at runtime as long as you inform the runtime code at compile time where to look for them.

Note that $O ‹drivespec› does not tell the compiler where to *compile* the overlay files, but only where the files will be located at runtime. $O B will inform the runtime code that the next overlay file to be opened will reside on the B disk drive.

Once given, a $O ‹drivespec› directive remains in force until the next $O ‹drivespec› directive is encountered. This means that if you use $OB (for example) to locate one overlay file to the B drive at runtime, other overlay files opened later during the compile will also be looked for on drive B unless you cancel the effect of the $OB directive. This is done by issuing a $O@ directive. "@" specifies the default disk drive. *Always issue a $O@ directive after the last procedure in an overlay file located to a specific disk drive with a previous $O ‹drivespec› directive.*

$R+/–:
INDEX RANGE
ERROR CHECK

Ordinarily, if you attempt to index an array outside of its legal bounds, no runtime error occurs. If indexing outside the bounds of an array trashes adjacent data items, the resulting bugs will be peculiar and rough to define. You have the option of turning on runtime index range error trapping, so that when an index range error happens, the Turbo Pascal runtime code will trap a runtime error and halt your program. The $R+/– directive turns this error trapping for index range errors on and off. $R+ turns index range error trapping on. $R– (the default) turns index range error trapping off.

Like all of Pascal's safeguards, range checking costs your program a little in terms of execution speed. For ease of debugging, you might turn index range trapping on while you're developing a program. Once you have thoroughly debugged your program, you might wish to recompile it with trapping turned off. Your program will then run a little faster.

**$V+/–:
STRING
VAR-PARAMETER
LENGTH
CHECKING**

All string types are defined to have a specific physical length. String types are defined as **String[20]**, **String[80]** and so on, with the length given in brackets after the identifier **String**. When you pass a string type to a function or procedure by reference (as a **VAR** parameter, in other words), the physical length of the formal parameter and the physical length of the actual parameter are required to be exactly the same. Attempting to plug a larger or smaller actual parameter into the formal parameter will generate a compile time error.

This restriction makes it awkward to write a procedure to handle string types of differing physical sizes. The $V+/– directive allows you to turn this restriction off and on. $V+ (the default) enforces this physical length matching restriction. $V– allows you to pass actual parameters of any length to a given formal parameter.

The consequences of passing an actual parameter *larger* than its formal parameter can be overwriting of adjacent data, very much like array index range errors.

**$U+/–: USER
INTERRUPT**

The $U+/– directive can also be very handy during program development. With $U+ in force, you can halt program execution at any time, even out of those dreaded endless loops, simply by pressing CTRL-C. With $U– in force (the default) CTRL-C will have no effect except during **READ** or **READLN** statements. (See above in connection with the $C+/– directive.)

Turning this user interrupt feature on will slow down your programs considerably—in practice, it's best used as a debugging aid to allow you to break out of endless loops without rebooting.

**$K+/–:
8086 STACK
CHECKING (8086
VERSIONS ONLY)**

This directive is only available in 8086 versions of the compiler. Ordinarily, the runtime code checks to see if space is available on the stack for local variables and value parameters before each call to a function or procedure. If space is not available, a runtime error FF will occur and execution will cease.

With $K+ (the default) in force, the compiler will generate code to make this check. With $K– in effect, that code will not be generated, and the runtime library will simply assume that space is always available on the stack. This will usually be true. However, in recursive applications where heavy use of the stack is expected, it may be a good idea to use $K+.

With $K– in force, a stack collision will almost always crash your system hard, requiring a reboot.

Turbo Pascal overlays

24.1   What an overlay is

No matter how rank a beginner you are, if you are serious about programming in Pascal you will eventually design and attempt to build a program that is too large to compile on your computer. This will happen considerably more quickly in a Z80 environment such as CP/M-80, where the most memory you will ever have is 64K. In an 8086 system, you can have a lot more elbow room, but in time your ambitions will overreach even the larger memory systems offered by 8086 machines.

The only answer is to break your program up into chunks and keep most of it on disk, calling it into memory only as the chunks are needed to actually execute. In Turbo Pascal, this is done using overlays.

An overlay system is a means of compiling a number of subprograms so that they occupy the same space in memory—but not at the same time. Suppose you have a main program and three large subprograms: an accounts payable subsystem, an accounts receivable subsystem, and an inventory manager. Each is a large procedure with local variables and procedures. Taken together, they comprise more code than will load and run on your computer at any one time. But each one alone will load and run comfortably. The solution is to make each of them an overlay procedure.

Your main program can then be quite small; in this case, it might be nothing more than a master menu that chooses between the three major subsystems. When the user chooses accounts payable at the Master Menu, the accounts payable procedure is loaded from disk and run. When the user later returns to the Master Menu and chooses the inventory manager, the inventory manager procedure is loaded from disk into the same memory space where the accounts payable procedure had been running previously.

Since the accounts payable procedure and inventory manager procedure are independent and do not call one another, they need not be in memory at the same time. Taking procedures from disk only as they are required is the essence of an overlaid application.

24.2   Compiling a program with overlays

A number of other language compilers implement overlays in one form or another, including Microsoft Pascal and Pascal/MT+. I have never seen an overlay system quite so easy to use as the one present in Turbo Pascal. Writing an overlaid application in Pascal/MT+, in particular, is a hair-raising experience, in which you must know every detail of the runtime memory map intimately, and manually calculate offsets into a common data area for overlay static variables, to keep them from stomping on one another. It is, in short, more trouble than it is worth.

The Turbo Pascal system of overlays, while somewhat less versatile than that of other compilers, is the essence of simplicity: The reserved word **OVERLAY** is added ahead of the declaration line for a function or a procedure that is to be made into an overlay. When the compiler encounters that procedure, it is compiled to a separate file on disk called an overlay file.

Having an overlay file with only one procedure in it is pointless; the idea is to get two or more procedures into the same overlay file. If the text procedure in the program also has the reserved word **OVERLAY** in front of its declaration line, that procedure will also be compiled into the overlay file. The compiler will continue to compile procedures into the overlay file as long as the procedures it encounters are declared with the **OVERLAY** word. As soon as it encounters a procedure or function *without* the **OVERLAY** word, the compiler closes the overlay file and continues compiling normally.

You can have multiple overlay areas within a single program (see Figure 24.1). The figure shows a program with two overlay areas

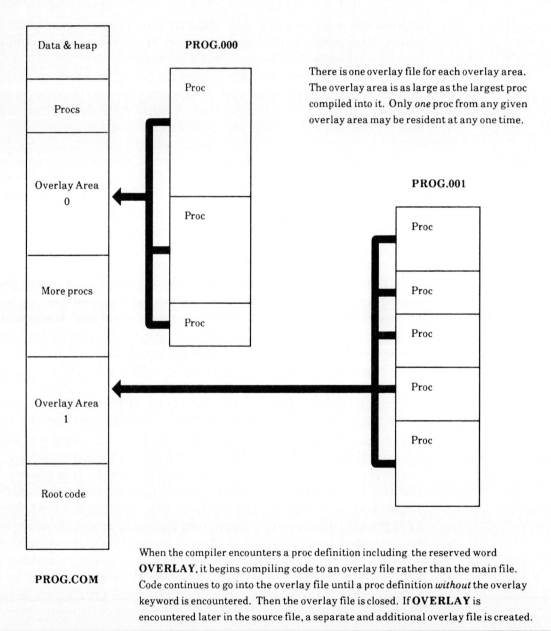

There is one overlay file for each overlay area. The overlay area is as large as the largest proc compiled into it. Only *one* proc from any given overlay area may be resident at any one time.

When the compiler encounters a proc definition including the reserved word **OVERLAY**, it begins compiling code to an overlay file rather than the main file. Code continues to go into the overlay file until a proc definition *without* the overlay keyword is encountered. Then the overlay file is closed. If **OVERLAY** is encountered later in the source file, a separate and additional overlay file is created.

FIGURE 24.1 Overlay areas and files

and two overlay files. In order to force two overlay areas, you must declare one or more procedures *without* the keyword **OVERLAY** between the two groups of procedures declared *with* the keyword **OVERLAY**.

An overlay area is made large enough to hold the largest overlay procedure compiled into its overlay file. When a smaller procedure from the overlay is called, it is loaded into the overlay area, and any difference between the size of the procedure and the size of the overlay area is simply unused space while that particular procedure is resident.

OVERLAY FILE NAMING CONVENTIONS

When an overlay file is opened, it is given the same name as the program file being compiled. Its file extension is a number, however. The first overlay file to be opened while compiling program **FOO.PAS** will be named **FOO.000**. The second overlay file to be opened (if any) will be named **FOO.001**. The third, if any, will be named **FOO.002**, and so on.

A SAMPLE PROGRAM WITH OVERLAYS

The following simple program will give you a taste for how overlays are used with Turbo Pascal. **OvlTest** contains four overlay procedures in two overlay areas. The four overlay procedures do nothing more than announce themselves when they load and begin running, but they represent a valid overlaid program design.

Note that all four overlay procedures would have been compiled into a single overlay file, were it not for the presence of the procedure **GetNumber** between procedures **Two** and **Three**. Since **GetNumber** is *not* declared with the reserved word **OVERLAY** it is compiled to the root file (**OVLTEST.COM**), and it serves to divide the two groups of overlay procedures into the two overlay areas.

```
1        {-----------------------------------------------------------}
2        {                       OverlayTest                         }
3        {                                                           }
4        {          Turbo Pascal overlay system demo program         }
5        {                                                           }
```

(continues)

```
 6           {                              by Jeff Duntemann          }
 7           {                              Turbo Pascal V3.0          }
 8           {                              Last update 2/1/86         }
 9           {                                                         }
10           {                                                         }
11           {                                                         }
12           {----------------------------------------------------------}
13
14           PROGRAM OverlayTest;
15
16           VAR
17             Quit   : Boolean;
18             Number : Integer;
19
20
21           OVERLAY PROCEDURE One;
22
23           BEGIN
24             Writeln('>>Hi!  Overlay procedure #1 at your service!')
25           END;
26
27
28           OVERLAY PROCEDURE Two;
29
30           BEGIN
31             Writeln('>>Number Two here.  May I help you?')
32           END;
33
34
35           FUNCTION GetNumber : Integer;
36
37           VAR
38             I  : Integer;
39             OK : Boolean;
40
41           BEGIN
42             REPEAT
43               GotoXY(43,18);
```

(continues)

```
44              ClrEOL;
45              Read(I);
46              IF (I >= 0) AND (I <= 4) THEN OK := True ELSE
47                BEGIN
48                  GotoXY(1,24);
49                  Writeln('Valid numbers are 0-4 only!');
50                  OK := False;
51                END
52            UNTIL OK;
53            GetNumber := I
54          END;


57      OVERLAY PROCEDURE Three;

59      BEGIN
60        Writeln('>>Numbah Three.  Whaddaya want?')
61      END;


64      OVERLAY PROCEDURE Four;

66      BEGIN
67        Writeln('>>Four''s on line--lay some work on me!')
68      END;


71      BEGIN  { MAIN }
72        CLRSCR;
73        REPEAT
74          GotoXY(1,18);
75          WRITE('>>>Enter a Number from 1-4 or 0 to Quit: ');
76          Number := GetNumber;
77          IF Number = 0 THEN Quit := True ELSE
78            BEGIN
79              Quit := False;
80              GotoXY(1,5); ClrEOL;
81              CASE Number OF
```

(continues)

```
82                    1 : One;
83                    2 : Two;
84                    3 : Three;
85                    4 : Four
86                END
87              END
88          UNTIL Quit;
89        END.
```

(concluded)

When you run **OvlTest**, you will be asked to enter a number from 0 to 4. 0 exits the program. The numbers 1 to 4 invoke overlay procedures **One**, **Two**, **Three**, and **Four**. The first time you invoke a procedure from either overlay area, you will see the disk activate while the procedures are loaded into memory. After the first time the disk will not activate. Why not?

Ordinarily it would, and in a program with larger overlay procedures the disk will always activate each time you invoke an overlay procedure. **OvlTest** is such a small program with such small overlay procedures that the initial disk access for either overlay area brings the entire overlay file into the disk buffer, and from that point on, the procedures are loaded from DOS's disk buffer rather than from the physical disk. This is a fluke caused by the size of **OvlTest**, *not* a special feature of Turbo Pascal!

24.3 Special considerations when using overlays

Overlay procedures may access global variables in the root program, just as though they were ordinary non-overlay procedures. Within overlay procedures, access to variables is subject only to Pascal's ordinary restrictions of scope (see Chapter 3).

Overlays can be used *only* when compiling to disk rather than memory. The reserved word **OVERLAY** will trigger compiler error #77 during a compile to memory. Go into the Options Menu and invoke the C (compile to .COM file) command before compiling a program that contains overlays.

Overlays may themselves have overlays; in other words, overlays may be nested (see Figure 24.2). A large procedure within an overlay

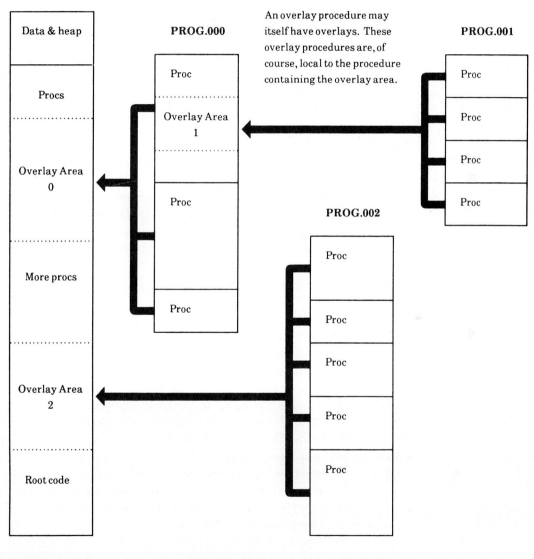

An overlay procedure may itself have overlays. These overlay procedures are, of course, local to the procedure containing the overlay area.

FIGURE 24.2 Nested overlays

file may itself declare overlay procedures. Overlay procedures declared within an overlay procedure are, of course, local to that procedure.

Overlay procedures within the same overlay area may *not* call one another. You must be careful in your design of an overlaid application not to get caught in a spot in which an overlay procedure must call another in the same overlay area. In such a case, you will probably have to move one of the two contending procedures out of the overlay file back into the main line program code.

Generally, you should try to design your overlaid applications with *large* chunks of code put out into overlay files. The previous example of an accounting package is a good one: The entire accounts payable section is set up as a procedure and put out to an overlay area, as is the accounts receivable section and the inventory section. Once you load accounts payable, you'll be using it for some period of time, and the initial delay for loading the accounts payable code from disk will seem unimportant.

What you want to avoid is putting out to disk procedures that are called frequently and used only for short periods of time in any one instance—the **GetString** procedure from Section 15.2 is a good example of such a procedure. If a data entry screen calls **GetString** to fill a data field and then immediately calls another overlay procedure in the same overlay area to verify the validity of the data just entered, and repeats this process 20 times to complete the 20 fields that make up the screen, a tremendous amount of disk thrashing will go on as the program first loads **GetString**, then loads the data validator, then reloads **GetString** and so on. In this case, the entire screen should be a procedure, with **GetString** part of the root program and the validator a local procedure within the screen procedure. Work with overlays for a while and you will get the idea. Design to minimize disk access. A few large overlays are much better than a great many little ones!

Unless you specify otherwise, the runtime code will look for overlay files on the default disk drive. You may place overlay files on any disk drive at runtime, however, as long as you specify at compile time where you intend to put them.

For Turbo Pascal V2.0, this is done with the $O <drivespec> compiler directive (see Section 23.4). To place an overlay file on a given disk drive, specify the drive with $ <drivespec> immediately before the *first* procedure in that overlay file. And don't forget to place the directive $@ immediately after the *last* procedure in that overlay file, to reset the overlay compile destination to the default disk drive, indicated by "@".

For Turbo Pascal V3.0 and later, the $O compiler directive has been replaced by a built-in procedure. This procedure has two names, **OvrPath** for PC/MS DOS environments, and **OvrDrive** for CP/M and CP/M-86.

OvrPath(Pathname : String) specifies a path to the directory where the overlay files reside. Any pathname valid under DOS may be used with **Ovrpath**. The path can include a valid disk drive specifier. Once **OvrPath** is invoked, subsequent calls to overlay procedures will look to that path for their overlay files. **OvrPath** may be called as often as necessary. Once an overlay path has been set with **OvrPath**, it may be reset to the current directory by executing **OvrPath('.')**. The period is an acceptable pathname for the current directory.

OvrDrive(DriveNum : Integer) is used in CP/M environments (both Z80 and 8086), which have a "flat" directory structure and do not employ pathnames. **OvrDrive** specifies which of the system's disk drives contain the overlay files. Drives are specified as numbers, using the following correspondence: Logged drive = 0, A: = 1, B: = 2, C: = 3, and so on.

Starting with Turbo Pascal V3.0, overlaid applications can be run from the Turbo Pascal Environment, without having to generate a .COM file and run from the DOS prompt. This applies to all implementations except CP/M-80. No special commands have to be given; simply compile and run as normal. Realize, of course, that you are still bound by memory restrictions running from the Turbo Pascal Environment, and that an overlaid application that runs as a .COM file will not necessarily run when compiled to memory.

Subprograms existing in overlay files cannot be recursive; that is, they cannot call themselves (see Section 14.3).

One final word about overlays: You can't use the very convenient search for runtime error feature of the Options Menu (see Section 23.3). The problem is that, in a program with overlays, a program counter value specifies only an offset from the beginning of the program code file—and in an overlaid program, two or more pieces of code may run at that location at one time or another. You may know the program counter at which your program failed, but you won't necessarily know which overlay file was loaded at the time of failure, and there is no way to make the editor pinpoint a runtime error location in one particular overlay procedure out of many.

As in many human endeavors, programming in Turbo Pascal gets more difficult as your programs grow more complex. Ideally, test a procedure thoroughly in the main code segment before farming it out into an overlay file.

Turbo-87 Pascal and Turbo-BCD Pascal

Two special versions of Turbo Pascal are available for computers that use the 8086 CPU. Both use a different real number format to provide faster and more accurate numeric results for particular types of programming projects. In this section we'll look at how Turbo-87 Pascal and Turbo-BCD Pascal differ from the standard Turbo Pascal for the 8086.

25.1 Turbo-87 Pascal

There is an empty 40-pin socket beside the 8088 CPU in every IBM PC and XT. This socket accepts Intel's 8087 Numeric Data Processor (NDP) chip, a "coprocessor," since it executes instructions with the cooperation of the 8088 CPU with which it resides essentially in parallel. The 8087 performs real number calculations in hardware, and therefore allows programs that do a lot of real number crunching to execute a great deal more quickly than programs running on the 8088 alone—up to 100 to 500 times more quickly, depending on the type of calculation to be done.

Making use of the 8087 requires that your programs be generated with specific 8087 instructions to call up the 8087 chip and communicate with it. Turbo-87 Pascal was written to provide those special 8087 instructions. Programs compiled under Turbo-87 Pascal will make use of the 8087 for all real number calculations.

From a program syntax standpoint, there is virtually no difference between Turbo Pascal and Turbo-87 Pascal. Any program that compiles correctly under Turbo Pascal for the 8086 will compile correctly under Turbo-87 Pascal. The only differences between the two are the size of the real number format and the available real number precision.

TURBO-87 8087 REAL NUMBERS

The standard Turbo Pascal allots six bytes to each real number variable (see Section 7.5). Turbo-87 allocates eight bytes to each real number variable, giving 8087 reals the awesome range of 10^{-307} to 10^{308}. (The IBM 370, by contrast, can only express a range of real numbers from 10^{-78} to 10^{76}.) In an 8-byte Turbo-87 real number, the high bit of the highest byte (in terms of address) acts as a sign bit. The border between mantissa and exponent does not respect byte boundaries. Do not try to interpret isolated parts of a Turbo-87 floating point real. For more information on the internal workings of 8087 real numbers, see Intel's Numerics Supplement to the *8086 Family Data Book*.

TURBO-87 CAUTIONS

Programs compiled under Turbo-87 Pascal cannot be run on a machine without an 8087. Trying to do so will probably crash your machine. Keep this in mind—if you give an 8087 program you developed to your user group, those without 8087's installed will be reaching for the reset switch.

The major problem with using Turbo-87 Pascal is that real number data written to files cannot be read by programs compiled under standard Turbo Pascal. The real number format is different, and the size of the real number fields in the file will be different. Files that need to be passed between Turbo Pascal programs and Turbo-87 programs will need to be run through some sort of file conversion utility.

Also, don't try to compile programs using Turbo-87 Pascal on a machine without an 8087 installed. The compiler will work normally until it attempts to generate code that modifies a real number variable. Then the compiler will hang. I know of no reason why this should be necessary, but it happens.

Finally, the **SizeOf** procedure will return 6 for standard reals and 8 for 8087 reals. This is one way for a program to determine if it was compiled for 8087 reals:

```
1          {<<<< CompiledFor8087 >>>>}
2
3
4          { Described in section 25.1 -- Last mod 2/1/86   }
5
6          FUNCTION CompiledFor8087 : Boolean;
7
8          VAR
9            R : Real;
10
11         BEGIN
12           IF Sizef(R) = 8 THEN CompiledFor8087 := True
13             ELSE CompiledFor8087 := False
14         END;
```

This is important because most programs that need not interchange real number data with other programs can be compiled interchangeably between standard Turbo Pascal and Turbo-87 Pascal. This means you can't simply **Writeln** a label in the corner of the "hello" screen of an application warning that this application was compiled for the 8087—the same source was used to compile *both* the 8087 and non-8087 object code. Using the above function, the program tests the size of its real numbers, and if it finds an 8-byte real, it can warn the user that if he does not have an 8087 chip installed, the application will crash. A safe exit to the operating system is then made possible by answering a yes/no question. Courtesy to the user is *always* in order!

25.2   Turbo-BCD Pascal

Turbo-BCD Pascal is another variant on standard Turbo Pascal that provides a different format of real numbers called BCD reals. BCD stands for Binary Coded Decimal, which alludes to their representation in memory. BCD reals would be better named (as they sometimes are) "business" or "financial" reals, because their only purpose is to represent decimal currency values with complete precision, literally from 1/100 of a cent through 1 quadrillion dollars.

INTERNAL REPRESENTA-TION OF BCD REALS

BCD reals are represented in 10 bytes. The lowermost byte in memory contains the exponent and sign. The sign bit is the high bit of this byte; a zero bit indicates positive and a one bit indicates that the number is negative. The remaining seven bits contain the exponent, given in binary with an offset of $3F. To evaluate the exponent, remove the sign bit and subtract $3F from the low seven bits. The difference is the exponent: in other words, the power of 10 by which the mantissa is multiplied.

For an example, consider the dollar value $154,502,677.95. A hex dump of this value, stored into a BCD real, is as follows:

```
48 00 00 00 50 79 67 02 45 15
```

The leftmost byte contains the exponent and sign; the rest is mantissa. Also remember that while the exponent byte is a binary quantity and displayed in hexadecimal, the values stored in the mantissa are in *decimal,* not hex!

Subtract $3F from $48; the difference is $09. This is your exponent. If you were to express the above value in scientific notation, it would be 0.15450267795 E 09. The decimal point falls nine places to the right of the most significant digit.

If the exponent of a BCD real is zero, the entire number is taken to be zero.

Interpreting the mantissa is a little trickier. The most significant digit is stored in the rightmost (highest in memory) byte, but the digits are always normalized; in other words, there are no leading zeroes—the most significant digit of the mantissa is *always* in the high byte, whether that digit represents the ones column or the millions column of the value of the real number. All order-of-magnitude information is stored in the exponent; the mantissa is significant digits *only*.

Within each byte are stored two digits, with the more significant digit in the high four bits of the byte. However, since the digits are normalized, a value of 4 will be coded as 40 (with the four in the higher half of the byte), because leading zeroes are not coded.

This will make more sense after a few examples:

```
40 00 00 00 00 00 00 00 00 10      BCD real for 1

41 00 00 00 00 00 00 00 00 10              10

41 00 00 00 00 00 00 00 00 40              40

42 00 00 00 00 00 00 00 00 10             100

42 00 00 00 00 00 00 00 40 10             104

42 00 00 00 00 00 00 00 90 11             119

43 00 00 00 00 00 00 00 99 99            9999
```

Note that the mantissas for 1, 10, and 100 are identical.

Knowing the internal format of BCD reals might be important for an additional reason: The standard functions **Sin**, **Cos**, **ArcTan**, **Ln**, **Exp**, and **Sqrt** are not available in Turbo-BCD. If you require such functions you will have to write them yourself, perhaps in assembly language.

Also, the predeclared constant **Pi** is not available in Turbo-BCD.

THE FORM FUNCTION

Turbo-BCD Pascal provides a new function, **Form**, not available in any other version of Turbo Pascal. **Form** is a field formatting function that allows you to display and print BCD reals, integers, and strings in formats specified by a formatting string. It is conceptually similar to the venerable **PRINT USING** statement in BASIC. It is predeclared this way:

```
FUNCTION Form(<format string>,<v>,<v>,<v>,...<v>) : String;
```

Each **<v>** is a real, integer, or string variable. The length of the string returned is the same length as **<format string>**.

Within the format string are one or more "fields," that is, sequences of characters that specify how a given variable is to be formatted into the returned string value. Fields are either string or numeric.

A string field is composed of sequences of "@" and "#" characters. If the field is composed entirely of "#" characters, the variable will be left justified within the field. If the field contains even one "@" character in any position, however, the string will be returned right justified within the field. If the string variable is longer than the field, only as many characters from the variable as there are characters in the field will be returned. This truncation always begins on the left, regardless of whether the field is left or right justified.

For example:

```
Form('############','Lost!'); returns 'Lost!       ' length 12
Form('@@@@@@@@@@@@','Lost!'); returns '       Lost!' length 12
Form('@###########','Lost!'); returns '       Lost!' length 12
Form('#####','Leftward');     returns 'Leftw'        length 5
Form('@@@@@','Leftward');     returns 'Leftw'        length 5
```

Keep in mind that although we're using string literals here for the sake of keeping the example readable, string variables can be used as well.

Numeric formatting offers you more options. A numeric field is made of one or more of the following characters: "#", "@", "$", ",", ".", "+", "-", and "*". If any other character is present in the field, the compiler will treat that as the end of the field, and no further formatting characters within that field will be recognized.

# indicates a digit position. If a numeric field is composed of "#" and no other characters, the value is right-justified in the field, and unused positions are blank-filled to the left. If the value is negative, a floating minus sign will be placed to the immediate left of the value and the dollar sign if one has been specified with the "$" character:

```
Form('##########',21171);   returns '     21171'
Form('##########',-563);    returns '      -563'
Form('$######.##',-99.95);  returns '   -$99.95'
```

@ indicates a digit position and enables zero-fill. If a "@" character appears at any point in a field, unused positions to the left of the numeric value are zero-filled. *No minus sign will be displayed for negative quantities unless a sign position specifier ("+" or "–") is included in the field!*

```
Form('@@@@@@@',2150);  returns '0002150'
Form('@######',599);   returns '0000599'
Form('@######',-45);   returns '0000045'
Form('-@#####',-45);   returns '-000045'
```

$ indicates a digit position and enables display of a floating dollar symbol. The "$" character need appear in the field only once to enable dollar symbol display, and it may appear anywhere in the field. The dollar symbol will float to the immediate left of the numeric value, but to the right of any floating minus sign:

```
Form('$########',124);   returns '    $124'
Form('########$',-124);  returns '-$124'
```

* indicates a digit position and enables asterisk-fill of unused positions. If "*" appears in any position in the field, unused positions to the left of the numeric value will be asterisk-filled. As with "@", no sign will be displayed for negative quantities unless a sign position specifier ("+" or "–") is included in the field.

```
Form('*#######$.##',2125.77);   returns '***$2125.77'
Form('$*******.##',-2125.77);   returns '***$2125.77'
```

+ and – are sign position specifiers. A "+" character in a field will display the sign of the numeric value, either positive ("+") or negative ("–"), at that position. A "–" in the field will display a "–" sign at that position if the numeric value is negative. If the numeric value is positive, no sign will be displayed, and the position will be treated as an unused position and blank-filled, zero-filled, or asterisk-filled as the rest of the field requires:

```
Form('+######$.##',2125.77);     returns '+  $2125.77'
Form('-######$.##',2125.77);     returns '   $2125.77'
Form('-*#####$.##',2125.77);     returns '***$2125.77'
Form('-*#####$.##',-2125.77);    returns '-**$2125.77'
Form('*######$.##+',2125.77);    returns '***$2125.77+'
```

. and , are decimal and comma position specifiers. Note that *both* commas and decimals may act as either numeric decimals or numeric separators. Several of the examples above have used the decimal specifier "." to indicate where in the field the decimal point is to be placed. Commas can also act as decimals, as they are used (infrequently) in some cultures. If there is no "." or "," in a field, a numeric value with a decimal part will be truncated to whole digits when displayed. If more than one comma or period exists in a field, the rightmost comma or period indicates the position of the decimal in the numeric value:

```
Form('*#####$,##',150.69);          returns '****$150,69'
Form('*###,###,##$.##',6545676.42); returns '**$6,545,676.42'
```

The **Form** function can be used anywhere a string value can be used.

Conclusion

There is a great deal more to be said about Turbo Pascal than can fit between the covers of a single paperback book. In *Complete Turbo Pascal* I have tried to teach you Pascal by way of the Turbo Pascal product. The examples have all been fairly plain and simple, because the idea has been to teach you a language, not necessarily to provide you with subtle and sophisticated programming tools.

However, as my two years of observing the Turbo Pascal mini-industry have shown, Turbo Pascal is capable of developing world class applications. Taking it to the cutting edge almost always involves going outside the "city limits" of Pascal proper into the myriad extensions Borland International has added to Niklaus Wirth's original language. Many of these extensions are extremely machine-specific, and for this reason you won't find instructions on using them in any traditional Pascal text. I have, in fact, barely touched on them here.

As companion volumes to *Complete Turbo Pascal,* I am writing a series of books that I call the Turbo Pascal Solutions Series. The idea is to present solutions to specific programming problems by way of Turbo Pascal. The Solutions Series will assume that you already know Turbo Pascal fairly well. What it will provide are algorithms and "toolkit" routines for solving common (and uncommon!) programming problems.

The first volume in the Turbo Pascal Solutions series, *Turbo Pascal Solutions,* will appear early in 1987. The second volume, *Turbo Pascal Solutions: Graphics* will include assembly language source for fast graphics manipulation and plenty of down-and-dirty (and unapologetically non-portable) graphics and animation tricks. With any luck you'll see it in mid-1987. Watch for them.

In the meantime, get down and hack Turbo!

APPENDICES

Appendix A: Third-party vendor products for Turbo Pascal

As might be suspected for any software product that sells 300,000 copies, a growing third-party industry has arisen around Borland International's Turbo Pascal. Below I will describe some of the products of which I was aware in early 1986. Obviously, by the time you read this there will be many more. Do keep your eyes open!

The Turbo Users Group (TUG) TUG LINES

Business office:

P.O. Box 1510
Poulsbo WA 98370

Editorial office:

P.O. Box 548
Silverdale WA 98383

Every major software package has its user group, and Turbo is no exception. TUG publishes a lively, fully typeset newsletter/magazine called TUG LINES, which has been an indispensable source of clever code, bug reports, slick tricks, and Borland gossip. The original cost has been $25 for six issues, but that may well change as the membership explodes in time with sales of the compiler. Do write to the editors (enclose an SASE) and ask for current information. But by all means *join it!*

PC DocuMate for Turbo Pascal

Systems Management Associates
3700 Computer Drive
Raleigh NC 27609
1-800-762-7874
(919) 787-7703

Available from the mfr. for $14.95 + $1.50 shipping.

This is a keyboard template for the IBM PC standard keyboard. It will *not* fit the Keytronics 5151B nor any keyboard without the "pencil ledge." It summarizes the invocation syntax for virtually all Turbo Pascal built-ins, gives tables for color codes, and so on. Saves an *enormous* amount of thumbing through the manual, especially while you're just getting to know Turbo Pascal. The template is a stiff rugged plastic, nicely typeset and easy to read. I have had one since it was released and recommend it *very* highly.

MetaWindow Graphics Library V3.0

Metagraphics
444 Castro Street, Suite 400
Mountain View CA 94041
(415) 964-1334

Available from the mfr. for $50.00. Shipping extra, contact them for details.

This is a "toolkit" of graphics functions and procedures of awesome speed and power. It was originally written for linkable languages like Microsoft Pascal and various C compilers, but was modified to be callable as an external from Turbo Pascal. The full library for all compilers is $150, but the Turbo-only portion is $50. Describing it here is difficult. It gives you windowing abilities, mouse tracking, line draw, point plot, graphics GET/PUT, curves and polygons, and lots more. MetaWindow was written in hand-optimized assembly code and is *very* fast. I have been using it extensively in developing my draw program IKONYX for about six months. It is virtually bug free, and the manufacturer has been very responsive to questions. If you intend to do any graphics work at all in Turbo Pascal, you must have this product.

Turbo Asynch

Blaise Computing, Inc.
2034 Blake Street
Berkeley CA 94704
(415) 540-5441

$99.95 from the manufacturer.

This library provides RS232C asynch communications support for Turbo Pascal. The software itself, like MetaWindow, is an exit-remain resident program that loads above DOS and is called by your compiled Turbo program. Turbo Asynch is interrupt driven and supports communications speeds of up to 9600 baud without character loss. It provides character-oriented communications and XON/XOFF file transmission protocol. I have not worked with it extensively (it is very new at this writing), but everything it claims to do, it does. I was only disappointed that it did not support XMODEM file transfer, but that may be added by the time you read this.

Turbolink
Turbolink Tools

Pathfinder Software Inc.
P.O. Box 43
Littleton CO 80160
800-835-2246 X123

$99.95 for Turbolink; $24.95 for Turbolink Tools; $5 shipping for each product.

This is a bizarre and diabolically clever little product that belongs in every Turbo hacker's library. It allows you to create up to nine Turbo programs that are up to 64K in size and link them together so that they run as though they were a single program. It also allows you to link programs created by Turbo, Compiled BASIC, or interpreted BASIC/BASICA. It defines ways of passing information between the various linked modules. Turbolink uses interrupt 18H. The rather arcane calling conventions take a little getting used to, but there is no other means I know of to do this.

Turbolink Tools contains a pair of utilities that I have not tried; however, they look good. Turbolink Adjustor alters the Turbolink interrupt (normally 18H) to whatever interrupt you choose. Turbo Inline Generator creates a Turbo Pascal–compatible INLINE statement from any DOS .COM file.

Turbo Pal

Quicksilver Software
P.O. Box 880887
San Diego CA 92108

$19.95

This is a software "blue card" for Turbo Pascal. Like a keyboard template, it exists more to jog your memory than to act as any sort of complete reference to the language. It is a memory-resident utility occupying 36K of RAM and using CTRL-F6 as its hot key. There is no facility for changing this, although I have suggested to the author that he ought to at least give the address of a patch-point for a different key combination.

When you press CTRL-F6, a screenful of keywords and brief explanations appears. You can use the arrow keys to bounce down through the collection, or you can enter the keyword you wish to check. It's simpler than that, actually—the software watches every keypress, and after two or three you're probably just where you want to be. In other words, if you're trying to reference the keyword **Circle**, you type a "C" and the cursor is moved *immediately* to **CASE**; type the "i" and the cursor moves immediately to **Circle**. Neat.

Not copy protected, and the author is working on a whole series of similar reference "cards" for other popular languages and products, including an "empty" card with instructions on how to fill it yourself to act as a reference to an unsupported product or one you have written yourself. Well worth $20.

Appendix B: Compile-time error messages

01: ';' expected. That old devil semicolon is missing. See Section 13.8
02: ':' expected.
03: ',' expected.
04: '(' expected.
05: ')' expected.
06: '=' expected.
07: ':=' expected.
08: '[' expected.
09: ']' expected.
10: '.' expected.
11: '..' expected.
12: BEGIN expected.
13: DO expected.
14: END expected.
15: OF expected.
16: PROCEDURE or FUNCTION expected.
17: THEN expected.
18: TO or DOWNTO expected.
20: Boolean expression expected.
21: File variable expected.
22: Integer constant expected.

23:   Integer expression expected.

24:   Integer variable expected.

25:   Integer or real constant expected.

26:   Integer or real expression expected.

27:   Integer or real variable expected.

28:   Pointer variable expected.

29:   Record variable expected.

30:   Simple type expected. This excludes reals, sets, records, arrays, files.

31:   Simple expression expected.

32:   String constant expected.

33:   String expression expected.

34:   String variable expected.

35:   Text file expected.

36:   Type identifier expected.

37:   Untyped file expected.

40:   Undefined label.

41:   Unknown identifier or syntax error.

42:   Undefined pointer type in preceding type definitions.

43:   Duplicate identifier or label.

44:   Type mismatch.

45:   Constant out of range.

46:   Constant and CASE selector type do not match.

47:   Operand type(s) does not match operator.

48:   Invalid result type. Functions may return only scalars, strings, and pointers. Records, files, sets, etc. are invalid.

49:   Invalid string length. Strings may not be longer than 255 characters.

50:   String constant length does not match type.

51:   Invalid subrange base type.

52:   Lower bound > upper bound.

53:   Reserved word. This results from any attempt to use a reserved word as though it were an identifier.

54:   Illegal assignment.

55:   String constant exceeds line. The open and close quote characters must be on the same line for string constant definition. For longer string constants you must concatenate two or more shorter strings.

56:   Error in integer constant.

57:   Error in real constant.

58: Illegal character in identifier.

60: Constants are not allowed here.

61: Files and pointers are not allowed here.

62: Structured variables are not allowed here.

63: Textfiles are not allowed here.

64: Textfiles and untyped files are not allowed here.

65: Untyped files are not allowed here.

66: I/O are not allowed here. This will come up if you try to write an enumerated type to a text file or to the screen.

67: Files must be VAR parameters.

68: File components may not be files. You cannot define a "file of files."

69: Invalid ordering of fields.

70: Set base type out of range.

71: Invalid GOTO. A GOTO cannot take you into a FOR loop.

72: Label not within current block. Turbo Pascal, unlike many Pascals, does not allow you to GOTO a label outside the current block.

73: Undeclared FORWARD procedure(s).

74: INLINE error.

75: Illegal use of ABSOLUTE.

76: Overlays cannot be forwarded. You cannot declare an overlay procedure as FORWARD.

77: Overlays not allowed in direct mode. This is no longer strictly true with Turbo 3.0.

90: File not found. An include file could not be located.

91: Unexpected end of source. Count your BEGINS and your ENDS. This error typically happens when there are more BEGINS than ENDS and the compiler thinks it is still in the middle of a compound statement when the terminating "END." appears.

92: Unable to create overlay file. Full or write-protected media on the overlay output path.

97: Too many nested WITHs. CP/M-80 only

98: Memory overflow. Too many declared variables for available memory.

99: Compiler overflow. You have run out of memory to hold code. Either break your program up into include files or overlays.

Appendix C: Runtime error messages

1:   Floating point real overflow. An intermediate calculation generated a value that cannot be represented in Turbo Pascal's real number format.

2:   Divide by zero attempted.

3:   Negative argument passed to SQRT built-in function.

4:   Zero or negative argument passed to LN built-in function.

10:   One of two problems: (1) You attempted to convert a string longer than one character to a character, or (2) a string concatenation yielded a string longer than 255 characters.

11:   An index value passed to COPY, DELETE, or INSERT was outside the range 1-255.

90:   An index expression for an array subscript was out of the legal range for that array.

91:   The value assigned to a subrange or scalar variable was out of legal range.

92:   The real value passed to ROUND or TRUNC was outside the range -32767 to 32768.

F0:   The requested overlay file was not found.

FF: The heap collided with the stack. There was insufficient free memory when one or the other grew. Often happens in programs making heavy use of both recursion and the heap.

Appendix D: I/O error messages

1: The file name passed to RESET, ERASE, EXECUTE, CHAIN, or RENAME does not exist.

2: File not open for input. You are trying to read from a file that was not previously opened via REWRITE or RESET; or, you may be trying to read from a file opened by RE-WRITE, or you are trying to read from device file LST, which is defined as output-only.

3: File not open for output. You are trying to write to a file that had not previously been opened for I/O with a RESET or REWRITE. Or, you are trying to write to a *text* file that was opened with RESET. Or, you are trying to write to device file KBD, which is defined as input-only.

4: You are trying to perform block file I/O on a file that has not yet been opened via RESET or REWRITE.

10: You read a string of invalid numeric format from a text file into a numeric variable.

20: You are trying to ERASE, RENAME, EXECUTE, or CHAIN to a file assigned to a logical device, for which these operations are invalid.

21: You are trying to use EXECUTE or CHAIN while running a program compiled into memory. Compile to a .COM or .CHN file and run your program again.

22: You are trying to assign a file name to a standard file like INPUT, OUTPUT, CON, TRM, KBD, LST, AUX, or USR.

90: The record length of a binary file does not match the length of the file variable you are assigning to it.

91: You are attempting to seek past physical end-of-file.

99: Unexpected EOF. A text file physically ended before a CTRL-Z marker character was encountered. Or, you attempted to sequentially read beyond EOF on a binary file. Or, READ or BLOCKREAD is unable to read the next sector of the file due to bad data on disks or a bad record count. Suspect all other possibilities first.

F0: Disk found to be full while WRITEing, CLOSEing or FLUSHing a file to disk.

F1: You are attempting to create a new file and there are no available directory entries left. Delete some unused files. You may only have 64 files in any one CP/M-80 disk directory.

F2: (Z80) You attempted to sequentially write record 65536 (or later) to a binary file. A Turbo Pascal binary file may have 65535 records max.

F3: Too many open files. (PC/MS DOS only) Expand the FILES= specifier in your CONFIG.SYS file. DOS cannot "handle" more than sixteen open files at once—if you need more than that, you're out of luck. Also, make sure that you close every file once you're through with it—once DOS allocates a file handle to a file, the handle is not released until the file is explicitly closed.

FF: File no longer on unit. You pulled a disk out of a drive while a file on that disk was open. This error occurs when you attempt to close or flush the file and the runtime cannot find the file on the unit where it used to exist.

Glossary

Jargon and technical terms that may puzzle a beginner

8087   Also known as "math coprocessor." An integrated circuit that plugs into an accessory socket in the IBM PC and certain other 8086/8088-based computers. It "takes over" when the CPU is called upon to perform certain floating point number functions including multiplication, division, and transcendental functions. It can increase processing speed for these functions by 10 to 200 times.

Absolute variable   A variable that is defined to exist at a specific address in RAM memory. Assigning a value to that variable places that value at a specific place in memory. This allows you easy accesss to "memory mapped" computer resources like screen buffers, which exist at certain memory addresses. Normally the programmer does not know where a given variable will exist in memory. In Turbo Pascal, variables are made absolute with the ABSOLUTE keyword.

Array   A line of identical data items that are given a single identifier and referenced individually by a number called an index. INTARRAY : ARRAY[0..9] OF INTEGER means that a line of ten integers numbered 0 through 9 has been allocated in memory and given the name INTARRAY. To reference the sixth integer in the array you would reference INTARRAY[5]. One individual data item in an array is called an element.

ASCII   The American Standard Code for Information Interchange. A code that represents letters, numbers, common symbols, and certain control functions like carriage return, line feed, and tab as 7-bit binary numbers. The codes range from 0 to 127.

Assembler   A program that converts marginally human-readable mnemonic keywords like MOV A,M into pure binary machine instructions. "Written in assembler" means written using assembler keywords. Code written in assembler is usually faster and more compact than code written in higher-level languages like Pascal.

Boolean   A data type contained in a single byte. It has two possible values: TRUE and FALSE. **Boolean** values contained in **boolean** variables or resulting from **boolean** expressions are used in programs to decide which of two different actions to take: one if the value is TRUE, and the other if the value is FALSE.

Bounds checking   The checking of array indices to determine if the index goes beyond the defined limits of the array. For example, to specify CHAR_ARRAY[275] of an array defined as ARRAY [0..128] OF CHAR would cause the bounds checking code (if enabled) to trigger a runtime bounds error.

Bug   A problem with a program once it has compiled correctly. A problem that is flagged by the compiler during compilation is called an **error**.

Case label   A constant (or list of constants, separated by commas) that labels one of several component statements in a CASE/OF statement. If the **case selector** expression evaluates to a value equal to a **case label**, the statement associated with the **case label** is executed:

```
CASE Chr(Keypress) OF
'A'         : <statement1>;
'Q'         : <statement2>;
'X','Y','Z' : <statement3>;
End;
```

In this example 'A', 'Q', and 'X','Y','Z' are all **case labels**.

Case selector   An expression yielding a value that is used to select one statement of several in a CASE/OF statement. If a **case label** is found to be equal to the value of the **case selector**, the statement associated with the **case label** will be executed. In the example given under **case label**, Chr(Keypress) is the **case selector**.

Chaining   The passing of control from one program to another program, which is stored on disk. The code that supports chaining must first load the program from disk into memory and then pass control to it. The Chain and Execute procedures accomplish this function in Turbo Pascal.

Closed interval   A range of some ordinal data type written as ‹start value›..‹end value›, usually used within a **set constructor** to specify a value included in a set. A **closed interval** includes the start value, end value, and all values falling between the two. These are all **closed intervals:** 'A'..'R', 17..44, RED..YELLOW

Comment delimiter   One of a pair of special symbols that enclose comments about the computer program of which they are a part. Anything within a pair of **comment delimiters** is ignored by the compiler. Turbo Pascal recognizes two styles of **comment delimiters:** (* *) and { }

Compiland   A distinct input to a **compiler** program. A compiland is a compilable source program.

Compiler   A program that takes as input a text file of keywords arranged according to some particular computer language's rules of syntax and writes as output a file containing some kind of machine-readable code. Turbo Pascal is a "native code" compiler in that its output file is pure machine code. The UCSD Pascal compiler outputs "pseudo-code," which is in turn interpreted by an interpreter program custom-written for a particular machine. Since only the interpreter program is machine-specific (and the pseudo-code is always the same), the same program compiled under UCSD Pascal can be run on many different machines. The price to be paid is mainly one of speed. P-Code is always slower than pure machine code.

Compiler directive   An instruction to the compiler that is embedded within the source code. This instruction may turn runtime error checking on and off, specify an include file, or some other task.

Console   A two-way I/O device that includes some sort of character input (usually the keyboard) and some sort of character output (usually a CRT screen). The console is the primary means of communicating with your computer.

Constant   An unchanging data value that is assigned a descriptive name at compile-time:

```
PI = 3.14159
```

A **constant**, once defined, cannot be changed as a variable can. In the example above, the compiler would substitute the literal value 3.14159 each time it encountered the constant PI. Thus, there is no distinct location in the data area named "PI" as there would be if "PI" were a variable.

Control variable   In a FOR loop, the variable that contains the ascending or descending count. It cannot be a formal variable, and it must be local to the block in which it is used. **I** is used below as a **control variable**:

```
FOR I := 100 DOWNTO 1 DO Sum := Sum + FactorArray[I];
```

Crash   A program or hardware failure that causes your computer to become completely unresponsive. It will ignore keyboard input until manually reset or powered off and then powered on again. A "head crash" on a hard disk means that the read/write head has come into contact with the disk platter itself, usually with disastrous results. Aerodynamic "flying" heads and other new technology have made this less frequent and less damaging.

Debugger   A special program that provides the ability to run another program in a special environment that allows starting and stopping the program at will at any point during execution. While the program is stopped, the programmer may inspect the values contained in program variables and perform other tests to determine what the program is doing while it is running.

Disassembler   A program that accepts as input a compiled program code file and creates from it a human-readable assembly code program listing. Sadly, disassemblers do not produce comments alongside the generated assembly language **mnemonics**.

Dynamic variables   Variables that are created and destroyed as needed by the program at runtime via the NEW(<pointer>) and DISPOSE(<pointer>) functions. **Dynamic variables** are given memory space out of a special region called the **heap**. Dynamic record variables containing pointers to other dynamic record variables may form a **linked list**, which is a convenient way of ordering and searching a list whose size is not known at compiletime.

Enumerated type   A programmer-defined ordinal data type consisting of a number of named constants:

```
Spectrum = (RED,ORANGE,YELLOW,GREEN,BLUE,INDIGO,VIOLET)
```

A variable of type Spectrum can have as a value any of the seven constants included in the type Spectrum:

```
VAR
    Color : Spectrum;

    Color := Orange;
```

An **enumerated type** can act as an array **index**, a set base type, or a **control variable** in a FOR loop.

Error   A problem with a program that is discovered during compilation, usually by the compiler. A problem with a program that is discovered after the program has been compiled correctly is called a **bug**.

Exception checking   Checking for errors (exceptions) that occur when a program is running. Such errors would include indexing an **array** beyond its bounds, dividing by zero, numeric overflow, and so on.

External   Existing outside a given separately-compiled program. In Turbo Pascal, subprograms (functions and procedures) may be declared as external. These subprograms are assembled separately with an assembler program (like Microsoft's MASM), and are loaded by the compiler into a Turbo Pascal program during compilation.

Field   Any of the several data items that are part of a larger data structure called a **record**. See **record**.

Global   Accessible from the entire program. As opposed to **local**, which means "private" to a function or procedure within that program.

Heap   An area of memory set aside to contain **dynamic variables**. Also called "heapspace" or "heapstore."

Hex   An abbreviated synonym for "hexadecimal." A hex number is a number expressed in base 16. In base 16, there are 16 digits. The digits that correspond to decimal numbers 10 through 15 are represented by letters: A,B,C,D,E,F. Each position in hex notation holds a value sixteen times the value of the position to its right. Hex 50 is equivalent to decimal 80, because $5 \times 16 = 8 \times 10$. Hex F6 is equivalent to decimal 246, because $(F \times 16) + 6 = (2 \times 100) + (4 \times 10) + 6$. A number preceded by a dollar sign ($) in Turbo Pascal is interpreted as being in hex notation.

Index   A number that is used to reference an individual array element within an array. (See **array**.) In the array reference INTARRAY [5], the 5 is the index of a particular element in the array.

Interrupt   A provision for stopping normal execution of a program, "saving" the condition of the computer at the moment of interruption, and then performing some unrelated (and usually brief) task on the computer. When that task is done, the original task is resumed. Interrupts are initiated by hardware signals only on the 8080/Z80; for the 8086/8088 they may also be originated by the software. Interrupt service procedures may be written in Turbo Pascal to perform tasks while the computer is in an interrupted state.

I/O   Shorthand for "Input/Output." **I/O** is the collective term for the channels through which a computer communicates with the outside world. These channels include disk drives, keyboards, printers, CRT screens, plotters, mice, and so on.

Linked list   A way of allocating data records in memory such that a pointer contained in the first record points to the second record, which contains a pointer that points to the third record, and so on. A **linked list** has the advantage of being as large or as small as needed, as opposed to an **array**, which is a fixed size set at compiletime.

Literal   A data value stated in the **source code** without being given a descriptive name and made a **constant**. 'A', 723, FALSE, 'Fungi from Yuggoth', and ['Y','y'] are all **literals**.

Local variable   A variable declared within a procedure or function, rather than in the variable declaration part of the program itself. A local variable may not be read or written to from outside the procedure or function in which it was declared.

Mnemonic   A tool for remembering assembly-language opcodes. Since binary or hex numbers are hard to remember, short acronyms stand for binary opcodes in assembly code work: NOP (short for "No-Op") stands for hex 00 in 8080 assembly language.

Null statement   Anywhere a statement may be placed in Pascal, it is legal to leave out a statement completely. This lack of a statement is called the **null statement**. It may act to reserve a position for a statement that may be written someday, or it may simply hold a place in a conditional statement for a logical condition that requires no work to be done:

```
IF NameOK THEN ELSE DisplayError
```

Between the THEN and ELSE keywords is a **null statement**. It is good practice to place the comment **{ Null }** anywhere you leave a **null statement** to make your intentions clear to the reader. Although it is "invisible," you must follow the **null**

statement with a semicolon in places where a nonnull statement would require a semicolon:

```
CASE ErrorCode OF
   0 : { Null };           { Everything's OK! }
   1 : SoundAlarm;      { We're about to crash... }
   2 : PowerDown;       { Hopeless; power down... }
```

Keep in mind that the comment { Null } is *not* the **null statement**!

Object code   A file of machine-readable codes that is the output of a **compiler** program. The purpose of a **compiler** is to translate **source code** into **object code**.

Ordinal Type   A type that has 255 or fewer possible values that exist in a definite order. For example, CHAR is an ordinal type because it has 255 different values that are ordered: A,B,C and so on. BYTE and BOOLEAN are also ordinal types. INTEGER is not; there are too many integers. Sets, arrays, and records are not, because they have no well-defined order. *Enumerated types* are always ordinal types.

Overlay   A code file that is stored on disk until needed, at which time the **overlay manager** loads the overlay onto disk and allows other parts of the program to use the code and variables contained within that overlay. Since many overlays may occupy the same address range in memory, a very large program may exist in relatively little memory since large parts of it remain on disk until needed. Some parts of the program (including the **overlay manager**) must always remain in memory. These parts taken together are called the **root**.

Overlay manager   A procedure that determines which overlays are currently in memory and which are on disk, and loads overlay files into memory when needed.

Port   A method of getting data into or out of a computer. A port is actually a code number (0-255 for 8080/Z80; 0-65535 for 8086) which when sent to the CPU will cause one or two bytes of data to be sent to or from memory via the system data bus.

Range checking   Checking a value to see if it falls within the legal range of values for a given data type. For example, type CHAR may have any value from 0 to 255. Trying to load CHR(455) into a CHAR variable would be a range error.

Record   A data type consisting of a number of different data items taken together and given an overall name:

```
NameRec = RECORD
              Name    : String80;
              Address : String80;
              Phone   : String80;
              Age     : Integer
           END;
VAR
    CustData : NameRec;
```

NameRec is a **record** data type. CustData is a **record**.. The individual data items within the **record** are called **fields**.

Recursion   The process of a procedure or function invoking itself. The secret is knowing when to stop.

Root   In an overlaid program, the portion of the program that always resides in memory. See **overlay**.

Semantic error   An error in the meaning of a Pascal expression or statement, rather than in the arrangement of the symbols making up the expression or statement. (That sort of error is called a **syntax error**.) Type conflicts and undeclared identifiers are the most common **semantic errors**.

Set constructor   A pair of brackets ([ ]) that contains the elements of a set: ['A'..'Z','0'..'9'] or [RED,INDIGO].

Source code   Also called "source file" or simply "the source." An ASCII text file created by a text editor like the Turbo Pascal editor, or by a standalone editor program like ED or WordStar. It contains the human-readable words that describe a Pascal program. The compiler transforms the **source code** into **object code**, which is a series of machine instructions enabling your computer to do some sort of task.

String   A data type consisting of an array of characters and a length counter. As characters are added to or deleted from the array, the length counter is updated to reflect the new character count. Several built-in functions and procedures operate upon strings in Turbo Pascal.

Subrange   A range of some ordinal type that falls completely within the range of legal values of that ordinal type. 1..10 is a subrange of type Integer. 'A'..'Z' is a subrange of type Char.

Syntax   The arrangement of Pascal keywords and symbols required for proper compilation is Pascal's **syntax**. A syntax error occurs when you arrange keywords and symbols in a way the compiler doesn't recognize. A BEGIN without a corresponding END or a missing semicolon are syntax errors.

Variant Record   A type of record that may have one of several different internal structures, depending on the value of a single field. All variant records have a constant part that is the same for all variants of that record type, and a variant part that is different for each variant.

Index of programs, procedures, and functions

NOTE: The names listed below are not in all cases the same as the names given in the text proper. Instead, longer names have been shortened to follow the convention for CP/M and MS DOS filenames. These shorter forms are the names under which the software appears in the listings diskette. (See front overleaf for ordering information, or check your local user group or CBBS.) The file extensions are defined as follows:

.PAS   A Pascal program
.SRC   A Pascal function or procedure
.ASM   An assembly-language routine
.BAT   A batch file
.DEF   A collection of type or constant definitions

Index

CAUZIN SOFTSTRIP® DATA STRIPS

Strips 1A–1D

GENERIC.PAS (Section 2.3)
WORDSTAT.PAS (Section 4.2)
SETSTUFF.SRC (Section 9.1)

Strips 2A–2B

CRTTEST.BAT (Section 13.9)
ROOTER1.PAS (Section 13.1)
ROOTER2.PAS (Section 13.1)
ISMONO.PAS (Section 13.9)
TRAPPER.PAS (Section 13.11)

Strips 3A–3E; 3F–3I

BOXSTUFF.SRC (Section 14.1)
GRAFEC.DEF (Section 14.1)
QUICKSORT.SRC (Section 14.4)
BOXTEST.PAS (Section 14.1)
SHELSORT.PAS (Section 14.2)
FACTRIAL.SRC (Section 14.4)
RANDOMS.KEY (Section 14.4)
SORTTEST.PAS (Section 14.4)

Strips 4A–4B; 4C–4E

CAPSLOCK.SRC (Section 15.1)
EVALUATOR.PAS (Section 15.1)
FREECASE.SRC (Section 15.3)
GETEXT.SRC (Section 15.1)
GETSTRING.SRC (Section 15.2)
SCREEN.PAS (Section 15.2)
RVRSNAME.SRC (Section 15.3)

Strips 5A–5B; 5C

BEEP.SRC (Section 16.11)
POWER.SRC (Section 16.4)
PULL.SRC (Section 16.10)
ROLLEM.PAS (Section 16.10)
UHUH.SRC (Section 16.11)

Strips 6A–6E; 6F

CLREGION.SRC (Section 17.2)
BOMBER.PAS (Section 17.5)
YES.SRC (Section 17.2)
CURSOFF.SRC (Section 17.2)
CURSON.SRC (Section 17.2)
FLPFLD.SRC (Section 17.2)
MONOTEST.SRC (Section 17.2)
PATTERN.PAS (Section 17.5)
WRITEAT.SRC. (Section 17.2)

Strips 7A–7C

GBOX.SRC (Section 17.4)
HATCHER.PAS (Section 17.4)
SPIRO.PAS (Section 17.4)

Strips 8A; 8B–8G; 8H

AVERAGE.PAS (Section 18.5)
CASE.PAS (Section 18.8)
FRIENDS.KEY (Section 18.10)
FRIENDSS.NAP (Section 18.10)
GFILE.PAS (Section 18.11)
HEXDUMP.PAS (Section 18.11)
KSEARCH.SRC (Section 18.10)
SHOWNAME.PAS (Section 18.10**)

Strips 9A–9D; 9E–9F

BUILDER.SRC (Section 19.2)
LISTDISP.SRC (Section 19.2)
LISTMAN.PAS (Section 19.3)
REALMAX.SRC (Section 19.2)
REALMEM.SRC (Section 19.1)
**SHOWDIR.PAS (Section 18.12)

Strips 10A–10D

BINARY.PAS (Section 20.4)
CLEARBIT.SRC (Section 20.4)
FREEBYTE.SRC (Section 20.6)
KEYSTAT.SRC (Section 20.6)
KEYSTAT2.SRC (Section 20.6)
SETBIT.SRC (Section 20.4)
VARDUMP.SRC (Section 20.2)
WHICH.PAS (Section 20.2)
WRITEHEX.SRC (Section 20.4)
WRITEHI.SRC (Section 20.4)

Strips 11A–11E; 11F–11J

FATPAD.PAS (Section 20.9)
ITERM.PAS (Section 20.8)
KEYSTAT3.SRC (Section 20.6)
MAKE.BAT (Section 20.9)
MOUSE.SRC (Section 20.6)
SCRNBLT.COM (Section 20.9)

Strips 12A; 12B–12F; 12G

SNAPSHOT.PIC (Section 20.9)

Strips 13A–13E; 13F

SCRN.BLT.ASM (Section 20.9)
PLOTTEST.PAS (Section 20.10)
PLOT.ASM (Section 20.10)
OVLTEST.PAS (Section 24.2)
CMPFOR87.SRC (Section 25.1)

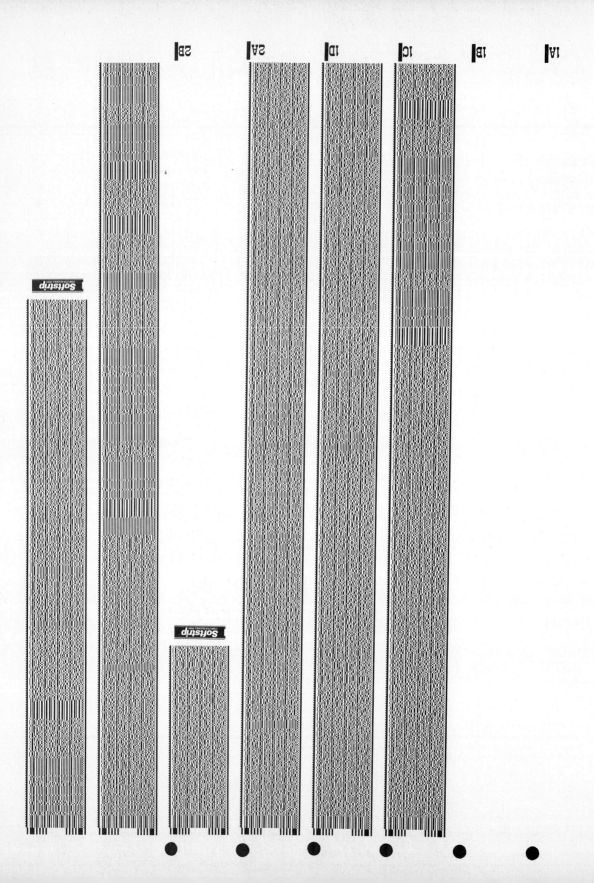

3A 3B 3C 3D 3E

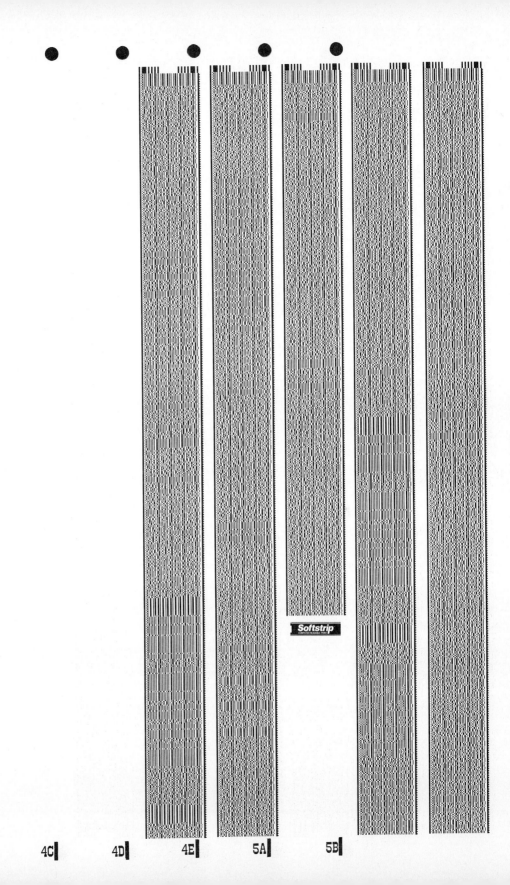

4C 4D 4E 5A 5B

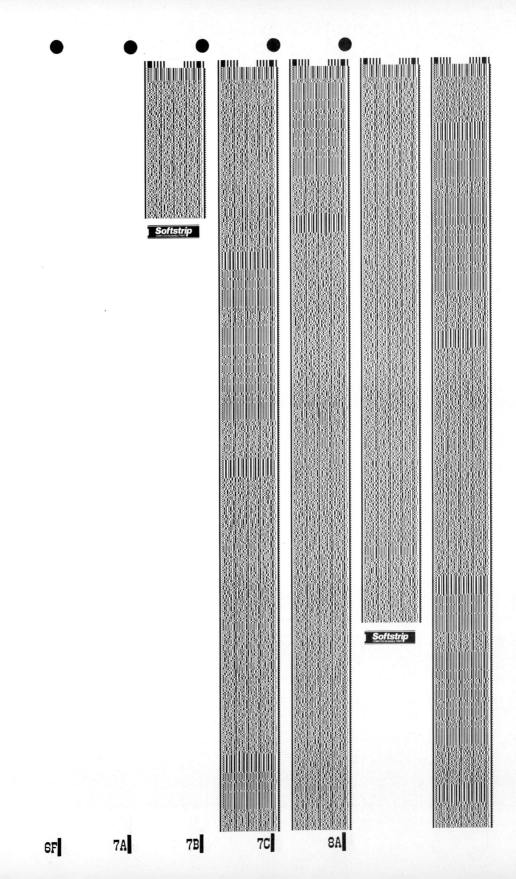

6F   7A   7B   7C   8A

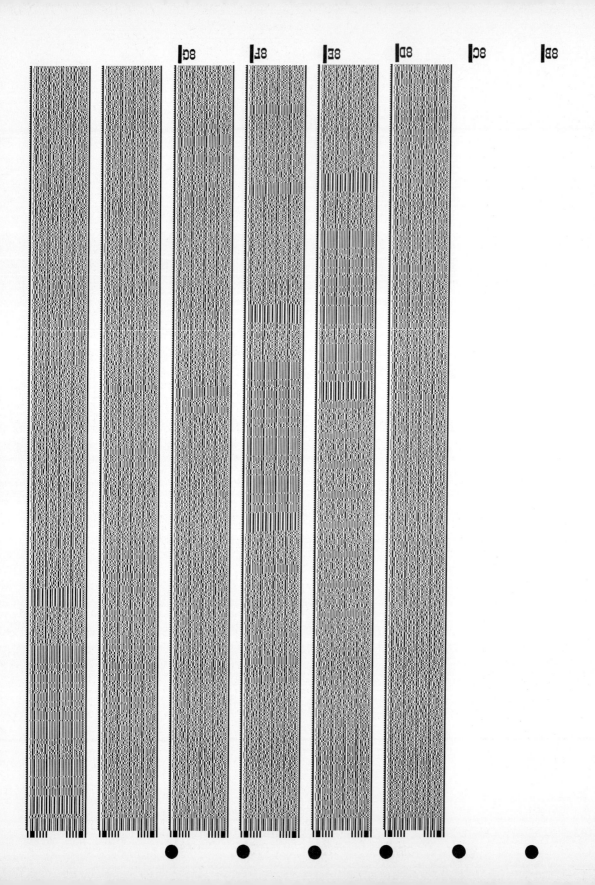

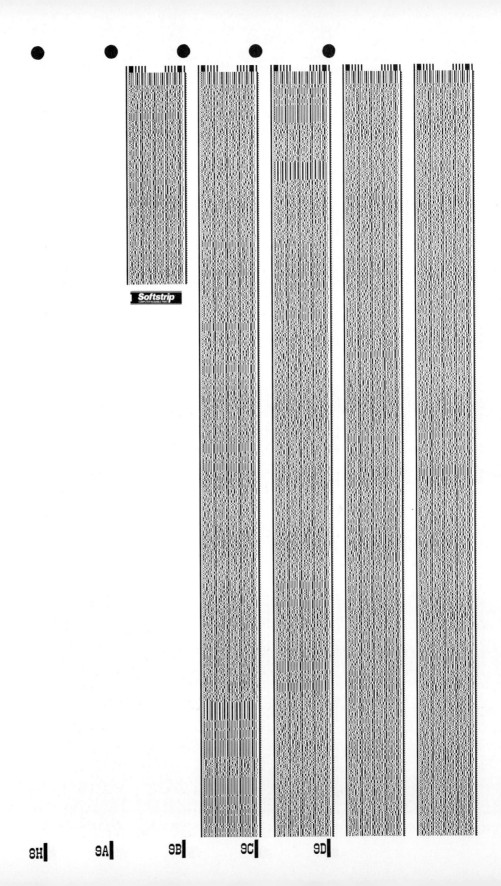

8H 9A 9B 9C 9D

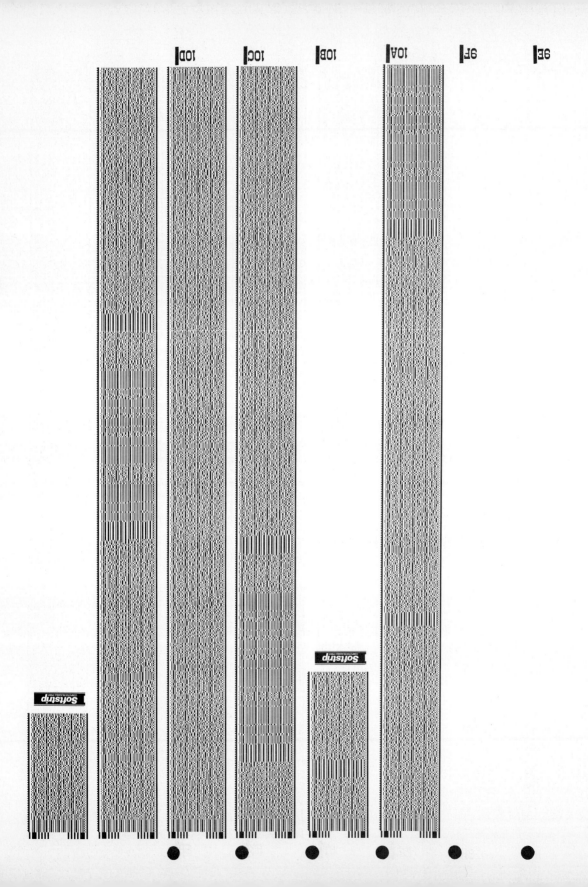

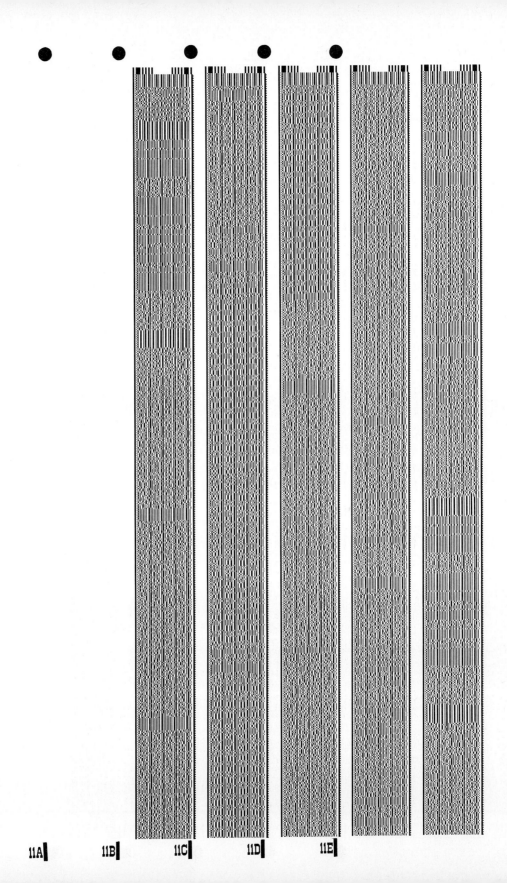

11A █   11B █   11C █   11D █   11E █

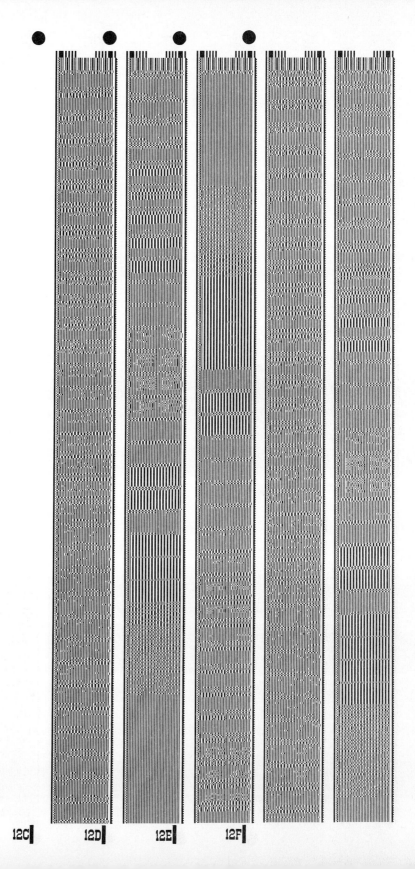

12B

12C

12D

12E

12F

13G   13F   13E   13D   13C   13B   13A   12G

13F

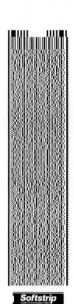

Softstrip

Has your computer read any good programs for you lately?

Picture yourself with the complete system. It would be simple, reliable, certainly a cost efficient means of distributing and retrieving the information you need. Stop dreaming, the system is available now! The cornerstone of the system is the Cauzin Softstrip® reader, a scanning device that is rapidly changing the shape of computer software.

Gone is the ordeal of keying in programs for hours. Gone too is the frustration of trying to debug those programs. And, what you save in time and money is just the beginning. For only $199.95 you get the Softstrip reader, a special storage base, a full one-year replacement warranty, a complete Accessory Kit containing all the connector cables and communications software you'll need to link the reader to your computer, and the StripWare™ Sampler, filled with programs from leading publishers and authors.

Once you become a Softstrip reader owner you'll receive FREE monthly featured programs and THE CAUZIN EFFECT NEWSLETTER. Each month, Cauzin publishes data strips in their advertisements in most major computer magazines. Soon, a variety of book publishers will be carrying data strips as well.

Another interesting feature of the System is it's universal file format...allowing data to be used by a variety of different computers, making disk incompatibility a less than fond memory. Now you can include your Lotus 1-2-3™ spreadsheet in a report that can be read directly into EXCEL™ on a Macintosh.

The good news doesn't stop there. If you order now, Cauzin will give you a FREE copy of its print utility called STRIPPER™ (a $19.95 value), which allows you to create your own strips. The program works with Epson® compatible and ImageWriter™ dot-matrix printers. Anything you can put on magnetic disk, you can put on Softstrip data strips. There are no limitations to the type of files; program code, computer language, sound or graphics. Use it to move data between different types of computers or to trade programs and data with associates.

Take the coupon below to your local dealer today for your FREE STRIPPER program. If there isn't one in your area, to order direct and take advantage of this limited time offer, call toll-free: 1-800-533-7323 (in Connecticut call 573-0150.)

A STRIPPER™ TO GO, PLEASE

This Certificate entitles the bearer to **One (1) FREE STRIPPER™ Package** with the purchase of a Cauzin Softstrip® reader.

Name _____

Address _____

City _____ State _____ Zip _____

Dealer Signature*
_____

Cauzin will underwrite replacement to dealer with verification signature.

Cauzin Systems, Inc. 835 South Main St. Waterbury, CT 06706

MORE PROGRAMMING BOOKS FROM SCOTT, FORESMAN AND COMPANY

The Complete Guide to IBM PC AT Assembly Language

Designed for experienced programmers new to assembly language, this third book in our popular series on the PC AT is a complete handbook for programming the AT in 80286 assembly language. Includes comprehensive instructions on constructing and running your own programs on the IBM PC, XT and AT. By Hahn. **$24.95**, 608 pages

Programming the Intel 80386

An indispensable guide for the many owners and users of 80386-based systems, this complete resource covers the chip's hardware layout and assembly language programming, includes and explains a detailed sample program in assembler, provides a large foldout diagram of the chip's pinout, and much more. By Smith, Shiell, and Johnson. **$21.95**, 256 pages

Advanced Programming Techniques in Modula-2

This book presents a wide variety of useful software tools and techniques for advanced Modula-2 programmers. After a brief overview of the language, you'll learn how to use Modula-2 for file conversion, file I/O, advanced mathematics, and more. By Ward. **$21.95**, 400 pages

Working with Xenix System V

Both a tutorial for new users of Xenix and a comprehensive reference guide, this book helps you use Microsoft Xenix System V productively on your IBM PC, XT, AT, or compatible. Includes a quick-reference command chart and a handy table comparing the key commands of Xenix and Unix System V. By Moore. **$19.95**, 256 pages

Using Your IBM PC AT

In a clear, nontechnical style, this valuable reference book guides you from the basics to advanced features of the AT, with special sections on DOS 3.0 and 3.1. Includes a handy summary of DOS commands and error messages. By Hahn. **$19.95**, 272 pages

Mastering Xenix on the IBM PC AT

A readable step-by-step tutorial on using the IBM Xenix operating system. This book introduces you to the major commands and options, the Xenix file system, the visual editor, the mail system, and more. Includes hundreds of examples. By Hahn. **$21.95**, 416 pages

HERE'S HOW TO ORDER

To order programming books from Scott, Foresman and Company, contact your local bookstore or computer store. Or, for greater convenience, simply mail in the handy order form below along with your payment.

Scott, Foresman and Company
Professional Publishing Group
1900 East Lake Avenue
Glenview, IL 60025

In Canada, contact
Macmillan of Canada
164 Commander Blvd.
Agincourt, Ontario
M1S 3C7

ORDER FORM

Please send me the following programming books from Scott, Foresman and Company:

_____ The Complete Guide to IBM PC AT Assembly
        Language, $24.95, 18263
_____ Programming the Intel 80386, $21.95, 18568
_____ Advanced Programming Techniques in Modula-2,
        $21.95, 18615
_____ Working with Xenix System V, $19.95, 18080
_____ Using Your IBM PC AT, $19.95, 18262
_____ Mastering Xenix on the IBM PC AT, $21.95, 18260

[   ] **Check here for a free catalog**
Please check method of payment:
[   ] Check/Money Order   [   ] MasterCard   [   ] VISA
Amount enclosed $_____
Credit Card No. _____ Exp. Date _____
Signature _____

Name (please print) _____
Address _____
City _____ State _____ Zip _____

Add applicable sales tax, plus 6% of Total for shipping.

Full payment must accompany your order.

Mail to:
Scott, Foresman and Company
Professional Publishing Group
1900 East Lake Avenue
Glenview, IL 60025

A18600